The INSPIRATIONAL WRITINGS of PAT ROBERTSON

The Secret Kingdom

Answers to Two Hundred of Life's Most Probing Questions

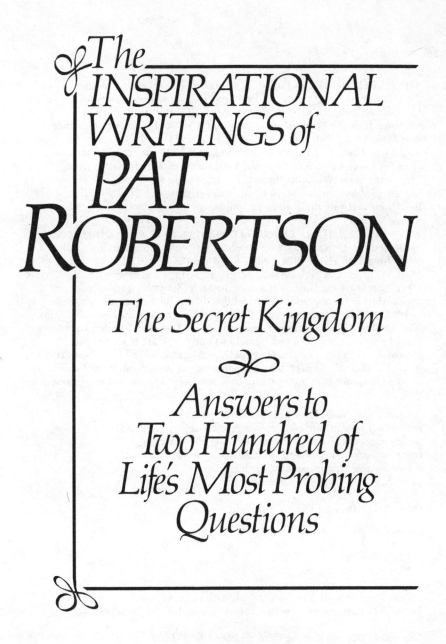

The
INSPIRATIONAL WRITINGS of
PAT ROBERTSON

The Secret Kingdom

Answers to Two Hundred of Life's Most Probing Questions

Published in 1989 by

Inspirational Press
A division of LDAP, Inc.
166 Fifth Avenue
New York, NY 10010

Inspirational Press is a registered trademark of LDAP, Inc.
Published by arrangement with Thomas Nelson, Inc., Publishers.

Library of Congress Catalog Card Number: 89-84150
ISBN: 0-88486-029-9

Printed in the United States of America.

Contents

THE
SECRET
KINGDOM

EXPANDED
EDITION

Pat Robertson
with Bob Slosser

Contents

Preface to the Expanded Edition

In the years since the writing of *The Secret Kingdom*, events in my own life, as well as in the life of the country and the world, have done nothing but convince me even more of the reality of the laws of the kingdom of God. I have seen every one of the laws that I discussed operating in the lives of individuals and nations. I believe men and women everywhere must open their hearts and minds and see the invisible world at work in the visible world. They must reject the notions of those who would try to persuade us that there is only a material world, that God does not figure in the affairs of men and nations.

That's why I was delighted when the editors at Thomas Nelson developed the idea of an expanded version of *The Secret Kingdom*—an integration of the study guide into the book itself. This will facilitate use of the book immeasurably and should enable more of us to seize upon the principles of the kingdom and to get our lives in line with them.

Let me give you just one example from my own life in the period since the first writing of the book that illustrates why I am so certain the Lord has opened His storehouse of wisdom to His people in recent times.

It was December 31, the year's end, and I was reviewing my personal financial contributions to the work of the Lord for the preceding twelve months. I had been carrying this desire to give my entire CBN salary back to the ministry, and I saw on that day that I was a few thousand dollars off the mark. But, unhappily, my bank account was quite low. There was barely enough to cover the amount required to complete the matching of my salary. On top of that, I knew I would have some bills coming due for my horses. I didn't have that many, but they sure seemed to eat the hay!

I leaned back in the armchair. "What am I going to do?" I spoke into the quietness of the room. "I want to do this. But am I taking a risk?"

I sat upright in the chair. "I'll do it!" And I wrote out this rather large check to CBN and mumbled half aloud, "There. It's done. I'm a dollar-a-year man."

Two weeks went by. Then out of the blue came a check, personally for me and not connected to the ministry. I looked at it in absolute surprise. I hadn't expected any such thing. Within seconds, the light flashed on. I grabbed my pen and did a few quick calculations on a yellow legal pad. The amount of the check was written six dollars of being twelve times the total of the check I'd written for CBN on December 31. Twelve times. Not double. Not triple. I looked up and smiled. "That's good measure, pressed down, and running over—just as the Bible promises," I said enthusiastically.

Then, more softly, I wondered, "Will we ever start trusting the Lord? He is always there. He never fails us."

You see, dear reader, Jesus clearly taught that a Law of Reciprocity operates within the kingdom of God. And since that kingdom—that invisible world—undergirds and penetrates the visible, material world, the Law of Reciprocity will operate in our lives today. The kingdom is here, as Jesus taught; it's in our midst.

We have learned that lesson over and over at the Christian Broadcasting Network, especially in the years since the writing of *The Secret Kingdom*. It's actually turned out that when we cry, "Lord, we need some money for this project,"

He will send someone knocking at our door saying, "We need help."

At first we complained when that would happen, but now after years of testing in this regard, we know the Lord has in so many words said: "I've given you the key to meeting your needs. Use it. Give to the needy, and I will give to you."

I remember well the time, just before our annual fund-raising telethon, when an extraordinarily worthwhile project was presented to us along with a request for $100,000. Despite our own need and the irony of giving such a large amount just as we were going to make our own appeal, we gave the $100,000. And, of course, that was the key: We made our goal on the telethon, far exceeding what we had achieved in previous years.

Perhaps the hardest lesson has come from watching the national and world economies run headlong into the laws of the kingdom. The laws were ignored, and the economies have suffered desperately.

We need only consider one phase of this to see the point. It centers on the Law of Use and the accompanying exponential curve—this time working negatively instead of positively. The vehicle was debt.

Let's consider the United States. Since I wrote *The Secret Kingdom*, the country's national debt has passed the second trillion-dollar mark. Think about it. From the founding of the nation it took us until 1981 to accumulate one trillion dollars of debt. But, because we were on the wrong side of the exponential curve, it took only five years to accumulate the second trillion. The third trillion will take only four years. Peter Grace, the chairman of the Grace Commission that undertook a serious but neglected study of government spending in America, has said that the United States will owe thirteen and a half trillion dollars by the year 2000! That is an impossible situation, arrived at by ignoring a major law of the kingdom of God—the Law of Use coupled with the exponential curve.

We see the same thing internationally, especially with the Third World countries. They have borrowed intolerable amounts and, with the compound-interest clock running, are sinking to a point beyond recovery. This is so serious as to threaten the entire world economy.

The dangers facing the world—and they've heightened since the writing of *The Secret Kingdom*—always lead me to reflection on another law of the kingdom. It's the one I call the Law of Greatness, or perhaps in everyday parlance "the principle of leadership." The world's leadership crisis has worsened in the last few years, and that may be as threatening as our violations of the Laws of Reciprocity and use. We need great leaders more than at any other time in history. The key has been given. We need only to use it.

If I am correct in believing that the last five years have intensified the truth of the kingdom laws, then we will all benefit from urgent use of this expanded edition. We need to dig deeply into what God has given us, and this combination text and study guide should definitely enhance that. The next five years will be even more important than the past five.

Pat Robertson
January 1, 1987

Introduction

The yellow moon hung low over the Atlantic. Two hundred feet from the narrow beach the surf boomed and crashed, streaking white in the crystal moonlight. Beyond the breakers a hundred sea gulls settled for the night, rising and falling in the dark swells.

I turned and looked north. Cape Henry, shadowy under the soft sky, stretched before me, a gathering of sand dunes named after the eldest son of King James I of England. It was utterly peaceful, clutching to itself a history little noticed as the noisy twentieth century raced toward conclusion. For that gentle corner of the Chesapeake Bay's great mouth had been the stage for a small drama of unusual significance to America.

On April 26, 1607, a small band of settlers arrived from England to lay claim to a new world, stepping from their boats into the fine sands of the cape, anxious and weary. Three days later, amazed by this big fresh land, they carefully carried ashore a rough, seven-foot oak cross and plunged it into the sand. As they knelt around it, their spiritual leader, an Anglican clergyman named Robert Hunt, reminded them of the admonition of the British Royal Council, derived from the words of the Holy Scripture: "Every plantation, which my Heavenly Father hath not planted, shall be rooted up."[1]

8

With face turned toward heaven, the priest then dedicated the vast new land and their future in it to the glory of Almighty God.

Revived, eager, and joyful, these brave pioneers reboarded their tiny ships and sailed around Cape Henry and into the mouth of a river they named in honor of their monarch, James. Before long they sighted an outcropping along the banks that seemed entirely suitable to their immediate needs and on May 3 founded Jamestown, the first permanent English settlement on the North American continent.

Their "plantation" was indeed not "rooted up." From it and later settlements in Massachusetts, Rhode Island, Pennsylvania, New York, and Maryland grew the most prosperous nation in humanity's history. Unparalleled freedom and creativity burst upon the earth.

As I surveyed that historical site and looked eastward at the Atlantic beneath that dazzling moon, I was gripped by the renewed realization that a dread disease had fastened itself upon the lands sending forth our forefathers. As I turned westward toward my car, my mind's eye swept across the huge country that lay before me. And I mourned more deeply because the same sickness was fastening itself upon my land, the new world so sincerely dedicated to God three hundred and seventy-five years ago.

Yes, the disease seemed epidemic throughout the earth. Could it be fatal? Was an "uprooting" to come?

So great are our problems that to think of them as incurable is not unreasonable. Thoughtful men frequently compare the recent course of Western civilization with the collapse of the ancient Roman Empire. Everywhere scholars, politicians, industrialists, financiers, sociologists, and futurists see grave trouble ahead. Yearningly, they look back to the optimistic beginnings of our country and the whispers seep from their pursed lips, "What went wrong? What happened to the hopes and aspirations of the pioneers? Were their brave struggles in vain?"

The thoughts accruing from many months of reading and meditation poured in upon me that night when I looked upon the Atlantic where the American dream had begun. I, like other concerned persons, seemed to have nothing but questions. Is our nation—our world—faced with collapse? Can we survive? Is our only choice between anarchy and dictatorship? Or is there an alternative?

More than any time in my life, I knew that night that we must urgently seek a third choice. I knew we would have to reach into the invisible world that has been there all along, a world far truer than any civilization in history. We have wasted too much time, decades of delay and doubt.

The challenges of my contemporaries rang in my ear:

Is there truly an invisible world of the spirit?

Is it possible to draw help from that invisible world?

Can there be a new world order?

Yes.

This book comes from convictions about those questions. Its purpose is to foster understanding of the invisible world, better described as an invisible kingdom, the kingdom of God. It has principles. They can be learned.

My recognition of this has come slowly, spanning several years, and is still expanding. First was a prayer for wisdom, spoken quite naively, perhaps in the manner of King David's son Solomon. I desperately wanted to understand—God, the world, the present, the future, the working of things.

Oddly, or so it might seem, my first awareness of the possible answer to that prayer dawned as my interest became fixed on the words of John the Baptist in the early pages of the New Testament: "'Repent, for the kingdom of heaven is at hand.'"[2]

I was struck by the words "at hand." What did they mean? Eventually my mind recalled similar words of Jesus, spoken the night of His betrayal as Judas approached with his rowdy gang: "'. . . the one who betrays Me is at hand!'"[3]

In this case, the meaning was obvious. Judas had arrived; he was there. John the Baptist, using the same words, had obviously meant the same thing. The kingdom had arrived; it was there, at hand.

This was revolutionary understanding, as simple as it may seem these six or seven years later. I had been instructed to regard our time as the age of the church, and it is that in a very real sense; but John the Baptist and later the Lord Jesus Christ declared the arrival of the kingdom of God. Somehow I had failed to take seriously the fact that the kingdom of God is the central teaching of Jesus. He began His earthly ministry by declaring the arrival of the kingdom,[4] and He ended it by "speaking of the things pertaining to the kingdom of God."[5] Indeed He described such teaching as His ultimate purpose: "'I must preach the kingdom of God to the other cities also, for I *was sent for this purpose.*'"[6]

That the kingdom of God was at the heart of the Lord's work is obvious, and furthermore He spoke of it as existing then and now, not to arrive at some far-distant time and place. The kingdom of God is in our midst.[7]

My constant prayers for wisdom brought additional insight over the weeks, months, and years, and I gradually perceived that Jesus had spoken quite precisely about how this kingdom worked. He was far from theoretical. He actually laid down specific principles, so sweeping that they might be better considered as laws, even at the risk of offending those who cringe at the merest hint of legalism. Jesus quite bluntly said, "If you do this, then this will happen." When He added no restrictions as to time, place, nationality, and the like, then they were laws, in the same sense as the natural laws established by God—those governing motion, gravity, sound and such. They simply work.

Sitting in a big stuffed chair morning after morning in my living room, poring over the Scriptures, praying, thinking, making notes on a yellow legal pad, I uncovered one, then two, and three, and more of these major principles. But, equally important, I put them to work in my life, my family's life, and the life of the Christian Broadcasting Network. I wasn't interested in abstraction. I wanted to determine if they worked.

They did. And they do. They, and they alone, can alter the world's slide into anarchy or dictatorship. They offer a third choice.

Scripture References

1 Compare Matthew 15:13, KJV
2 Matthew 3:2
3 Matthew 26:46
4 Matthew 4:17
5 Acts 1:3, KJV
6 Luke 4:43
7 Luke 17:21

I TWO DOMAINS

1. The Visible World

The world is in crisis. That's the way *Newsweek* and *Time* magazines say it.

The ax is already laid at the root of the trees.[1] That's the way the Bible says it.

They're describing the same thing, merely from different viewpoints. The world has reached the stage where disaster looms on every hand. Everything seems to be going wrong, and the forecast is worse.

The key words in any description of our plight are economy, defense, energy, crime, poverty, morality, education, hunger, and pollution. Volumes are written on each. And each carries the same theme—hopelessness. The great cosmic clock appears to have wound down.

All about use we see "fear in a handful of dust," in Eliot's words, as man stares horror-stricken at

> A heap of broken images, where the sun beats,
> And the dead tree gives no shelter, the cricket
>   no relief,
> And the dry stone no sound of water.[2]

We cry out for solutions to problems too big for us. Our governments are on the verge of collapse; our finance is

13

chaotic, our atmosphere polluted, our populations so massive that millions starve. Fear reigns.

Our condition is not difficult to understand. And the purpose of this book is not to dwell on that condition, but rather to explore reliable remedies. Nonetheless, to understand the encompassing nature of those remedies, we should take a few moments to set the stage of the visible world. We need only trace a few strands of the hangman's noose that seems poised over our heads, beginning with the most immediately destructive, the threat of nuclear holocaust.

Age of Terror

Let us go back to 1940. Three physicists—Enrico Fermi, Leo Szilard, and Eugene Wigner—working in a makeshift laboratory in a handball court under the grandstand at the University of Chicago, split the atom and thereby confirmed the theoretical formula of Albert Einstein: $E = MC^2$. The split, or fission, caused a multiplication of energy in the order of six million to one.

At last man had found a source of cheap and abundant energy for the world forever. A new industrial revolution was at hand. Age-old territorial disputes would end. Wars would cease. The poor could be warmed, sheltered, fed. No nation need be without.

History records a different outcome. The work of those three deeply religious men evolved into an age of terror, not an age of abundance. There was Hiroshima. Then Nagasaki.

That was only the beginning. Physicists quickly perfected nuclear fusion and a release of energy of fifty million to one. Utilizing hydrogen, a fuel as abundant as the waters of the seas, this process held promise as the energy source of the millenium. There need be no fossil fuel shortage, no air pollution, no fabulously wealthy OPEC oil cartel, and no desperately poor Third World.

The utopia did not come. Instead we have hydrogen bombs rated in millions of tons of TNT. The superpower nations, during the fifties and sixties, built arsenals capable of destroying all life on earth. A balance of terror developed between the United States and the Soviet Union bearing the terrifying acronym MAD—Mutual Assured Destruction.

Then came the seventies. The United States, wearied by its struggle in Southeast Asia, gradually dismantled its military capability, delaying the start of weapons systems commensurate with advanced technology. The Soviet Union, meanwhile, pushed its flagging economy to the breaking point to build the most awesome array of weapons ever assembled by a nation in peacetime.

Instead of balance, the world of the eighties is faced with an imbalance of terror in favor of a malevolent dictatorship bent on world domination.

Aggravating the danger is the internal weakness of the Soviet Union. Its economy is falling apart. Its citizens see Marxism as a failure. Its leadership is old. In short, Communism does not appear to work.

A widely held view in the West is that these seemingly over-whelming difficulties might force the failing Soviet leaders to begin a military adventure simply to continue in power.

Given this view, plus the unquestioned Soviet military power, along with the vulnerability of the governments controlling Middle East oil, our age appears to have in place the ingredients to touch off World War III.

Age of terror is an apt description. But there is a solution, as we will see.

The Struggle for Energy

Intertwined with the age of terror is the concern for sufficient energy to fuel the gulping planet. It is almost as ominous as the nuclear threat, despite the deceptive ebb and flow in short-range supply and demand.

In 1950 there were 2.51 billion people in the world. By 1980 the figure has soared to 4.41 billion. The demand for everything from food to factories skyrocketed.

But nothing exploded like the demand for energy. In 1950 the world used the equivalent of 2.66 billion metric tons of coal. In 1980 consumption was 9.5 *billion* metric tons.

In thirty years the population had not quite doubled; energy use had more than tripled. We were running wild with everything that required fuel.

This massive growth presented a simple truth as the decade of the eighties got underway: The planet does not contain enough nonrenewable and renewable sources of energy to supply indefinitely the basic needs and growing aspirations of a world population that continues to explode.

It seems clear that if we do not make drastic cuts, we face the following perilous prospects:

—Those possessing dwindling energy sources will extract ever-increasing prices. This trend will hold true in the long run, even when temporary conditions cause occasional price drops that give the world a false sense of security. If recent patterns continue, the cost of energy will place such insupportable burdens on worldwide industry and financial markets that money supplies will be imprudently increased. This could set off hyperinflation and lead to worldwide financial collapse.

—To prolong high-energy lifestyles, the developed nations may use military force to seize dwindling resources. This could be expected to pit the United States against the Soviet Union ultimately, with all the risks of nuclear war or of surrender to intimidation.

—As oil import costs continue to mount, industrially developed nations will show more and more strain as they try to maintain a balance of trade. Aggressive financial actions, including punitive trade measures, seem certain and will heighten world tension.

—The prognosis is even worse for the weaker nations. They simply do not have the money to buy oil and pay interest on their huge debts at the same time. Many face bankruptcy already. Such default by any of several nations can cause suffering internally and global economic confusion externally. It could trigger a worldwide bank collapse, for example, unless the United States is willing to bail out the country in trouble.

—America's cities pose a unique danger that has wide-ranging potential, traceable in large part to energy consumption and high costs. The mammoth office buildings, shopping centers, and apartment houses of New York, Detroit, Chicago, Cleveland, Boston, Philadelphia, and other cities are energy gluttons. The rising operating costs have been staggering. Compounding this financial burden is the fact that physical plants of these cities—the sewers, water lines, and other underground support utilities, plus the roads, bridges, and other systems above ground—have far exceeded their life expectancies. The cities don't have the money for proper maintenance and replacement. Time bombs are ticking away both above and below ground. Should they begin to explode, the cities will be brought to their knees. The social and economic consequences nationally and globally will be staggering.

—Imprudent substitution of hazardous, untested energy sources in the face of diminishing traditional sources could present the world with intolerable environmental problems affecting all of life. Yet rigid regulation could inhibit exploration, discovery, and creativity needed to overcome shortages. The dilemma breeds deep strife.

—The reluctance and/or inability of car manufacturers to respond to worldwide energy problems threw a major portion of American industry into a tailspin that threatened the wider economy. By the early eighties, foreign car manufacturers, led by the Japanese, had seized 28 percent of U.S. domestic auto business. Many major American industries, in fact, have been badly hurt in recent years by foreign competition and trade practices. Anger and discontent are mounting.

The struggle for energy and the manifold ramifications of that struggle have propelled the world to the brink of upheaval. Even the tiniest of international movements has the potential for escalating.

We will see, however, that there are alternatives.

Economic Disaster

Picking up another related thread, we learn that the lesser-developed nations of the world owed more than $500 billion to banks and wealthier nations early in 1981. Annual interest on those loans approached $100 billion, which was $35 billion more than the total debt of those nations only eight years earlier. Tragically, they are being forced to borrow simply to pay interest. A number of loans are being refinanced so the nations do not appear to be in default.

During this period, Poland was in the news as its people suffered the penalty of reaching for freedom from Soviet-led repression. That country's disastrous financial condition is typical of that of many other countries of the world. In 1982 it owed $24 billion of the $89 billion owed to the West by Russia and the East Bloc countries. Strife-torn, it still cannot pay its debts and yet has to ask for more.

It seems certain, with so many countries in a condition like Poland's, that one day a scene similar to the following will be played out:

A sweaty-palmed finance minister from Zaire or Turkey or East Germany will sit in a room in Switzerland or Germany or France and be told by several dignified bankers that his country's loans are in default. No more money is available. When word leaks out, the canny finance minister from oil-rich Kuwait, Abu Dhabi, Saudi Arabia, Iraq, or Libya could quietly withdraw his country's deposits from the banks in question. When word of this withdrawal is circulated, a wild scramble to get cash out of weakening banks could result.

Major institutions could fall like dominoes overnight. Eurodollar certificates of deposit could be wiped out, along with other large domestic certificates. Broad-based money market funds could lose virtually all their bank assets. There would very possibly have to be a nationwide freeze on bank withdrawals in this country to prevent a collapse of the banking system. Bonds, stocks, gold, silver, and jewels would fall like stones. Trade and commerce could be brought to a standstill.

Only a multinational effort to print a trillion or more dollars could save off fiscal disaster. And this rescue would merely accelerate post-World War I, German-style hyperinflation, followed eventually by a worse crash.

In 1974–75 the world economy lurched, and several big banks and real estate operations failed; but the system held together. In 1980 it lurched again. That time silver crashed and the bond market lost $300 billion. Many financial institutions became technically insolvent as the market value of their bond and mortgage portfolios plunged in the wake of a 21 percent prime interest rate. One major bank failed and Chrysler became a government ward, but the system survived.

Another lurch seems to be building. Banks have neither restored liquidity as they had after the mid-seventies problem, nor have their portfolios improved as much as desired. Nonbank businesses are illiquid and overextended with short-term loans made in hopes that interest rates would drop.

Furthermore, the U. S. government continues to borrow to cover budget deficits. Inflation, although dipping at least temporarily, still remains high. It seems built into the system at every level. Prices do not actually fall; their rate of increase merely slows.

Questions are inevitable. Are major business and financial institutions, as well as individuals, bound for bankruptcy? Will this trigger the sort of doomsday scenario described above?

There are options, as we will see.

A Tailspin in Morality

As the eighties unfolds, nothing portrays our world crisis more clearly than man's internal and moral condition. The unmistakable scent of what the Bible calls the Antichrist spirit is in the air. It was present at the tower of Babel and at Sodom and Gomorrah. It was present in the French Revolution and in Nazi Germany. And it is present in Europe and the United States today.

The signs of this spirit are clear. They emerge in this fashion: A significant minority, then an actual majority, of the people in a society begin to throw off the restraints of history, then the restraints of written law, then accepted standards of morality, then established religion, and, finally, God Himself.

As the rebellion gains momentum, the participants grow bolder. Those practices that once were considered shameful and unlawful move into the open. Soon the practitioners are aggressive, militant. As each societal standard falls, another comes under attack. The pressure is relentless. Established institutions crumble. Ultimately the struggle that began as a cry for "freedom of expression" grows into all-out war against the rights of advocates of traditional morality. The latter are hated, reviled, isolated, and then persecuted.

Honor, decency, honesty, self-control, sexual restraint, family values, and sacrifice are replaced by gluttony, sensuality, bizarre sexual practices, cruelty, profligacy, dishonesty, delinquency, drunkenness, drug-induced euphoria, fraud, waste, debauched currency, and rampant inflation.

The people then search for a deity that will both permit and personify their basest desires. At Babel it was a tower, man's attempt to glorify himself. In ancient Mediterranean cultures, like those of Sodom and Gomorrah, it was a god or goddess of sex. In France, it was the goddess of reason; in Germany, Hitler and the Nazi party; in Europe and especially in the United States, the god of central government under the religion of secular humanism.

The pattern is always the same. So is the result. No society falling under the grip of the Antichrist spirit has survived. First comes a period of lawlessness and virtual anarchy, then an economic collapse followed by a reign of terror. Then comes a strong dictator who plunders society for his personal aggrandizement; he dreams of worldwide empire and storms into war. Eventually come defeat and collapse.

In some cases God intervenes directly to destroy the Antichrist society before it reaches full flower. In others, the society destroys itself. Sometimes a righteous nation takes action; in others the task is performed by stronger barbarians. But always there is destruction.

In the United States, trends, also reflected in other countries are well defined:

—Organized crime is the largest industry in the land. With gross revenues of $150 billion, the profits of crime eclipse the profits of the American oil or auto industries, producing power and influence that compromise and corrupt the fabric of society. The impact of illegal drug use, as only one example, is staggering. In 1981 cocaine grossed $35 billion and marijuana $24 billion, establishing that Americans spent more on those two illegal drugs than they contributed to all charities, education, and religion combined.

—The sexual revolution has snaked it way into the schools, the homes, and virtually all of society. Traditional standards regarding nudity, fornication, adultery, homosexuality, incest, and sadomasochism have been under firece attack and many are crumbling. Educators deluded by humanism are offering sex education without moral standards to children; some courses appear to advocate masturbation, premarital sex, and homosexuality. Motion pictures, television, and the publishing industry pour the excesses of unbridled gratification into communities and homes.

—From this rampant hedonism has emerged permission to minimize the inconvenient side effects of sexual pleasure. The Supreme Court ruled that the thing conceived through sexual relations between two humans is not itself a human and therefore may be destroyed prior to the fourth month of pregnancy. The killing of unborn infants through abortion has thus proceeded at the rate of 1.2 million a year.

—At the same time, family life has been battered. In the decade of the seventies, the number of couples living together outside of marriage doubled, and divorce reached a rate of one for every two marriages. But data were not crystallized for the marred lives of children caught in the breakup of families, for the suicides of young and old unable to survive the trauma of sudden rootlessness, for the wasted lives of despair.

Financial morality has been corrupted as the government, exalted by humanist philosophy, has become god and provider. In 1941 the population of the United States was 133.7 million; government spending was $13.6 billion. Forty years later the population had grown by 72 percent, to 229.3 million; federal spending had grown by 4,762 percent, to $661.2 billion. We have already touched on the result: federal debt exceeding $1 trillion, ever-increasing inflation, and domestic and world economies in danger of collapse.

—As self-restraint and regard for God rapidly diminish under the assault of secular humanism, a new rule of law has been emerging. Judges are less inclined to make decisions based on the Bible, the Constitution, natural laws, or precedent. Instead, they often impose as a rule of law whatever seems sociologically expedient or whatever reflects the prevailing sentiment of the ruling elite. As Justice Charles Evans Hughes declared early in the century, "The Constitution is what the judges say it is," pointing to a trend in which a government based on men's opinions would supersede a government based on laws. Lawlessness has thus come a long way.

But we will see that there is a remedy.

Revolt Against God

Underlying all the threads we have examined as integral to the deepening crisis coming upon the world—and we have examined only a fraction of them—is one that transcends all others. It is the increased disregard for the Creator of the world.

Shortly after the turn of the century, a false view of reality began to take hold in America. Although its name did not become well known immediately, humanism spread into all aspects of life and became the dominant philosophical view about the time of World War II. Today millions of people openly embrace it, and many millions more follow along under its influence.

Francis A. Schaeffer, the Christian philosopher-theologian, described humanism's influence this way:

> ... the humanist world view includes many thousands of adherents and today controls the consensus in society, much of the media, much of what is taught in our schools, and much of the arbitrary law being produced by the various departments of government.
>
> The term humanism used in this wider, more prevalent way means Man beginning from himself, with no knowledge except what he himself can discover and no standards outside of himself. In this view Man is the measure of all things, as the Enlightenment expressed it.
>
> ... Since [the humanists'] concept of Man is mistaken, their concept of society and of law is mistaken, and they have no sufficient base for either society or law.
>
> They have reduced Man to even less than his natural finiteness by seing him only as a complex arrangement of molecules, made complex by blind chance. Instead of seeing him as something great who is significant even in his sinning, they see Man in his essence only as an intrinsically competitive animal, that has no other basic operating principle than natural selection brought about by the strongest, the fittest, ending on top. And they see Man as acting in this way both individually and collectively as society.[3]

Thus, for a vast number of people, God has been removed from the center of things, and man has taken His place. All things exist for man and his pleasure.

In a church-state dialogue sponsored in 1981 by the Virginia Council of Churches, a professor of humanistic studies summed up the direction of American leadership most clearly: "We must throw off the tyranny of the concept that the Bible is the Word of God. We must be freed from the tyranny of thought that comes from Martin Luther, John Calvin, Zwingli, and John Knox."

He discarded the Bible as the authoritative guide for faith and conduct, casting with it such long-accepted truths as the doctrine of man's sinfulness, the doctrine of eternal reward and eternal punishment, the necessity for repentance and justification by faith in Jesus Christ, and the necessity for holy living to please God. Such astounding recommendations can only be grasped when one recalls the words of *Humanist Manifesto I* and *II* (produced in 1933 and 1973), which denied the "existence of a supernatural God who hears and answers prayer."

With all standards and yardsticks removed, society first eased, then rushed toward the extremes of hedonism and nihilism, with increasing numbers finding fulfillment in "doing their own thing."

"If it feels good, do it," comes the advice of everyone from parents to psychologists. This, they say, is freedom.

Meanwhile, as we noted earlier, nothing works. Bodies wear out early as sickness and disease soar. Never has there been so much cancer, so much heart disease. Brains, too, wear out. Never have emotional and mental breakdowns run so high; never have suicides reached such levels. Schools fail; businesses fail; governments fail.

Yes, humanism and its society are failing, although seemingly few have perceived the depth of that failure. Most see only symptoms, not the underlying sickness.

Inevitable Conclusions

The fear has become widespread that our society—and the world's—is beyond repair. There is confusion everywhere.

At times the confusion approaches chaos. It seems clear that we will slide further into chaos, the jungle of anarchy— "I've got mine; to heck with you"—"do unto others before they can do unto you"—"every man for himself." Or we in desperation will yield to dictatorship. Which will it be?

It matters not that both of the prevailing philosophies of materialism have been proven corrupt and ineffective. Communism says materialism is the goal but the state should control it. Capitalism strives for materialism, but the strong control it. Both move toward dictatorship, oligarchical or individual.

Eventually a strong man must be chosen as both systems fail—unless we turn to the third choice that is available to us.

What will we do?

Study Guide

Key Scripture: Matt. 24:4–12

Key Idea: Fear reigns in the visible world.

1. Pat Robertson points out that "The key words in any description of our plight are economy, defense, energy, crime, poverty, morality, education, hunger, and pollution." What is today's underlying theme in each of these areas, according to Pat? _____
Briefly describe one area of life in your community that mirrors the international hopelessness at the local level.

2. What does the prophetic word of Jesus in Matthew 24:4–12 say will characterize the end times?

3. List the five strands of the noose hanging over our head, according to the author.

   a.   d.
   b.   e.
   c.

Facing the Issues

1. "Instead of balance, the world of the eighties is faced with an imbalance of terror in favor of a malevolent dictatorship bent on world domination." List up to three

recent developments in weapons systems that illustrate this statement by the author.

2. "The planet does not contain enough nonrenewable and renewable sources of energy to supply the basic needs and growing aspirations of [the world's growing] population." What developments have locked us into a high level of energy use?

3. "Are major business and financial institutions, as well as individuals, bound for bankruptcy? Will this trigger the . . . doomsday scenario?" What developments in the financial institutions of today seem to underline this statement?

4. "The signs of the spirit are clear. They emerge in this fashion: A significant minority, then an actual majority, of the people in a society begin to throw off the restraints of history, then the restraints of written law, then accepted standards of morality, then established religion, and, finally, God Himself." Indicate some of the "signs of the times" illustrating this statement.

5. "Thus, for a vast number of people, God has been removed from the center of things, and man has taken His place. All things exist for man and his pleasure." What are two key steps that precede this condition?

Making It Happen

If we look at the visible world only, we get a very bleak picture of the future for humanity. The root cause of all the world's problems is mankind's increasing rejection of God. And to the extent that we hold any part of our lives back from the Lord's control, we are a part of what's wrong with the world. As you examine your own life in the light of this fact, ask the Holy Spirit to show you that part of yourself that you have been most unwilling to submit to His authority, and say a heartfelt prayer of surrender now.

Scripture References

1 Matthew 3:10
2 From "The Waste Land," T. S. Eliot, 1922
3 Francis A. Schaeffer, *A Christian Manifesto* (Chicago: Crossway, 1981), pp. 24, 26

2. The Invisible World

Fortunately, a Voice speaks steadily and clearly into the turmoil and dread of the day, a Voice that contradicts our finitude and limitation and restriction. It says, "'But seek first His kingdom and His righteousness; and all these things shall be added to you.'"[1]

Obviously the words are those of Jesus, climaxing a teaching about food, clothing, shelter, and all the "things" needed for life. God, His heavenly Father, was able and eager to provide the necessities for happy, successful living on the planet Earth if the people merely turned to the right place—His kingdom.

His point immediately established a fact that the world has in large measure refused to consider—the fact that an invisible world undergirds, surrounds, and interpenetrates the visible world in which we live. Indeed, it controls the visible world, for it is unrestricted, unlimited, infinite.

The problem of the world, and of many Christians, has not been simply refusing to acknowledge the possibility of such a kingdom, but failing to perceive that it exists *right now*, not in some far-off time or far-off place called heaven. This is so strange because Jesus spent virtually all of His earthly ministry telling people that the kingdom of God had come and then explaining its workings.

For reasons that are beyond our comprehension, even we Christians missed it as we soaked up the good news of salvation, the fullness of the Holy Spirit, the fellowship of the church, and the *future* millenium. In fact, it is embarrassing today, as we begin to glimpse the core of what Jesus was doing, to note that practically everything He said pertained to the "kingdom." For example, His first utterance in His public ministry, according to Matthew, was: "'Repent, for the kingdom of heaven is at hand.'"[2]

Each of the gospel writers said it similarly. "The time has come," Jesus declared, in essence. "The kingdom is here, and I've come to open it to you and to show you how it works."

His pattern recalls the days following the anointing of Saul as Israel's first king when it became necessary for the prophet Samuel to teach how things should work: "Then Samuel told the people the manner of the kingdom, and wrote it in a book, and laid it up before the Lord. . . . "[3] Jesus did much the same, teaching His followers "the manner of the kingdom," but leaving it to others to put it in writing.

Many of us are now discovering this central purpose of our Lord, perceiving that the kingdom of God, though invisible, is right now nonetheless real, nonetheless powerful. We are much like the servant of Elisha who went outside the tent one morning and saw Syrian troops ready to close in on them from every side.

"We're surrounded!" he yelled.

But Elisha calmly asked the Lord to open the young man's eyes. Then he saw into the invisible world. Chariots of fire, the heavenly host, were everywhere about them, protecting Elisha. As the prophet had said, "'. . . those who are with us are more than those who are with them.'"[4]

Yes, the kingdom of God is here—now. And the message of the Bible is that we can and should look from this visible world, which is finite, into the invisible world, which is infinite. We should look from a world filled with impossibilities into one filled with possibilities.

We should do more than look, however, if we believe the Scriptures. We should enter. We should reach from the visible into the invisible and bring that secret kingdom into the visible through its principles—principles that can be adopted at this moment.

"The kingdom of God is like this . . . ," Jesus said, in effect. "It operates this way. . . ." "If you want this, then do this. . . ." Over and over.

So real is this invisible world, that when Jesus comes to earth the second time things will be turned inside out— through a sort of skinning process, you might say—and the invisible will become visible. The kingdom of God and its subjects will be manifested—unveiled. In the language of Paul's letter to the Romans: ". . . the creation waits eagerly for the revealing of the sons of God."[5] It "groans and suffers"—"standing on tiptoe," according to J. B. Phillips' translation—as it yearns for that unveiling.

The apostles had a foretaste of the inside-out effect during their days with Jesus. First came a statement by the Lord that has puzzled many Bible readers through the centuries: "'Truly I say to you, there are some of those who are standing here who shall not taste death until they see the Son of Man coming in His kingdom.'"[6]

A most marvelous event occurred six days later. We refer to it as the Transfiguration. Taking Peter, James, and John with Him, Jesus went to a high mountain.

> And He was transfigured before them; and His face shone like the sun, and His garments became as white as light. And behold, Moses and Elijah appeared to them, talking with Him. And Peter answered and said to Jesus, "Lord, it is good for us to be here; if You wish, I will make three tabernacles here, one for You, and one for Moses, and one for Elijah." While he was still speaking, behold, a bright cloud overshadowed them; and behold, a voice out of the cloud, saying, "This is My beloved Son, with whom I am well-pleased; listen to Him!" And when the disciples heard this, they fell on their faces and were much afraid. And lifting up their eyes, they saw no one, except Jesus Himself alone.[7]

The Lord became like lightning, shining white, and what had been invisible within Him became visible. The inside became the outside. The Law (Moses) and the prophets (Elijah) were fulfilled, and the Son of Man (Jesus) came visibly in His kingdom, in power and glory.

The disciples had a taste of what the kingdom will be at its manifestation. But what they saw at that moment had been resident in Jesus all the time. It had merely been invisible, but no less real and powerful. And that is what the Lord was telling His followers to lay hold of when He instructed them to seek the kingdom *first* so all of their needs would be met.

"Reach into the invisible and apply it to the visible," He said. "'For all things are possible with God.'"[8]

The Unlimited World of Jesus

Almighty God has been warning for thousands of years that because of our foolishness we will face crises. We are face to face with nuclear terror, a massive energy shortage, an insoluble economic crisis, debilitating moral bank-ruptcy, and other impossible difficulties. But Jesus explained that we are limited in our ability to cope with such problems only because we insist on living according to the ways of a world that is limited.

In effect he has said, "That need not remain so. An unlimited world surrounds you.

"Your are finite; it is infinite.

"You are mortal; it is immortal.

"You are filled with impossibilities; it is filled with possibilities."

That was the world of Jesus, even when He came as a man to live on this finite earth. He was careful to say: "'... the Son can do nothing of Himself, unless it is something He sees the Father doing; for whatever the Father does, these things the Son also does in like manner.'"[9]

The invisible world of His Father was Jesus' world throughout His incarnation. It was a world where everything was beautiful. And He became upset when His disciples failed to follow His example.

Once, when they were in the middle of the Sea of Galilee on a boat journey Jesus had instructed them to make, a storm arose; and their mission was near failure as their little vessel was swamped and showed signs of sinking. They rushed to wake Him from a much-needed nap. He was visibly perplexed. Why hadn't they been able to cope with the situation? They had failed to see into the invisible world where there were no impediments to the Lord's mission, and they had allowed themselves to be limited by world conditions.

So Jesus Himself arose and spoke to the storm, calming it. He then asked a rather humbling question: "'Why are you timid, you men of little faith?'"[10]

They had refused to reach into the world of the possible. And Jesus was angry, frustrated by the unwillingness of those He loved to accept the truth of what He had told them. One cannot help but wonder about His frustration as His followers seem so impotent to overcome the visible world today.

A Major Lesson

The Gospel according to Mark contains one of the Lord's most compact, yet most comprehensive, teachings about how to manifest the power of the invisible world in the visible today. Although we will be exploring the passage in more detail later, it is so significant for our initial understanding of the kingdom that we need to look at it in part now.

Jesus set the stage for the teaching when, on the way with His disciples to the temple to deal with the mockery practiced there under the guise of worship, He walked up to a fig tree in leaf, examined it for fruit, found none, and said: "'May no one ever eat fruit from you again!'"[11]

We must understand immediately that Jesus was not being capricious or petulant. He didn't simply lose His temper. The fig tree, as is so often the case in Scripture, symbolized Israel in biblical times; and when He cursed it, He was symbolically addressing a religious system that was often outwardly showy and inwardly fruitless. It was a system that practiced money changing and the selling of doves for sacrifice within the temple walls but gave the people little to feed their souls. He cursed that practice, too, as the Scripture goes on to report, and drove the money changers from the premises: "'Is it not written, "My house shall be called a house of prayer for all the nations"? But you have made it a robbers' den.'"[12]

No, He was not showing off. As with everything in His brief time on earth, the Lord made a point of tremendous significance. The next morning it came to light.

Jesus and His disciples passed the fig tree on the way back into Jerusalem and it had died, withered under His curse. Still failing to perceive the invisible world but yet observing its effects, Peter blurted out, "Look, the fig tree you cursed is all dried up!"

Then came the simplest insight into the deepest phenomenon: "And Jesus answered saying to them, 'Have faith in God.'"[13]

Those four words burst through the frontiers of heaven, laying bare the invisible kingdom. *Have faith in God.* We must totally believe in and trust Almighty God. We must know that One sits on the throne of the universe, as John saw in his great vision in the Book of the Revelation;[14] and He controls everything to the uttermost. He is without peer. He is omnipotent, omniscient, and omnipresent—the only free, unrestricted being in the universe.

Kathryn Kuhlman often said during her powerful ministry, "I sometimes think we're too familiar with God." She was right. Many times it seems we are trying to make Him into a toy that we can wind up and get to do our bidding. We sing Him little songs and utter all manner of things that threaten to demean His utter sovereignty. Kathryn's point was that God is God Almighty, the Great I Am. He created the sun and the moon and the earth and the solar system. It is staggering! He merely said, "Let there be light"[15] and the power of a billion hydrogen bombs began to move, rolling from one end of the solar system to the other. The distances and the energy are awesome. And they clearly illustrate the truth that a power exists in the universe transcending anything finite man's tiny mind can imagine. Paul the apostle put it into words, but even they are inadequate: "Now to Him who is able to do exceeding abundantly beyond all that we ask or think. . . ."[16]

That is God. And Jesus said, "Have faith in Him." Touch Him, He said, and anything is possible.

The Lord wants us in league with His Father. His teachings make it plain that total faith and trust in God—for every breath and every second—are to produce a oneness with Him. We are to see with Him, think with Him, as Jesus did, so that we can say along with Jesus that we do only what we see the Father doing. That way, we will reach into the invisible world even though living in the visible.

In the fig tree episode, Jesus went on to explain another point that will be dealt with fully in another chapter, but for now we will simply reflect on it:

> "Truly I say to you, whosoever says to this mountain, 'Be taken up and cast into the sea,' and does not doubt in his heart, but believes that what he says is going to happen, it shall be *granted* him. Therefore I say to you, all things for which you pray and ask, believe that you have received them, and they shall be *granted* you."[17]

In short, Jesus told His disciples that if they truly had faith in God, believed in His absolute sovereignty and mighty power, and entered into league with Him, they would become participants in the same energy and power that prevailed at the creation. They would work as God works; be fellow workers with Him, in the words of Paul.[18]

Yes, Jesus said, there is an invisible world, but we can see into it and touch it—here, now. God works; He wants us to work.

Principles of the Kingdom

Having been trained and surrounded by Christians who did not concern themselves especially with the Lord's teachings on the reality of the kingdom here and now, I didn't begin to catch glimpses of this reality in any meaningful way until the mid-seventies. I, too, had dwelt pretty much on the good news of salvation and the work of the Holy Spirit in believers' lives, and that truly is good news. But there is much more.

By mid-decade, I was wrestling with John the Baptist's insistence that "the kingdom of heaven is at hand."[19] As I have said, I soon saw he was reporting that the kingdom was here—here on earth—obviously because Jesus Christ was here.

I mused over this for many weeks and months, tracking through the Scriptures, praying for wisdom, and talking with one or two friends. As I badgered the Lord for wisdom, I began to realize there are principles in the kingdom as enunciated by Jesus Christ and that they are as valid for our lives as the laws of thermodynamics or the law of gravity. The physical laws are immutable, and I soon saw that the kingdom laws are equally so.

How can we determine those principles? They are found in the Bible. When we see a statement of Jesus that is not qualified as to time or recipient, then we have uncovered a universal truth. If He uses the terms "whosoever" or "whatsoever" or some other sweeping generalization, we should be especially alert. He is probably declaring a truth that will apply in every situation, in every part of the world, in every time.

It sounds so simple, and it is. Not every word spoken by the Lord had direct application for everyone; some were restricted. But others were without restriction—a "house divided against itself shall not stand,"[20] for example.

Once we perceive this secret, we realize anew that the Bible is not an impractical book of theology, but rather a practical book of life containing a system of thought and conduct that will guarantee success. And it will be true success, true happiness, true prosperity, not the fleeting, flashy, inconsistent success the world usually settles for.

The Bible, quite bluntly, is a workable guidebook for politics, government, business, families, and all the affairs of mankind.

There are dozens of these principles sprinkled throughout, and they are all marvelous. But there are several broad, overriding ones that I like to think of as "laws" of the kingdom. They span all of life, often overlapping and supplementing one another, but never contradicting. We will be probing into those major ones that hold special potential for revolutionizing our time and world.

They give us an alternative in our current world dilemma.

Now Is the Time

Think for a moment about those strange words of Jesus: "'seek first His kingdom and His righteousness; and all these things shall be added to you.'"[21]

So many of us see the words and are conscience-stricken. But for the wrong reasons.

We say, "Oh, if I could only bring myself to pray a lot and read the Bible and go to church every day, then God would like me and I would be His, and He would send His blessing to me."

We are not even certain we understand what we mean when we say "blessing."

Jesus was much more concrete than that. He was saying, "The kingdom of God rules in the affairs of men. It has principles for living, and they will bring success." Indeed, they will bring forth the kinds of things the world needs so desperately—the food, the shelter, the clothing, the fuel, the happiness, the health, the peace.

"But you shouldn't spend all your time and concentration seeking those things," He said in effect. "Seek the kingdom, understand the way it works, and then, as day follows night and as spring follows winter, the evidences of earthly success will follow you."

If we press this through to its logical conclusion, possibilities for life will rise up that we long ago relegated to the musty, unused portions of our Bibles, thinking of them as those promises made for a future time referred to as "the millenium." We will see that many of those conditions—those blessings we feared might turn out to be lofty Bible language that would pass us by—can be experienced in large measure right now. For they exist in the kingdom now. And we are speaking of reaching into that kingdom and letting its principles govern us right now.

Only God will inaugurate the visible reign on earth of His Son and those who will rule with Him,[22] but His word for the last two thousand years has been to "prepare the way."[23] His purpose is that His people know Him and learn how His secret kingdom functions. For the most part, we have fallen far short. But the word persists, and we can readily expect the willing fulfillment of some of the millenium blessings, like those foreseen by the prophet Isaiah, if we will follow His instructions:

> They will not hurt or destroy in all My holy mountain,
> For the earth will be full of the knowledge of the Lord
> As the waters cover the sea.[24]

> . . . they will hammer their swords into plowshares, and their
> spears into pruning hooks.
> Nation will not lift up sword against nation,
> And never again will they learn war.[25]

There *can* be peace; there *can* be plenty; there *can* be freedom. They will come the minute human beings accept the principles of the invisible world and begin to live by them in the visible world.

Can mankind do that? We will see how.

Study Guide

Key Scripture: Matt. 6:33

Key Idea: The fear that dominates the visible world can be overcome by faith in the One who established the invisible world.

1. What is the dramatic new reality according to Matthew 4:17?

2. Describe the new reality experienced by Elisha's servant in 2 Kings 6:8–17.

3. What was the atmosphere in the new reality described in Matthew 17:2–6, 8?

4. What is the contrast between the visible world and the invisible world according to the author on page 32? What experiences of the disciples illustrate this?

5. What do we learn about the role of faith in the invisible kingdom from the experience of Jesus' disciples in the boat?

6. How do we know a statement of Jesus has application for all time?

7. In what way do we become a part of the invisible world, according to Matthew 6:33?

Making It Happen

"If we press this through to its logical conclusion, possibilities for life will rise up that we long ago relegated to the musty, unused portions of our Bibles, thinking of them as those promises made for a future time referred to as 'the Millennium.'" Prayerfully read Matthew 6:33 again. Let the Holy Spirit guide you in describing one "possibility for life" through which you can participate this week in the invisible world, instead of being held captive by fear, like those who focus on the visible world.

Scripture References

1 Matthew 6:33
2 Matthew 4:17
3 1 Samuel 10:25, KJV
4 2 Kings 6:16
5 Romans 8:19
6 Matthew 16:28
7 Matthew 17:2–6, 8
8 Mark 10:27
9 John 5:19
10 Matthew 8:26
11 Mark 11:14
12 Mark 11:17
13 Mark 11:22
14 See Revelation 4:2
15 Genesis 1:14
16 Ephesians 3:20
17 Mark 11:23, 24
18 1 Corinthians 3:9
19 Matthew 3:2
20 Matthew 12:25
21 Matthew 6:33
22 See Revelation 20:4
23 Matthew 3:3

3. Seeing and Entering

In New Testament times, there was a man who perceived there was more to Jesus than met the eye. He may have heard John the Baptist refer to Him as one who "'existed before me.'"[1] The strange prophet, who lived alone in the desert, had even called Him "'the son of God.'"[2] Jesus of Nazareth was real and down-to-earth. Yet there was something other-worldly about Him. He spoke with authority, like the authority of Jehovah written about in the scrolls.[3] He must have been sent from heaven.[4]

One night this man, Nicodemus,[5] a ruler of the Jews, found Jesus alone and managed to talk with Him, which was hard to do because of the crowds. He may have been glad no one would see him.

He fumbled a bit for something to say and then blurted out: "Rabbi, we know you've come from God as a teacher, for no one can do the signs You do unless God is with him."

It was an awkward start, but it summarized what he was feeling. Nicodemus wanted to know God, and he instinctively realized that Jesus could give him teaching that would lead directly to God.

The Lord skipped small talk and went to the heart of Nicodemus' concern, preserving for all generations an understanding of the indispensable initial step toward life in an invisible world that governs all else. The kingdom of God is not really a place—at least not yet—but rather a state of being in which men, women, and children have yielded all sovereignty to the one and only true sovereign, Almighty God. It is the rule of God in the hearts, minds, and wills of people—the state in which the unlimited power and blessing of the unlimited Lord are forthcoming.

The natural eye cannot see this domain, and Jesus quickly explained that. He probably spoke softly, but distinctly. "'. . . unless one is born again, he cannot *see* the kingdom of God.'"[6]

Nicodemus was startled. What kind of a remark was that? So, getting bolder, he answered back more directly than he had begun: "How can a man be born when he is old? He cannot enter a second time into his mother's womb and be born, can he?'"[7]

The poor man had wanted to glimpse the invisible world and had been told how, but it went right by him, as it probably would have most of us. But Jesus really had told him how to peer into the throne room of God, from which the universe is directed. It should be noted, however, that He referred first to "seeing" the kingdom. Next, He took it a step further: "'. . . unless one is born of water and the Spirit, he cannot *enter* the kingdom of God.'"[8]

Jesus knew His man. Nicodemus wanted it all. He had suspected this very special rabbi, although visibly a flesh-and-blood man, was somehow living at that moment in Contact with God. So Jesus laid it out for him.

God is spirit. Those who would know Him—who would worship Him—must do so in spirit.[9] Since the Fall left man spiritually dead,[10] we must be reborn. Flesh begets flesh and spirit begets spirit,[11] so this rebirth must be accomplished by God the Holy Spirit. After that, being children of God,[12] we are able to engage in communion and fellowship with Him, as Adam did in the original kingdom in the Garden of Eden.[13]

Nicodemus' amazement soared, so Jesus pressed on with many deep things of the spirit—the things that men and women everywhere must make a part of themselves if they are to begin to deal successfully with our world in crisis:

> "Do not marvel that I said to you, 'You must be born again.' The wind blows where it wishes and you hear the sound of it, but do not know where it comes from and where it is going; so is everyone who is born of the Spirit." Nicodemus answered and said to Him, "How can these things be?" Jesus answered and said to him, "Are you the teacher of Israel, and do not understand these things? Truly, truly, I say to you, we speak that which we know, and bear witness of that which we have seen; and you do not receive our witness. If I told you earthly things and you do not believe, how shall you believe if I tell you heavenly things? And no one has ascended into heaven, but He who descended from heaven, even the son of Man. And as Moses lifted up the serpent in the wilderness, even so must the Son of Man be lifted up; that whoever believes may in Him have eternal life. For God so loved the world, that He gave His only begotten Son, that whoever believes in Him should not perish, but have eternal life."[14]

The New Testament evidence is that Nicodemus did eventually believe,[15] accepting entry into the secret kingdom even while coping with the trials of the visible one.

Like millions and millions of others, this once-timid man received Jesus into his life, accepting Him for who He was—God incarnate, the Word become flesh, Savior of the world, Lord of all. Forgiven for his sins, he was reconciled to God Almighty and enabled to perceive the "heavenly things" Jesus had spoken of, to gain access to the kingdom of God.

He was, in short, born again—born from above, as some translators prefer, born of the Spirit. He could say with Paul the apostle who later wrote:

> Now we have received, not the spirit of the world, but the Spirit who is from God, that we might *know the things freely given to us by God*, which things we also speak, not in words taught by human wisdom, but in those taught by the Spirit, combining spiritual thoughts with spiritual words.[16]

Both Nicodemus and Paul discovered that the kingdom of heaven is based on an invisible, spiritual reality, capable of visible, physical effects.

This is the reality that the world craves so badly.

Rebirth Is a Beginning

Unhappily, evangelical Christians have for too long reduced the born-again experience to the issue of being "saved." Salvation is an important issue, obviously, and must never be deemphasized. But rebirth must be seen as a beginning, not an arrival. It provides access to the invisible world, the kingdom of God, of which we are to learn and experience and then share with others. Jesus Himself said it clearly before His ascension:

> "All authority has been given to Me in heaven and on earth. Go therefore and *make disciples* of all the nations, baptizing them in the name of the Father and the Son and the Holy Spirit, *teaching them to observe all that I commanded you*; and lo, I am with you always, even to the end of the age."[17]

The commission was to make followers and learners—converts—and to *teach* them the principles of the kingdom. Entry into the body of believers was not enough. They were to learn how to live in this world, although their residence was in the kingdom. The invisible was to rule the visible. Christ has authority over both.

We have fallen short. Occasionally we have perceived God's hand at work in the world. But we have not striven to understand how the kingdom functions nor have we fully participated in its manifestation on earth.

We *must* hear this before it is too late: Jesus has opened to us the truths of the secret world of God! He has given us entrance into a world of indescribable power.

The atom gives us a clue as to what we're dealing with. We can't see an atom; solid matter looks like solid matter.

But atomic theory convinces us the atoms are there, pressed together into material substance at some point in time. And with Einstein's $E = MC^2$, we have discovered that this means matter is energy—sheer power capable of blowing up the world. yet all we see is the matter, even though the energy controls the matter.

Now this terribly great power is a tiny fraction of what we touch when we touch God's power. And it, too, is unseen—totally undiscerned—by one who has not been born again. The unspiritual man or woman regards such possibilities as foolishness.[18] And even many who have been born anew by the Spirit, though possessing the internal eyesight to see and believe in the invisible realm, refrain from appropriating its power for their daily lives. Having "seen" the kingdom, but not having fully "entered" in, they allow the conditions of the world to dominate them, contrary to the instructions of the Lord. The rebirth should give us the power to prevail over circumstances surrounding us.

Jesus gave us an additional piece of insight on this score. If we are to enter into the kingdom, taking full hold of that which is available, then we must "become like children,'" He said.[19] That is hard for our sophisticated generation, for it requires simple trust. A child is willing to leap ahead and seize any opportunity his father lays before him. So it must be with Christians and their heavenly Father, who gladly offers them the inexhaustible riches and power of His kingdom.[20] Indeed, He is pressing them upon us, if we will only respond confidently, joyfully, exuberantly—like little children.

An Issue of Truth

In light of the critical condition of the world, we need to examine even more philosophically why we are falling short in the matter of entering into the kingdom after rebirth. For if Christians miss the mark, how will the *world* learn?

Let's look at the logic of the problem. It leads us right into the issue of truth; and if there is anything the people of the world are looking for, it's truth.

First, we should recall the teachings of the Lord delivered through His encounter with a woman of Samaria. It is remarkable that this discourse, containing spiritual instruction with practical physical effects, involved one from the despised Samaritans, a people of mixed Assyrian and Jewish blood resulting from the Assyrian invasion of the Israelites' land centuries earlier. The Lord, a Jew, obviously wanted to show that His message extended to all people. We pick up the conversation in the middle of profound insights into the Holy Spirit, eternal life, adultery, worship, and ministry to the world, with Jesus speaking:

> ". . . an hour is coming, and now is, when the true worshipers shall worship the Father in spirit and *truth*; for such people the Father seeks to be His worshipers. God is spirit, and those who worship Him must worship in spirit and *truth*."[21]

That alone sounds right and good, but how does one practically do it?

Fortunately Jesus also said the following in a discussion with His disciples: "'I am the way, and the *truth*, and the life. . . .'"[22]

Putting those two revelations together, we see that we are to bring ourselves into line with a standard that is true. Jesus is the *truth*, so, being born of His Spirit, we are to conform to Him. We are to walk in His will. Only then can we worship God in spirit and truth. Only then can we move in truth. Note how essential He said this was: "'Not everyone who says to Me, "Lord, Lord," will enter the kingdom of heaven; but *he who does the will of My Father* who is in heaven.'"[23]

We need to be clear on this. Truth is the very centerpiece of the kingdom and its principles. We must be certain of the essential rightness of the principles, as opposed to other views. They lead to a new system of life that is better than any other system, the most practical possible, providing peace of mind, health, happiness, abundance, joy, and life everlasting. But we believe them because they are *true*.

Consider the following dialogue between Jesus and Pontius Pilate, the Roman governor at the time of the Lord's arrest and crucifixion:

> Then Pilate went back into the palace and called for Jesus to be brought to him. "Are you the King of the Jews?" he asked him. "'King' as *you* use the word or as the *Jews* use it?" Jesus asked. "Am I a Jew?" Pilate retorted. "Your own people and their chief priests brought you here. Why? What have you done?" Then Jesus answered "I am not an earthly king. If I were, my followers would have fought when I was arrested by the Jewish leaders. But my kingdom is not of the world." Pilate replied, "But you are a king then?" "Yes," Jesus said. "I was born for that purpose. *And I came to bring truth to the world. All who love the truth are my followers.*"[24]

Yes, there is a kingdom. Jesus said it is founded on truth. He, the Truth, is king of it. Everyone who loves the truth—Him—and wants to follow the truth is a member of that kingdom.

> ". . . He who sent Me is true; and the things which I heard from Him, these I speak to the world. . . . If you abide in My word, then you are truly disciples of Mine; and you shall know *the truth*, and *the truth shall make you free.*"[25]

Not only is He true, the Lord said, but the things He teaches are true. And if we accept and practice these truths, we will be free, another condition the people of the world so desperately seek. I want to emphasize what it is that makes us free. It is not merely the acceptance of Jesus and His atonement, but *the doing of the truth*—putting into practice the principles of the kingdom.

As I said, we too often stop short. We must start with the crucifixion and the resurrection, but we must follow through with the practice of the principles, the laws of life. For God said thousands of years ago:

". . . I will give you a new heart and put a new spirit within you;
and I will remove the heart of stone from your flesh and give
you a heart of flesh. And I will put My spirit within you *and
cause you to walk in My statutes, and you will be careful to
observe my ordinances.*"[26]

He has gone to great lengths over many centuries to
plant within our hearts His ways, His truth, His principles.
What he has done surpasses the old covenant of law and
regulation handed down to the people of Israel at Mount
Sinai. Jesus has fulfilled the written law, placing it within
His subjects, but they must live out the principles.

Applying this to our personal conduct, we see that
speaking the truth is central. Its importance must never be
minimized. Just as Jesus is the king of truth, the Holy Spirit
(the Lord and giver of life) is called "the Spirit of truth."[27]
Where He abides there is truth. At the same time, Satan (the
adversary) is described as "the father of lies."[28]

Although true speech is only a part of ultimate truth, it
is no mere coincidence that the apostle John tells us God's
final heaven will exclude anyone who "maketh a lie."[29] All
liars, he declares, "shall have their part in the lake which
burneth with fire and brimstone."[30] Telling the truth is a
serious matter!

In the world we see conduct that flies flagrantly in the
face of these warnings. The Soviet Union, an atheistic society, gives over an entire section of its secret police to
"disinformation"—the systematic spreading of lies through
the free press of its adversaries. So frequent has the use of
the big lie become in dictatorial societies that George Or-
well in his book *1984* portrayed the ultimate dictatorship as
one in which there was no truth, only a reordering of facts
in "newspeak."

In the United States, regard for truth still exists in some
quarters, although it is clearly diminishing along with regard for absolute values. Perjury—the willful telling of a lie
while under lawful oath—is a felony and stands as a secular
affirmation of the kingdom's demand for truth.

How sad that in some instances we find church people

who actually seek to further God's kingdom by the use of falsehood, building up with one hand but tearing down with the other. Exaggeration, embellishment, and even fabrication have become instruments of evangelism in some quarters. A tragic indictment is that the term "evangelistically speaking" is the euphemism some have chosen to describe flagrant misrepresentation of fact.

We must see that the Lord does not need our embellishment to accomplish His purpose or to glorify His name. We do Him—and ourselves—a disservice when we depart from the truth.

Jesus Understands

Jesus and His Ways are true. As the One by whom and for whom all things were created,[31] He understands precisely how the world works. His teachings, which so many in the world have tried to relegate to the categories of goody-goody daydreaming or pietistic navel-gazing, are functional.

The world yearns for peace; He can provide it. The world wants love; He has the formula. The world wants riches, honor, and full life; He promises them all.

But there are requisites. One must be born again by accepting the free gift of salvation that He alone provides, learn from Him, and put His principles into practice.

What are the key laws or principles that govern the deepest desires and needs of mankind? They embody the truths that we will be examining and illustrating in detail in the following chapters, along with the virtues and subprinciples flowing through them.

We will see that the truths of Jesus have the characteristic of the "truths" of the American Declaration of Independence—they are "self-evident." We will begin to understand why a society that abandons these laws, which are self-evident, will collapse. And equally evident will be the reasons why a society that voluntarily adheres to such laws can be expected to prosper.

Do not forget: The One proclaiming the laws knows how both the visible world and the invisible kingdom work!

Study Guide

Key Scripture: John 13:1–16; 1 Cor. 2:12–13

Key Idea: "We *must* hear this before it is too late: Jesus has opened to us the truths of the secret world of God! He has given us entrance into a world of indescribable power" (p. 53).

You are at a crossroads in your life. For twenty years you have been accumulating skills and seniority in a major national company. Promotion beyond your present position comes only to those who literally lose their life for the company. You know what it has cost others in broken marriages and alienated adolescents.

At the same time you are aware that your skills are in high demand if you were to form your own consulting business. Yet the risk of failure is ever-present when you leave the cocoon of the major national company. In fact, starting a new venture could be just as time-consuming as going for broke in the company.

What is the difference between your making this decision and a person who does not know Jesus Christ as personal Savior making the same decision?

Entering the New Reality

1. Read John 3:1–16 carefully. What are the two objections Nicodemus raises to Christ's teaching on the new birth?

   a.

   b.

2. According to verse 12, what is the difference between Nicodemus's understanding of things and Jesus' understanding of how the spiritual world works?

3. How does a person enter the secret kingdom, according to verses 5, 15–16?

4. What is the new reality we enter when we are born again, according to 1 Corinthians 2:12–13?

5. Into what kind of activity does our new position in the secret kingdom take us? (see Matt. 28:18–20.)

6. What is the secret for successful activity in the invisible kingdom of God? (See pp. 51, 52.)

7. On a scale of 1 to 5, rate the following qualities and their importance in the kingdom (5 being the highest value).

Become like children	1	2	3	4	5
Highly developed skills	1	2	3	4	5
Being truthful	1	2	3	4	5
Commitment to sharing Christ	1	2	3	4	5
Absolute truthfulness	1	2	3	4	5
Childlike faith	1	2	3	4	5
Willingness to learn	1	2	3	4	5

Making it Happen

It's obvious that the truth is very important to God and that truth as we're to live it is exemplified in the life of Jesus

Christ. During the next week, read through the biblical book of Mark, focusing on Jesus as a model of truthfulness. Note especially what He said about Himself, how He related to God the Father and to people, and the priorities by which He lived from day to day.

Scripture References

1 John 1:30
2 John 1:34
3 See Matthew 7:29
4 See Matthew 16:16
5 See John 3:1–21
6 John 3:3
7 John 3:4
8 John 3:5
9 See John 4:24
10 See Genesis 2:17
11 See John 3:6
12 See John 1:12, 13
13 See Genesis 1, 2
14 John 3:8–16
15 John 19:38–42
16 1 Corinthians 2:12, 13
17 Matthew 28:18–20
18 See 1 Corinthians 2:14
19 Matthew 18:3
20 Luke 12:32
21 John 4: 23, 24
22 John 14:6
23 Matthew 7:21
24 John 18:33–37, TLB
25 John 8:26, 31, 32
26 Ezekiel 36:26, 27
27 John 14:17
28 John 8:44
29 Revelation 21:27, KJV
30 Revelation 21:8, KJV
31 See Colossians 1:16

4. How God's Kingdom Works

To understand how the kingdom of heaven works and how it holds sway over the visible world, we must place two facts in the brightest light.

First, there is absolute abundance in the kingdom of God.

Second, it is possible to have total favor with the ruler of that abundance.

On the first point, Jesus, telling His disciples that they were being permitted to know the secrets of the kingdom,[1] set forth the truth of abundance with a parable about a sower.[2] The seed that fell on good ground, He said, yielded crops of a hundredfold, sixtyfold, and thirtyfold. *That* is abundance—returns of 10,000, 6,000, and 3,000 percent. You see, there is no economic recession, no shortage, in the kingdom of God.

Throughout our forests, we see this truth touching the physical world. Consider the profusion of seed that comes from a maple tree. Look at the multiplicity of colors in a sunset; there are more hues than we can name. Plant life, marine life, bird life—there is no end, almost as though God had sent abundance into the universe as testimony to His own infinitude.

Because He is the only truly free being in the universe, His kingdom is a sphere of total possibility. Jesus emphasized this when He multiplied the loaves and fishes, taking a little boy's lunch and feeding more than five thousand hungry people.[3] God is never diminished by circumstances.

Neither is He limited by His own universe or the natural laws He Himself established. Pantheists attempt to convince us that God is merely *in* nature. But were that true, He would be limited. No, He is above the laws of nature and any restrictions that those laws might try to impose. He can create from nothing, or He can take existing matter and transform it. His is a total world—total health, total life, total energy, total strength, total provision.

In the matter of favor, Jesus, of course, was our perfect illustration of God's bestowal: "And Jesus kept increasing in wisdom and stature, and in *favor* with God and men."[4]

Within a few short years, God presented the supreme token of this grace at the time of the baptism of Jesus in the River Jordan: ". . . and the Holy Spirit descended upon Him in bodily form like a dove, and a voice came out of heaven, 'Thou art My beloved son, in Thee I am well-pleased.'"[5]

This, God the Father was saying, was the One He had spoken of and promised for centuries. He was going to pour out His grace and blessing on His only begotten Son and on those who belong to Him.

First, we need to recognize that when the Bible speaks of God's "grace," it is speaking of His "favor." In the New Testament, the Greek word for grace is *charis*, perhaps best defined as "the unmerited favor of God."

This favor, the apostle Paul said, allows us to stand before God Himself.[6] It is our sole means of access to the throne of the kingdom.[7] Think of it: If we have access to the Father, standing before Him in His favor, then we have the prospect of continuous blessing. Indeed, Paul wrote that the prospect was for·*increasing* blessing:

> But God, being rich in mercy, because of His great love with which He loved us, even when we were dead in our transgressions, made us alive together with Christ (by grace you have

been saved), and raised us up with Him, and seated us with
Him in the heavenly places, in Christ Jesus, in order that *in the
ages to come He might show the surpassing riches of His grace*
in kindness toward us in Christ Jesus.[8]

Now when God blesses us and keeps us, and lets His face
shine upon us, and is gracious to us,[9] then before men we
appear in a light that far transcends any of our natural abilities. He can cause our plans to succeed. He can cause people
to like us. He can cause us to be preferred and chosen above
others of equal talent. He can protect our children. He can
guard our property. He can cause His angels to aid us.

How well I remember the day in the late sixties when
God showed forth this favor in my life in a practical, worka-
day manner. CBN was in urgent need of $3 million worth of
modern equipment that would allow us to broadcast with
the power and quality needed if we were to do what the Lord
had called us to do. With absolutely no worldly credentials
or the support that would normally be required to do business at this level, I began negotiations with one of the
world's leading electronics manufacturers. There was no
reason to expect a successful outcome.

But God had other plans. In the most remarkable, yet
smooth and calm manner, I received total favor from this
giant company and arranged for our equipment needs to be
met for a period of years at the finest terms imaginable.
Others in the industry were envious, for I had received
every concession in price, down payment, and credit terms
that it was possible to get.

You see, God had let His face shine upon us and was
gracious to us. We had favor with Him in the invisible
world, and since He ruled even the visible world that tried
to ignore Him, He gave us favor there as well.

A Partnership

With those two truths of abundance and favor established, we are ready for the fact that God has entered into a

partnership with redeemed man. He has given us the potential of cooperating with His Spirit in the whole work of the kingdom. Prayer is the link between finite man and the infinite purposes of God. In its ultimate sense, it consists of determining God's will and then doing it on earth. It does *not* consist merely of asking for what *we* want. To pray in the truest sense means to put our lives into total conformity with what God desires.

We begin this process by dropping our own preconceived ideas and entering His presence by grace to wait upon Him. Our thought should be: "Lord, what do *You* want? What are *You* doing?" As George Mueller, the great British man of faith, said, "Have no mind of your own in the matter."

The Lord's chastisement of the false prophets, recorded in the Book of Jeremiah, illustrates the importance of this. Warning the people against those prophets who were speaking visions of their own imaginations and not from the mouth of God, He asked: "'But who has stood in the council of the LORD,/That he should see and hear His word?/Who has given heed to His word and listened?'"[10] They were to be alone with the Lord, to see and to hear what He was doing. They were not to put their own ideas first.

So it should be with us when we pray. We should stand in the Spirit in the invisible kingdom; there we will see and hear, and our role in the partnership can become active.

If we turn again to the account of Jesus and the fig tree as recorded in Mark's Gospel, which we touched on in chapter two, this becomes clear. We should recall that Jesus, discussing the power that withered the tree, said that the first thing required was "faith in God," absolute trust and confidence that He is God Almighty, unlimited and infinite. Implied was the fact that He speaks to His people, revealing what He is doing. Then Jesus said this:

> For verily I say unto you, that whosoever shall say unto this mountain, Be thou removed, and be thou cast into the sea; and shall not doubt in his heart, but shall believe that those things which he saith shall come to pass; he shall have whatsoever he saith.[11]

If we fully believe God and have discerned His will, Christ said that we may translate that will from the invisible world to the visible by the spoken word. In short, God uses the spoken word to translate spiritual energy—sheer power—into the material.

The most vivid illustration, of course, was the creation of the world. God spoke to the void and said, "'Let there be light.'"[12] and there was light. The same with the firmament and the waters and the dry land; the same with everything that was created.[13] All things were made by the Word.[14] And that which was spoken was energized by the Spirit, moving upon the face of the waters,[15] shaping matter, which is itself energy, into God's predetermined patterns.

In like manner, our partnership with God is fulfilled when we speak His word in the power of the Holy Spirit. As Jesus taught: "'Therefore I say unto you, What things soever ye desire, when ye pray, believe that ye receive them, and ye shall have them.'"[16] Thus He took us right back to where He began. Have faith in God, know who He is, know what He is doing, trust His favor upon us, participate with Him. What we say in His name should then come to pass.

The Missing Link

For the vast majority of Christians throughout history, the "speaking" has been the missing link between what we believe and what we do. We have lost the understanding of how God Almighty works, how His Son works, and how we are to work once we enter into the unobstructed view of God that Jesus provides in the kingdom.

The thing that clouds our view is sin. But once the sin is forgiven, we are to enter bodily into the throne room of grace and commune with God by the Spirit, who communicates with our spirit. It's a bit like turning into a radio or television station. You get on the right frequency and you pick up a program. So it is with listening to the Lord. He is speaking constantly, but we are often on the wrong frequency.

Once He has spoken to us, we are to speak after Him. If we do, miracles occur. If we don't, usually nothing will happen. For, in the material world, God has chosen to enter into partnership with us, his co-laborers, whom He is grooming for the perfect, visible establishment of His kingdom on earth.

Right now, in this life, He would have us stop cajoling and begging. He would have us live in the kingdom, in harmony with Him, receiving His thoughts by the Spirit. As the apostle Paul said, ". . . We have the mind of Christ."[17] So speak that mind, Jesus was saying in the fig tree episode. Speak His thoughts. Don't be afraid. Don't doubt. "For God has not given us a spirit of timidity, but of power and love and discipline."[18]

We must see that, by living in the kingdom now, we enter back into what man lost in the Garden of Eden. We return to the authority God gave us at the Creation. Like Adam, we hear the Lord's voice revealing the secrets of the world. And, as He speaks, we speak after Him in the manner of Ezekiel in his vision in the valley of dry bones.

> Again He said to me, "Prophesy over the bones, and say to them, 'O dry bones, hear the word of the Lord.'"[19]

The prophet listened as the Lord said He intended to give the bones life, sinews, flesh, skin, and breath. Then it was Ezekiel's turn.

> So I *prophesied* as I was commanded; and as *I prophesied*, there was a noise, and behold, a rattling; and the bones came together, bone to its bone. And I looked, and behold, sinews were on them, and flesh grew, and skin covered them; but there was no breath in them. Then He said to me, "Prophesy to the breath, prophesy, son of man, and say to the breath, 'Thus says the LORD GOD, "Come from the four winds, O breath, and breathe on these slain, that they come to life."'" So I *prophesied* as He commanded me, and the breath came into them, and they came to life, and stood on their feet, an exceedingly great army.[20]

In this Old Testament episode, Ezekiel learned what I call the word of faith, which didn't receive full development until the New Testament was written. The lesson was this: Through our words, we translate the will of God in the invisible kingdom to the visible situation that confronts us. We speak to money, and it comes. We speak to storms, and they cease. We speak to crops, and they flourish.

Although I will discuss this miraculous phenomenon in detail later, the simple truth is that God's word, spoken into a situation, will perform His purpose: "So shall My word be which goes forth from My mouth;/It shall not return to Me empty,/Without accomplishing what I desire,/And without succeeding in the matter for which I sent it."[21]

The Way It Will Be

Some day, when the kingdom is fully manifested, the speaking will not be necessary. The thought will become the deed, as it is in heaven today.

On my television program, "The 700 Club," I did an interview with Dr. Richard E. Eby, a well-known California obstetrician and gynecologist, that illustrates the point vividly. In 1972, he said, he fell from a second-story balcony and split his skull. He told me that he died (whether for minutes or hours, he doesn't know) but miraculously returned to life and today is perfectly healthy and normal.

During the experience, Dr. Eby related, his spirit left his body and apparently went to heaven, or paradise. As one would expect, he found it to be a most beautiful place. At one stage he entered a field of flowers and as he walked along, he was overwhelmed by their beauty. "Wouldn't it be wonderful if I had a bunch and could smell them?" he thought. But as he started to bend over, he looked at his hand, and it was already full of flowers.

At another point, he was thinking how good it would be to go to a distant valley and, behold, he was there.

As a scientific man, he naturally analyzed these experiences carefully and concluded that in heaven the mere thought produces the action. As the psalmist declared: "Delight yourself in the Lord;/And He will give you the desires of your heart."[22]

In heaven, Dr. Eby was delighting himself in the Lord, doing His perfect will, and the yearnings of his heart were immediately fulfilled. He didn't have to speak them. On earth a translation is required, but not so in the ultimate kingdom. One day we will not need telephones, mass transit, or computers as the speed of thought eclipses the speed of light. But now we need the spoken word.

What Is Faith?

As we have emphasized several times, the covering statement for the entire matter of how the kingdom works is "Have faith in God." Faith governs all. But it is frequently misunderstood.

The Bible says bluntly:

> Now faith is the assurance of things hoped for, the conviction of things not seen. For by it the men of old gained approval. By faith we understand that the worlds were prepared by the word of God, so that what is seen was not made out of things which are visible. . . . And without faith it is impossible to please Him, for he who comes to God must believe that He is, and that He is a rewarder of those who seek Him.[23]

The Living Bible's paraphrase is helpful:

> What is Faith? It is the confident assurance that something we want is going to happen. It is the certainty that what we hope for is waiting for us, even though we cannot see it up ahead. . . .[24]

Said another way, faith is the title deed to things we can't see. When we buy property, we meet with the seller and papers are drawn up. We receive a deed and it says we own a stated piece of property. The minute it is signed, we own the property. We don't have to go to it; we don't have to see it. It's ours. We have a title deed.

The same with faith. We have a title deed to what God has promised. Our role is to believe in our hearts that it has been accomplished, according to what God has given us the deed to, and then to speak it. We can't force it. We can't sit around a room with a group and work it up. We can receive it only from God. The Bible says: "So then faith cometh by hearing, and hearing by the word of God."[25]

We hear the Lord's Word; it builds in our hearts, and the light goes on. "It's mine!" Deep down inside, there will be no doubt. That is what the Lord meant when He referred in the fig tree episode to the one who speaks to the mountain and "does not doubt in his heart." The mountain will move if the Lord has spoken.

The Bible also cautions about double-mindedness:

> . . . let him ask in faith without any doubting, for the one who doubts is like the surf of the sea driven and tossed by the wind. For let not that man expect that he will receive anything from the Lord, being a double-minded man, unstable in all his ways.[26]

There can be no equivocating, no going back and forth. So many of us hear something from the Lord, we believe it briefly, but the wind blows and the storm pounds and our faith in what God said vanishes like the mist. We need to counter by speaking the word God has given and then simply accepting it.

I must add a word, however, to drive home a subtle point. Our faith throughout all of this must be in the Lord— "have faith in God," Jesus said—and not in our ability, our stubborn strength. Our faith is not to be *in our faith*: "Trust in the LORD with all your heart,/And do not lean on your own understanding."[27]

For the Lord, while structuring most of His dealings with man around the point of faith, made plain that His insistence on faith was not quantitative, but qualitative. He said we would move mountains if we had faith the size of a mustard seed.[28] We don't need a mountain of faith to move a mountain of dirt or even a mountain of world problems.

The object and reality of the faith are the issues. We don't need stubbornness, but confidence.

> . . . this is the confidence which we have before Him, that, if we ask anything according to His will, He hears us. And if we know that He hears us in whatever we ask, we know that we have the requests which we have asked from Him.[29]

The Importance of Right Thinking

We begin to see that in the kingdom:
—Spirit controls matter.
—Lesser authority yields to greater authority.
—The mind is the ultimate conduit of the spirit.
—Speech is the intermediate conduit between spirit and matter and between greater and lesser authority.

That which the writers of the many "success" books call "positive mental attitude," or PMA, is indeed important. Because our minds are the agents our spirits use in influencing the world around us, it is patently clear the negative attitudes can vitiate our most valiant attempts. Conversely, positive thinking will more often than not lead to successful action.

Unfortunately, such people as Napoleon Hill, who wrote *Think and Grow Rich*, have gleaned only a few of the truths of the kingdom of God. They try to gain the kingdom without submitting themselves to the King.

Some of the metaphysical principles of the kingdom, taken by themselves, can produce fantastic temporal benefits. But without the lordship of Jesus, these benefits are both transitory and harmful. In fact, many of the advocates of mind over matter ultimately end in hellish spiritism. "'What will a man be profited, if he gains the whole world, and forfeits his soul? . . .'"[30]

Many sincere followers of Jesus Christ destroy their

effectiveness in this world because they do not understand the laws of spiritual authority and the way this authority is transmitted. They especially are not aware of the power of what they say.

Solomon wrote: "From the fruit of a man's mouth he enjoys good. . . ."[31] In other words, when you confess blessing, favor, victory, and success, those things will come to you.

But the majority of Christians ignore this truth. "How do you feel?" we ask someone.

"I feel terrible," he replies, not realizing he has commanded his body to be sick.

"Can you do it?"we ask.

"I can't do that," he replies, not knowing he has limited God and himself by his words.

"I can't get out of debt," someone says. He has just commanded his debt to continue.

We call such negative assertions "realistic appraisals" of the situation. But they aren't realistic, for they ignore the power of God, the authority of the invisible world of the spirit, and the grant of power made by God to His children.

A much more realistic assertion was made by the apostle Paul when he boldly declared: "I can do all things through Him who strengthens me."[32]

Pettiness, overemphasis on minutiae, fear of failure, constant complaining, murmuring—all inhibit the realization of kingdom conditions. As a man thinks in his heart, so he is.[33]

Many atheletes and men of physical accomplishment have realized this principle. Ben Hogan, the golfer, was one. As he approached a shot, in his mind's eye he would see himself swinging the club and the ball traveling in a perfect arc, landing in a particular spot. He set the pattern in his mind. And then he followed through with his body. His success was spectacular.

The same has been true with runners and jumpers. God has given us minds and bodies that work that way. Our bodies will obey our minds, for the most part. Added to that is the fact that our spirits can be in touch with God. Now if our spirits govern our minds and our minds govern our bodies, then God in the invisible world governs us in the visible world.

At the same time, the Lord has called for us to be honest and truthful in the innermost being,[34] so we are not to delude ourselves and to say something is true when it is not. We are not to engage in superstition or silliness. We merely are to have confidence that with Him all things are possible.

Perhaps the most dramatic example of proper thinking, speaking, and doing came to my attention through "The 700 Club." It involved Leslie, May, and Joe Lemke and an extraordinary true-life story of love.

The story began in 1952 when May, a nurse-governess with a reputation for unusual ability with children, was asked to take care of a six-month-old baby named Leslie who was retarded, who had cerebral palsy, and whose eyes had been removed because they were diseased. Leslie was not expected to live long.

The Lord gave May a great love for Leslie, and she began to treat him like a normal baby. She taught him to feed from a nursing bottle by making loud sucking noises against his cheek. Soon she gave up everything else to take care of the child. "I have a job to do for Jesus now," she said, "and I'm going to do it."

By the time he was ten, Leslie could move only a hand and friends advised May that she was wasting her time. But she refused to concede. "I'm doing something for an innocent boy who will be something some day," she said. "I believe in God, and He will do it."

She carried the boy around and spoke her love into his ear, holding him and squeezing him continuing to treat him like a normal child. Eventually he learned to stand by holding onto a fence, and then to walk by following it.

Throughout it all, May prayed constantly for Leslie. Before long, she added a thought to her petitions, repeating it to the Lord several times a day: "Dear Lord, the Bible says you gave each of us a talent. Please help me find the talent in this poor boy who lies there most of the day and does nothing."

May noticed that the boy seemed to respond to musical sounds like the plucking of a string or a cord. So she and her husband, Joe, bought a piano; and she played him all kinds of music, using the radio and records. Leslie listened for hours, seemingly in deep concentration.

After four years of praying for the boy's "talent" to be revealed, May and Joe were awakened at 3:00 A.M. one night by the sound of piano music. They found Leslie sitting at the piano playing beautifully, like a trained musician. He was sixteen years old.

Over the next ten years, the boy learned dozens of songs—classical, popular, jazz—and has even learned to sing with the playing. His talent was fully manifested through May's constant love and confession that nothing is impossible with God. She discerned God's purpose and spoke it into being, thoroughly rejecting negativism.

A Necessary Ingredient

Perhaps history's biggest roadblock to effective demonstration of the invisible kingdom is found in negativism. For in the final analysis, it reveals the absence of *unity*, about which I will have more to say in conjunction with other principles. But at this point, we need to see that the kingdom of God works through the phenomenon of harmony.

To begin with, entrance into the kingdom, totally dependent upon grace and not upon any kind of status or merit, immediately establishes a basic equality among people. No one can say, "I've earned a better place than you." Growing from that logically is a new relationship between individuals. It is one based on the will of the Father, surpassing existing national, racial, familial, or church relationships. The Lord Jesus was precise on this: "'. . . whoever does the will of My Father who is in heaven, he is My brother and sister and mother.'"[35]

That statement transcended the Lord's own family relationships, and it transcends ours. The kingdom thus is a family. Jesus is our elder brother; His Father is our father. That cuts across all lines. My mother can be a black woman who does the will of the Father. My brother can be a Chinese who does likewise, or a Jew, or an Arab.

How we need to see this! All strife and turmoil in the world can be eliminated simply by its fulfillment. The Middle East can be at peace. Latin America can be at peace. The aged and the young can be at peace.

This wholly unique concept of love and family relationships can produce that which has escaped man's grasp from the beginning. But peace will not be the only fruit of such transferral of kingdom life to this world. Paul the apostle wrote of the "fruit of the Spirit" that would grow in a climate of unity—"love, joy, peace, patience, kindness, goodness, faithfulness, gentleness, self-control."[36] Against such characteristics there is no law, Paul added. None is needed.

The Scripture's classic illustration of the transfer of kingdom power to the visible world when there is unity comes in a well-known but underutilized portion of Matthew's Gospel.

> "Again I say to you, that if two of you agree on earth about anything that they may ask, it shall be done for them by My Father who is in heaven. For where two or three have gathered together in My name, there I am in their midst."[37]

The full implication of the point is that when there is no unity of purpose, no crossover of barriers, then the power is not activated.

Prospects for Improvement

I am confident that we will see the kingdom of God working more in the visible world as the Lord continues to bring people to Himself. Should the world experience the great revival of faith in Jesus Christ that I am expecting, then it would be reasonable to see an increase in the exercise of these truths of the kingdom. This, I am sure, will enable the world to transcend many of the limitations we are experiencing now.

For example, it is clear that we are going to run out of fossil fuels, even though at times we experience some relief in the oil and gas shortage. We can't keep burning limited resources forever. But we have some very big oceans, and they contain hydrogen. Sooner or later, God may give to one or more of His people a concept for running cars on such water. He will simply allow a peek into the invisible world to see His purpose. Then a faithful one will speak and act according to the revelation, and the concept will take life.

I believe we can expect this in the area of building materials, perhaps to replace steel and other items in short supply. I am sure there will be foodstuffs we haven't dreamed of, perhaps new living space to accommodate vast populations. The limits are not found in what we see, feel, and taste. They are in our hearts and our willingness to stand in that place where we have an unclouded view of what the Lord is doing.

Thoughts like these invariably cause concern about whether someone who is not prospering or indeed is suffering in slums and poverty is violating the truths of the kingdom. Such questions must not be dismissed hastily. For there is suffering in the world and seemingly many Christians are living short of the ideals we are discussing and are in great distress.

What can we say? I am convinced that if a person is *continuously* in sickness, poverty, or other physical and mental straits, then he is missing the truths of the kingdom. He has either failed to grasp the points we have been making in this chapter about the operation of the kingdom or is not living according to the major principles we will be exploring. He has missed the prosperity I believe the Scripture promises.

True, there is suffering, even in God's will, but as with the cross of Christ, it doesn't last forever.

It is important, however, that we not try to equate scriptural prosperity with riches. We are speaking of the Lord's blessing, not great material wealth. Some people are not capable of handling money or other wealth. Some would be destroyed by pride. So God prospers according to His wisdom, according to the true need of those involved.

Nonetheless, I believe Christians can escape any ghetto to which they have been confined, real or imagined. God will make a way. He will provide methods with which to reverse conditions and attitudes. Shortage will turn to abundance, hostility to favor.

As for tragedy and seemingly inevitable mishap, the Bible says:

> The steps of a good man are ordered by the LORD: and he delighteth in his way. Though he fall down, *he shall not be utterly cast down*: for the LORD upholdeth him with his hand.[38]

Furthermore, it says the wicked will try to harm the righteous, but "the Lord will not leave him in his hand."[39] There may be difficult days and even stumbling, but God's arm will be there to deliver the faithful.

Study Guide

Key Scripture: Eph. 2:4–7

Key Idea: As members of God's invisible kingdom, we can experience His blessing as we work in partnership with Him.

1. "God has sent abundance into the universe as testimony to His own infinitude" (p. 55). Describe one example of God's superabundance in the world you live in.

2. Write out in your own words the spiritual abundance described in Ephesians 2:4–7.

3. What attitude puts us into partnership with God, according to Mark 11:23 (kjv)? (See also pp. 57–59).

4. What sets us free to think God's thoughts after him according to the apostle Paul in Colossians 3:1–4?

5. How can we unleash God's activity in our lives when we think God's thoughts? (See pp. 59–61.)

6. "We have a title deed to what God has promised. Our role is to believe in our hearts that it has been accomplished, according to what God has given us the deed to, and then to speak it. We can't force it. We can't sit around a room with a group and work it up. We can receive it only from God" (p. 63). Describe one situation in your life where you can apply this.

7. What is the biblical version of a "positive mental attitude," according to page 65?

Making It Happen

Santos (not his real name) lived in a Mexican ghetto in the West. By the time he was sixteen he had personally witnessed eight men being killed, had participated in gang brutality, and had slashed a man who challenged him across the face with his knife. The violence was so extreme that no policeman dared enter his community. One day he was introduced to Christ through a radio program in Spanish.

Soon he was out on the street, preaching against the violence. He learned to read and write in Spanish. Eventually he became a prison guard, preaching wherever he could. Gradually he saw God make great changes in his community.

What condition in your community needs changing? How can you become the instrument for change as you draw on the power of God?

Scripture References

1 See Matthew 13:11
2 See Matthew 13:3–8
3 See Matthew 14:16–21
4 Luke 2:52
5 Luke 3:22
6 See Ephesians 2:8–18
7 See Hebrews 4:14–16
8 Ephesians 2:4–7
9 See Numbers 6:24, 25
10 Jeremiah 23:18
11 Mark 11:23, KJV
12 Genesis 1:3
13 See Genesis 1
14 See John 1:3
15 See Genesis 1:2
16 Mark 11:24, KJV
17 1 Corinthians 2:16
18 2 Timothy 1:7
19 Ezekiel 37:4
20 Ezekiel 37:7–10
21 Isaiah 55:11
22 Psalm 37:4
23 Hebrews 11:1–3, 6
24 Hebrews 11: 1, TLB
25 Romans 10:17, KJV
26 James 1:6–8
27 Proverb 3:5
28 See Matthew 17:20

29 1 John 5:14, 15
30 Matthew 16:26
31 Proverb 13:2
32 Philippians 4:13
33 See Proverb 23:7, KJV
34 See Psalm 51:6
35 Matthew 12:50
36 Galatians 5:22, 23
37 Matthew 18:19, 20
38 Psalm 37:23, 24, KJV
39 Psalm 37:33

5. Progressive Happiness

As we have seen, the kingdom of heaven exists now, here. Although it is spiritual and invisible, it governs the material and visible. It is inhabited by people who have been born again spiritually. It operates in a specified manner.

Now we see that it also has a constitution, a system of fundamental principles and virtues to determine the quality and conduct of life. That constitution is contained in what has come to be known as the Sermon on the Mount, presented by Jesus quite early in His public ministry, probably within the first year.

It clearly sums up a new way of life. It demands an inner revolution of attitude and outlook. It turns ordinary ideas upside down. It sets the stage for a new world order.

This constitution has a preamble. We label its eight points as the Beatitudes, which is fitting since they truly do guarantee "blessedness" or "happiness." Happy are those who live by them.

They also show us a lot about the nature of God, the one ruling the kingdom.

Complemented by principles and virtues set forth throughout Scripture, they provide the underpinning and framework for real life, even during a time of transition from the old, discredited order into the emerging future.

As we explore these well-known, yet still-alien words, we should peer between and behind them to perceive the Lord Himself. For the Beatitudes demonstrate the nature of God in a sweeping foundational way.

We should start by remembering that God's name, Yahweh, is no mere label but is significant of the real personality of the one bearing it. It stems from the Hebrew word for "to be," and some authorities believe it may be the so-called hiph'il tense, which would mean "He who causes everything to be."

At any rate, He revealed Himself to the covenant people as I AM.[1] It was almost like a blank check. God said, "I am ____," and His people were to fill in the blank according to their need. If they needed peace, He was Jehovah-shalom—"I am your peace."[2] If they needed victory, He was Jehovah-nissi—"I am your banner, your victory."[3] If they needed help of any kind, as Abraham so desperately did when he was being tested regarding his son, Isaac, then He was Jehovah-jireh—"I am your provider."[4]

The point we should remember, which is the one the Beatitudes demonstrate so simply, is that God revealed Himself, His nature, His power and His will at the point of the need. The people had to recognize and acknowledge their need.

This is an overriding lesson of the Beatitudes, which is essential to life in the kingdom. The one who feels he has need of nothing *will receive nothing.* He will never experience the full name and nature of God. He will never know His peace and comfort; he will never know His victory; he will never know His provision of every need of life. Indeed, he will never know His salvation and experience the name God gave to His Son—Jesus, which means "I Am Salvation."

No, the self-sufficient, the self-righteous will not experience the kingdom of heaven. The void within them will not be filled if they do not cry out, "God Almighty, come and meet the deepest need in my life."

Let's look at the Beatitudes themselves,[5] taking note of their progressive nature in the working of an individual's life.

Spiritual Beggars

> "Blessed are the poor in spirit, for theirs is the kingdom of heaven."

As with each of the points, the Lord began with a word that is preserved for us in the New Testament as *makarios* which we render usually as "blessed" or "happy." Therefore, each of the points contains a guideline to happiness, which our world desperately craves.

"Happy are the poor in spirit." What a contradiction this seems! But upon closer examination it becomes clear. First we must understand that the Lord meant more than merely "poor." His words conveyed the meaning "beggarly." Happy are the beggars in spirit, the spiritual beggars, those who know they are needy and are not afraid to say so, as we noted above.

The Lord's teaching at another time made the point most dramatically. Contrasting a shame-stricken publican (or tax-gatherer) with a proud Pharisee, He revealed a man who was poor in spirit.

> "And the publican, standing afar off, would not lift up so much as his eyes upon heaven, but smote upon his breast, saying, God be merciful to me a sinner. I tell you, this man went down to his house justified rather than the other: for everyone that exalteth himself shall be abased; and he that humbleth himself shall be exalted."[6]

He was exalted right into the kingdom, into perfect happiness. He had been empty, but he was filled, simply because he was ready to acknowledge that he needed God and was willing to beg for help. The kingdom was his, right then—"theirs *is* the kingdom." He had taken the first step in the progression demonstrated in the Beatitudes.

The Intercessors

"Blessed are those who mourn, for they shall be comforted."

This contradiction seems more extreme than the first. Happy are those who mourn. How can it be?

We find help from the writings of Paul, in which he told of a "godly sorrow" that works repentance.[7] This is what Jesus was pointing to. For "repentance" means "afterthought" or "reconsideration." A man is to be repentant, to have an afterthought, to reconsider. He is to be sorry for his sins; he is never to be self-satisfied. As the psalmist wrote:

> The sacrifices of God are a broken spirit;
> A broken and contrite heart, O God, Thou wilt not despise.[8]

So the Lord's message in this second Beatitude was, in essence, "if you want the comfort of God surrounding you, you must come to a place where you mourn for your sins." But He pressed it beyond that; He wanted us to mourn for the sins of people around us, too. The world does not want to mourn; it wants to laugh all the time. But rather than thumbing our noses at the world, we are to mourn, to hurt, to cry out for the lost.

We have the biblical account of Lot in Sodom and Gomorrah, where greed, drunkenness, homosexuality, and corruption were rampant. Lot, a "righteous man," was not merely angered by the filthy deeds of the wicked; he was "vexed" and "tormented" in his soul.[9] He mourned over their deeds. And God comforted him by sending angels to preserve him when those cities were destroyed.[10]

Do you see the progression? The kingdom becomes ours; we are in it. Immediately, the magnitude of our sin falls upon us, even though the Lord has forgiven us. In quick succession, we then see the sin of others—our relatives and friends who are not saved, indeed, the whole world. We are burdened with concern for others. We mourn. We become intercessors.

A philosophy has swept the earth that says, in effect, "I'm OK; you're OK." Without Jesus's salvation there is no room in His kingdom for such thinking. Complacency is an abomination. We have only to recall the lesson He gave when speaking of His second coming. It will be just like the days of Noah, He said.

> "For as in those days which were before the flood they were eating and drinking, they were marrying and giving in marriage, until the day that Noah entered the ark, and they did not understand until the flood came and took them all away, so shall the coming of the Son of Man be."[11]

He deplored the people's complacency over the condition of the world. In the kingdom, this must give way to concern and mourning. Then we can expect the fulfillment of Jeremiah's prophecy: "'. . . For I will turn their mourning into joy,/And will comfort them, and I give them joy for their sorrow.'"[12]

A Matter of Control

"Blessed are the meek, for they shall inherit the earth."

This next step in the progression is one of the most misunderstood verses in the Bible. Conjuring up images of the famous cartoon character Caspar Milquetoast, it has convinced many that Jesus wanted His people to be dull, obsequious, spineless, and stupid. This, of course, runs contrary to everything we find about the men and women of God on the pages of Scripture. They were strong, vocal, and often brilliant.

Our problem has been with the word "meek." It *does* mean "humble" and "gentle," even "docile." But the definition cannot stop there. Biblical meekness does not call for the abject surrender of one's character or personal integrity.

It calls for a total yielding of the reins of life from one's own hands to God's hands. But it doesn't stop there either. The meek exercise discipline, which results in their being kept continuously under God's control.

Thus, a meek man is a disciplined man who is under the control of God. He is like Moses, a strong, bold leader who at the same time was described as the meekest man on earth.[13] Having seen his sin and that of others, the meek person takes the next step and places himself under God's control and discipline. He serves God. But, remember, God will not seize control. He will govern a life only if it is constantly yielded to him, and that requires constant discipline. God is not interested in building robots.

Happy is the man who is under control—of God and of himself. Earlier I mentioned Paul's reminder to his beloved Timothy that they had received a spirit of "power and love and *discipline* [or self-control]," not of "timidity."[14] This is what the Lord was talking about. One with this virtue will inherit the earth.

So often Christians have been mislead into thinking that once they are born again, nothing is required. This, as we will see, is damaging. The Lord and all those who wrote of Him made clear that rebirth was only the beginning, to be followed by discipline, work, and suffering. Obviously the drunk, the drug addict, the lustful, the slothful do not have the discipline to rule the earth and to correct its evils. No, it is for the meek, the disciplined—those who are controlled by God, who follow His Son, who struggle. Remember these powerful words: "'. . . from the days of John the Baptist until now the kingdom of heaven suffers violence, and violent men take it by force.'"[15] Zealous men force their way in. That's what it means. Though the Milquetoasts fall by the wayside, God's meek men and women will inherit the earth.

A Work of the Spirit

"Blessed are those who hunger and thirst for righteousness, for they shall be satisfied [filled]."

God is righteousness. To be righteous is to be Godlike. Jesus said we should hunger and thirst after righteousness. It is a free gift,[16] but we must seek it. We should desire in every fiber to be Christlike in nature. For such can be ours. According to the Bible, God planted the Spirit of His Son within us when we received Him, not being satisfied that we merely be adopted children, but that we also have Christ's very nature *within* us.[17] We, setting our life's course in pursuit of Him, must yearn for this nature, this righteousness and holiness, to flood us. Having had the righteousness of Jesus *imputed* to us, we now should desire to have that righteousness *imparted* to us, actually living it out. If we remain unrighteous, the Bible says, we will miss the kingdom.

> Or do you not know that the unrighteous shall not inherit the kingdom of God? Do not be deceived; neither fornicators, nor idolaters, nor adulterers, nor effeminate, nor homosexuals, nor thieves, nor the covetous, nor drunkards, nor revilers, nor swindlers, shall inherit the kingdom of God.[18]

"I want to know more of God"—that should be our cry. "I want His Spirit to possess more of me. I want to be more effective. I want to see His kingdom come on earth."

With that cry of hunger and thirst for God, for more of His power, we in fact are crying out for an anointing of the Holy Spirit for service, which the Bible calls baptism in the Holy Spirit. This actually fulfills the next step in the progression of development revealed in the Beatitudes, providing an empowerment for serving God.

Jesus described it this way: "'. . . you shall receive power when the Holy Spirit has come upon you; and you shall be My witnesses both in Jerusalem, and in all Judea and Samaria, and even to the remotest part of the earth.'"[19] You will indeed be effective—being filled with the miraculous power of God Himself—simply because you hungered and thirsted for Him.

Yes, Jesus said, you will be filled and satisfied. Interestingly, the Greek word that we translated "filled" is *chortazo*,[20] which carries the implication of "gorged." We won't merely have a little, the Lord said; we will be gorged with righteousness, power, and everything good in the kingdom.

This obviously is the perfect fulfillment of "'seek, and you will find.'"[21]

The Flow of Mercy

"Blessed are the merciful, for they shall receive mercy."

Most of us grasp this one, but we may fall short in seeing its magnitude.

The root Greek word for mercy is *eleos*, containing the sense of compassion and tenderness, of kindness and beneficence. It flows from the greater to the lesser: God is merciful to man; a wealthy man is merciful to a poorer man.

Thus we see a further progression in the Beatitudes. We begin to think toward men as God thinks toward us, extending our work out into the world. Having received mercy from One greater than we are, we are to give mercy to those we are in a position to favor.

Although our motivation should be purer than this, the fact is that as we show compassion to someone below us, there is always someone upstream to do the same for us—either men or God Himself. Behind this is a broader law that we will examine at greater length.

The Ultimate Happiness

"Blessed are the pure in heart, for they shall see God."

From the Middle Ages came the idea that "the highest good," the *summum bonum*, was the "beatific vision." The ultimate happiness was to see God. There could be nothing greater. It was its own reward—an end, not a means.

In this Beatitude, Jesus showed the way for the fulfillment of that truth, elevating to its climax the progression of experience we have observed in these teachings.

If the highest good, the supreme happiness, is to see God—and it is—then purity in heart is required. Again, we grasp this simple statement rather quickly, but frequently its greatness passes over our heads.

In the Bible the word "pure" often means clean and untainted, but it is also used to describe gold that is without alloy or unadulterated. So the Lord was saying more than "blessed are those who have clean hearts." He was additionally saying "blessed are those whose hearts are single and undivided, whose devotion is without mixture."

As for the word "heart," it means the center of our being, the core of our spirituality and deepest motivations. It is the real person.

It is not uncommon for people to want God, at least part of the time or with part of themselves, while at the same time wanting money and fame and all the world has to give. That won't do if you want to see God and receive the ultimate happiness, Jesus said.

Again, we need to see the insistence on unity and wholeness that filled the Lord's ministry. If your eye is unclear or dark, then your whole body will be full of darkness, He said, adding: "'No one can serve two masters; for either he will hate the one and love the other, or he will hold to one and despise the other. You cannot serve God and mammon.'"[22]

We must focus on heaven or on earth. If it is the former, we will find the highest good.

The Way of Inheritance

"Blessed are the peacemakers, for they shall be called sons of God."

Most of us would indeed be happy were we the children of a reigning monarch with power to act in his name and eventually to rule. Well, that can be the case, and the monarch is known as the "King of Kings"[23] whose realm is all of creation.

Now a child of God is an heir of God,[24] the recipient of authority, possession, wealth, and even the kingdom itself. In short, he is the inheritor of everything that exists.

But, Jesus said, to progress to that status you must be a "peacemaker." And that is one who stops conflict and war.

The Lord Himself was the unique peacemaker, bringing peace between man and God.[25] In His name we are to do the same. We are to be going throughout the earth saying to all men, "Your sins are pardoned. You can be reconciled to God." As Paul taught:

> Now all these things are from God, who reconciled us to Himself through Christ, and gave us the ministry of reconciliation, namely, that God was in Christ reconciling the world to Himself, not counting their trespasses against them, and He has committed to us the word of reconciliation. Therefore, we are ambassadors for Christ, as though God were entreating through us; we beg you on behalf of Christ, be reconciled to God.[26]

Indeed, we as peacemakers should be *begging* people to accept that which God has already done, since reconciliation is a two-way street requiring a response from both parties. For the world still echoes with the song of the heavenly host on a quiet night two thousand years ago: "'peace, good will toward men.'"[27] Each Christmas Eve, even the hardest hearts quiver at the prospect. Man craves God and peace from his deepest recesses.

However, the sons of God, the peacemakers, do not stop at the point of peace with God. They work for peace between men. They themselves are not warriors, and they counsel others to stop fighting among themselves. Their goal is peace among individuals and among nations as they constantly strive to bring conflicting groups together and seek harmony and love, not at the expense of godly principle, but through godly relationships.

These will be blessed, for they do the will and the work of the Father, as sons and daughters. They will mature as heirs, and they will inherit their Father's estate, the kingdom.

Persecution Will Come

"Blessed are those who have been persecuted for the sake of righteousness, for theirs is the kingdom of heaven.

"Blessed are you when men cast insults at you, and persecute you, and say all kinds of evil against you falsely, on account of Me."[28]

A new world order is near. It is called the eternal kingdom of heaven, to be brought about by God Almighty. Only certain people will live in it. And it is the Lord's intention that those people practice living in it right now, doing His will and experiencing the blessings at this time.

As they do so, however—bringing every thought captive and exercising the authority of the kingdom—they will become visible for who they are, and opposition will mount. Abuse will come. It came to Jesus; it came to the early saints.

But, this Beatitude says, they will be happy as they continue in their remarkable realm. Indeed, wrote the apostle Peter, they will be experiencing genuine maturity: "If you are reviled for the name of Christ, you are blessed, because *the Spirit of glory and of God rests upon you.*"[29] The blessing can hardly be greater than that in this life.

Many people innocently ask, "But why would anyone want to persecute people if they're loving and kind?"

The answer lies deep in the innermost parts of unregenerate man. He is offended by the beauty of others, by their brightness, their happiness, their prosperity. He prefers a dark, worried countenance to a clear, carefree one. He simply loves darkness more than light, which is a specific disclosure of Scripture.[30]

The Bible says those who are following Christ bear a fragrance that is distinguishable both to the believer and the unbeliever. To one, it is the sweet aroma of life; to the other, the stench of death.[31] Such a person produces either appreciation or offense. The offense has at times turned to rage and persecution.

The Greek root behind the word we translate "persecute" means "to pursue," in the manner one would chase a fox or rabbit in a hunt, and pursuit is sometimes what results from the world's rage and persecution. "We must drive them from our midst," people roar. "We must search them out and destroy them." Before his conversion, Paul the apostle did the same thing to the Christians as his offense turned to fury.[32]

But whether it be rage of merely rudeness, Jesus said we would be happy. "When men lie about you, when they curse you, when they throw you into prison because you remind them of God," He said, "be glad, rejoice, jump up and down, for the kingdom is yours. It is already yours."

The progression has reached fullness.

Study Guide

Key Scripture: Matt. 5:3–12

Key Idea: "A new world order is near. It is called the eternal kingdom of heaven, to be brought about by God Almighty. Only certain people will live in it. And it is the Lord's intention that those people practice living in it right now, doing His will and experiencing the blessings at this time" (p. 85).

Dr. E. V. Hill, the internationally acclaimed pastor of New Shiloh Baptist Church in south central Los Angeles, reported that he had grown up in a community in Texas where for thirty years they had no murders and no major crime. Founded by ex-slaves after the Civil War, the town "lived by the Bible," according to Dr. Hill. Imagine yourself sitting on the first town council, facing responsibility for setting up the rule of law. Which would you choose, the Ten Commandments or the Beatitudes? _____

Which of the Beatitudes would you consider key in interpersonal relationships in such a community?

Getting God's Perspective

1. The Hebrews never pronounced the name of God, considering it too sacred to even say aloud. Yet what are three ways in which God revealed Himself to His own in the Old Testament? (See Gen. 22:14; Ex. 17:15; Judg. 6:24.)

   a.

   b.

   c.

2. What did God reveal about Himself at these times of need in the lives of the Old Testament saints?

   a. His _____

   b. His _____

   c. His _____

3. What is the one condition necessary to receiving God in a time of need?

Blessed Contradictions (Matt. 5:3–4)

1. "No, the self-sufficient, the self-righteous will not experience the kingdom of heaven. The void within them

will not be filled if they do not cry out, 'God Almighty, come and meet the deepest need in my life'" (p. 76). What two people in Luke 18:11–14 illustrate this statement?

2. What, according to Matthew 5:3, is the primary condition for getting into the kingdom?

3. How does this contradict the way man looks at things?

4. What is the contradiction in verse 4?

5. What attitude described in Psalm 51:17 explains the contradiction?

6. What is the progression normally experienced by the person becoming a Christian? (See p. 78–79.)

A Matter of Control (Matt. 5:5)

After reading the section on pages 79 and 80, answer the following questions:

a. Caspar Milquetoast would have made a good Christian.   Yes No

b. Jacob exhibited meekness when he ran from Esau.   Yes No

c. The meekest man on earth was Moses.   Yes No

d. The meek man runs his own life.   Yes No

e. The self-disciplined person will inherit the earth.
Yes No

f. When self is in control, Satan often gains control.
Yes No

Some Hunger! (*Matt. 5:6*)

Write our your personal prayer in response to Jesus'
teaching in verse 6.

The Flow of Mercy (*Matt. 5:7*)

1. What happens, according to Matthew 18:23–35, if the
flow of mercy is not passed on?

2. Why should we show mercy toward others? (See Eph.
2:4–7.)

3. Describe one situation during the past week in which
you did not show mercy—or in which you were able to
show mercy.

The Ultimate Happiness (*Matt. 5:8*)

1. If you are really honest with yourself, how would you
have to complete the following sentence? "I want God
and _____
_____"

2. Write out Matthew 6:24 in your own words so it fits
your situation, substituting the word or phrase you
listed in number one for the word *mammon.*

3. What will you need to do, according to 1 John 1:9, to achieve purity of heart right now?

True Sons of God (Matt. 5–9)

1. If you were honest about it, how would people describe you today? _____ peacemaker _____ troublemaker _____ uninvolved

2. What is our first responsibility as peacemakers (reconcilers) according to 2 Corinthians 5:18–20?

3. Describe one situation where you can be a peacemaker through "godly relationships."

Persecution Is Normal (Matt. 5:10–12)

1. What is it about Christians that raises opposition? (See p. 85.)

2. What do we learn about the benefits of persecution from 1 Peter 4:14?

3. Why should we rejoice when we experience persecution? (See v. 12.)

Making It Happen

Ask the Holy Spirit to show you a plan of action from one of the following:

- Confess to God a sin He has shown you.
- Ask forgiveness of someone to whom you were unmerciful.
- Write a letter or call someone with whom you need to reestablish peace.
- Make a personal commitment to accept God's control in your life.

Scripture References

1 See Exodus 3:14
2 See Judges 6:24
3 See Exodus 17:15
4 See Genesis 22:14
5 See Matthew 5:3–12
6 Luke 18:13, 14, KJV
7 2 Corinthians 7:10, KJV
8 Psalm 51:17
9 2 Peter 2:6–8, KJV and NASB
10 See Genesis 19:1–26
11 Matthew 24:38, 39
12 Jeremiah 31:13
13 See Numbers 12:3, KJV
14 2 Timothy 1:7
15 Matthew 11:12
16 See Romans 5:17
17 See Galatians 4:4–7; 2 Peter 1:3, 4
18 1 Corinthians 6:9, 10
19 Acts 1:8
20 Matthew 5:6
21 Luke 11:9
22 Matthew 6:24
23 Revelation 19:16
24 See Romans 8:17
25 See Romans 5:1
26 2 Corinthians 5:18–20
27 Luke 2:14, KJV

28 Matthew 5:10, 11
29 1 Peter 4:14
30 See John 3:19
31 See 2 Corinthians 2:15, 16
32 See Acts 8:3

6. Upside Down

From the constitution of the kingdom of God, which so clearly reverses normal world thinking, we see that one virtue comes ahead of all others in the invisible realm. It is humility.

How can humility underlie happiness, prosperity, and fulfillment?

In my own case, the deep significance of this virtue unfolded in my constant search for wisdom from God. For, as we will see, wisdom and humility are thoroughly intertwined.

At one point, the following words sprang to life in my spirit: "'. . . God *resisteth* the proud, but giveth grace unto the humble.'"[1] The power of those words is devastating if you trace the logic. Not only does God help those with genuine humility, but also He actively *opposes* those who are proud.

Of course, the definition of humble that is easiest for most of us to grasp is that it is the opposite of proud. Most of us seem to know what pride is. God insists that we be the very opposite if we are to receive His favor and blessing; otherwise He is against us.

Thus it became clear to me that if we desire to live in the kingdom of God, to receive God's favor, we must make humility the number one virtue. It is foundational.

Jesus, the very Son of God, existing in the form of God, took on the likeness of man without diminishing His deity and "humbled Himself by becoming obedient to the point of death, even death on a cross."[2] And His Father *favored* that humility in this manner. "Therefore also God highly *exalted* Him, and bestowed on Him the name which is above every name. . . ."[3]

The Old Testament prepares us for such a consequence with words like: "The reward of humility and the fear of the LORD/ Are riches, honor and life."[4]

Those humble before God, obedient and reverent toward Him and His will, are the victorious ones, the ones elevated to the rewards that the world scrambles after—riches, honor, life. Just consider the competition, the greed, the worry, the abuse, the killing expended in the race for those benefits. People worldwide want (1) enough to live on, (2) recognition and approval of what they do, and (3) good health and long life. To the humble and obedient, these blessings come naturally.

The path of the proud is perfectly clear from Scripture, for without question pride is the greatest sin there is in the eyes of God. It thwarts His goodness toward man.

The proud man says, "I'll do it my way. I'm sufficient. I can control my destiny. I'm the captain of my soul, the master of my fate." There is nothing spiritually beggarly about him, nothing regretful about his inner condition, nothing hungering to be Godlike. In short, he lacks humility; and he receives nothing from the Lord, as we saw in discussing God's nature. His rewards, which are from men, are like vapor; they vanish suddenly, imperceptibly. For the wisdom of the Scripture says, "Pride goes before destruction/ And a haughty spirit before stumbling."[5]

Where there is pride, there will always be a fall. It is inevitable. We see it all about us, on a large scale and on small. Nations and individuals are slipping. They become arrogant; they cut off advice from old and respected friends; they go alone, and they fall.

As we strive to look into the invisible world to see God, to hear what He is saying, it is essential that we always bear in mind that our knowledge of that world comes primarily through His disclosure. *He* must reveal. Otherwise, we cannot see. Recollection of that should keep us humble, even though our confidence rests in the fact that He said He would be found by those who diligently seek Him.[6] The proud, however, cannot bring themselves to seek, for that requires coming in from a lower position; and they have been conditioned otherwise.

Solomon Was Right

As I said, humility is closely entwined with wisdom, which was the object of my diligent search years ago. I had been impressed with Solomon's reply to the Lord's offer one night following King David's death, "'Ask what I shall give you.'"[7]

Can you imagine how most of us would have replied? But the Bible shows that Solomon revealed great humility in even approaching God, describing himself as a little child. "'. . . I do not know how to go out or come in,'" he said.[8] "'Give me now wisdom and knowledge . . . for who can rule this great people of Thine?'"[9]

The Lord's response laid bare the pattern prevailing in the kingdom of heaven.

> "'. . . Because you had this in mind, and did not ask for riches, wealth, or honor, or the life of those who hate you, nor have you even asked for long life, but you have asked for yourself wisdom and knowledge, that you may rule My people, over whom I have made you king, wisdom and knowledge have been granted to you. And I will give you riches and wealth and honor, such as none of the kings who were before you possessed, nor those who will come after you.'"[10]

Echoing throughout were the words of Christ centuries later. "Seek first His kingdom and His righteousness; and all these things shall be added to you."[11]

I have become convinced that wisdom is the key to the

secrets of the kingdom of God. It leads to favor. But the starting point is humility, as Solomon knew. For humility reveals fear of, or reverence for, the Lord.

The Book of Proverbs reveals the next step: "The fear of the LORD is the beginning of wisdom,/And the knowledge of the Holy One is understanding."[12]

The cycle is complete—from humility, to fear of the Lord, to wisdom, to knowledge of the Holy One.

Wisdom, or spiritual understanding, *is* knowledge of the Holy One. And that is what we are seeking—knowledge of God, knowledge of His will and purpose, knowledge of the invisible world and how it works, knowledge of how to reach into it and bring its blessing and prosperity into our visible world.

In its ultimate sense, wisdom is understanding that an action taken today will be proven in the future to have been a correct one. And God provides that understanding.

To the people of Israel, God presented a body of Law that was to be their wisdom, an external expression of His will. If they followed those rules and principles in their society, then many years later people would look back and say they had acted wisely. Unfortunately, they were inconsistent and often improperly motivated, and God's wisdom was not fully realized in their lives.

Through the incarnation of Christ and the coming of the Holy Spirit to dwell within believers, the wisdom of God took on an internal expression, with which we are now dealing. Obviously, like the Israelites, we have not been consistent or sincere in all of our efforts to manifest it.

But this wisdom from God is still available. Knowing that He governs all things, present and future, we can approach Him with pure hearts and say: "Show me how to run my life. Show me how the world works. Show me Your ways, Your principles, for running this enormously complex universe. I want to conform to what You do, to Your will, Your purpose, Your plan."

At that point we are seeking truth, and He will grant us wisdom for that. His entire purpose is to have us conform to truth. His wisdom will come; His principles will work. We will act, and the future will bear us out. People will say, "My, wasn't that man wise? Where did he get such wisdom?"

And all the while, it came from God.

Lesson From the Garden

It is helpful to recognize that the entire point of conflict in the Garden of Eden came from God's attempt to teach Adam and Eve wisdom. It was not that God wanted to prevent them from obtaining knowledge by forbidding them to eat from the tree of the knowledge of good and evil. His purpose was that they would gain wisdom by obeying Him. Day after day they were to pass that tree, saying, "If I eat the fruit from there, that will be evil; if I refrain from eating it, that will be good." They were to learn good and evil simply from having that tree in their midst.

We know that they ate, did evil, and failed to obtain what God intended. For good is doing what God wants; it reveals wisdom. Evil is doing what He does not want; it reveals foolishness.

God was, and still is, looking for people who will do what He wants, people with wisdom, that He may enter into their lives, their visible world, and favor them. No problem, no shortage, no crisis is beyond His ability.

But instead He encountered, and still encounters, foolishness fed by pride.

Three Crucial Virtues

The three cardinal virtues in the kingdom of God are *faith, hope,* and *love.* We've already spoken of the centrality of faith in seeing, entering, and experiencing the kingdom; but it is also interwoven with the virtues of hope and love. Paul the apostle more than once put them together in describing the Christian life and ministry: "But now abide faith, hope, love, these three; but the greatest of these is love."[13]

Faith is essential to the functioning of a civilization. We daily reveal faith in the laws of the creation. How could the world function if it didn't have faith that there would be a tomorrow? How could medical doctors and scientists function without faith in an orderly universe? How could we exist without faith, to some degree, in other people? How could we conduct business without faith in the marketplace and the rules of commerce? Nothing would work without some kind of faith.

Since we as spiritual beings are saved by the grace of God "through faith,"[14] it is obvious that faith is indispensable in any relationship with the Lord. Without it, we don't even know God exists. We are lost in our sins and are unable to see or to enter the invisible world, let alone transfer its blessings into this visible one.

As for hope, we need to make a distinction between it and faith. Hope is the ability to transfer our reliance from ourselves to God. It is founded on the sovereignty of God, His total independence of circumstances, His limitlessness.

It does not develop in us until our faith is tried, until under pressure we realize there is a Creator who will work things out for those with whom He is pleased. The apostle Paul described the progression:

> Therefore having been justified by faith, we have peace with God through our Lord Jesus Christ, through whom also we have obtained our introduction by faith into this grace in which we stand; and we exult in *hope* of the glory of God. And not only this, but we also exult in our tribulations, knowing that tribulation brings about perseverance; and perseverance, proven character; and proven character, *hope*.[15]

God's purpose is that our faith be tested, expressly to refine and strengthen it. Our endurance purifies and toughens our character; resolute hope in God and His plan results.

Note how Paul concludes the development of his thought: ". . . and hope does not disappoint."[16]

Why is this true? Because hope shaped on the anvil rests in Him and in the moral rightness of His ultimate purpose—that the wicked will fall and the righteous will be rewarded.[17] Any expectation of the transfer of the blessings of the kingdom into our lives depends on it.

Finally, there must be love, which Paul described as the greatest of the trinity of virtues. Interestingly, it grows out of the other two. Hope grows out of faith, and love grows out of hope.

When a person has hope, when he knows that his future is assured, he stops struggling to maintain his own sphere of dominance; he stops fighting other people. He is willing to let the moral law of God work to defend his place. Then he is free to have concern for the well-being of others. He is no longer threatened and can give himself, his possessions, his life to someone else and know that God will make it right.

This process—and it usually is that rather than an immediate change—was radical in my life. Stepping from the role of aggressive, competitive young lawyer who was just beginning the climb up the power ladder in a major international corporation, to the role of a man whose hope is secured by Almighty God completely altered my life and lifestyle. That hope released my ability to love—to love *real* people in *concrete* ways, not merely abstractly. Those in corporate halls were no longer shallow faces; folks in the hard, dirty streets of New York City were no longer the masses. They were people. I had been set free to express my concern for them, which eventually led my family and me to share our lives—our food, our clothing, our shelter—with others in one of the most wretched sections of New York. Our concern took on visible expression.

The Lord's experience with the cross was the ultimate expression of hope and love, of course. He had no visible assurance that He wouldn't be found absolutely foolish. He could have turned out to have been the most tragic figure in history, but He had hope in the rightness and goodness of His Father. He was free to love His people and to die for them.

Hope and love are what we must have, Paul said, if we are to experience the power of God in the world today. Love is the strongest force possible. The reason is simple: God *is* love. No negative can overcome that positive. The perpetrators of hate and darkness have tried since the beginning, but the light from Him has prevailed.[18]

Love is so overwhelming that it nullifies the physical principle under which every action produces an opposite, equal reaction. If someone pushes someone else, the latter will push hard in return, and escalation develops, usually to the point of violence. But Jesus said, "Absorb the push. Break the cycle. Overcome evil with good."[19]

We need to see that He wasn't advocating merely defense, but rather the perfect offense with the only weapon capable of absorbing and defeating evil. If someone demands you to go one mile, you can fight him; you can go sullenly and curse him all the way, feeling beaten and rejected. Or you can go on the attack and follow the charter of the kingdom: "'And whoever shall force you to go one mile, go with him two.'"[20] Love will thus heap burning coals on his head, and the conviction of the Lord will work in His life for good.[21]

Yes, any of us who yearn to see our world changed and have been disappointed by the relative importance of the people of God must examine ourselves regarding the virtue of love. For the picture painted by Paul in one of his most famous discourses has to convince us that, were love to underlie all of our thoughts, words, and deeds—our use of the principles of God—then the world *would* be changed.

> Love is patient, love is kind, and is not jealous; love does not brag and is not arrogant, does not act unbecomingly; it docs not seek its own, is not provoked, does not take into account a wrong suffered, does not rejoice in unrighteousness, but rejoices with the truth; bears all things, believes all things, hopes all things, endures all things. Love never fails . . .[22]

Eventually, Paul said, all else will pass away. The special gifts and talents, the wonderful endowments from on high—they will all run their course. But love endures forever, bridging eternity.

Holy Paradoxes

I trust it is abundantly clear that the constitution of the kingdom of God (the priorities of anyone who would experience the power and blessings of life there) is riddled with paradox. One can almost hear the Lord chuckle as the world looks in disbelief at what would appear to be anti-principles, in light of the way most people and nations conduct their affairs.

The world says hate your enemies. The kingdom says love your enemies.

The world says hit back. The kingdom says do good to those who mistreat you.

The world says hold onto your life at any cost. The kingdom says lose your life and you will find it.

The world says a young and beautiful body is essential. The kingdom says even a grain of wheat must die if it is to have life.

The world says push yourself to the top. The kingdom says serve if you want to lead.

The world says you are number one. The kingdom says many who are first will be last and the last first.

The world says acquire gold and silver. The kingdom says store up treasure in heaven if you would be rich.

The world says exploit the masses. The kingdom says do good to the poor.

Sadly, the church itself has often been a leader among those blinded to the paradoxes of the kingdom of God. So many times congregations have fled from the inner city, where they are so desperately needed, to comfortable suburbs, where they could luxuriate and not have to face the poor and their problems. Or they have served a political or social movement rather than the needy. Or they have embraced the management techniques of corporations rather than the government techniques of God. In short, they lost the sound of truth.

If we live for this world—if we seek to grasp it—then we will die to the kingdom. But if we lose ourselves in love and service for others, then we will find ourselves in the kingdom.

The temptations of worldly thinking are great, but they must be resisted even at the cost of appearing foolish by embracing truths that are paradoxical to conventional wisdom.

You see, one major paradox that we must accept as we try to change the world is this: The people of God are to live out the Beatitudes and the virtues of humility, wisdom, faith, hope, and love while at the same time becoming leaders.

"'You are the light of the world . . . ,'" Jesus said.[23] In darkness, a light does not follow; it leads.

Yes, the humble, the disciplined, the wise, the faithful, the hopeful, the loving—they are to lead. *That* is a holy paradox.

And how will it be brought to pass? The laws of the kingdom will show us.

Study Guide

Key Scripture: 2 Chr. 1:11–12; Rom. 5:1–4; 1 Cor. 13:4–8

Key Idea: "One major paradox that we must accept as we try to change the world is this: The people of God are to live out the Beatitudes and the virtues of humility, wisdom, faith, hope, and love while at the same time becoming leaders" (p. 103).

In a 1983 interview with Barbara Walters, Dear Abby (Eppie Lederer) made the following statements: "I'm supposed to fix everything. Sometimes I can't fix anything, and I've learned that, so I accept my limitations . . . I refuse to allow myself to be miserable. . . . And I've learned that it's good not to be bitter. Hostility doesn't pay off. The payoff is how you feel about yourself in your gut. Do the decent thing."

The above reveals what kind of woman, in your opinion?

How would you describe yourself if you were asked to make a statement about yourself?

Laying the Foundation

1. Pat Robertson writes, "If we desire to live in the kingdom of God, to receive God's favor, we must make humility the number one virtue" (p. 94). Read Philippians 2:5–8 to answer the following questions.

   a. Who is the number one illustration of humility in action?

   b. What is the contrast in Jesus between verses 5 and 8?

   c. Who initiates the action in verse 7?

   d. What was Jesus' reward for His example of humility, according to verse 9?

2. What are the three most keenly felt needs of people everywhere? Compare your answer with Pat's on page 95.

3. Why, according to Proverbs 16:18, is the self-made, self-assured man not a success in the kingdom of God?

4. Who is our primary source of knowledge about the world?

5. Why do the proud have such a tough time finding the Lord?

Paging Mr. Solomon

1. Imagine the telephone ringing in your home one evening and a pleasant voice saying, "Congratulations, you have won $1,000,000 tax free." List three things you would do with that money.

    a.

    b.

    c.

2. Read 2 Chronicles 1:6–12 and write down what Solomon asked for himself.

3. Now look back at your answer to the first question. What does your answer tell you about your priorities in comparison to Solomon's?

4. How does Jesus describe what our priorities ought to be in Matthew 6:33?

5. What will setting such a priority lead to, according to Proverbs 9:10?

6. What is the relationship between humility, the fear of the Lord, and wisdom? (See pp. 96–98.)

7. How do we internalize the wisdom of God as believers?

8. What kind of people is God looking for? (See p. 98.)

The Big Three

1. Consider a typical day. You roll out of bed, clean up, and head for the kitchen (or a coffee shop). After lingering over a cup of coffee you jump in the car to go to the office. At break time you insert a couple of coins into the coffee machine and walk off with a steaming cup. You pick up the telephone to call the head office. At lunch you go out with a couple of associates and grab a bite at the local pizza parlor. With only half the day gone, how many actions have been taken strictly by faith? List at least five.

   a.

   b.

   c.

   d.

   e.

2. What is an even more important step of faith we need to take, according to Romans 5:1?

3. What is the role of hope in the life of the believer? (See Rom. 5:1–5 and the last paragraph on p. 99.)

4. What five things are present in the life of the person with hope? (See paragraph 3 on p. 100.)

   a.

   b.

c.

d.

e.

5. Pat Robertson writes, "Love is so overwhelming that it nullifies the physical principle under which every action produces an opposite, equal action" (p. 101). What practical steps did Jesus recommend to His followers? (See Matt. 5:39–42.)

a.

b.

c.

d.

6. Describe one area in your life where living out 1 Corinthians 13:4–8 in the power of the Holy Spirit would make this kind of difference.

Making It Happen

1. Write down one situation during the past week in which you lived like a person of the world, according to the list of paradoxes on pages 102 and 103.

2. Describe one area where you are going to seek God's wisdom and act in total dependence upon Him.

Scripture References

1 James 4:6, KJV
2 Philippians 2:8
3 Philippians 2:9
4 Proverb 22:4
5 Proverb 16:18
6 See Jeremiah 29:13, 14
7 2 Chronicles 1:7
8 1 Kings 3:7
9 2 Chronicles 1:10
10 2 Chronicles 1:11, 12
11 Matthew 6:33
12 Proverb 9:10
13 1 Corinthians 13:13
14 Ephesians 2:8
15 Romans 5:1–4
16 Romans 5:5
17 See Psalm 37:9
18 See John 1:5
19 See Romans 12:21
20 Matthew 5:41
21 See Romans 12:20
22 1 Corinthians 13:4–8
23 Matthew 5:14

II LAWS OF THE KINGDOM

7. The Law of Reciprocity

One simple declaration by Jesus revealed a law that will change the world: "'Give, and it will be given to you . . .'"[1]

Eight words. They form a spiritual principle that touches every relationship, every condition of man, whether spiritual or physical. They are pivotal in any hope we have of relieving the world's worsening crises.

Jesus expanded the universality of this theme throughout His ministry, varying subject matter and application. His point was so encompassing that it demanded many illustrations. In the discourse from which we get the eight words, we find this expansion: "'. . . just as you want people to treat you, treat them in the same way.'"[2] And from that, of course, came what the world describes as the Golden Rule: "Do unto others as you would have them do unto you."

Jesus went on, putting a frame around the eight key words in this manner:

"Be merciful, just as your Father is merciful. And do not judge
and you will not be judged: and do not condemn, and you will
not be condemned; pardon, and you will be pardoned. Give,
and it will be given to you; good measure, pressed down,
shaken together, running over, they will pour into your lap. For
by your standard of measure it will be measured to you in
return."[3]

By putting this together with the world's greatest teaching on love, repeated from the Old Testament by Jesus as
the heart of God's will, we establish the perfect "law" for
conduct: "'. . . You shall love your neighbor as yourself.'"[4]

A Universal Principle

The Law of Reciprocity, a kingdom principle revealed in
these teachings of the Lord, is relatively easy for us to identify
since it is so visibly pervasive in the physical world. As we
noted in the previous chapter, a basic law of physics says that
for every action there is an equal and opposite reaction. The
jet age in which we live is founded on it.

Scientists some years ago must have said, "If we can
push a jet of hot air out the back end of an engine, there has
to be an equal and opposite reaction going forward. Now, if
we can attach this to an airplane, the thrust will be unprecedented."

Of course the logical, parallel step produced rocket
engines able to generate enough backward thrust to provide
forward speeds necessary to break the hold of gravity and
send machines and men into outer space.

In the interpersonal realm, we find the same principle
prevailing. If you smile at someone, he most likely will
smile back. If you strike someone, the chances are he will
hit you back. If you express kindness, you are almost certain
to have someone express kindness in return. If you are
critical of everything and everyone, you can expect to receive critical judgment from others.

A number of years ago, not long after our family moved to the Tidewater area of Virginia to begin the Christian Broadcasting Network, I remarked to my uncle, a man of admirable maturity, "The people in Tidewater are so very nice, far more so than I had even expected."

My uncle's eyes twinkled and he spoke a powerful, homespun version of the Law of Reciprocity that I hope I never forget: "I tell you what, young man, you will find nice people anywhere you go if you're nice to them."

It is a principle built into the universe. Even international relations respond to it. We Americans saw it at work from the earliest days of the conflict that escalated into the Vietnam War. The escalation was gradual at first. The North Vietnamese and Viet Cong would push at our allies and us. And we would push back, a little harder. They would retaliate, harder, and then back we would come. In such fashion, the United States participated in a dragged-out war that sapped its resources and resolve, simply because of an unwillingness on either side to break the cycle.

This should have been done in one of two ways.

First, we could have loved the enemy and all Southeast Asians, giving them food, clothing, and housing, and doing everything possible to establish them in freedom and the love of God. Love is able to absorb evil actions without fighting back, thus disrupting the cycle of tit for tat. Great faith and courage would have been required while awaiting reciprocal love.

Second, we could have hit the enemy so fast and so devastatingly as to nullify reciprocal action. Because of the ultimate infallibility of the Law of Reciprocity, however, it seems almost certain that the latter course would have at a point in history, perhaps distant, produced reciprocity from some source. Recall, for instance, the low estate to which biblical Babylon fell from its days of great, but frequently cruel, empire.

The point, however, is that the Law of Reciprocity functions in international relations—for good or for evil. It is immutable.

The Individual Level

I want to look first at the personal level, for that is where our walk with God must begin. The Christian faith *is* personal, although it quickly spreads to the interpersonal, the national, and the international. It is rarely private for long.

Nonetheless, individuals today are in crisis, and the Law of Reciprocity is important to them.

Jesus, as we have seen, said, "Give, and it shall be given unto you; good measure, pressed down, and shaken together, and running over, shall men give into your bosom. . . ."[5] What words for those today who are suffering economically, threatened with unemployment or foreclosure! They, quite bluntly, need money. The stories are much the same: "What do I do? I'm using everything I have, and still my bills aren't paid. It seems I've been in debt forever."

As simple as it might look, the Law of Reciprocity is the solution. The world sees such thinking as foolishness, but the Lord says it is wisdom—because it is founded on truth.

As we hear Christ's words, "'Give, and it will be given to you,'"[6] they take us immediately to "'seek ye first His kingdom . . . and all these things shall be added to you.'"[7] We saw that "all these things" comprise what one needs to live.

Giving is foundational. You have to give of yourself. You have to give of your money. You have to give of your time. And this foundational truth works in both the invisible and the visible worlds.

It is not complicated. If you want a higher salary in your job, you have to give more. Those with good salaries are not people who sit back and scheme and spend all their time thinking of ways to promote themselves. The people who are recognized in an organization are those who work harder, think more creatively, and act more forcefully in behalf of the enterprise. They give. They are rewarded.

So many people in our age go for a job with one thought in mind: "What will I get out of it?" Their only concerns are salary, fringe benefits, and title. They are takers, not givers. And takers do not go to the head of the list. The top people are those who say, "I want to do this to help you. Your company has a product that I can help make successful. I have a plan that I'm certain will work." They are givers.

We tend to justify our shortcomings in comparison with these people by hinting at "lucky breaks" or "knowing the right people." But we're wrong. Invariably, those who give concepts, extra time, personal concern, and the like are the receivers. They are giving to an organization—and, indirectly, to individuals in that organization—and they are bound to benefit.

The hard work and overtime must also be accompanied by a proper attitude, of course. Those who give meanness or anger or trouble will get it back. "'Do not judge lest you be judged,'"[8] the Lord said, which drives directly at attitudes. Anyone who is critical, constantly faulting others and cutting associates, will not rise to the top. He will get back what he gives. The one who makes his department look good, including his boss, is the one who will get the salary increase he needs. ". . . By your standard of measure it will be measured to you in return."[9] That's a law.

We cannot talk about a need for money without running headlong into the matter of giving to the Lord. Since everything is His—the cattle on a thousand hills, silver, gold, governments—He obviously is the one we should be turning to in our need. "Give, and it shall be given to you," Jesus said. And that includes our dealing with God Almighty.

The prophet Malachi was precise in speaking the thoughts of the Lord regarding such dealings.

"From the days of your fathers you have turned aside from My statutes, and have not kept them. Return to Me, and I will return to you," says the LORD of hosts. "But you say, 'How shall we return?' Will a man rob God? Yet you are robbing Me! But you say, 'How have we robbed Thee?' *In tithes and offerings.* You are cursed with a curse, for you are robbing Me, the whole nation of you! *Bring the whole tithe* into the storehouse, so that there may be food in My house, and *test Me now in this,*" says the LORD of hosts, "*if I will not open for you the windows of heaven, and pour out for you a blessing until it overflows.*"[10]

The passage shows how seriously the Lord God takes the matter of giving. Obviously, He owns everything. He doesn't really need our tithes and offerings, but He has gone to great lengths to teach us how things work. If we want to release the superabundance of the kingdom of heaven, we must first give. Our Father is more than ready to fulfill His side of the Law of Reciprocity. One can almost imagine His heavenly host standing on tiptoe, brimming with anticipation, gleeful, awaiting the opportunity to release the treasures so badly needed in our visible world.

Note the promise of abundance in Malachi's words. Some translators render the promised blessing as so great that "you won't have enough room to take it in."[11] In the world, we measure return in percentages of six or eight or ten, and sometimes fifteen and twenty. In the kingdom, as we noted earlier, the measures are 3000 percent, 6000 percent, and 10,000 percent—thirty, sixty, and a hundredfold.

That is a beautiful promise for those facing economic distress today. "Test me," says the Lord. "Prove me."

I am as certain of this as of anything in my life: If you are in financial trouble, the smartest thing you can do is to start giving money away. Give tithes and offerings to the Lord. Give time. Give work. Give love. That sounds crazy. But we have seen how the plan of God is filled with paradox. If you need money, then begin to give away some of whatever you have. Your return, poured into your lap, will be great, pressed down and running over.

A Case in Chile

A missionary to Chile shared some insights into this law of the kingdom some time ago. As pastor of a group of extremely poor peasants, he did everything he could to minister to their needs. He revealed what he considered to be the full counsel of the Lord, teaching the Bible as the Word of God and leading them into many significant and deep understandings.

But one day the Lord spoke as clearly as if He had been

standing face to face with him. "You have not declared my whole truth to these people," He said.

"But Lord," the missionary replied. "I don't understand. I've taught them about justification by faith and forgiveness of sins and baptism in the Holy Spirit, about miracles and walking in Your power. I've taught them about the church, about history, about doctrine. I've taught them about godliness and holy living, about the Second Coming.

"What, my Lord, have I failed to teach them?"

He waited a moment. The voice was very clear. "You have not declared my tithe to them."

The missionary was stunned. "But Lord, these are very poor people! They hardly have enough to live. I can't ask them to tithe. They have nothing."

Again, a silent moment. "You must declare to them my tithe."

He was a faithful, obedient man. And the debate ended.

The next Sunday morning, with heavy heart, he stepped into the pulpit of the little rustic church in that poor, backward community, took a deep breath, and began.

"My beloved brethren," he said, looking into the open, uplifted faces of his flock, "God has shown me that I haven't been faithful in declaring to you His whole counsel. There is something you have not been doing that I must tell you about. You have not been tithing to the Lord."

And he began a trek through the Scriptures with them that lasted nearly an hour. He explained everything, including the Malachi portions urging that the Lord be proven on the matter.

The next Sunday, it was their turn. In they came, obedient to the Word. They didn't have money, so they brought eggs, chickens, leather goods, woven articles, and all manner of things from their poor peasant homes. The altar area was heaped high.

The missionary felt badly about taking the gifts, but he too was faithful, so he sold some and used the money for the work of the church. He distributed some of the gifts to the destitute in the neighborhood and kept some for his own sustenance, in lieu of income.

The same thing happened Sunday after Sunday. The people tithed.

It wasn't long before the effects of drought were seen throughout the countryside. Poverty gripped the people of the land worse than ever. Crops failed; buildings deteriorated; gloom covered everything.

But, miraculously, this was not so with the members of that little church. Their crops flourished as though supernaturally watered. But more than that, the yields were extraordinary, bounteous, healthy, flavorful. Their fields were green, while those around were withering. Their livestock were sleek and strong. Relative abundance replaced abject poverty.

They even had an overflow of crops and goods that could be sold, and before long their tithes included money. They were able to build a much-needed new meeting house.

Despite his misgivings, the missionary and his people had learned that no matter how desperate the situation, no matter how deep the impoverishment, the principles of the kingdom can turn deprivation into abundance.

They touch the visible world.

What Is a Tithe?

Lest we become rigid and legalistic, we need to understand the tithe quantitatively. The word, of course, means a "tenth." People quibble over such questions as whether it is before or after taxes, whether it should go to a single ministry, whether it should be put ahead of absolute necessities, and the like. Such niggling misses the point.

The Lord cherishes a ready giver whose heart puts Him and His service ahead of everything. St. Paul had a lot to declare on this point:

> Now this I say, he who sows sparingly shall also reap sparingly; and he who sows bountifully shall also reap bountifully. Let each one do just as he has purposed in his heart; not grudgingly or under compulsion; for God loves a cheerful giver. And God

is able to make all grace abound to you, that always having all
sufficiency in everything, you may have an abundance for
every good deed. . . . you will be enriched in everything for all
liberality. . . .[12]

According to the dictionary, the original definition of
tithe was one-tenth of the annual produce of one's land or of
one's annual income. According to the Bible, that is merely
the *starting place* of giving to the Lord. The Malachi passage
refers to "tithes and offerings." One might say, then, that
there is no offering until the tithe has been paid; it is the
expected, minimum amount.

So a lot of people who practice this critical spiritual law
give far more than ten percent of their income to the Lord's
work. it's all His anyhow, they recognize. King David voiced
this when he said:

"Both riches and honor come from Thee, and Thou dost rule
over all. . . . But who am I and who are my people that we
should be able to offer as generously as this? For all things
come from Thee, and from The hand we have given Thee."[13]

He also wrote in one of his great psalms:

The earth is the LORD's, and the fulness thereof; the world, and
they that dwell therein.[14]

Therefore, many people ignore any ten percent cutoff
and give out of the abundance of their provision. I know one
New Jersey florist who had been thoroughly blessed by the
Lord as he exercised the principles we are exploring in this
book, and he frequently gave ninety percent of his annual
income to the service of God. And the prosperity simply
mounted. He was not able to outgive the Lord. That law is
built into the kingdom. It never changes.

One of the saddest things that can happen to people
comes about so naturally. When hard times come, when
they are thrown out of work or inflation runs wild, the first
place they cut is often their tithe. Usually their intentions
are good. "I'll make it up next week," they rationalize. And

God lets them go. He does not pressure. But that is the worst thing they can do. That, I believe, is the time to step up your giving. That is the time you need something from God. "Prove me," the Lord says. "'Give, and it will be given to you . . . .'"15

One of the many men who served the Lord in the rescue missions and other street ministries during the Depression of the thirties has reported very moving accounts about those who would pass through the soup kitchen—broken, smashed men, virtually destroyed—where he would often ask them about their spiritual lives.

"Tell me, friend, were you faithful to the Lord with your tithes?" he would inquire.

And the man would shake his head no, clutching his cup and plate in front of him, staring vacantly ahead.

And he'd ask the next one, "When you were prosperous and all was well with you, did you give to the Lord? Were you faithful with your tithe?"

The man would shake his head no.

Never once, this worker reported, did he find a man living in poverty who had been faithful to the Lord and His principle of giving. And that fits exactly with what David said thousands of years ago: "I have been young, and now I am old; Yet I have not seen the righteous forsaken, Or his descendants begging bread."16

We must not misunderstand any of this to say that should there be a general economic collapse, we will see Christians riding in Rolls-Royces, wearing big jewels and rich furs, and living in mansions while everyone else lives in poverty. That would be contrary to the nature of God. It merely means that, if we have been faithful to the Lord, given to Him, given to the poor, given to our neighbor, then we will receive according to the prosperity of the Lord, not the prosperity of the ungodly.

We will experience the fulfillment of seeking first the kingdom of God and having the things necessary for life given to us additionally, even matter-of-factly, if you will.

Those who ignore God's principles, on the other hand, can be expected in a moment, a flash, to find themselves totally stripped of what they thought was theirs.

> Yet a little while and the wicked man will be no more;
> And you will look carefully for his place, and he will not be there.
> But the humble will inherit the land,
> And will delight themselves in abundant prosperity.[17]

The Example of Slavery

As we have noted, the Law of Reciprocity works in all the affairs of men. It can work for our good, or it can work for our harm. Americans saw it fulfilled in racial relationships, with roots going back to the days of slavery.

In one of the horrors of history, our representatives went to Africa, seized human beings, stored them in ships, and brought them here to treat like property. We sold them and put them out as forced labor, mistreating them, breaking up families, and ignoring their rights and dignity as people created in the image of God.

"'Give, and it will be given to you. . . .'"

It took a hundred years, but our land has been reaping what it sowed. I many cases, blacks were forced into a matriarchal society as men were totally destroyed emotionally, psychologically, and spiritually. Women struggled to put bread on the table for their children, who soon perceived the cause of their suffering and were ripe for hatred.

Guilt and resentment often overtook the whites. The sides of conflict were locked in. And it came. A good nation was battered, its regions divided, its people torn.

Even though education has been improved, rights defended, and poverty relieved, the suffering continues. The government itself teeters under the threat of bankruptcy as it is unable to meet the demands of sickness, unemployment, welfare, inner-city redevelopment, and other social distress, much of it traceable to the deprivation of the black man centuries ago.

Signs of a possible turnaround through proper use of the Law of Reciprocity, which again identifies slavery as the cause of much that went wrong in America, can be seen in the economic recovery of the South. For many years, the southern economy foundered, hostage to the northern banking and commercial interests, because the region did not have properly trained and educated people capable and desirous of working in factories and offices. Without these wage earners, there were also few customers for southern manufacturers, and prosperity eluded all.

But once the South began to give freedom to the black people, providing education and taking other steps to lift their standard of living, the economy edged upward and soon reached boom level in many places. The South prospered as it never had.

Quite simply, the society had cursed itself. But the Law of Reciprocity, still lacking in many dimensions of life, had made it possible to reverse the curse.

I saw the very opposite of the national racial experience unfold on the streets of Portsmouth, Virginia, one day in 1960, only to be snuffed out, all through the working of the reciprocity principle.

A friend, Dick Simmons, was visiting shortly after my family and I had moved to Tidewater, and he asked if we could go preach on the streets in some of the poor sections of the city. We ended up going to a shopping center in the middle of an area of recent racial violence.

We began by engaging a number of black youths in conversation, and before long several dozen had gathered. Dick preached to them about Jesus. The Holy Spirit moved upon all of us, and after a few minutes. Dick said, "Now if you want to meet Jesus, the one I'm talking about, you can do that right here, right now. You bow your head and kneel right here on the sidewalk and pray, and ask Jesus to come into your life."

What a unique gathering that was! In the middle of one of the city's tensest areas, where violence had already erupted, love and peace and beauty descended. Here were two white men giving love and knowledge and experience— giving the truth of the gospel—to a group of deprived, volatile black youngsters, and what did we get in return? We received love and kindness and warmth back from them.

In an instant, even as the youngsters were praying the sinner's prayer and lives were being changed, everything exploded into a surrealistic movie scene. Two cars of police with trained dogs wheeled to a stop. Men and dogs piled out and charged the kneeling black youngsters. The policemen had jumped to a hasty conclusion, promoted by a phone call from a bystander, that a racial protest was mounting, and they intended to break it up. They chased the youngsters across the street as growls and yells filled the air.

In a twinkling, the Law of Reciprocity set in. The youngsters began to throw rocks at the policemen. Yells turned to curses. And the violence escalated, with all the potential of the devastation that shattered American cities in the sixties.

Dick and I had given love; we had received love. The police had given harshness; they had received harshness. Unhappily the latter pattern prevailed through most of the land.

Potential for the World

Convinced that the Law of Reciprocity could bring relief, if not total solution, to the major problems of the world, I began shortly after dawn one morning early in the decade to make notes on these problems. In less than an hour I had covered the spectrum: The Law of Reciprocity without question affects the way people and nations live with each other. It has the potential to bring peace to the world.

Following are merely a few of the issues I jotted down, but they are widespread enough to make the case. Remember, under the Law of Reciprocity, men everywhere would operate under the principle of giving what they expect to receive, treating others the way they want to be treated, and loving their neighbors as themselves.

War. The need for standing armies would be removed as nations give as they receive and love their neighbors as themselves. The threat of invasion would be gone. Defense appropriations would be unnecessary. Huge governmental spending and the cruelty of high inflation and high taxes would be relieved.

Trade. There would be no need for tariff barriers because nations and companies would not be dumping products and damaging domestic industries. Trade would occur as needed and desired, fostered by healthy, imaginative competition, uninterrupted by runaway greed. Terms like "Third World" would become meaningless.

Injustice. Incredible extremes of wealth and poverty would be evened out simply by human kindness and generosity. The unjust privileges of wealth and other types of status would diminish, melting away envy, jealousy, greedy ambition, and perverted competitiveness.

Crime. Burglary, theft, and vandalism would vanish, along with personal assaults, murder, rape, and kidnapping. Narcotics usage and traffic would cease. Business and securities fraud would pass, cheating at every level would fade, along with price-fixing, monopoly and cartel abuse, and influence peddling. International terrorism would end. Prisons would become obsolete.

Pollution. Air, water, and land could be cleaned up. There would be no more factories belching acid smoke into the air and draining chemical waste into rivers. Beer cans, bottles, and garbage would vanish from the roadsides and campsites. Parks would retain their beauty. Wildlife would flourish.

Productivity. As the Japanese have learned from their change of heart after World War II, moving from a people known for cheap merchandise to one prospering from excellence, nations would see their economies improve radically through increased productivity in every sector. Employers and employees alike would see sharp changes in their motivation, satisfaction, and collective prosperity. There would be no more shoddy products, no more dangerous construction in which buildings collapse and hundreds are injured or killed, no more unsafe toys to maim children.

Government. Huge governmental bureaucracy would disappear as overdrawn, rigid regulation and enforcement becomes unnecessary, along with most of the social services. As men begin to treat one another as God intended, the governments could concentrate on those relatively few things that must be done collectively.

Renegades Excluded

Many people rightly ask, "Can this law be made to work in the world today? Can we simply begin to live this way?"

I believe the answer is yes, with an exception.

The Law of Reciprocity when practiced by law-abiding people and nations will not work with a totally lawless renegade. To begin to practice this principle with one such as that is extraordinarily dangerous, and a distinction must be made.

However, if you analyze it, you will see that even this exception is a fulfillment of the reciprocity principle. As the renegade gives (living outside law and decency) so will he receive from the entire society, in force. He will be ostracized. That, in a sense, was God's answer to the problem when He called forth His people Israel. They were not to temporize. The renegade was removed from society and rendered incapable of such conduct through very harsh punishment.[18]

For us, the example is found in the New Testament. Jesus did not turn the other cheek to the devil or anyone governed by the devil through His ministry. Instead, He exercised His authority. As James said: ". . . Resist the devil and he will flee from you."[19] Oppose him and those belonging to him. They are renegades.

It should be noted that the need to act quickly against the renegade in our society explains why the Law of Reciprocity does not encompass pacifism. For domestic tranquility, there must be a police force and a system of justice capable of bringing sure and swift punishment upon those who rebel against society. Injustice in the administration of the law will bring on revolution. But lack of diligence in the punishment of crime will promote anarchy.

So also in the international realm, the family of peace-loving nations must be able to protect itself against renegades. The Law of Reciprocity would forbid two equals from beginning a fight to settle a dispute. However, a miscreant is not the equal of law-abiding persons. A rogue nation is not the equal of the family of nations. A rebellious child is not the equal of his parents. In each of these cases, the lawful and just application of discipline or restraint does not violate the Law of Reciprocity. Such discipline is in fact a God-given, albeit temporary, method of dealing with evil in a still imperfect world.

But in all other cases, I believe we should exercise the Law of Reciprocity to the fullest, even among those not yet committed personally to God Almighty. For it is a principle that will work in the visible world—now.

Study Guide

Key Scripture: Luke 6:31, 35–38

Key Idea: "Giving is foundational. You have to give of yourself. You have to give of your money. You have to give of your time. And this foundational truth works in both the invisible and visible worlds" (p. 112).

Pat Fleck was making his second attempt to gain a seat in Congress held by a long-term congressman. The first attempt had revealed a surprisingly strong base of support for Pat. He felt that this time around he had an excellent chance to unseat the incumbent.

A graduate of a reputable business school, Pat had gained most of his administrative experience in an international Christian organization, and this made him vulnerable to charges that he was inexperienced in the "real world." Between elections he had focused on building strong constituency support and on developing visibility for his platform. Yet Pat had also monitored the voting record of the incumbent closely, trying to determine vulnerable areas. In the process he had uncovered a particularly juicy bit of information about the personal life of the incumbent, which he knew would incense the conservative voters and help him gain higher visibility in the news media. Though Pat's campaign manager was all for using the information, Pat hesitated. He was aware of what James said in his epistle about gossip. As the campaign heated up, the pressure on Pat to use the information grew. He was not gaining voter support as quickly as he had hoped, and a little scandal would go a long way.

How would the incumbent congressman's campaign strategy change if Pat Fleck were to release information that would reflect negatively on the moral character of the incumbent?

What Jesus Taught

"And just as you want men to treat you, treat them in the same way. . . . But love your enemies, and do good, and lend, expecting nothing in return; and your reward will be great, and you will be sons of the Most High; for He Himself is kind to ungrateful and evil men. Be merciful, just as your Father is merciful. And do not pass judgment and you will not be judged; and do not condemn, and you shall not be condemned; pardon, and you will be pardoned. Give, and it will be given to you; good measure, pressed down, shaken together, running over, they will pour into your lap. For whatever measure you deal out to others, it will be dealt to you in return" (Luke 6:31, 35–38).

1. Write down the foundational and universal principle of Jesus in your own words.

2. Match the life experience on the left with the teaching of Jesus on the right.

   a. Your neighbor's dog attacks your child.
   —Give, and it will be given to you.

   b. You hear an elder in the church has been seen with another woman.
   —Love your enemies.

   c. Your sister always expects you to host the family gatherings.
   —Be merciful.

   d. Your boss expects you to take work home regularly.
   —Judge not.

   e. A murderer who accepted Christ in prison is up for parole.
   —Expect nothing in return.

The Universal Principle

"A basic law of physics says that for every action there is an equal and oppostie reaction" (p. 110). This can be proved in a variety of physical phenomena, such as jet engines and rocket engines. Consider the following situations and, based on your reaction, put an X under Yes or No.

	Yes	No
1. When involved in an accident not your fault you should let the other driver know what you think of him/her.	___	___
2. When the neighbor's dog gets through the fence, take it back on a rope and threaten to sue if it happens again.	___	___

3. When the city sets plans in motion to
   annex your area, organize a protest march.   ___   ___
4. When a black family moves into your
   neighborhood, take them a welcome cake.   ___   ___
5. When your pastor loses his cool in an
   elders' meeting, take him out for lunch to
   discover what is really troubling him.   ___   ___

Briefly describe one situation in your community where you can put the Law of Reciprocity into action in a positive way.

Facing the Issues

1. Kurt had been most successful in every business position he had taken, with two positions as vice-president of medium-sized companies heading his resumé. At his last place of employment he had discovered clearly unethical business practices sanctioned by the board. He had resigned when no one seemed to listen to his protests. He was sure that God would help find another job quickly. Yet one year later he still had no job, despite sending out dozens of resumés and going to interviews. Then he was offered a job at a Christian organization at an hourly rate much too low to support his family.

   Should Kurt take the job, based on the Law of Reciprocity taught by Jesus in Luke 6:38? Give reasons for or against.

2. John believed that God deserved a tenth of his income. Yet he knew if he gave it this month his son would not get the glasses he needed desperately to do better in school. If you were John, what would you do. Base your answer on Malachi 3:7–10.

3. Pat Robertson writes, "If we want to release the super-abundance of the kingdom of heaven, we must first give. Our Father is more than ready to fulfill His side of the Law of Reciprocity" (p. 114). What one word describes the attitude we need to have if we are to live like this?

Facing the New Reality

1. As a result of slavery, "a good nation was battered, its regions divided, its people torn" is the way Pat Robertson describes the United States of the Civl War era. How does he interpret the effect of the divine Law of Reciprocity in the South today?

2. "The Law of Reciprocity without question affects the way people and nations live with each other. It has the potential of bringing peace to the world" (p. 121). What would happen in the following areas if this Law of Reciprocity were implemented?

   a. War

   b. Trade

   c. Injustice

   d. Crime

   e. Pollution

   f. Productivity

   g. Government

3. When will the Law of Reciprocity not work?

Making It Happen

1. When facing issues that require implementing the Law of Reciprocity, what special advantage do believers have according to Romans 8:31–37?

2. Write out one area in your life where you can begin acting in keeping with the Law of Reciprocity.

Scripture References

1 Luke 6:38
2 Luke 6:31
3 Luke 6:36–38
4 Matthew 22:39, see also Leviticus 19:18
5 Luke 6:38, KJV
6 Luke 6:38
7 Matthew 6:33
8 Matthew 7:1
9 Luke 6:38
10 Malachi 3:7–10
11 Malachi 3:10, TLB
12 2 Corinthians 9:6–8, 11
13 1 Chronicles 29:12, 14
14 Psalm 24:1, KJV
15 Luke 6:38
16 Psalm 37:25
17 Psalm 37:10, 11
18 E.g., Exodus 21, 22; Leviticus 18:24, 20:1–27, 21:9
19 James 4:7

8. The Law of Use

An exceptional urgency seemed to have gripped the Lord's ministry by the time He reached the teaching we will examine at this point. He had so much to impart and seemingly so little time to do it. Everything was speeding up.

In the midst of rapid-fire teachings about the kingdom of heaven, He began this story:

> "For it is just like a man about to go on a journey, who called his own slaves, and entrusted his possessions to them. And to one he gave five talents, to another, two, and to another, one, each according to his own ability; and he went on his journey."[1]

Then unfolds the development of what I have come to call the Law of Use. Servant number one received five talents. The parable says he went out and "'traded with them.'" We can imagine what happened. Perhaps he bought some commodities, sold them at a profit, and reinvested the entire amount. Or perhaps he took a journey and returned with valuable goods, and he added to the value of those goods through work he or someone else did to them. Regardless, he worked with his master's money and eventually doubled it.

The man with the two talents acted similarly. He may have bought wool, handed it over to a weaver, and then sold the woven cloth at a profit, only to quickly reinvest it and keep all the money working. Eventually he had doubled the amount left with him.

The third slave acted differently, however. The parable says he took the single talent, dug a hole, and buried it. He was afraid, Jesus said—afraid that if he went out and bought wool or oil or some such item, a depression would come and he would lose the money. Or maybe robbers would steal it. Or maybe someone would outsmart him or cheat him, say, at the weights and balances. Perhaps he would make a wrong decision. So, impotent with fear, he preserved his lord's investment by hiding it in a safe place.

After a long time, the lord returned and called the slaves to him. "Tell me," he said after a brief exchange, "how did you do with my money?"

The first servant quickly replied, "Master, I took the five talents and I traded with them. I bought and sold, and even wheeled and dealed a little bit, and I made five more talents. Here is the original and five additional."

He had covered his overhead and still doubled the amount.

The master was pleased: "'. . . Well done, good and faithful slave; you were faithful with a few things. I will put you in charge of many things; enter into the joy of your master.'"

The next servant stepped forward and reported: "Lord, I took your two talents, and I went out and bought and sold. I entered into some business transactions, and I took some risks, but I made money. I've got two more talents. Here are the two you gave me and two additional."

The lord replied in the same way he had to the man with five talents.

Then it was the third man's turn. "Tell me what you've done with my money while I've been gone," the master said.

"Lord, I knew you were a hard man," he began. "You reap where you don't sow. You gather where you don't even plant. So I was afraid. I figured the best thing to do was play it safe, so I wrapped the talent up nicely and hid it. Here it is; I didn't lose anything."

Most of us today can sympathize with this fellow. After

all, if you're a trustce over somebody else's property, you have to be careful. You can't take risks. It's even worse in an economically volatile world like ours.

What did the master do in this illustration to prepare us for the kingdom?

> "... 'You wicked, lazy slave, you knew that I reap where I did not sow, and gather where I scattered no seed. Then you ought to have put my money in the bank, and on my arrival I would have received my money back with interest. . . . cast out the worthless slave into the outer darkness; in that place there shall be weeping and gnashing of teeth."[2]

The man was considered wicked—sinful, given to evil—because he refused to take what his lord had given him and put it to work, improving upon it.

Note that quantity wasn't the key. Their use of what they had been given was what mattered. Proper use gave them entry into the place of joy. Improper use barred the third man.

However, the startling point of the parable is the following conclusion: "... 'to everyone who has shall more be given, and he shall have an abundance; but from the one who does not have, even what he does have shall be taken away.'"[3] During my extended time of seeking wisdom from God, the magnitude of that sentence crystallized for me. I perceived that it presented a principle, a law, that was as important for day-to-day life as any there is.

"'To everyone who has shall more be given.'" It seems shocking, particularly to those tending toward a welfare state or socialism, as so many in the world do today. We have a poor man with only onc talent and another who has improved his lot, and we take the one away from the former and give it to the one who already has ten. It goes against the grain, simply because we have failed to see how important God views our use of what He has given us.

Despite our preconceived attitudes toward social justicc, God's Law of Use controls the ultimate distribution of wealth. We must be willing to take the world as He made it and live in it to the fullest. For He says, in fact, that if we are willing to do that—if we are willing to use what He has given us—we will have more. But if we are not willing to use what He has given us, we will lose it.

As we will see, this is not mean or unfair. It is the way *God* wants the world to be. And as we begin to understand the Law of Use, we will soon realize that this is the only way it can be.

Muscles Respond, Too

Our bodies give us a perfect illustration of the working of the Law of Use. For instance, let's say you would like to learn to do push-ups. Perhaps you've never been able to do them well.

I will assume the Lord has given you the strength to do one, perhaps only the kind from the knees, called a woman's pushup; but you can do that. And so you take what you have, and you put it to work. Do one a day for a week or two and before long you'll find it's not hard. Then go to two, and do two for a week or two. They'll get easier, and then you can move to three, and so on. Before long you'll be doing ten, and you'll start to wonder, "Why did I think these were so hard?"

Do you see the same principle? To everyone who has, and who uses what he has, more shall be given.

Now, you could do the very opposite. You could take what you have, refuse to use it, and ultimately lose it. For instance, you could tape you hand to your side in such a way that you would be unable to move it. If you left it there, totally unused, for six months, the muscles would wither and an arm that had had unlimited potential would be useless. Even what you had would have been taken away.

The same would hold true for the development of your mind and resultant skills. If you were a doctor, say, and wanted to master a particular type of treatment, you would begin simply with the knowledge you had. You could study everything available, and you could practice your knowledge, simply at first, perhaps under close supervision. You could stay at it for a year or two and before long, you would master the subject. You would have expertise and a specialty that others would covet, all acquired through using what you already had.

Of course, if you thoroughly neglected study and abstained totally from practice, you would gradually reach a point of deterioration and incompetence where no one would want to trust himself in your hands. You would lose what you started with.

So also in our spiritual lives. If we pray, read the Bible, and exercise the understanding we already have, we will grow. If we don't, we will weaken and diminish in effectiveness.

Carver and the Peanut

One of the geniuses of our country was a black man named George Washington Carver. He perfectly illustrated the Law of Use in a different fashion.

One day he went before the Lord in prayer and said, "Mr. Creator, show me the secrets of Your universe."

It was a big request, but he believed in asking boldly.

He received a bold answer, although it might not have seemed so at first.

"Little man," God said, "you're not big enough to know the secrets of My universe."

One can almost feel the sense of repudiation. However, God was not finished with His reply. "But I'll show you the secret of the peanut."

From the universe to the peanut! "Take it apart," God said.

Undaunted and obedient, Carver did just that. He took the peanut apart and discovered several hundred elements in that little seed.

Still God wasn't finished. "Start putting it back together again, in different form," the Lord instructed.

He did. And from that work came food of many kinds,

plastics, paint, oil, and seemingly endless products. He revolutionized Southern agriculture and industry all by using what God had given—boldly, creatively, patiently.

The Exponential Curve

Working hand in hand with the Law of Use is a mathematical phenomenon known as the exponential curve. Actually Jesus set forth the first step in such a curve when He told the parable of the talents. It fits perfectly into our principle.

The Lord told how two of the servants doubled what had been given to them. Had they done that at regular intervals, such as annually, then their increases, placed on a graph, would have established an exponential curve that would have proved astounding.

For example, if they began with $100 and continued to double the amount each year, the graph would proceed along at a rather ho-hum level for a few years and then it would skyrocket. At the end of twenty years, the $100 would have grown to $50 million. In just five more years, it would have soared to $1.6 billion. By the thirty-five mark, it would be $1.6 trillion, and at the end of fifty years, it would be $12.8 quadrillion, which is more money than exists in the world.

This shows dramatically what can happen through a joining of the Law of Use with the exponential curve, simply accomplishing at a set rate what Jesus was teaching in the parable.

Of course, such 100 percent increases are not necessary for the exponential curve to be effective with this law. Take the $100 and compound it at six percent for fifty years and it is transformed into nearly $2,800. Increase the percentage to 15 or 20 percent and you end up with several hundred thousand dollars.

So phenomenal is this principle that Baron Rothschild, the financier, once described compound interest as "the eighth wonder of the world." Bankers throughout history have enriched themselves enormously by way of this "wonder." The key is consistency and longevity, to the point where the exponential curve makes its sharp upward turn, and the escalation defies the imagination.

Certainly, the Lord Jesus did not intend to lay down for us a principle whose purpose was to allow the rich to get richer and the poor to get poorer. No, He was showing how the world works and how, through diligent, patient exercise of the gifts He is constantly bestowing, we can enter into the prosperity and abundance of the invisible world.

We need to see that the truths He disclosed are available to everyone—now. The sad fact is that not everyone—not even those committed to Him—will enter in. We are too much like the servant who took his talent and buried it.

The problem often is that we will look at someone successful in a field we would like to be in and say, "I wish I were like him." We want to have the success without having applied the Law of Use and the exponential curve. We want to go from obscurity and poverty to fame and riches in one quick jump. First we have to take what He has given and multiply it, steadily and patiently. Success will come.

To want full accomplishment immediately is lust. It is a sin and calls for violation of the pattern of God. It is wanting something for nothing. Socialism and communism feed on such lust, calling for taking from the rich and giving to the poor, for leveling society in such a way as to deprive individuals of the learning and maturity necessary to handle abundance.

So many well-meaning people have in fact done harm to individuals and indeed to nations by short-cutting God's plan and short-circuiting the blessings intended. They want to give everyone everything immediately, not only stirring up lust, but also fulfilling it, and ultimately harming those they want to help.

God's way is the way of gradual, sure growth and maturity, moving toward perfection. It can be compared to an airplane during takeoff. If the trajectory is too low, then time will overtake it, the plane will run out of runway and crash, or it will get a few feet off the ground and not rise fast enough to avoid the trees or buildings.

People are the same. If their goals are too low, too stretched out and easy, they will never rise to any significant potential before time overtakes them.

On the other hand, if the pilot sets the exponent in his takeoff pattern too high an the plane rises too steeply, it is likely to stall and crash.

The same is true with people. Set your economic growth too high, and you will stall; try to make your child learn too much too fast, and he will become discouraged and give up; try to do fifty push-ups without practice, and you will encounter agony.

Thus, although there is nothing but abundance in the kingdom of heaven and nothing is impossible with God, the Lord's plan is for us to set realistic goals with what He has given us. He wants us to have goals that are demanding enough to keep us occupied, but are not overtaxing, and to stick with them long enough for them to come to fruition.

We find clues to this in other parables of the Lord.

> ". . . The kingdom of heaven is like a mustard seed, which a man took and sowed in his field; and this is smaller than all other seeds; but when it is full grown, it is larger than the garden plants, and becomes a tree, so that the birds of the air come and nest in its branches."[4]

The black mustard of the East starts with the tiniest seed imaginable, but from that tiny beginning comes a strong plant often running to heights as tall as a man on horseback. So it can be with the things to us to use.

Similarly Jesus told of what might be called *unconscious* growth from small beginnings:

> And He was saying, "The kingdom of God is like a man who casts seed upon the soil; and goes to bed at night and gets up by day, and the seed sprouts up and grows—how, he himself does not know. The soil produces crops by itself; first the blade, then the head, then the mature grain in the head. But when the crop permits, he immediately puts in the sickle, because the harvest has come."[5]

We must never despise small beginnings. The increase will come, almost unconsciously, imperceptibly, in the early stages; but suddenly there will be a burst of growth as the exponential rate takes hold and reaches maturity. Before long, it's harvest time.

Remember, everyone has something. With some, it's music. With some, it's athletics. With some, it's technical skill. Even a quadriplegic confined to bed cannot feel left out of this marvelous principle. Perhaps more important than anything else, he can consistently exercise the great gift of prayer, maturing to remarkable depths and affecting the entire world.

Wrong Side of the Curve

One of the tragedies of man is that he frequently gets himself on the wrong side of the exponential curve; it can work against us as well as for us. This happens to individuals and it happens to nations.

The United States and many of its citizens are examples at this very time. Singly and collectively we have allowed the exponential curve to plunge us into enormous debt. In most cases, the beginnings were innocent, but the exponential rate is merciless if it's working against you. It can destroy you if you are borrowing money and paying high interest rates. Vast numbers of Americans are caught in such traps right now, and our government has been suffering under an increasingly impossible burden for years.

This, of course, comes from the lust and covetousness I mentioned, the insistence on having everything now. "I want my furniture *now*," the housewife cries. Meanwhile her husband demands his new, bigger car—now. Neither wants to await the accumulation of the resources necessary to avoid sending compound interest careening into action. On a wider scale, our national attitude views many luxuries as necessities. We override the Law of Use when we attempt to put the biggest, most modern television sets and gadgetry in every home and apartment through consumer debt or even through welfare laws. The national debt soars, credit card bills reach astronomical heights, and the exponential curve zooms upward to hopelessness and collapse.

Jesus Himself, coming in the flesh as man and suffering temptation just as we do, ran into a test on this score early in His public ministry. It came during His temptation in the wilderness: "Again, the devil took Him to a very high mountain, and showed Him all the kingdoms of the world, and their glory; and he said to Him, 'All these things will I give You, if You fall down and worship me.'"[6]

Satan, described in the New Testament as "'the ruler of the world'" (although destined to be cast out),[7] promised Him everything, right then, if He would just do it his way. But the Lord said He would do it God's way—gradually, the way of sacrifice and suffering, the way of work, the way of the cross.

The law of Satan's kingdom is: Have it now, with a splash. Quick money, quick things, quick success.

In God's kingdom, the Law of Use governs, providing genuine and lasting security, genuine and lasting prosperity.

Because of the power of the Law of Use and the exponential curve—along with man's seemingly incurable weaknesses—God many centuries ago established two rules for the people of Israel of which we should be aware.

First, he decreed that the Israelites were not to take usury of one another: "'You shall not charge interest to your countrymen: interest on money, food, or anything that may be loaned at interest.'"[8]

They were permitted to charge interest to foreigners, which would agree with the parable of the talents in the New Testament, apparently because the Lord intended to give them dominance over other nations: "'For the LORD your God shall bless you as He has promised you, and *you will lend to many nations*, but you will not borrow; and *you will rule over many nations*, but they will not rule over you.'"[9]

Modern experience has shown that usury ultimately leads to subservience; and God did not want that for His people, but rather intended for them to rule.

Second, God set up a year of jubilee for his people to counteract the fact that a few eventually gain control of all wealth and land. In short, He directed that every fifty years all debt be canceled, all accumulated property be redistributed, and the cycle of use begin again.

It was part of His marvelous plan under which the land would have a sabbath year to the Lord. For six years, the land would be worked, "'but during the seventh year the land shall have a sabbath rest, a sabbath to the LORD.'"[10] Then He laid out the jubilee plan:

> 'You are also to count off seven sabbaths of years for yourself, seven times seven years, so that you have the time of the seven sabbaths of years, namely, forty-nine years. You shall then sound a ram's horn abroad on the tenth day of the seventh month; on the day of atonement you shall sound a horn all through your land. You shall thus consecrate the fiftieth year and *proclaim a release* through the land to all its inhabitants. It shall be a jubilee for you, and each of you shall return to his family.'[11]

The "release" or "liberty" was multifaceted and touched much of the life of the Israelites, specifically remitting indebtedness. It was as though God said to a man who perhaps was twenty at the beginning of the cycle and who is now seventy: "You've had your day in the sun, your time of opportunity, so now you should step aside, cancel the debts, and let people start over again."

I believe it is quite possible the year of jubilee will be the only way out, short of collapse for our world in its current economic slide. The United States government, and indeed all governments, have gotten on the wrong side of the exponential curve and the Law of Use and have reached the point of insupportable debt. Trying to meet the demands of the people who are screaming "We want it now!" the governments, along with individuals, have run at major deficits, borrowing huge sums of money, always at compound interest. Early in the decade, the estimated worldwide debt was $10 trillion, with interest payments reaching the point where nations cannot meet them. The United

States itself owed $1 trillion, and efforts to correct its economic trends set off dangerous convulsions.

Notwithstanding the sneers of many in the banking community, it may be that God's way will be the only one open to us—a year of jubilee to straighten out the mess.

We should also be fully aware of the fact that finance is not the only area in which the exponential curve can work against us. We need only look at the snowballing evils of pornography, adultery, divorce, alcoholism, and drug addiction to grasp this. Such evil began small and steadily increased, almost unconsciously it seems, until the unprecedented surge of recent years and today's raging floodtide.

The Most Powerful Principle

In the previous chapter, I said the Law of Reciprocity was probably the most encompassing of the kingdom principles, virtually undergirding every aspect of life and revealing a course of conduct that could change the world.

The Law of Use, meanwhile, coupled with the exponential curve is probably the most powerful of the principles in terms of day-to-day life. It is the fundamental law for the growth and development—or the decline—of all organizations and societies in both the invisible and the visible worlds. Beginning with the cradle, it touches everything—child development, intellectual development, professional development, physical development, social development, and on and on.

Together the Law of Reciprocity and the Law of Use are the core of the way the world works, the invisible world and the visible one.

We have already explored major areas touched by the Law of Use and the exponential curve, but we need to see the never-ending, ever-increasing potential. There is, in fact, a principle of increasing opportunity. For example, the man with $100 has certain vistas of opportunity before him. By applying the Law of Use, he can increase that sum to $1000, and immediately his opportunities for expanded use of the law are increased. Quite simply, the man with $1000 has more clout than the man with $100.

If he presses on with the Law of Use, he will rise to the $10,000 level and his vistas widen; then $100,000 and he finds bank doors and credit open to him that he hadn't dreamed of. A million dollars opens an entirely new class of opportunity, and so it goes—never-ending opportunity for the person involved in the Law of Use.

The broadcasting world works the same way. To him who is faithful in a little will more be given. A person who has worked his way up to ownership of five stations has a far easier time acquiring a sixth than the person just starting out has in acquiring the first. The former is experienced and knowledgeable. He knows when and how to move. He has access to money markets that the inexperienced, struggling beginner lacks.

So it is with people in science. The one who has mastered fundamental and intermediate theorems is far more capable of going on to an advanced theorem than is the youngster who hasn't had his first high school science course.

In politics, the person who has successfully run for a city council seat is more likely to succeed in a race for mayor than someone who is unknown and untested. The mayor is then in a stronger position to move to the state legislature than the beginner, and on up the line to governor, senator, and perhaps president.

The same holds true for spiritual life. The opportunities steadily increase as we move from one level of understanding and maturity to the next. Mastery of one small principle of the faith opens up new horizons for even wider growth. Prayer and intercession for our families build us up for prayer and intercession for our church, and then our town, our state, and our nation. Similarly, public ministry to fifty people will open opportunities for ministry to one hundred. We are then far better prepared to minister to one thousand, then ten thousand, then twenty thousand.

No, we are not to despise small beginnings, but rather to exercise the eternally established Law of Use.

I am convinced that this law—put to work with the commitment, the virtues, and the accompanying subprinciples—can produce giant steps toward easing and ultimately removing the crises that grip the world. It will touch world hunger, the economic quagmire, energy depletion, Third World needs, educational and social injustice, church evangelism, moral decadence, disease, and inadequate health care.

The only thing lacking is for us to hear with understanding the words spoken by God to Moses regarding the sanctuary Israel was to construct for the Lord: "'According to all that I am going to show you, as the *pattern* of the tabernacle and the *pattern* of all its furniture, *just so you shall construct it.*'"[12]

"Do it my way," says the Lord. He has given a pattern for the secret kingdom. We merely need to follow it.

Study Guide

Key Scripture: Matt. 25:14–30

Key Idea: "God's Law of Use controls the ultimate distribution of wealth. We must be willing to take the world as he made it and live in it to the fullest. For He says, in fact, that if we are willing to do that—if we are willing to use what He has given us—we will have more. But if we are not willing to use what He has given us, we will lose it" (pp. 133–134).

You are a reasonably healthy person in your mid-fifties. In your research you become acquainted with a fine group at the local college. One Saturday they invite you to go cross-country skiing with them. It's been some years since you were on skis, but you are sure you can still manage well enough to have some fun. After all, you don't want to be known as a spoilsport. What will happen to you as you relax before the roaring fire in the lodge after three hours on skis? Or in a similar vein, two hours on the tennis court?

Read Matthew 25:14–30. What principle of life does Jesus illustrate with the parable of the talents, according to Pat Robertson?

Why is the man with one talent considered "wicked, lazy . . . worthless"?

Facing the Issues

1. In what three areas of your life will disuse result in loss?

   a.

   b.

   c.

2. Considering the example of George Washington Carver, what could be the "peanut" in your life? _____

The Exponential Curve

1. Write out in your own words how the exponential curve works in the area of finances.

2. In his campaigns to teach people in Third World countries to read, Frank Laubach emphasized that each person who learned to read should teach one other person to read. What could happen if each person who accepted Christ as personal Savior were to lead one other person to faith in Christ, considering the effect of the exponential curve?

3. Why does Pat Robertson call wanting full accomplishment immediately a sin? (See p. 137.)

4. Pat Robertson writes, "So many well-meaning people have in fact done harm to individuals and indeed to nations by short-cutting God's plan and short-circuiting the blessings intended" (p. 137). Describe one area in which we as a nation are doing that.

   Describe one way in which you may be doing that.

5. "He [God] wants us to have goals that are demanding enough to keep us occupied, but are not overtaxing, and to stick with them long enough for them to come to fruition" (p. 138). List one situation in your community, your church, or your personal life where you need to implement this principle.

Wrong Side of the Curve

1. What is the law of Satan's kingdom? (See Matt. 4:8–9.)

2. In what ways can this principle lead to our destruction as a nation?

3. Do you consider the command in Deuteronomy 23:19 practical today? _____
   Give the reasons for your answer.

4. Does the Year of Jubilee described in Leviticus 25:8–10 have application today? _____
   Why or why not? (See p. 141.)

Making It Happen

1. What is the "principle of increasing opportunity"? (See pp. 142–143.)

2. Your goal is a seat in the Senate. What will you have to get involved in before you run for the Senate?

3. What would happen if you applied the Law of Use and the principle of increasing opportunity to your prayer life?

4. List two steps you will need to take to capitalize on the Law of Use in your personal finances.

   a.

   b.

Wrap-Up

"I am convinced that this law—put to work with the commitment, the virtues, and the accompanying subprinciples—can produce giant steps toward easing and ultimately removing the crises that grip the world. It will touch world hunger, the economic quagmire, energy depletion, Third World needs, educational and social justice, church evangelism, moral decadence, disease, and inadequate health care" (p. 144).

Scripture References

1 Matthew 25:14, 15ff
2 Matthew 25:26, 27, 30
3 Matthew 25:29
4 Matthew 13:31, 32
5 Mark 4:26-29
6 Matthew 4:8, 9
7 John 12:31,14:30
8 Deuteronomy 23:19
9 Deuteronomy 15:6
10 Leviticus 25:4
11 Leviticus 25:8-10

9. The Law of Perserverance

We've caught glimpses of it in previous chapters, but we need to see clearly that the ways of the universe yield to perseverance.

We see it in the simple, homely story of the chick and the egg. The baby chick, approaching full life, finds himself in a nice, safe environment, dark and quiet. His home, the egg, keeps him warm and cuddly; he feels just perfect.

Soon, however, he becomes aware that the shell keeping him so comfortable and safe is also circumscribing his life. He begins to feel restricted.

You see, there is something in life that says, "I have to grow." Humans and animals have planted within them the need to be free and to grow.

So the little chick begins pecking at the shell. He doesn't understand it, but things have been set up so that he has to peck and peck and peck. He works very hard, gaining strength hour by hour from that God-ordained struggle. Before long, he has attained the strength and the endurance to cope with a new environment, and he breaks through the shell. He pecks some more, and soon he is free, ready for a new level of life.

People have tried to help little chicks speed the process of cracking the shell and opening it for them. But, short-circuiting God's process, they kill the chicks. They are stillborn, unable to handle for even a few moments the rigors of a new environment.

God's principle is what I call the Law of Perseverance. It is critical to success in life generally and to life in the kingdom especially.

Certain risks go with new life and growth—the risks of freedom, we might say—but God prepares us for those risks, through perseverance and struggle, building our muscles, as it were, for each new phase. To refuse to struggle is to stand still, to stagnate.

Jesus taught the Law of Perseverance in a passage well-known to most Christians:

> "Ask, and it shall be given to you; seek, and you shall find; knock, and it shall be opened to you. For everyone who asks receives, and he who seeks finds, and to him who knocks it shall be opened. Or what man is there among you, when his son shall ask him for a loaf, will give him a stone? Or if he shall ask for a fish, he will not give him a snake, will he? If you then, being evil, know how to give good gifts to your children, how much more shall your Father who is in heaven give what is good to those who ask Him!"[1]

We grasp His meaning more fully when we understand that the verbs "asks," "seeks," and "knocks" were written in the Greek present imperative and are to be understood in this manner: "*Keep asking*, and it shall be given to you; *keep seeking*, and you shall find; *keep knocking*, and it shall be opened to you." The Father gives "what is good to those who *keep asking* Him."

He also said, as we have noted, that "'. . . the kingdom of heaven suffers violence, and violent men take it by force.'"[2] It does not come easily. The little chick we spoke of was violent; he had to be. Most of the secrets of God come forth with effort; the blessings of God are the same.

Some Christians have been taught that all one has to do to get things from God is to speak the word of faith, believe, and receive. That comes close to the truth, but it neglects the universal Law of Perseverance. God slowly yields the good things of the kingdom and the world to those who struggle. Jacob, for instance, wrestled all night with an angel before he became Israel, a prince with God. Abraham waited one hundred years before he received Isaac, the child of promise. The people of Judah waited and struggled seventy years in captivity before God brought them home.

This does not negate the necessity for asking in faith, the believing, and the receiving. But many times those steps are only the beginning of the process. The fulfillment may take years.

Jesus gave this illustration of perseverance:

> Now He was telling them a parable to show that at all times they ought to pray and not to lose heart, saying, "There was in a certain city a judge who did not fear God, and did not respect man. And there was a widow in that city, and she kept coming to him, saying, 'Give me legal protection from my opponent.' And for a while he was unwilling; but afterward he said to himself, 'Even though I do not fear God nor respect man, yet because this widow bothers me, I will give her legal protection, lest by continually coming she wear me out.'" And the Lord said, "Hear what the unrighteous judge said; now shall not God bring about justice for His elect, who cry to Him day and night, and will He delay long over them? I tell you that He will bring about justice for them speedily. However, when the Son of Man comes, will He find faith on the earth?"[3]

Jesus knew men inside out. He knew our tendency to give up quickly, to become inconsistent and lackadaisical. Yet He pleaded with us to persist, in prayer and in all aspects of life.

> And He said to them, "Suppose one of you shall have a friend, an shall go to him at midnight, and say to him, 'Friend, lend me three loaves; for a friend of mine has come to me from a journey, and I have nothing to set before him'; and from inside he shall answer and say, 'Do not bother me; the door has alrcady bccn shut and my children and I are in bed; I cannot get up and give you anything.' I tell you, even though he will not get up and give him anything because he is his friend, yet

because of his persistence he will get up and give him as much
as he needs."[4]

Keep on asking, He said, keep on seeking, and keep on
knocking. Don't be afraid even to make a ruckus. God prefers that to slothfulness and indolence. He wants people
who will travail and perhaps stumble a bit, but keep on
going forward, just like a toddler who's trying to learn to
walk. The child builds muscles and learns. One day he will
run.

In the early, trying days of the church, according to the
Book of Acts, Paul and Barnabas traveled through Lystra,
Iconium, and Antioch "strengthening the souls of the disci-
ples, encouraging them to continue in the faith, and saying,
'Through many tribulations we must enter the kingdom of
God.'"[5]

There was to be conflict, they said, using a word that
most translators have rendered "tribulation" but which carries the idea of "pressure," especially pressure on the spirit.
This pressure, or tribulation, was understood in New Testament times to build stamina and staying power, leading to
fullness of character.

We are to remember that there is an adversary. He is
called Satan. One of his favorite techniques in the unrelenting effort to trip the people of God is to foster discouragement and depression. That is why the Bible says repeatedly
that Christians are to be patient, to hold on, to persist.

Satan is continuously pouring into our ears such negatives as these: "You're not accomplishing anything. . . .
You're on the wrong course. . . . You don't have the necessary skill and ability. . . . Everyone else has failed so why do
you think you'll succeed? . . . Those promises you thought
were from God are nothing. . . . You're unworthy. . . ."

So we often grow discouraged and quit. Then the principles of the kingdom cease to function in our lives. And we
fail.

The ultimate personal failure, of course, is suicide. It is
the number two killer in our nation's youth, next to automobile accidents. So many people have given up in hope-

lessness, finding their problems overwhelming, the world a mess beyond repair, the possibilities of life too dark. And they slip into the horror of taking their lives, which truly are not theirs to take.

Even the great prophet Elijah reached such despair. Having experienced one of his great triumphs, the defeat of the priests of Baal through a powerful miracle of God, he obviously was exhausted mentally, emotionally, and physically. Jezebel was trying to kill him. He fell into gloom.

"'It is enough . . . ,'" he cried out. "'O LORD, take my life, for I am not better than my fathers.'"[6]

But God would not let him give up. Neither does He want us to quit.

Instead, we are to be constantly alert against discouragement and depression. We are to be aware of what our enemy is trying to do. We are to reject him and he will flee. God will not let trial and temptation overcome us if we will stand, but rather will make a way of victory for us.[7] He wants us to persevere and will make it possible.

Lessons of History

Had God given us no more insight than the Law of Perseverance together with the Laws of Reciprocity and Use, we would have enough to change the world. We need only think of examples from our own national history.

Consider Abraham Lincoln. He became one of the greatest governmental and moral leaders in American history. But the achievements didn't come until he had passed through many personal failures, including bankruptcies and endless humiliating labors to make ends meet. The struggles, the battles, the wounds—they equipped him for the environment in which he would make his greatest contribution.

Consider Thomas Edison. This greatest of inventors went through hundreds of experiments that were failures before he achieved success with the electric light. He attributed his incredible accomplishments to "two percent inspiration and nintey-eight percent perspiration"—a formula for struggle and perseverance.

Consider the Wright Brothers. On the lonely sands of North Carolina's outer banks, they battled the elements, the ridicule of men, the lack of resources. They built; they failed; they rebuilt and failed again. Finally, they flew. And the world was changed.

In my own life's work, through the grace of God, I learned the centrality of perseverance. In 1959 my family and I arrived in Tidewater with $70 and a God-planted desire to establish a broadcasting ministry that would glorify the Lord. We went through two years of personal and corporate struggle before getting on the air with our first station. Then came ten years more of striving, anguish, and hardship before we obtained our second station. Steadily the growth increased, as we persevered and learned the lessons of the kingdom.

In that pressure cooker, which in so many ways resembled the trials of the chick with the egg, we matured to the point of readiness for a worldwide ministry. With hindsight, it is amusing to note how the Lord forced us to use everything He had given us to its very limit before He provided something new. Before establishing us in our new Virginia Beach international center, He had us using every nook and cranny and every foot of property available to us. We had trailers lined up all over the land, jammed with people and activity. We had rented property all over Tidewater, taxing our ingenuity and patience daily. Through it all, we were getting ready for the next phase of our work; we were being strengthened for a new environment and new challenges. We were getting maturity the only way a Christian can get it.

In 1979 I examined CBN's history and found that in those twenty years, the Lord had taken our initial $70 and caused it to double exponentially every year during that time. By sheer mercy and grace, He had led us in the Laws of Reciprocity, Use, and Perseverance.

Had He led us otherwise, dumping on us too quickly the responsibility for a worldwide ministry and budgets of tens of millions of dollars, we would have crumbled. But He is wise enough to lead his people according to His laws even before we are able to know and articulate them.

As the great Bible teacher Donald Gray Barnhouse put it, "God uses oak trees, not mushrooms." Are not perseverance and strength the great virtues of oak trees?

Study Guide

Key Scripture: Matt. 7:7–11; Luke 11:5–8; 18:1–8

Key Idea: "Certain risks go with new life and growth—the risks of freedom, we might say—but God prepares us for those risks through perseverance and struggle, building our muscles, as it were, for each new phase" (p. 150).

The grunts and groans of men exercising on Nautilus machines mingled with the music of the aerobics in the next room. Hardly the place where you'd expect a woman in her seventies, yet there she was, moving from machine to machine.

"When I started I had a tough time with ten pounds. Now I'm on forty pounds," she told a much younger woman on the equipment next to her. "And that seems easy already."

The regulars on Monday morning recognized the progress, for they had seen her come faithfully several times a week for months. The fact was that she was passing much younger men in her progress because she was not only regular but clearly persistent in her effort at self-improvement.

Describe one area of your life where perseverance bore fruit.

Facing the Issues

The Necessity of Effort

Read Matthew 7:7–11 and tell why asking, seeking, and knocking pay off.

What law of the kingdom takes effect when we keep on asking, seeking, and knocking?

The Necessity of Struggle

1. Pat Robertson writes, "Most of the secrets of God come forth with effort; the blessings of God are the same" (p. 150). Give three examples illustrating the importance of perseverance despite struggle. (See p. 151.)

   a.

   b.

   c.

2. What step is asking, seeking, and knocking in faith? How soon may we expect fulfillment?

3. After reading Luke 18:1–18, put down one experience in your life, where you acted like the widow. Then name one situation in which you will need to demonstrate a similar perseverance.

The Necessity of Conflict

1. "Jesus knew our tendency to give up quickly, to become inconsistent and lackadaisical" (p. 151). How does Jesus, who lives in us today, feel when we are like that?

2. What would have happened if the man whose friend arrived at midnight (see Luke 11:5–8) had been afraid of possible conflict with his friend?

3. What happened when Prime Minister Chamberlain was unwilling to face the possibility of conflict with Hitler over the German Führer's expansionist tactics?

4. What did John Mark do when he faced the possibility of conflict on his first trip with Uncle Barnabas and the apostle Paul? (Compare Acts 13:13; 15:38.)

5. What can we as Christians expect, according to Paul in Acts 14:22?

The Necessity of Awareness

1. "One of his (Satan's) favorite techniques in the unrelenting effort to trip the people of God is to foster discouragement and depression" (p. 152). What are some of the things the Adversary says to us?

2. What was at the root of Elijah's discouragement in 1 Kings 19:4? Why is his depression so surprising? (See chap. 18.)

3. What should give us confidence in our battle against Satan's attempts to discourage our perseverance? (See 1 Cor. 10:13; 2 Tim. 1:12.)

Perseverance Pays Off

1. What did Abraham Lincoln, Thomas Edison, and the Wright Brothers have in common? (See pp. 153–154.)

2. How did God prepare Pat Robertson for leadership in the Christian communications field?

Making It Happen

Focus on one area of your life where perseverance will be needed. Write it down on a piece of paper and place it in your wallet or purse. Now complete the sentence, "I resolve that I will lay hold of God's power by faith to _____
_____ "

Scripture References

1 Matthew 7:7–11
2 Matthew 11:12
3 Luke 18:1–8
4 Luke 11:5–8
5 Acts 14:22
6 1 Kings 19:4
7 See 1 Corinthians 10:13

10. The Law of Responsibility

Flowing in the same stream with the Laws of Reciprocity, Use, and Perseverance is the Law of Responsibility. Jesus summed it up succinctly: ". . . unto whomsoever much is given, of him shall be much required: and to whom men have committed much, of him they will ask the more."[1]

Using a parable on watchfulness and preparation, He made clear that rejection of this law leads to suffering. Those who are given understanding, ability, goods, money, authority, or fame have a responsibility that the less favored do not bear; failure to fulfill it produces fearful punishment.[2]

Jesus was precise in showing that the parable was for the favored in every category, spiritual and physical, those living in the invisible world and those living in the visible.

Whatever level of opportunity is given to us, both God and man expect us to give a certain standard to performance. Favor carries with it responsibility. As the favor increases, the responsibility increases.

If, for example, I am the steward of $1000 for someone, that person will expect a profit of about $100. But if I'm the steward of General Motors and report a profit of $100, I will be forced to resign in disgrace.

If I'm a tennis player who manages to get on the courts, say, on Saturday afternoons and can hit the ball well enough to get by, my friends will be satisfied. But if I'm given the skill and opportunity to advance to world class and then perform like a weekend player, people will be disappointed and my stature will diminish severely.

Rubinstein, the pianist, capsulized this principle when he remarked that should he fail to practice one day, he would know it; should he skip practice for two days, the critics would know it; but should that extend to three days, "the whole world knows it." A part-time church pianist might get away with a bit of a letdown, but not an internationally acclaimed musician. More is required of the professional.

Exercise of the Law of Use will bring success, especially if done in tandem with the Law of Perseverance, but the rewards of those two laws *demand* observance of the Law of Responsibility. We need to see this even before we expect God to fulfill His promises regarding the other principles. It is very wrong if we ask God for something and then don't accept the responsibility that goes with it.

Harry Truman said it well when remarking on the burden of the presidency: "If you can't stand the heat, get out of the kitchen." The presidency of the United States carries heavy responsibilities, he related; and if one doesn't want to face the responsibilities, he should not seek the favor of the people in the first place. For, as he said at another time, "There is no end to the chain of responsibility that binds [the President], and he is never allowed to forget that he is President." The sign on his Oval Office desk said: "The buck stops here."

At CBN, we have found the burden of favor to be a responsibility never to be forgotten. For example, the Lord blessed us deeply one year, allowing us to lead 75,000 people to acceptance of salvation through Jesus Christ. From that point on, there is no way we or our supporters could be satisfied with leading one thousand people to the Lord, despite the fact that one thousand salvations in one year is an astounding achievement. No, the Lord has given us much—equipment, personnel, opportunity—and much is required, both by God and by man. That's the way it works.

The Church Should Listen

Leaders of the church should be especially careful to rise to the responsibility given to them, for the Scripture is so clear on this point as to be somewhat frigthening. I am always stopped momentarily when I read the words of James regarding teachers: "Let not many of you become teachers, my brethren, knowing that as such we shall incur a stricter jugment."[3]

Those who have been shown enough to teach can be expected to practice what they teach, at the very least. The office carries a great responsibility.

Paul's letters to Timothy and Titus show the great expectations of God and man from those desiring to be overseers ("bishops" in the older translations).

> It is a trustworthy statement: if any man aspires to the office of overseer [or bishop], it is a fine work he desires to do. An overseer, then, must be above reproach, the husband of one wife, temperate, prudent, respectable, hospitable, able to teach, not addicted to wine or pugnacious, but gentle, uncontentious, free from the love of money. He must be one who manages his own household well, keeping his children under control with all dignity (but if a man does not know how to manage his own household, how will he take care of the church of God?); and not a new convert, lest he become conceited and fall into the condemnation incurred by the devil. And he must have a good reputation with those outside the church, so that he may not fall into reproach and the snare of the devil.[4]

He goes on to point out that those seeking the lesser office of deacon, while not required to measure up to the full responsibility of overseer or bishop, must nevertheless bear a burden greater than that of most, first being "tested" and found "beyond reproach."[5]

Christ's first disciples, especially the Twelve, carried

extraordinary burdens and responsibilities, as the New Testament shows in detail. They had been "'given the mystery of the kingdom of God'"[6] by the Lord Himself while others heard only in parables. This great gift, in a sense, carried with it the load of the world; and those apostles paid a great price—ridicule, ostracism, persecution, martyrdom—for the opportunity of spreading the gospel. Their sense of responsibility was always before them. In his letter to the Romans, Paul summed up that responsibility with these words: "I am under obligation both to Greeks and to barbarians, both to the wise and to the foolish."[7]

Even the ordinary, little-known people who have received the inexpressibly rich gift of eternal life—by grace through faith—are called to a life far more responsible and demanding than they led before. Knowing the Lord, who is "'the way, the truth, and the life.'"[8] sets a standard for us in the sight of God and people that we should always keep in mind. Paul referred to it as knowing how to conduct yourself "in the household of God, which is the church of the living God, the pillar and support of the truth."[9] It is a significant responsibility each Christian must meet. We need only look at the Great Commission given by Jesus to His people just before His ascension.

> "All authority has been given to Me in heaven and on earth. Go therefore and make disciples of all the nations, baptising them in the name of the Father and the Son and the Holy Spirit, teaching them to observe all that I commanded you. . . ."[10]

Even though He had said He Himself would build His church,[11] the responsibility for carrying that plan forward for the entire world was put into the hands of His people. *That* is responsibility.

Rank and Responsibility

Early in the nineteenth century, a French duke, Gaston Pierre Marc, wrote in a collection of *Maxims and Reflec-*

tions a two-word statement that has become part of our language: *"Noblesse oblige."* Despite historical abuses, it expresses the essence of the Law of Responsibility. "Nobility obliges" or, better, "nobility obligates" states the obligation of people of high rank, position, or favor to behave nobly, kindly, and responsibly toward others.

The idea, of course, did not originate with the Frenchman. The ancient Greeks reflected such attitudes in their writings, as shown by Euripides—"The nobly born must nobly meet his fate"[12]—and by Sophocles—"Nobly to live, or else nobly to die, befits proud birth."[13]

Men have known almost instinctively that as accomplishment and position rise, so do responsibility and burden. With each achievement, society raises its expectation a notch.

With the British of the nineteenth century, the concept of *noblesse oblige* reached its zenith, sometimes for good, sometimes for not-so-good. Regardless of mistakes, the British nobility perceived that if they were to have their country houses and servants, their privileges and honors, they in turn had to be responsible for the working people.

In the case of Great Britian as a whole, she felt a responsibility for the entire world, a duty to Pax Brittania—the British peace—on every continent. She called it the burden of empire, sending young men and women to India and the four corners of the earth, challenging any she felt would disrupt the peace of the world.

In a pattern that would be repeated, Russia threatened to enter Afghanistan in the late nineteenth century as a move toward a warm-water port in the Middle East. The British, accepting the responsibility accompanying their position as the world's greatest power, challenged the Russians and prevailed. To them, it was *noblesse oblige*, protecting the people from invaders, pirates, and brigands. To others, it often was unadulterated colonialism, in which people were exploited, confined to subservience and poverty. Both views contained truth. Humility and purity, among other virtues, were lacking. Nonetheless, Victorian

Britain instinctively realized that the Law of Responsibility was a foundational corollary to her preeminent position in the nineteenth-century world.

The U.S. Faltered

Contrasted with the British leaning toward *noblesse oblige* were the frequent failures of responsibility by the government of the United States during the second half of this century. To begin with, Americans during most of their history worked hard under the Law of Use. They were frugal, disciplined, and moral. Furthermore, they persevered, and following World War II became the strongest power on earth. With that stature came responsibility, especially, in my judgment, the responsibility to accomplish two goals: to order the world economy and to keep world peace.

On the first, we began to fail rapidly in the sixties, refusing to measure up to the responsibility. We were profligate in our spending, igniting the timebomb of inflation, which we exported overseas since every other currency was tied into the American dollar. We printed money faster and faster, sending more abroad than we got back through sales of our own goods, eventually reaching a point where more than $600 billion of our money was held in foreign banks. This showed little sense of duty, strength, courage, or determination.

In 1971, shirking our responsibility even more, we went off the gold standard, having little choice in light of overseas claims against our currency. Thus inflation exploded across the world.

Second, as the leader of the free world, we faltered in our duty to lead in keeping the peace. It became especially critical after the Vietnam debacle, in which our course cost us severely in morale, determination, economic strength, and lives of thousands of valiant youths. From that point on, our neglect went on the downhill slalom. We neglected to keep the peace in Africa, allowing the Communist-led world to take several countries in an unprecedented display of international burglary. We allowed similiar conduct in Latin America, where Communists took over Nicaragua and moved upon El Salvador and other countries.

All of this merely solidified a trend that had been building momentum since the end of World War II. For multifaceted reasons, we Americans seem to have no stomach for the full burden of leadership and responsibility demanded of someone to whom much has been given. We apparently want the position of power but not all the sacrifices of duty that accompany it. Because of historical and cultural factors, we have not developed a national fiber of *noblesse oblige.*

Yet, God and man insist on it. The parable told by Jesus about the slave who was made steward over his master's possessions said this about failure to fulfill responsibility: "'And that slave who knew his master's will and did not get ready or act in accord with his will, shall receive many lashes. . . .'"[14]

In the eighties we are experiencing the pains of our neglect, beleaguered at every turn.

The Issue of Capitalism

Although I believe communism and capitalism in their most extreme, secular manifestations are equally doomed to failure, likely to result in tragic dictatorship, I at the same time believe free enterprise is the economic system most nearly meeting humanity's God-given need for freedom in existence. When greed and materialism displace all spiritual and moral values, capitalism breaks down into ugliness.

In his instructive and provocative book, *Wealth and Poverty,*[15] widely circulated in the early days of the Reagan Administration, George Gilder makes a convincing argument that capitalism at least *sets out* to fulfill generally what I am calling the Laws of Reciprocity and Use.

"Giving is the vital impulse and moral center of capitalism," he argues, adding:

Capitalists are motivated not chiefly by the desire to consume wealth or indulge their appetites, but by the freedom and power to consummate their entrepreneurial ideas. Whether piling up coconuts or designing new computers, they are movers and shakers, doers and givers, obsessed with positive visions of change and opportunity. They are men with an urge to understand and act, to master something and transform it, to work out a puzzle and profit from it, to figure out a part of nature and society and turn it to the common good. They are inventors and explorers, boosters and problem solvers; they take infinite pains and they strike fast.

Then he drives to the heart of the criticism leveled at the capitalists—their preoccupation with money. But his answers are logical and need to be heard.

Are they greedier than doctors or writers or professors of sociology or assistant secretaries of energy or commissars of wheat? Yes, their goals seem more mercenary. But this is only because money is their very means of production. Just as the sociologist requires books and free time and the bureaucrat needs arbitrary power, the capitalist needs capital . . . Capitalists need capital to fulfill their role in launching and financing enterprise. Are they self-interested? Presumably. But the crucial fact about them is their deep interest and engagement in the world beyond themselves, impelled by their imagination, optimism and faith.

His assessment is on target, I believe. Capitalism satisfies the freedom-loving side of humanity. It has an inherent quality of giving, of breaking through into new levels of experience. It uses that which it has and fully exploits the exponential curve, and perseverance is one of its tested virtues.

But what about responsibility? As success grows, the responsibility grows. Has the level of fulfillment of that responsibility kept pace? That is the problem.

His argument, while touching on "religious" factors, becomes muddy on the point of God and faith. He is imprecise, as in the case of the last word in the above-quoted passage. What precisely is the "faith" in? Everything else rests on that foundation. Imprecision will produce shakiness ultimately. Jesus said, "'Have faith in God.'"[16] It was the umbrella for all activities.

If the faith is in God, then this quite naturally flavors the question of responsibility. Faith in God presumably will produce an acknowledgment of responsibility toward God—and an ongoing and rising responsibility toward men. This is where the capitalists most frequently stumble.

And they are not alone. Other conservatives have fallen short, too. This is exemplified by the evangelical Christians, who so often find themselves in league with economic and political conservatives. They have been given great understanding, and often they have given much in return. However, they have concentrated almost exclusively on personal salvation, nelgecting responsibility for intelligent public policy, international affairs, the poor, the oppressed. To whom much enlightenment has been given, much will be required.

We in the developed world—capitalists, evangelicals, everyone—will be held accountable for all that has been given. The people in Africa and South America will not be held to the same level of accountability simply because they have not received as much.

Just think of the Western world! Think of the revelations in law, justice, science, medicine, technology, religion. Think of the rewards that have come through capitalism and evangelical Christianity, as merely two examples. Those revelations, those rewards, govern what is demanded of us—by God and by men.

The responsibility is great. And this may not be comprehended to the fullest by Gilder and his fellow conservatives and capitalists. We all need to hear Isaiah, who in his great prophecy spelled out this responsibility, mincing no words in reporting God's instructions. We will look at only one section of them,[17] for they alone are enough to set us in motion with the Law of Responsibility.

> Shout with the voice of a trumpet blast, tell my people of their sins! Yet they act so pious! They come to the Temple every day and are so delighted to hear the reading of my laws—just as

though they would obey them—just as though they don't despise the commandments of their God! How anxious they are
to worship correctly; oh, how they love the Temple services!

The words echo throughout the New Testament. How
God deplores those who hear His word and do not *do* it![18]
They wonder why they don't see power in their lives. Isaiah
looks at the kinds of questions they throw at God.

"We have fasted before you," they say. "Why aren't you impressed? Why don't you see our sacrifices? Why don't you hear
our prayers? We have done much penance, and you don't even
notice it!" I'll tell you why! Because you are living in evil
pleasure even while you are fasting, and *you keep right on
oppressing your workers.* Look, what good is fasting when *you
keep on fighting and quarreling?* This kind of fasting will never
get you anywhere with me. . . .

No, the Lord says, your revelation carries a responsibility, to Him and to people. He hits the point on workers hard.

No, the kind of fast I want is that you stop *oppressing* those
who work for you and treat them fairly and give them what
they earn.

Then He broadens it.

I want you to share your food with the hungry and bring right
into your own homes those who are helpless, poor and destitute. Clothe those who are cold and don't hide from relatives
who need your help.

Fulfill your responsibility at the level to which He has
raised you, God says, and He will raise you even higher.

If you do these things, God will shed His own glorious light
upon you. He will heal you; your godliness will lead you
forward, and goodness will be a shield before you, and the glory
of the Lord will protect you from behind. Then, when you call,
the Lord will answer. "Yes, I am here," he will quickly reply. All
you need to do is to stop oppressing the weak, and to stop
making false accusations and spreading vicious rumors!

From the beginning of the Scriptures to the end, a theme flows relentlessly: *God is the enemy of oppression.* So must His people be. In His behalf, Isaiah pounds at the issues even more boldly.

> *Feed the hungry! Help those in trouble!* . . . And the Lord will . . . satisfy you with all good things . . . and you will be like a well-watered garden, like an ever-flowing spring.

Give, and it will be given to you. Fulfill your responsibility at your current level if you would rise to a higher one. Blessing carries responsibility.

Unending commitment to that truth would advance the cause of capitalism and free enterprise immensely, carrying it perhaps past the dangers of anarchy and dictatorship. It would also advance the cause of evangelical Christianty, perhaps to the point of winning the world, a feat that has thus far eluded us.

Study Guide

Key Scripture: Is. 58:1–11; Luke 12:42–48; 1 Tim. 3:1–7

Key Idea: "Whatever level of opportunity is given to us, both God and man expect us to give a certain standard of performance. Favor carries with it responsibility. As the favor increases, the responsibility increases" (p. 160).

The letter looked ordinary enough when you took it out of the mailbox. True, the upper left hand corner carried a long corporate name, but you thought nothing of it. Yet as you started reading the letter you recognized this was no ordinary letter. Suddenly you had to sit down and the lines got blurry, for the letter informed you that you had inherited property and a bank account worth millions. What would be the most difficult aspect of such a gift?

List three major benefits you have inherited simply by being born in this country.

a.

b.

c.

What is your responsibility in the light of these benefits?

Facing the Issues

1. What is the law expressed in Luke 12:48?

2. How does the Law of Responsibility relate to the Law of Use and the Law of Perseverance? (See p. 161.)

The Church

1. Who carries an especially heavy burden of responsibility according to James 3:1?

2. What areas of life require a high level of personal responsibility when you are in a position of leadership? (See 1 Tim. 3:1–7.)

3. For whom did Paul feel responsible? (see Rom. 1:14.)

4. What level of responsibility is ours simply by the fact that we are Christians? (See Matt. 28:18–20.)

The Society and the Nation

1. What did the British consider "the burden of empire?"
   (See p. 164.)

2. "Americans during most of their history worked hard under the Law of Use" (p. 165). What were the results of that?

3. In what two areas have we failed to measure up to our responsibility as a worldwide power?

   a.

   b.

4. How would you describe "the full burden of leadership" in the world today? (See p. 166.)

The Issue of Capitalism

1. When are both communism and capitalism doomed to failure? (see p. 166.)

2. When does capitalism break down into ugliness?

3. What are the key benefits of capitalism? (See p. 167.)

4. How will faith in God affect our participation in the economic system? (See p. 168.)

5. What are six areas in which the Western world has made significant contributions? How does this affect our level of responsibility?

Making It Happen

Read Isaiah 58:1–11. Now respond to the following:
1. Describe one action suggested by Isaiah for which you need to repent in prayer right now.

2. Write out one course of action you need to initiate immediately to bring your activity into line with God's commands. This may be in your home, office, or community.

3. What promise can you claim for yourself as you initiate the action described above?

Scripture References

1 Luke 12:48, KJV
2 See Luke 12:46–48
3 James 3:1
4 1 Timothy 3:1–7
5 1 Timothy 3:10
6 Mark 4:11
7 Romans 1:14
8 John 14:6
9 1 Timothy 3:15
10 Matthew 28:18–20
11 See Matthew 16:18
12 Euripides, *Alcymene*, c 485–406 B.C.
13 Sophocles, *Ajax*, c.495–405 B.C.
14 Luke 12:47
15 George Gilder, *Wealth and Poverty* (New York: Bantam, 1982), pp. 30, 31 ff
16 Mark 11:22
17 Isaiah 58:1–11, TLB
18 See James 1:22–25

11. The Law of Greatness

All people desire to be great.

Because of human frailty, however, this can turn out badly, especially if we think in terms of comparison with others, for that usually spells pride.

But to think more deeply than that is possible. Pride is still a hazard, but one can set goals of accomplishing tasks rather than of performing better than someone else. It's a fine line, but it exists.

Jesus, pointing to that line, spoke of the possibilities of greatness—a purity of greatness, we might say. Indeed, He set forth a two-part principle that I have labeled the Law of Greatness. The world needs it desperately at this hour.

It is easy to forget that the people surrounding Jesus during His earthly ministry were just that—people. Plain, simple, ordinary people. They exhibited the frailties of all of us. For example, at one point, acting a bit like twentieth-century kids quarreling over who's the greatest shortstop in the American League, the disciples came to the Lord and asked, "'Who then is the greatest in the kingdom of heaven?'"

The answer was remarkable, flying in the face of everything we expect in our day.

> And He called a child to Himself and set him before them, and said, "Truly I say to you, unless you are converted and become like children, you shall not enter the kingdom of heaven. Whoever then humbles himself as this child, *he is the greatest in the kingdom of heaven.*"[1]

At another time, they fell into a dispute over which of *them* was regarded as the greatest. They, like us, were very concerned about their status from time to time. But the Lord showed great patience with them.

> And He said to them, "The kings of the Gentiles lord it over them; and those who have authority over them are called 'Benefactors.' But not so with you, but *let him who is the greatest among you become as the youngest, and the leader as the servant.* For who is greater, the one who reclines at the table, or the one who serves? Is it not the one who reclines at the table? But I am among you as *the one who serves.*"[2]

Every time the question arose, the answer was the same two-pronged directive: If you want to be great, become like a *child* and become a *servant.* And that answer reverberates down through human experience to our day, yet so few of us grasp it.

"Oh, that was OK for what He was doing then," we say, "but He didn't understand what it was going to be like in the modern world."

Or we mumble something like, "That may be all right for church, but you'll get killed in the real world."

If you're honest, you have to admit those remarks seem true as the twentieth century winds down. Knowledge has exploded all over the planet and even onto other planets; man is doing things never dreamed possible. Furthermore, we are in a life-and-death struggle for minds and bodies. Greatness will be measured by success in that explosion and struggle. A little child won't stand a chance.

We all rationalize that way. And we are all in a mess as a result. We should look at what Jesus was showing us.

What is there about a little child that He wants us to copy? If they're very little, they cry a lot and seem to be pretty much governed by what their stomachs tell them. If they have pain, they cry; if they're wet, they cry. As they grow, they're apt to be spoiled by their families. They may become extraordinarily self-centered; they may whine a lot. In time, they may become unruly and undisciplined. All parents know the pattern.

Is this what Jesus wanted us to be?

No, He had something else in mind. He spoke of three qualities that under normal circumstances predominate in little children: They are trusting. They are teachable. They are humble.

To being with, little children trust their mothers and fathers. They have to. A baby relies upon his mother to feed him, trusting that she is not going to put poison in his mouth. As he grows, he believes in his parents, usually certain that his daddy is absolutely the greatest man in the world. We all know that many things can work to warp that trust, but basically all children, if treated the way God would have parents treat their offspring, will have incredible faith in their mothers and fathers. They won't worry about being fed, clothed, or housed. They will simply trust that their parents will meet their needs.

Such total trust in the provision and protection of God is the first giant step toward greatness.

As for being teachable, children, most significantly, will listen. They have voracious appetites for learning, and, since they're starting from zero, they know the best way to feed those appetites is to listen. They may ask a lot of questions, but they listen to the answers. "Daddy, why is the grass green? Daddy, why are the birds flying? Daddy, why is the car running?"

It never stops. Their minds are set in the inquiry mode.

Too often parents become annoyed, but they need to understand that this is a mark of intelligence. It is desirable and pleasing to the Creator. A child between the ages of four and five will learn more in that one year than a student will in four years of college.

This teachableness has an interesting side effect that I'm sure Jesus had in mind. Children, hungry to learn, will experiment. They are quick to master new ideas, new languages, new techniques. Their minds are open. If we think of this in the context of God's instruction to Adam and Eve to master and subdue the earth,[3] we see the importance of such inquiry and openness.

They are steps toward greatness.

Then, little children are humble—at least until someone spoils them. You seldom see a young child vaunting himself like something special. This virtue is eventually corrupted by a society that has become increasingly warped through the centuries, but in his very early years a child doesn't care if his dad is a prince or a pauper, highly educated or lacking in training. All he cares is that that man is Daddy and he loves him. Usually this carries over to attitudes toward others; he loves people as people, regardless of social status.

Quite simply, children love life, until we train this quality out of them. When you watch them play, they are free; they throw themselves into situations with abandon, even getting a little reckless. And they'll throw themselves into your arms with absolute delight. While fully content in the fact that their parents are sovereign—it's so good and natural that they never even think to challenge it—they are free to be free.

They wear no masks. They're innocent, transparent, and genuine. Become like them and you're on the road to greatness.

The New Testament is jammed with urgings toward humility, and we have noted the importance of this virtue in simply moving toward the kingdom of God. But we should observe that Jesus, in a parallel passage on greatness, reemphasized that insistence on humility. It is a virtue with more than passing importance. After having said that "'the greatest among you shall be your servant,'"[4] He continued: "'And whoever exalts himself shall be humbled; and *whoever humbles himself shall be exalted.'"*[5]

With that principle, Christ was pointing to a truth that Solomon had unfolded in a different way: "The reward of humility and the fear of the LORD/Are riches, honor and life."[6] Greatness, summed up as "riches, honor and life," is the reward of those who are humble, which is the necessary ingredient for fearing the Lord. And that, psychology confirms, is what men long for—financial reward, recognition, and a good, satisfying life. It all awaits the little child, epitome of the humble.

So, in short, Jesus said greatness begins with being trusting, being teachable, and being humble. The three traits go together—not merely in children, but in adults as well. The trusting person puts away criticism and skepticism, and becomes open. He doesn't have to be right all the time. Then he is able to learn—from God, from people, from circumstances. He'll listen; he'll try new things. And *that* is the humble person.

Do you see the circle? Trust. Teachableness. Humility. They run from one to another, backward and forward.

The businessman who becomes like a child in this regard will rise to greatness. So will the scientist. So will the minister.

A Difficult Concept

In the second episode we examined at the beginning of this chapter, Jesus added another criterion for greatness. Quite paradoxically, He said the secret of greatness is service. If you reflect on it, you see that it fits well with being childlike, but it begins to rub. It goes against the grain of society.

That is why we should be serious and careful on this subject. We are dealing with a law that turns everything upside down. Little children soon yearn to grow up so they can "be somebody." But Jesus says, "Be a child if you really want to *be* somebody." Servants, meanwhile, usually hate their position, yearning to earn enough to have their *own* servants. But Jesus says, "No, become a servant if you wish to be truly great."

This pushes us into a corner where we have to ask, "Do I really want this?" We should weigh it carefully, for the Lord said to count the cost of the things we set out to do.[7]

If you're an average workingman, you may have been striving all your life to escape any image of servanthood, trying to rise to the point, perhaps, where you work for yourself and not for someone else.

If you're a black man or woman, you've known the effects of the struggle against slavery all your life, and the most onerous recollection you have is your race's all-too-frequent relegation to the role of household servant. Can anyone challenge the black's desire to attain to the higher professions and cast off once and for all the idea of serving someone?

If you've experienced management-labor relations, you understand that no manager has any true desire to be a servant of the labor ranks, and no laboring man will accept the slightest hint that he's a servant of management or anyone else. Such thinking is anathema to both parties.

If you're a politician, you smile indulgently when someone refers to you as a "public servant"; you really prefer the role of celebrity.

If you're a minister of the gospel, "successful" and well-known on the speaking circuit or perhaps on television, the chances are great that you're far more comfortable signing autographs and sitting at head tables than being a servant to the flock.

You see, there will be a cost if we seek true greatness. For our attitudes—wrong ones—are well solidified, despite the fact that we have had examples of true greatness over the years.

My generation considered Albert Schweitzer to be a great man, and most—even those who disagreed with his theology—would acknowledge that his was true greatness. Why? Because he became like a little child and like a servant. He gave his life for the sick, the oppressed. He was trusting, teachable, and humble. He was a servant.

A scientist, musician, philosopher, and theologian, he left what the world would have considered to be the road to greatness in Germany and went to Africa to labor among primitive, underprivileged people in a little village. Establishing a hospital, he lived his life out in full service to others, continually learning, continually enthusiastic, continually innocent.

Even the modern world came to understand that his greatness was somehow different from the greatness most men sought. Year after year, he was numbered at the top of the list of outstanding people.

Similarly, polls measuring the ten most admired women in the world place a remarkable Roman Catholic nun, Mother Theresa of Calcutta, at the top. This is a woman who has given up everything, in a materialistic world's terms, to go among the poor, downtrodden masses of India to feed them, clothe them, house them, and love them.

Hers is a role of a servant through and through, a refusal to lord it over anyone, and yet we somehow know she has achieved greatness.

Stepping back through history, we encounter Father Damien, the Belgian priest who gave himself entirely to service to the leper colony on the Hawaiian island of Molokai in the mid-nineteenth century. His was true greatness.

And there is Hudson Taylor, the missionary who turned away from a life of comfort in Britain to throw himself into service of the suffering and lost Chinese. His greatness still rings in the annals of missionary service.

And there was Florence Nightingale, the English nurse who served heroically in the Crimean War and became known as the founder of modern nursing.

These unusual humanitarians were among those who found the key to success through the Law of Greatness.

It Works in Business

The business world, too, has produced greatness. And we need to understand that the principles set forth by Jesus are pragmatic and effective in the hard-nosed give-and-take of free enterprise.

Henry Ford was a good illustration. He wanted to make inexpensive, efficient transportation available to as many people as possible. So he came up with the Model T. Before long he was serving thousands with cheap transportation. The more he served, the more money he made, and the greater his business became. He became the greatest figure in the auto industry.

The Law of Greatness did not gain a permanent foothold in the American car industry, however. Confrontations gradually replaced service. Management and labor lost all semblance of unity, and the thought of serving one another became a joke. The industry also confronted the public, steadily losing awareness about changes in society, consumer economics, and fuel outlook. It designed cars the way *it* wanted them.

The early tolling of the death bell went largely unnoticed.

Eventually deterioration in the concept of service reached a point where car manufacturers decided that fully effective quality control at the factories was too expensive. Their surveys convinced them that they would be better off to repair mistakes at the dealership level.

So the cars came off the line with little things untended. The buyers drove them a short while and something would malfunction. When they took them back, the dealers made the repairs and sent the bill to the manufacturer. Almost inevitably something else would happen to the same car, and the process would be repeated. It was terribly inconvenient for car buyers, but it was less expensive for the manufacturer.

The tolling of the bell grew louder as the principle of service fell by the roadside.

This, as we noted in an earlier chapter, was not the case in Japan. There, thoughts of service penetrated deeper into the industrial consciousness. The desire grew to end shoddiness and to give customers the best products on the road. The industry would serve the people.

Secondly, management and labor began to work at the idea of becoming servants of one another. Companies took pains to instill in their managers the thought that they were servants of the workers. "We're here to make their jobs better, to improve their environment, to solve their problems," they repeated. Furthermore, they became like little children and listened to their workers. "We want to learn from you," management said, and before long workers were each submitting eighteen and nineteen suggestions a year for improving the work process; and management was adopting at least 80 percent.

The employees, meanwhile, were constantly reinforced in their understanding, through attitudes and material rewards, that they were servants of the customers and the society.

Serving is a concept that works at every level, even in an enterprise as massive as the automobile industry of a major, very prosperous nation. For, as the world knows, the Japanese auto industry overwhelmed everyone, even gaining a foothold in America that resulted in a major share of sales.

The principle works in other industries, too. J. C. Penney, for example, embraced the concept of giving a square deal to everyone—honest merchandise, honest measure, honest price. With that in mind, he developed a giant chain of stores across America, becoming a great man in merchandising.

It Is Needed Now

So a life principle emerges. Those who serve others—whether in religion, philanthropy, education, science, art, government, or business—are the great ones. Indeed, the deeper the sacrifice or the broader the scope of service, the greater the individual becomes.

And rarely will our society award the status of greatness to those who lust for personal power and seek to exalt themselves. How often we hear applied to such persons the phrases "petty tyrant . . . little Caesar . . . self-seeking . . . ruthless . . . vain." And though occasionally these people rise to prominence, they never touch greatness. Invariably the Law of Reciprocity brings them down.

Looking around us in the eighties, we would probably find a consensus that if ever greatness was needed in the world, it is now. We have few statesmen of international stature, for example. Instead of greatness of spirit, we find meanness. Our vision is dim.

We frankly need leadership at every level, especially in the international realm, as Armageddon looms closer with each passing day. We need men and women to lead our nation in taking on the responsibilities and the risks of serving other nations, helping them to achieve their potential, helping them with education, agriculture, and industry. We need to cast off paternalism and exploitation.

We need to dare to live the Beatitudes at this level, to be trusting, teachable, and humble, to discover perhaps for the first time in history how a man who is a servant can lead.

In addition to being spiritually and biblically sound, this course has a very practical result. The nation that does the most for others will be the one growing in greatness, the one other nations, as customers, will turn to, the one whose products will sweep around the world. That nation will be exalted, elevated, enlarged as the Laws of Reciprocity and Use take hold.

As with nations, so with all of us.

Study Guide

Key Scripture: Matt. 18:1–4; Luke 22:24–27

Key Idea: "Those who serve others—whether in religion, philanthropy, education, science, art, government, or business—are the great ones. Indeed, the deeper the sacrifice or the broader the scope of service, the greater the individual becomes" (p. 183.)

John drove a bus in a medium-sized city that had been able to get the system going as a result of federal block grants to regional transportation systems. The city was highly unionized because of a strong labor force. To keep his job, John had joined the drivers' union as well.

Suddenly the federal grants dried up. There was no one to pick up the subsidy needed to keep the bus system going. Some hard decisions would have to be made by the city government, as well as the management and employees of the bus system.

John was determined to be part of the solution, rather than the problem. Yet what could he, one believer, do to help avert a total collapse of the bus system? If you were John, what steps would you be willing to take?

Now compare your responses with those suggested as we study the Law of Greatness.

Facing the Issues

If you are like most people you have favorites in the various areas of entertainment, sports, and the church. Because of people like you and me expressing ourselves, a category of people called superstars develops. And even among the superstars are those who are in a class all by themselves. Is this a new phenomenon, a twentieth century accident of the mass media's growth? (Read Matt. 18:1-4.)

1. What was the disciples' concern?

2. Rather than reproach them for their concern, what did Jesus do?

3. According to Pat Robertson, what are the three qualities of a child that we should copy?

   a.

   b.

   c.

4. What is the first giant step toward greatness? (See the middle of p. 177.)

5. How does an unspoiled child normally react to other people? (See p. 178.)

6. Complete the equation:
   The trusting person + the teachable person + the humble person = _____ person

7. Complete the sentence: I recognize that of the three characteristics of a child that lead to greatness, I need to focus most on being _____

Being a Servant

1. After you have read Luke 22:24–27, describe the character trait that Jesus says will lead to greatness.

2. Why does Pat Robertson consider this a law that turns everything upside down? (See p. 179.)

3. How would this principle of the Law of Greatness apply to John, the bus driver?

4. If you are a husband and wife, how can you more clearly be a servant to your partner? Name a specific area where

it would make a big difference if you were genuinely a servant in the way Jesus was.

A Case in Point

1. Why did the Law of Greatness not gain a permanent foothold in the American auto industry? (See p. 182.)

2. According to Pat Robertson, in the Japanese auto industry "employees were constantly reinforced in their understanding, through attitudes and material rewards, that they were servants of the customers and the society" (p. 183). How did this affect the striving for improved work performance?

Making It Happen

In a recent interview in the newsmagazine *Maclean's*, Alvin Toffler, the world's best-known futurist, said, "Much of what we were taught in the past about how to succeed will not turn out to be false. . . . People who were extremely successful in the Second Wave style may find that works against them. . . . Now you go into a Third Wave company and you find yourself not with one boss but with two or three for different functions. And you yourself may be the boss on some project" (*Maclean's*, May 2, 1983, p. 10).

In what ways has the person living according to the two principles of the Law of Greatness been prepared for the new generation of leadership?

a. He is _____

b. He is _____

c. He is _____

d. He is a _____

e. He is living out the principles Jesus embodied in the
_____
_____

Describe one situation where you can in the power of the Holy Spirit exhibit these characteristics and really make a difference.

Scripture References

1 Matthew 18:2–4
2 Luke 22:25–27
3 See Genesis 1:28
4 Matthew 18:4 (paraphrased)
5 Matthew 23:12
6 Proverbs 22:4
7 See Luke 14:28

12. The Law of Unity

From the beginning of His revelation to mankind, God has held forth a difficult principle that flows naturally into and out of the concept of serving. Men have continually stumbled over it.

I call it the Law of Unity. It is simple to understand, and devastatingly difficult to obey. But it is essential. God has been trying to explain that to us for thousands of years.

Unity is central to the way the world works. Perhaps the most powerful illustration of that is found in God Himself, in the Bible's account of creation. "Then God said, 'Let *Us* make man in *Our* image, according to *Our* likeness. . . .'"[1]

This is the only part of the Creation where such language is used and, admittedly, we don't know with great precision what the Lord was inspiring the writer to communicate. He probably was referring to the Godhead, the Trinity, when He spoke of "Us." But He could have been speaking to the angelic court of God or perhaps even the multifaceted majesty of God. Regardless, there was some form of conversation involving more than one Person, and *there was unity.*

Although the passage presents many significant facts, this is the one we should see here: Within the Godhead (or the court of heaven) there was agreement and harmony. God moves in unity.

Thus, the principle is first stated: Great creativity occurs where there is unity. God's unfathomable power is released where there is harmony.

The early Genesis accounts add another piece of insight in this regard. After man had refused to obey God and live under His sovereignty, the half-truth of Satan, the liar and deceiver, came to pass: Adam and Eve became '"like God."'[2] We are not able to comprehend the seriousness of that moment. It was history's terrible tragedy. Man, the delight of God's heart, had fallen. And we read these words:

> Then the LORD God said, "Behold, the man has become like one of *Us*, knowing good and evil; and now, lest he stretch out his hand, and take also from the tree of life, and eat, and live forever"—therefore the LORD God sent him out from the garden of Eden. . . .[3]

Judgment flowed from unity. Just as the magnificent power of creation had sprung from the perfect harmony of heaven, so had the dreadful power of judgment and justice come from the awesome unity of the Almighty.

The examples are clear. God moves in unity. Harmony is central to the unleashing of God's incredible power.

Furthermore, unity in the invisible world governs the visible world. If it works in heaven, it works on earth. "'Thy kingdom come. Thy will be done. *On earth as it is in heaven.*'"[4]

This operation of the Law of Unity on earth was the point of one of the Lord's most-quoted statements:

> "Again I say to you, that if *two of you agree on earth about anything* that they may ask, *it shall be done* for them by My Father who is in heaven. For where two or three have gathered together in My name, there I am in their midst."[5]

He was calling for agreement, but not merely for agreement's sake. He was calling for unity. Since He would be in their midst when they gathered to consider some issue, they would be expected to agree with Him. Their unity would be an external manifestation of their internal agreement. Since He was there, He would bring them to harmony if they genuinely laid aside their own preconceptions and centered on Him.

Then, and only then, would power flow, just as at the Creation. For unity is the fountainhead of God's creative power.

There is a multiplication factor in that unity too. We see it in a song of Moses spoken to all of Israel as he approached the end of his life. One standing on the Rock, he said, would chase a thousand of the enemy, while two would put ten thousand to flight.[6] Unity does not cause a mere doubling or tripling of power; the progression explodes.

The Early Church

The biblical accounts of unity within the early church show the power of the Law of Unity. For example, the fledgling assembly (the *ekklesia* or church) continued to stick together after Christ's crucifixion, resurrection, and ascension—still weak, still uncertain, still afraid. But an enlightening verse says, "These all *with one mind* were continually devoting themselves to prayer. . . ."[7] They were in accord in unity.

Then, the Bible says, power flowed through and from that unity. The Holy Spirit, the giver of life and power, was sent forth upon the people of God as never before. The church was on its way.

At another critical stage, we see the launching of the missionary outreach that was to change the world as the people reached unity and harmony. This occurred in Antioch, where the Lord's followers were first called Christians.[8]

Now there were at Antioch, in the church that was there, prophets and teachers: Barnabas, and Simeon who was called Niget, and Lucius of Cyrene, and Manaen who had been brought up with Herod the tetrarch, and Saul. And while they were ministering to the Lord and fasting, the Holy Spirit said, "Set apart for Me Barnabas and Saul for the work to which I have called them." Then, when they had fasted and prayed and laid their hands on them, they sent them away.[9]

The Lord acted in that setting of harmony, in which those great and diverse leaders centered in on Christ— "ministering" to Him, worshiping Him, turning their full devotion upon Him, feasting upon Him rather than upon ordinary food. He called out Saul, whose name was changed to Paul,[10] and Barnabas, the "Son of Encouragement" whose name had already been changed from Joseph, and sent them forth in power.[11]

We see in all of these reports evidence that people will not hear the voice of God clearly unless the unity of the Spirit is maintained. Disunity will cause the Spirit to flee.

If we need further support for the point, we have only to look at the recent history of the church. Division and disunity have been its most distinguishing characteristics, with the result that it has been impotent to move the world. It has lacked the power that flows from unity. It is small wonder that Jesus, on the night of his betrayal, prayed so movingly and powerfully for the harmony of His people, asking that they might be "'perfected in unity.'"[12] He knew how critical it was.

For Good or For Evil

A fascinating aspect of unity is that it apparently generates a power that can work for good or for evil, at least for a time. We find this illustrated early in the Bible in the story of the Tower of Babel.

After the Flood, we read, "the whole earth used the same language and the same words."[13] The people were becoming gradually unified and beginning to work in harmony. They discovered the use of bricks and mortar, for example, and set out to build themselves a city with a great tower "whose top will reach into heaven." They wanted to make "a name" for themselves and to grow as a unified force.[14]

If we read carefully, we see that their motive reflected pride. Their plan actually constituted man's first effort to glorify himself. They wanted to build a memorial to themselves, a symbolic assault on heaven in defiance of God.

God viewed this as sin, and Scripture records His reaction as follows:

> "... Behold, they are *one people*, and they all have the same language. And this is what they began to do, and now *nothing which they purpose to do will be impossible* for them. Come, let Us go down and there confuse their language, that they may not understand one another's speech." So the LORD scattered them abroad from there over the face of the whole earth. ...[15]

God Almighty saw that the people were of one mind and one language; they were unified. Nothing would be impossible for them, whether for good or for evil.

God's assessment is blunt: Mankind in unity becomes absolutely overwhelming.

There are those who might think God's action against Babel was harsh and unreasonable, so we must make sure we comprehend the truth of the episode. The Lord instantly understood that the people's intention was to unify in glorifying man, which meant the same thing as unifying in rebellion against God. The Bible, as we have seen, tells us that God resists the proud but gives favor to the humble. Indeed, He resists pride in any form. Any expression of rebellious pride, especially the pride of a unified group, wherever found, will ultimately draw opposition from Him.

It is noteworthy that pride, which leads to the glorification of man, continues in the world today in a subtler, yet similar manner. It goes under the label of secular humanism, which, in truth, is a religion of man. Its intention is to build great towers, as it were, to the glory of man. Moving slowly, but persistently, across the earth and capitalizing on the natural pride of man, it has been gaining adherents. Its final aim is the rejection of the centrality of God and the removal of religious freedom from society. The unity of its believers has given it unprecedented force in our time.

Bible believers draw confidence, however, from the fact that the Scripture announces that such forces as those gathered under the banner of humanism or those who rallied at Babel, as long as they remain in opposition to God, will be defeated. The Bible places them under the name of "Babylon," which is doomed to annihilation.[16] It is noteworthy that the presumed site of the Tower of Babel was at or near historical Babylon.

The lesson we are to learn from all of this is that the Lord God takes the matter of unity very seriously. We, His people, should do no less.

Unity of Quest

Unity must begin with the individual. If you are going to experience the power that can change the world, you must be unified within yourself. You must have internal harmony. In the Bible, James addresses this point specifically. A "double-minded man," he says, will not receive anything from the Lord.[17]

One mind believing or desiring one thing and in the same person another mind believing or desiring something else will not work. And there can be no doubting, James added, ". . . for the one who doubts is like the surf of the sea driven and tossed by the wind."[18]

Instead, the Bible says, you must be as Abraham was when, at a hundred years of age and sonless, he was told he would be the father of many nations. He did not "waver" regarding the promise, but remained fully assured that God would perform what He had said.[19]

Abraham had unified his quest in life. He did not fall victim to spiritual schizophrenia, which wracks so many in their walk with the Lord. People can be torn between the pursuit of worldly goals and the pursuit of the Christian life. They can't make up their minds which to put first, needing desperately to hear the words of David: "My heart is fixed, O God, my heart is fixed. . . ."[20]

The well-known story of Mary and Martha illustrates the problem.

> Now as they were traveling along, He entered a certain village; and a woman named Martha welcomed Him into her home. And she had a sister called Mary, who moreover was listening to the Lord's word, seated at His feet. But Martha was distracted with all her preparations; and she came up to Him, and said, "Lord, do You not care that my sister has left me to do all the serving alone? Then tell her to help me." But the Lord answered and said to her, "Martha, Martha, you are worried and bothered about so many things; but only a few things are necessary, really only one, for Mary has chosen the good part, which shall not be taken away from her."[21]

We must not interpret that passage as approval of laziness or irresponsibility. Jesus loved Martha and her willingness to serve, but He was concerned about her attitude, her internal unity. Mary had "'chosen the good part'"; her quest had been unified. If need be, she would sacrifice all else for it. But Martha wanted to be recognized as a follower of Jesus *and* as a good organizer *and* as a good cook. She wasn't single-minded, and she had no peace. She was "'worried and bothered about so many things.'"

We cannot serve two masters.[22] We can not put our spouse and Jesus first in our lives at the same time. We cannot put our job ahead of everything and serve Jesus as Lord at the same time. Our problem is that we make a gap between the two, seeing them as two masters, and try to put each one first. That leads to schizophrenia and breakdowns.

The solution, of course, is to be single-minded. Put Jesus first, and then He will say, "Love your wife as I loved the church."[23] A spouse can get no greater love than that. Similarly, put Jesus first and He will say, "When you undertake a task, do it with all your might."[24] A job can get no more attention than that.

Single-mindedness is the solution to the internal desperation so many people regularly experience. It removes the terrible burden and dark heaviness that weigh upon the chest as they teeter on the fringes of nervous collapse.

A Collective Principle Also

The Bible is precise in showing that what is true for the individual is true for the family, the group, the organization, and the nation. When the Pharisees accused Him of being in league with Satan, Jesus countered with the following universal principle: ". . . 'Any kingdom divided against itself is laid waste; and any city or house divided against itself shall not stand.'"[25]

His point was simple. Without internal unity in a group—whether a family, a business, or a political entity—that group will ultimately collapse. Vacillation and dissension will lead to tearing and destruction.

Jesus, in this verse, was talking about the kingdom of Satan, showing that such universal principles as the Law of Unity apply everywhere. They are broader than religion. Even works of evil will collapse unless the evil forces are unified.

Unity produces strength; disunity produces weakness. Obviously, this was not a New Testament revelation. The Lord's words quickly remind us of the teachings of the man credited with unimaginable wisdom, Solomon: "He who troubles his own house will inherit wind. . . ."[26] This proverb was thoroughly supported throughout biblical history. Houses of leadership would often fall to scheming and fighting among themselves, and then the leadership would crumble.

In my generation, the name of Kennedy immediately comes to mind when we consider the strength derived from unity within a house or clan. Working together and for the good of the family or for one of its members, the Kennedys of Massachusetts achieved remarkable political success. The power of the individual was geometrically multiplied by the harmony of the group. We have fewer and fewer examples of such family unity.

The same is true of the business world. We need only think of those businesses that have fallen on hard times because they abandoned clear-cut unity of mission in favor of diversification. A great electronics company floundered because it tried to make large computers. A chemical company ran into trouble when it tried to be a land developer.

Successful organizations, as well as successful individuals, are those unified around a relatively simple statement of goals and mission. A double-minded man is "unstable in all his ways."[27] So is a double-minded business.

At the national level, the problem is just as great. Turning back into history we see the roots of modern-day Italy, whose turmoil may be greater than any developed country in the world despite its conspicuous marks of great civilization. Before the time of Garibaldi's efforts to unify Italy in the nineteenth century, that land witnessed the struggle of little city-states to prevail over one another and maintain their autonomy. Garibaldi brought them together in a fragile alliance; but following the wars in our century and the conditions in modern Europe, Italy is probably best described as "the sick man" of the continent, owing almost exclusively to the absence of harmony.

The factions in that nation simply will not come together. The house is divided. Consequently, the economy is sick; the society with its unbelievable terrorism and crime is unstable; governmental services falter. Life is a shambles.

In the United States, the history is different and the symptoms vary, but the disease is the same. From its founding until about 1960, Americans were united by at least a common ethic. Essentially, the country had been founded as a Christian nation, adopting biblical principles and governing itself pretty much under biblical countenance. There was a work ethic and moral restraint based on an underlying philosophical system of honor and decency that prevailed even in the face of frequent and flagrant violations.

Today, the United States struggles under a social philosophy of pluralism. There is no unified reality. Many disparate, frequently cacophonous voices echo from one shore to another. Confusion is triumphant.

A "700 Club" guest once asked a question typically heard in the current atmosphere: "Whatever happened to the concept that 'I am my brother's keeper'?"

The answer was easy. It vanished with the Christian ethic. Such concepts spring from a God-centered society, but we no longer have that unifying force. We now are fragmented, and each fragment spawns its own jealousy and self-concern. If this continues and the rival factions increase and strengthen, the country will fall quite simply from violation of the Law of Unity.

Unity With Diversity

It is important we understand that unity springing from the truth of the kingdom of God does not insist on, or even desire, uniformity. Lessons from the Bible about the unity of the Godhead make this abundantly clear. There is diversity even with the oneness of the Trinity.

We see this point in the lives of Christ's disciples, too. They were unified in their quest; but they were a diverse lot, thoroughly nonconformist in several instances.

Paul the apostle taught on this in a spiritual lesson that has physical applications:

> Now there are *varieties* of gifts, but the same Spirit. And there are *varieties* of ministries, and the same Lord. And there are *varieties* of effects, but the same God who works all things in all persons. But to each one is given the manifestation of the Spirit for the common good.[28]

Variety is God's way, he said, even invoking the Trinity to make the point—Spirit, Lord, God. Variety and diversity serve God's purpose, working distinctively and pointedly to arrive at the common good.

No, in families, businesses, churches, and nations, the Lord is not seeking a collection of robots. He is seeking people with varying personalities, talents, and styles who are unified in purpose and will work toward the common good.

Using His principles harmoniously, they can overcome the crises of our century.

Keenly aware of this the night before He was crucified, Jesus prayed to His Father in this manner:

> "I do not ask in behalf of these alone, but for those also who believe in Me through their word; *that they may all be one;* even as Thou, Father, art in Me, and I in Thee, that they also may be in Us; that the world may believe that Thou didst send Me. And the glory which Thou hast given Me I have given to them; *that they may be one, just as We are one;* I in them, and Thou in Me, that they may be perfected in unity, that the world may know that Thou didst send Me, and didst love them, even as Thou didst love Me."[29]

He knew that the fulfillment of the purposes of God would require unity. Without it, there would be no flow of power to save the world and to perfect the people of God.

Study Guide

Key Scripture: Gen. 1:26; 11:6–8; Matt. 18:19–20; John 17:20–23; Acts 13:1–3; 1 Cor. 12:4–7

Key Idea: God moves in unity. Harmony is central to the unleashing of God's incredible power.

1. What would happen if you were riding along on a bicycle and your brain sent one set of signals to the legs and a set of different signals to your arms? You'd end up in a tangled heap along the edge of the road. Now read Genesis 1:26. Why are the earth, sun, and moon moving in synchronous orbits and the rest of nature in similar harmonious patterns?

2. Pat Robertson writes, "Great creativity occurs where there is unity" (p. 191). If this is true, how should we react to some of the art, literature, and music of recent decades?

3. Again, if the above is not true, what should be our goal if we believe Christians should be producing great literature, great art, and great music to honor God?

4. What else, according to Genesis 3:22–23, flows from the unity of the Godhead?

5. What happens, according to Matthew 18:19–20, when the Body of Christ unites in prayer?

6. In an earlier lesson we learned about the exponential curve. What effect does this have upon the Law of Unity according to Deuteronomy 32:30?

The Law in Action

1. According to Pat Robertson, "people will not hear the voice of God clearly unless the unity of the Spirit is maintained" (p. 193). In what two ways is this illustrated in the early church according to Acts 1:14, 13:1–3?
   a.

   b.

2. First Central Church in a California community has outgrown present facilities, which are reasonably cen-

tral to where the people live. Some of the people want the church to locate considerably east of where it now meets, others want it several miles south. Deep down in his heart the pastor believes the church ought to locate in the southern area. What can he do to unleash the power of God in the church?

For Good or for Evil

1. "Mankind in unity becomes absolutely overwhelming" (p. 194). What effort by man illustrates this? (See Gen. 11:1–4.)

2. Why was the unity of that day so obnoxious to God?

3. How have men and women of the past few decades sought to raise a new monument to themselves in our school systems? (See p. 194.)

4. What should give us courage and hope in tackling man's efforts at self-glorification? (See Rev. 14:8.)

Facing the Issues

Internal Harmony

1. What is absolutely essential to success spiritually? (See James 1:6–8.)

2. Ken had been in Christian work most of his working years, achieving significant success as a leader. One day a Christian friend asked him to become president of a

business firm, offering him a salary in excess of $100,000.

   a. List three reasons why Ken should seriously consider the offer.

   b. List three reasons why Ken should stay as head of the Christian ministry.

   c. How might the experience of Mary and Martha in Luke 10:38–42 apply to Ken's situation?

   d. What could create the "internal desperation" Pat Robertson mentions on page 196 if Ken decides to stay with the Christian ministry?

   e. Write out a goal for your life that will give it the single focus Pat Robertson describes as necessary to success.

Group Harmony

1. List the three areas of group interaction described by Pat Robertson on pages 197–198 that require unity.

2. Write out your prayer for unity in the following areas of your life:

   a. Your family

   b. Your church

   c. Your country

Making It Happen

1. If 1 Corinthians 12:4–7 is accepted as true by you, what will be your attitude toward people who differ with you in your spiritual family, the church?

2. Write down what you consider your gift from God to serve in your earthly family, your spiritual family, and your community.

3. What is one area where you have contributed to disunity? What are you doing to do about it?

Wrap-Up

"He [Jesus] knew that the fulfillment of the purposes of God would require unity. Without it, there would be no flow of power to save the world and to perfect the people of God" (p. 200).

Scripture References

1 Genesis 1:26
2 Genesis 3:5
3 Genesis 3:22, 23
4 Matthew 6:10
5 Matthew 18:19, 20
6 See Deuteronomy 32:30
7 Acts 1:14
8 See Acts 11:26
9 Acts 13:1–3
10 See Acts 13:1, 9
11 See Acts 4:33, 36
12 John 17:23
13 Genesis 11:1
14 Genesis 11:4
15 Genesis 11:6–8
16 See Revelation 14:8
17 James 1:6–8
18 James 1:6
19 See Romans 4:13–21
20 Psalm 57:7, KJV
21 Luke 10:38–42
22 See Matthew 6:24
23 See Ephesians 5:25
24 Ecclesiastes 9:10 (paraphrased)
25 Matthew 12:25
26 Proverb 11:29
27 James 1:8
28 1 Corinthians 12:4–7
29 John 17:20–23

13. The Law of Miracles

Now to the miraculous.

We have seen how the kingdom works.

We have looked briefly at how our physical world appears to be approaching the outer limits of survival through its violation of the laws of the spiritual world on which everything we know ultimately stands.

We have considered how the invisible nature of that spiritual world does not diminish its reality, but merely governs who will understand it.

We have spoken of reaching into that spiritual world, touching the truth and power of God, and transferring them into the physical world. This is possible even as we hurtle toward that moment when the kingdom of God will burst into visibility and supplant all the kingdoms and powers on earth.

It is this point of reaching into the invisible and seeing its effects manifest in the visible that we should examine more closely. There is a Law of Miracles. It governs the question of God's willingness to disrupt His natural order to accomplish His purpose. When He does disrupt that natural order, the result is a miracle, a contravention of the natural laws through which he usually works moment by moment. He overrides the way in which things normally operate.

Since God is almighty, the only absolutely free person in the universe, not bound even by His own creation, He is perfectly able at any time to change the way things are done. He can heal a body instantly; He can still a storm, and He can move a mountain. Those are miracles.

Even then, however, He works within principles, and they frame the Law of Miracles.

Because of the desperate condition of our world, we still need miracles today. That means we need to understand the law and act on it, for Jesus introduced a new order of normality at the Day of Pentecost. With the power of the Holy Spirit, miracles were to be normal. He expected His followers to do even greater things than He did.[1] After all, during His incarnation He rebuked them for failing to do miracles like walking on water and casting out demons. And He praised an outsider, a Roman centurion, who perceived Christ's spiritual authority and discerned the relationship between the spiritual and the natural. "Just say the word and my servant will be healed," the centurion declared.

Jesus marveled at the Roman's understanding. "'. . . I have not found such great faith with anyone in Israel,'" He said.[2]

That is what we must recover.

The Umbrella of Faith

"Have faith in God."[3] In chapter four, we saw that to understand how the kingdom works, we have to *begin* there. That was the umbrella given by Jesus in explaining the cursing of the fig tree. We have to *end* there, too.

Through the process of rebirth—by grace through faith—we are to see and enter into the kingdom of heaven, where the miraculous power resides. As the Lord explained to Nicodemus, this is the world of the Spirit, which is like the wind, invisible, yet frequently revealing its effects. We cannot see the wind itself, but we can see the things it moves. With the kingdom, we too observe its effects. Furthermore, we gain access to its power through our faith in Jesus Christ, through our rebirth.

We might think of ourselves as a people dying of thirst. But off in a distance there is a pool of water, a reservoir with a dam and beautiful pebble-lined banks. We can see the green trees and lush grass in its vicinity, but we can't see the reservoir itself. We desperately need to get to it.

By accepting Jesus, all that He is, all that He has done—by being born again—we gain access to this marvelous reservoir, this thirst-quenching pool of water, the kingdom of God. We are given access to an entirely new world, a hertofore invisible world—the secret kingdom.

"Have faith in God," Jesus said. Believe that God exists, trust Him, expect Him to enter into communion with you, to show you His will and purpose. Use the water in the reservoir. Remember that faith is the title deed to that pool of power.

It is all ours, if we know the *rules of miracles*.

First, we are to take our eyes off the circumstances and the impossibilities and to look upon God and the possibilities.

We have good examples from the history of God's people for this. Remember Joshua and Caleb.[4] Representing the twelve tribes of Israel, they and ten others were sent as spies to determine if the people should enter the land promised to them by God. They stayed forty days and returned with reports of a marvelous land of milk and honey, but it was peopled with giants living in fortified cities.

"They are too strong for us," ten of the spies said.

But Caleb and Joshua, who were to figure prominently in Israel's future, were enthusiastic and eager to move ahead. "It doesn't matter how many giants there are. The Lord is with us." They looked at God and not at the circumstances, reflecting the attitude He expected of His people.

Yet the ten others prevailed, exploiting the fears of the Israelites existing since their flight from Egypt. They succumbed to their crisis, ignoring the principles of the miraculous, and failed to take what was theirs.

The biblical story of Jonathan, the son of King Saul, shows us how to focus on God rather than circumstances.[5] He and his young armor-bearer, looking at a great field of enemy Philistine soldiers, put out a sign to see if God was with them. He was. So they moved to the attack, declaring that it was no harder for the Lord to win with a few than with many. Their refusal to be deterred by seemingly impossible circumstances led to an important victory by the entire army of Israel.

Second, we are not to doubt in our hearts.

We have seen that spirit controls matter, that lesser authority yields to greater authority, and that the mind and the voice are the instruments by which the will of the spirit is transmitted to the environment.

For miracles to happen through us, God's will must first be transmitted by the Holy Spirit to our spirits. Then, Jesus declared, we must not doubt in our hearts. The inmost center of our beings—which the Bible alternately terms the "heart" or the "spirit"—must be focused on the objective. Our hearts must be fully persuaded, without any doubt. We must be like Abraham, who against all hope believed God would grant him a son by his wife Sarah. "He staggered not at the promise of God through unbelief; but was strong in faith, giving glory to God; and being fully persuaded that, what he had promised, he was able also to perform."[6]

In fact, the persuasion in our spirit must be so strong that it seems to us the desired result has already taken place. As Jesus put it, "believe that you have received" and you will have what you say.

I experienced this extraordinary *present* possession of a *future* miracle before I acquired CBN's first television station. Although my available capital was only $70, and I was without a job, and although I did not own a television set and was without any knowledge of broadcasting, motion pictures, or theater, the purchase of a station became for me a present reality. Even now it is hard to describe my inner experience at that time. The persuasion in my spirit was so real that purchasing a station with $70 seemed as possible as buying a bag of groceries at a supermarket.

As an official of RCA later told me, "You sounded so positive that we thought you had the money in the bank."

To those around me who could see only the *visible* reality, I was on a fool's errand. The things I was attempting were clearly impossible. But God had given me a measure of faith, and my spirit counted God's resources as part of my reality. As Jesus said: "'With men it is impossible, but with God all things are possible.'"[7]

The tentative, the hesitant, the fearful, the overly cautious, the half-hearted, and the half-persuaded will never know miracle power. They will never experience success or victory in the visible or the invisible worlds. The goals they seek will always elude them, and they will never understand why. Never, at least, until they understand that their divided minds and spirits are actually projecting the seeds of failure into every situation.

The Time to Speak

When Mark told in his gospel of the cursing of the fig tree, he was careful to include the voice. Jesus *spoke* to the fig tree, and He told the disciples to *command* the mountain, which would do what they said if they didn't doubt in their hearts.

Scripture tells us further that Jesus stilled a storm by *speaking* to it,[8] raised three dead people by *speaking* to them,[9] cast out demons by *speaking* to them,[10] cleansed a leper by *speaking* to him,[11] and healed a Roman officer's servant by *speaking a word from a remote location.*[12]

Prayer for Jesus was communing with the Father, listening to the Father, watching the Father. What was the Father doing? What did He desire? Insight from the Father unified the heart and mind of the Son. Then, taking the authority that was His, the Son spoke the word of the Father. And the miracle happened.

So we see that miracles begin with certainty that God is present and that He has a purpose. Then we, His people, translate that purpose into the physical world by invoking

His unlimited power. We do it with our mouths, speaking the word of the Lord to the mountain, to the disease, to the storm, to the demons, to the finances that God wants to send to us.

We do not pray further, unless the situation specifically calls for prayer. In one instance, Jesus said, "'This kind [of unclean spirit] cannot come out by anything but prayer.'"[13] That means we pray in those cases. Jesus also prayed at the tomb of Lazarus, but He made it plain that He was doing so for the people to recognize that God was performing the miracle. Then He Himself approached the tomb and uttered the words "'Lazarus, come forth,'"[14] executing God's will by speaking.

Prayer is extremely important, and we are never to neglect it. Jesus gave us example after example, going off by Himself to pray, often for hours. And the Scripture writers are relentless in their admonitions to pray. Paul went so far as to tell us to pray without ceasing.[15]

But once God's will is disclosed, then is the time to shift to speaking.

Because of the great power the Lord has given to speech, it is terribly important that we Christians not use our mouths to speak slander, profanity, lust, or foolishness. The last point is delicate. We are not to think that the Lord lacks humor or that we should not have fun. It means merely that we should avoid jokes and foolishness about sacred things, for that comes dangerously close to violation of the third commandment: "'You shall not take the name of the LORD your God in vain.'"[16]

Why should the Lord be so deeply concerned about our use of His name that He would include the issue in the Ten Commandments? He was giving us insight into the power of speech. We have in our mouths the power to kill or to make alive. We must not take it lightly.

This significance explains why, on the Day of Pentecost when the power of the Holy Spirit came upon the disciples, an evidence of their anointing was their speaking in tongues.[17] Their voices were empowered by the Holy Spirit, a miracle that continues to be experienced by people of God today through what is known as the baptism of the Holy Spirit. From there, the disciples entered into ministry more miraculous than any they had known. They had been clothed with power from on high.[18] Their speech was a critical factor—again, not to be taken lightly.

The Major Hindrance

Having faith, seeing, refusing to doubt, speaking—all are critically important parts of the Law of Miracles. But Jesus made another point in the episode with the fig tree. Many people wish He hadn't.

> "And whenever you stand praying, forgive, if you have anything against anyone; so that your Father also who is in heaven may forgive you your transgressions. But if you do not forgive, neither will your Father who is in heaven forgive your transgressions."[19]

With those few words, He set forth the major hindrance to the working of miracles in the visible world—the lack of forgiveness. Men and women, Christian and non-Christian, carry grudges. Any power of God within them is eaten up by resentment.

Is there any wonder that we see so little of the miraculous intervention of God in the affairs of the world?

We noted earlier that our initial view of God and our entrance into kingdom blessings depend on being born again and allowing the Lord to remove the cloud of sin between us and God. That unobstructed view must continue if we are to evidence the miraculous. Being born again merely sets the process in motion; we must then walk step by step in a state of forgiveness. John the apostle said it this way: ". . . if we walk in the light as He Himself is in the light, we have fellowship with one another, and the blood of Jesus His Son [continuously] cleanses us from all sin."[20]

He went on to say that the one who hates his brother, who is not in a state of forgiveness with him, walks in the darkness and doesn't know where he's going. Thus walking in the light equates to living in proper relationships, which also means that we can be cleansed of our sins. The blood of Jesus does not cleanse in the dark or in a state of unforgiveness. Without forgiveness, our view of God and His kingdom is clouded. We will see no miracles.

In this matter, the Lord does not appear to be speaking of the loss of eternal salvation, for we have learned that this comes by grace through faith, not works. He is not saying a grudge will prevent you from ultimately going to heaven; He can be expected to deal with that at the proper time. Rather, He is declaring that if we want to experience now the miraculous power, say, of moving mountains, it is imperative that we live in a condition of forgiveness. Unforgiveness is not a characteristic acceptable in the kingdom of God. It contradicts the doctrine of forgiveness itself.

If all the law and all the prophets hang on loving God with the entire being and loving our neighbors as ourselves,[21] then unforgiveness can shatter everything. It reveals, among other things, the horrible sin of pride. For only the humble can forgive—those who surrender anger, feelings, and reputation to the will of God.

No Small Matter

We must see that these concerns are for our own good. Resentment, for example, eats into a person like cancer. Indeed, it often causes sickness, both spiritual and physical, that can be debilitating and defy medical treatment. That is why the Lord dealt with the issue so many times.

One well-known dialogue occurred with Peter right after a bit of instruction on unity: "Then Peter came and said to Him, 'Lord, how often shall my brother sin against me and I forgive him? Up to seven times?' Jesus said to him, 'I do not say to you, up to seven times, but up to seventy times seven.'"[22]

Increasing the impact of the lesson, the Lord went on to tell a parable about a nobleman's slave who was forgiven a debt of $10 million after coming close to being sold along with his family on the slave market to recover the money. The man turned around and seized another slave who owed him $100 and had him thrown into prison for nonpayment. Here is how Jesus concluded the parable:

> "Then summoning him [the first man], his lord said to him, 'You wicked slave, I forgave you all that debt because you entreated me. Should you not also have had mercy on your fellow slave, even as I had mercy on you?' And his lord, moved with anger, handed him over to the torturers until he should repay all that was owed him. So shall My heavenly Father also do to you, if each of you does not forgive his brother from your heart."[23]

It is no small matter, and I regret that the church through the years has not dealt more forcefully with it. As members of the kingdom, totally indebted to our loving heavenly Father, we must maintain an attitude and an atmosphere that promote harmony with our brothers. If we refuse to do that, we do not receive the blessings from our Father, and we block the flow of miraculous power.

Our principal weapon in the crises we face in the world is love, and love operates only in a state of forgiveness and reconciliation. Pettiness must go, and jealousy and pride and lack of concern for others and neglect of the poor and needy.

A Friend's Illustration

I have a close friend, leader of one of the outstanding ministries in the world, who told me a story from his own life that reinforces the reality of the Law of Miracles as well as any I know.

At death, his father left him a fortune in property. In that period of grief and legal confusion, a family friend stepped in and legally, yet questionably, gained control of a part of the property.

My friend, when he realized what had happened, became angry and a seed of bitterness took root in him. A deep and churning resentment grew, worsening as he reflected on the nature of man that would allow him to take advantage of those who trusted him.

One day God showed my friend that if he was to continue in his ministry and to experience the miracle that had marked his walk with the Lord, he would have to deal with this resentment. He would have to forgive the man.

That was a difficult instruction from the Lord. The man was guilty. He had done something wrong to make money. Yet God said, "You must forgive him."

So, despite the spiritual struggle, my friend telephoned the man and arranged a meeting. I'm sure the man expected a confrontation and perhaps a shouting match; that's the way those things usually work out. But my friend, Spirit-filled and familiar with the purposes of God, followed through and said: "I want to ask your forgiveness. I've harbored resentment against you over what happened to the property. I've actually hated you. But I've been wrong and I've repented before God, and I totally forgive you for anything you may have done. And now I ask your forgiveness."

It was more than the man could stand. He began to weep, and the uniqueness of the moment broke him internally. Someone he had treated badly was actually asking him for forgiveness! It was upside down.

My friend immediately felt the flow of God's power in his own life. He was thoroughly free.

The two embraced and were reconciled.

In a matter of days, my friend received a call from an official of a corporation that owned a store on another piece of his property. The corporation had closed the store, and the future of the building and lease were unsettled. However, the official said, "You've been so nice to us that we're going to give you the store."

Again, things were upside down. That sort of thing simply was not done.

My friend, without lifting a finger, had overnight received a building worth far more than the piece of property that he had been denied in the previous episode. There was no quarreling or legal fighting. God had moved miraculously, once the roadblock of unforgiveness had been removed.

Furthermore, my friend's ministry, which centers on the miracle-working power of God, has flourished. Continuous forgiveness and continuous love—they are crucial in the Law of Miracles.

Miracles Are Available

If we would live in the kingdom of God today, by grace through faith, we would see far more miracles. We need only look at Paul's relatively compact, but nonetheless illuminating, instructions to the early Corinthian church to discover the miracle experiences that were considered normal.[24] He spoke of the "manifestations" that the unblocked presence of the Holy Spirit within God's people would bring forth, declaring that these were for the "common good."[25] There was nothing elitist or abnormal about them.

> For to one is given the *word of wisdom* through the Spirit, and to another the *word of knowledge* according to the same Spirit; to another *faith* by the same Spirit, and to another *gifts of healing* by the one Spirit, and to another the *effecting of miracles*, and to another *prophecy*, and to another the *distinguishing of spirits*, to another *various kinds of tongues*, and to another the *interpretation of tongues*.[26]

These are the supernatural evidences of God's favor and grace. They are among the effects of the blowing of the Spirit in our lives that the Lord was talking about with Nicodemus. You can't see the Spirit, which He likened to the wind; but you do see His effects.[27] When the wind blows, tree leaves move. When the Spirit blows other things move as well.

In my unending quest for wisdom, it turned out that the "word of wisdom" was a miracle of God that developed special meaning for me. All the gifts of the Spirit are exceedingly important when springing from faith, hope, and love;

but the supernatural bestowal of the word of wisdom is to be cherished.

The word of wisdom, as I indicated in chapter five when talking about wisdom in a broader sense, is a glimpse into the future regarding a specific event or truth. It is an unveiling.

Many people think prophecy is futuristic, and it often is. But not always. Prophecy specifically is "forth-telling"—speaking forth the Word of God. Quite often it deals with the present, or perhaps even the past.

I was praying one day in 1969, and the Lord spoke plainly to my inner man: "The stock market is going to crash."

This was startling, for I hadn't even been thinking about the stock market. Then He added, "Only the securities of your government will be safe."

In 1969 the stock market went to pieces and, in fact, has remained in a chaotic condition. It goes up and down, leaving people uncertain as to its stability.

That revelation has, I believe, application in the present, when a worldwide financial collapse seems imminent. It did not directly affect me or the ministry, but it was of great importance to the people of the country we were trying to reach with the gospel.

And the Lord has steadily increased this miraculous manifestation in my life and in ways more directly affecting the ministry than the performance of the stock market.

One day some years later, at a prayer meeting regarding an upcoming telethon in which we needed to raise the funds to meet the budget of our expanding outreach, the Lord spoke a word of wisdom as part of a prophecy. He responded to our concern about the burden we carried if we were to fulfill the mission He had given us.

I was speaking in prophecy about the presence of the Lord in what we were doing, and then the word of wisdom came regarding the telethon several days thence: "It will be so marvelous that you will not believe that it is happening. And yet this is going to happen before your eyes; and when it does happen, do not give credit to yourself, to your program people, to your computer operators, or to any of the things you have done. But give Me credit because I am telling you now that I am going to do it. And when it's over, you will see it and you will know who did it."

Of course, the word was fulfilled and we dramatically exceeded our goal. He met our need and the need of the people we were ministering to.

And we could give no one else the credit. Despite the difficulty of the circumstances, we were in God's will, and He was with us. According to the pattern revealed by the prophet Isaiah, He had proclaimed the "new things" He was doing, even before they sprang forth.[28]

Probably the most frequent occurrence of the miraculous in my life has involved the word of knowledge, touching on physical or emotional healing or other interventions by the Lord in the lives of people. Such a word quite simply reveals information the natural mind would not know, about a condition or a circumstance in which God is acting. And there have been memorable times when, quite unwittingly on my part, the "word of knowledge" has actually been an unveiling of something that was to occur in the future—a "word of wisdom."

For example, a woman in California was watching the "700 Club" while sitting in a great deal of discomfort from a broken ankle encased in a cast. She heard me say on the air, "There's a woman in a cast. She has broken her ankle, and God is healing her."

The woman immediately knew, in a burst of faith in her spirit, that those words had been spoken for her. She rose from the chair, removed the cast, and, with increasing confidence, began to put weight on the broken foot and then to jump on it. The ankle bone had been healed.

The thing she did not know was that she had been watching a program taped a week earlier and shown in her area at that time. Further checking uncovered that I had actually spoken the words about her ankle before it had been broken. In a word of wisdom, I had spoken about something that was yet to occur.

The Lord has caused this to happen many times over the years in my ministry.

He wants each of us to reach up into the invisible world and allow Him to perform miracles through us in the visible world. He will do it without limits of time or circumstances. He waits for us to practice the principles He has set forth in Scripture.

The University Miracle

One of the most miraculous moves in my life, covering numerous laws of the kingdom and spanning an inordinate amount of time, involved the establishment of CBN University, a complex of graduate schools now underway at our Virginia Beach center.

I had wanted to buy five acres in the city of Virginia Beach, which was burgeoning, as a possible headquarters site; but the owner of the land I was interested in refused to sell a portion of the 143-acre tract.

But the situation changed the day I was sitting in the coffee shop of the Grand Hotel in Anaheim, California. Invited to a conference at the Melodyland Christian Center, I had arrived late for the opening luncheon and was eating alone. When my meal of cantaloupe and cottage cheese arrived, I bowed my head to say grace—and the Lord began to speak to me about the site three thousand miles away. People around me in the busy shop must have thought I was terribly grateful for that cantaloupe, for I remained in the posture of prayer for a long time.

"I want you to buy the land," the Lord said. "Buy it *all*," He said. "I want you to build a school there for My glory, as well as the headquarters building you need."

I had not thought of a school before. True, we desperately needed a headquarters building. But did we need 143 acres?

When I returned to Virginia, I called the banker holding the major mortgage on the property and told him I wanted to buy the entire site and build a school on it. "Praise the Lord!" he exclaimed.

I hadn't been able to get anywhere with my small thinking about five acres, but suddenly I had acquired what God had directed—an interstate site worth $2.9 million, with nothing down, no principal payments for two years, and the balance at eight percent interest payable over twenty-three years. The terms could hardly have been more favorable! Furthermore, the Lord wasn't finished. He later gave us an adjoining site of 140 acres at prices that seemed miraculous.

The magnificent center standing on that property today is eloquent testimony to the power of God and the operation of the Law of Miracles. And, although I didn't know it at the time, the story had begun long before my California dialogue with the Lord. I eventually learned the following facts.

First, seven years before our acquisition of the site for the center, an Assembly of God minister had seen and shared with a friend of mine a vision of an international center on that same land. It would be a center reaching out to the world with the gospel. It would have students and dormitories, among other things, and would serve missionaries from around the world.

Second, at a point just ten miles from the site I had purchased, the first permanent English settlers in America had planted a cross on the sandy shore and claimed the land for God's glory and for the spread of the gospel. After 370 years, the ultramodern television facility with worldwide capabilities began to fulfill their dreams.

But that was not the only tie to those English settlers. I learned that a college had been part of their vision. Indeed, they had planned Henrico College as a school to teach the gospel and train young men and women for Christian service, hoping to reach the world through education. The plans for the college did not succeed. But the settlers believed the vision would last, as revealed in an introduction to a sermon pertaining to the overall settlement activity: "This work is of God and will therefore stand. It may be hindered, but it cannot be overthrown. . . ." They expected their descendants to rise to the challenge.

Interestingly, I am a descendant of the surgeon who came to Virginia in 1619 with the people who were to build Henrico College.

God had a plan. If miracles were required to fulfill it, then He performed miracles—all according to the laws of His kingdom.

Study Guide

Key Scripture: Num. 13:1–14:10; 1 Sam. 14:1–15; Mark 10:27; 11:25–26; John 14:12; Rom. 4:20–21; 1 Cor. 12:8–10

Key Idea: "Because of the desperate conditions of our world, we still need miracles today. That means we need to understand the law and act on it, for Jesus introduced a new order of normality at the Day of Pentecost" (p. 207).

1. Pat Robertson writes, "Since God is almighty, the only absolutely free person in the universe, not bound even by His own creation, He is perfectly able at any time to change the way things are done" (p. 207). Considering your condition right now physically, or your environment at home or at work, where would you like to see God perform a miracle. Write it down, and let's see if you are willing to meet the conditions God has set for acting through miracles.

2. What does the Law of Miracles govern? (See p. 206.)

Facing the Issues

1. How do we enter the kingdom of God, where the miraculous power resides? (See John 3:3.)

2. What is the title deed to the pool of power?

3. What are the two rules of miracles?

4. Look back at the situation you listed in *Setting the Stage*. If you were to describe your attitude, would it be that of Caleb and Joshua, the ten spies, or Jonathan?

5. "For miracles to happen through us, God's will must first be transmitted by the Holy Spirit to our spirits" (p. 209). How does this condition compare with your experience concerning the miracle you desire?

6. What does Pat Robertson's experience with RCA teach us about God's miracle-working power? Compare with Mark 10:27.

7. Underline the term that describes your attitude toward the miracle you would like God to do.

tentative	overly cautious
hesitant	half-hearted
fearful	half-persuaded
positive	fully persuaded

The Time to Speak

1. How did Jesus prepare His heart for God's miracle-working power to flow through Him? (See p. 210.)

2. What action by Jesus is common to the miracles He performed in Mark 4:39; 9:25; Matthew 8:3,13; 9:23–25?

3. When and how have you spoken out of your faith that God would perform a miracle?

4. Read James 3:8–11. Does it make sense to speak out to enlist God's miracle-working power in the light of your speech habits during the past weeks? If not, list the speech that is displeasing to God, then follow John's advice in 1 John 1:9.

5. What was the evidence that God's miracle power had come down on the Day of Pentecost?

The Major Hindrance

1. "Men and women, Christian and non-Christian, carry grudges. Any power of God within them is eaten up by resentment" (p. 212). Right now, whom do you resent? Against whom are you carrying a grudge? What do you need to do according to Mark 11:25–26?

2. What sin does unforgiveness reveal in your life? And who alone can forgive, surrender anger, feelings, and repudiation to the will of God?

3. What should we do when the person who has hurt us sets out again to deliberately hurt us after we have forgiven him or her? (See Matt. 18:21–22.)

4. What is the Christian's principal weapon?

5. How did Pat's friend (see p. 215) gain the release of God's power in his life?

6. Complete the following sentence: I will go to _____ and ask forgiveness for _____

Miracles Are Available

1. What do we learn about the availability of God's power in 1 Corinthians 12:8–10?

2. "He wants each of us to reach up into the invisible world and allow Him to perform miracles through us in the visible world. He will do it without limits of time or circumstance.He waits for us to practice the principles He has set forth in Scripture" (p. 219). Restate the principles you have learned from this study about activating God's miracle power in your life.

Making It Happen

Call up a friend or member of your family and share what faith goal you have set and how you expect God will act. If helpful, write down your prayer enlisting God's power in your specific situation. Be sure to follow through on the commitments you made earlier in this study.

Scripture References

1 See John 14:12
2 Matthew 8:10
3 Mark 11:22
4 See Numbers 13, 14
5 See 1 Samuel 14:1–15
6 Romans 4:20, 21, KJV
7 Mark 10:27
8 See Mark 4:39
9 See Matthew 9:23–25; Luke 7:11–16; John 11:34
10 See Mark 9:25
11 See Matthew 8:3
12 See Matthew 8:13
13 Mark 9:29
14 John 11:43
15 See 1 Thessalonians 5:17
16 Exodus 20:7
17 See Acts 2:4
18 See Luke 24:49
19 Mark 11:25, 26 (many manuscripts do not contain verse 26)
20 1 John 1:7
21 See Matthew 22:37–40
22 Matthew 18:21, 22
23 Matthew 18:32–35
24 See 1 Corinthians 12–14
25 1 Corinthians 12:8–10
26 1 Corinthians 12:8–10
27 See John 3:8
28 See Isaiah 42:9

14. The Law of Dominion

I was praying and fasting some years ago, seeking to understand God's purpose more fully. I heard His voice, level and conversational, "What do I desire for man?"

A bit surprised, I replied, "I don't know, Lord. You know.'

"Look at Genesis, and you'll see," He said.

Genesis is one of the longest books in the Bible, but I opened it at the beginning. In a few moments I read this:

> And God said, Let us make man in our image, after our likeness: and *let them have dominion* over the fish of the sea, and over the fowl of the air, and over the cattle, and over all the earth, and over every creeping thing that creepeth upon the earth. So God created man . . .[1]

"Let them have dominion." My eyes went over it several times. Then I knew the Lord's purpose. He wanted man to have dominion—then and now.

It was very clear. This was a kingdom law. God wants man to have authority over the earth. He wants him to rule the way he was created to rule.

You cannot help but juxtapose this desire of God with today's reality. The thousands of letters that pour into CBN, the pages of the newspapers, the screens of our television sets reveal anything but a people maintaining authority over their environment.

Christians especially show the symptoms of a defeated people. Many are sick, depressed, needy. They live in fear and confusion. Where, observers fairly ask, is the conquering army sung about in the great church hymns? Where is the blessing promised in the Bible from beginning to end? Was Jesus wrong when He said, "I will build my church; and the gates of hell shall not prevail against it"?[2]

No, Jesus was not wrong. Hell will *not* prevail. But we are seeing an Old Testament warning lived out among the people of God, and indeed all mankind: "My people perish for want of knowledge."[3] Men haven't been taught the Law of Dominion and the other principles of the kingdom. They are miserable.

But they can change immediately.

As in the Beginning

Almighty God wants us to recapture the dominion man held in the beginning. He has gone to great lengths to make that possible, sending His own Son as the second Adam to restore what was lost in Eden.

Remember, at the time of creation man exercised authority, under God's sovereignty, over everything. He was God's surrogate, His steward or regent.

The Genesis account uses two colorful words to describe this. One, *radah*, we translate "dominion." Man was to have dominion. The word means to "rule over" or "tread down," as with grapes. It comes from a Hebrew root meaning "spread out" or "prostrate." The picture we get from it is one of all the creation spread out before man, whose dominion would extend wherever his feet trod.

The other word, *kabash*, is translated "subdue." Man was told to subdue the earth. The root means "to trample under foot," as one would do when washing dirty clothes. Therefore, in *kabash* we have in part the concept of separating good from evil by force.

With the first word, *radah*, God gives man the authority to govern all that is willing to be governed. With the second, *kabash*, He grants man authority over the untamed and the rebellious. In both instances, God gave man a sweeping and total mandate of dominion over this planet and everything in it.

But stewardship requires responsibility. And implicit in the grant was a requirement that man order the planet according to God's will and for God's purposes. This was a grant of freedom, not of license. As subsequent history proved, God's intention was that His world be governed and subdued by those who themselves were governed by God. But man, as we know, did not want to remain under God's sovereignty. He wanted to be *like God* without having anyone to tell him what to do.

The progression toward the Fall is enlightening. First, note that God, after giving man dominion over the fish, the fowl, the cattle, and all the earth, specified that this authority extended to "every creeping thing that creepeth upon the earth."[4] Man specifically had dominion over serpents.

Then, we ask, what happened when Eve was faced with a challenge by the serpent? She faltered and allowed the serpent to convince her that God's grant of sovereignty was faulty. She refused to exercise her authority, and, worse than that, the serpent took authority over and manipulated her. Worse yet, with that first erosion, mankind allowed virtually all of his dominion to slip away.

It was the Law of Use in operation: Refuse to use what you have been given and you will lose it. Since that time, Satan has been exercising a type of dominion over human beings, deceiving them, destroying them.

God wants man to repossess that original dominion. He is ready to cause the Law of Use to work in our favor, if we will but begin to exercise what has been given.

We need to understand that God did not actually take the dominion away from man. He simply took away man's access to Him because of sin. Man still had dominion, but he lost the relationship and understanding necessary to exercise it properly. From there, the condition deteriorated as man voluntarily gave himself to the dominion of others.

As a result, man has for ages been neglecting and even misusing that which he was told to rule and subdue. He has, in effect, raped the creation rather than taken care of it. He has lost the humility and discipline to exercise dominion as God intended. He has exercised it arrogantly, or not at all. He hasn't been a servant of the creation—the animals, the oceans and rivers and streams, the forests, the mountains, the resources. He has violated the Law of Responsibility.

It is clear that God is saying, "I gave man dominion over the earth, but he lost it. Now I desire mature sons and daughters who will in My name exercise dominion over the earth and will subdue Satan, the unruly, and the rebellious. Take back my world from those who would loot it and abuse it. Rule as I would rule."

Application to the World

Included in God's grant of dominion to man was sovereignty over flowers, vegetables, and fruit. The mandate was all-inclusive: ". . . 'Behold, I have given you every plant yielding seed that is on the surface of all the earth, and every tree which has fruit yielding seed; it shall be food for you. . . .'"[5]

In one of the tragic ironies of all history, the Fall meant not only that man became a slave of Satan and his own base passions, but also that a sizable portion of mankind would become slaves of flowers, vegetables, and fruit. We have learned that those three can be cruel taskmasters. Last year in the United States, the tobacco plant caused the death of nearly 350,000 people, according to the Surgeon General. Corn, barley, rye, and grapes hold twenty million in alcoholic bondage. Together, these last four contribute to the death of 26,000 on our highways each year. But even that pales into insignificance compared with their fearful toll on human strength, creativity, and happiness.

Yet even more deadly is the hold that a weed, *cannabis*—called in Latin America "Mary Jane" or marijuana—has taken on the youth of our land, destroying their brains and their futures in exchange for a few moments of exhilaration. And we shudder at the fortunes that change hands and the crimes that are committed by those under the dominion of the seeds of the coca plants or the flowers of the opium poppy.

Last year in the United States, the cost of tobacco was $25 billion; alcohol $37 billion; marijuana $24 billion; and cocaine $35 billion. The cost of crime perpetrated by those addicted to heroin was at least $25 billion more. And well over half of America's staggering $250 billion medical bill can be attributed to illnesses induced by slavery to these items—vegetables, flowers, and fruit. Those statistics can reveal only a part of man's slavery. They are only illustrative of the financial toll we pay each year for our loss of dominion.

Yet attempts to set men free from this slavery are often met with derision and hostility. It does not matter that death and degradation are the outcome. Men outside the kingdom clutch their "pleasures" to their bosoms as if they were good, holy, and sacred rights.

You see, when man broke free of God's authority, he lost control of himself. Without a clear relationship with God, he became unable to see where he was going; and he soon became captive of what the Bible calls "the world, the flesh, and the devil." His own fears, his animal drives, his lusts, drove him. The devil, a malevolent power, played upon his base desires to seduce and entrap him. Then, as the human race grew, each man became a slave of mob psychology—the tyranny of the warped consensus of a sinful world.

Before the world can be freed from bondage, man must be made free from himself. This is why Jesus told the Jews of His day: ". . . 'If you abide in My word, then you are truly disciples of Mine; and you shall know the truth, and the truth shall make you free.'"[6]

Again, the writer of the letter to the Hebrews, speaking

of the effect of the death of Jesus for mankind, said: ". . . that through death He might render powerless him who had the power of death, that is, the devil; and might deliver *those who through fear of death were subject to slavery all their lives.*"[7]

When man, through Jesus, reasserts God's dominion over himself, then he is capable of reasserting his God-given dominion over everything else. That is the way everything on earth will be freed from the cycle of despair, cruelty, bondage, and death.

I furthermore believe the Lord would have man subdue the natural forces in the universe. Jesus, who was our example as well as our Redeemer, did this, as we have discussed in earlier chapters.

Without in any way advocating fanaticism, I believe God would enable man, under His sovereignty, to deal successfully with the conditions that threaten the world with catastrophic earthquakes. Scripture makes plain that God uses natural disasters as judgment upon mankind; but I am convinced that were man to turn from his wicked ways and seek the Lord, he would be able to take dominion over the faults in the earth's structure and render them harmless. For the words of Jesus spoken to the tumultuous waters of Galilee still echo down through history with great power and authority: "'Peace, be still.'"[8]

Similarly, man, taking his rightful place under God, would subdue the causes of drought and famine. World hunger would cease.

God's Fellow Workers

The concept of man's dominion over the created order is too much for us to comprehend unless we get a secure grip on the fact that the Lord thinks of us as fellow workers with Him in the development and operation of His kingdom.

Mark, in his gospel, tells how the disciples went out after Christ's ascension and "preached everywhere, while the Lord *worked with them.*"[9]

Paul, in his first letter to the Corinthians, reminded them that it was perfectly proper for both him and Apollos to be ministering to them. "We are God's *fellow workers* . . . ,"[10] he said.

Later, in a passage describing Christians as "ambassadors for Christ" to whom God has committed the message of reconciliation, he spoke of "*working together* with Him."[11]

You see, the Bible's view is that God, in a mystery too great for us to fathom, has chosen to use men to carry the truth around the world. To accomplish this, He had to give them authority.

In addition, the Bible speaks of that time when God's kingdom and His Christ will visibly rule on earth. "If we endure," Paul wrote, pointing to the Law of Perseverance, "we shall also *reign with Him*."[12] That will involve exceptional authority. God wants us to prepare for it.

We see this exemplified in the accounts of the Lord's sending His disciples out to minister: "And He called the twelve together, and gave them *power* and *authority* over all the demons, and to heal diseases. And He sent them out to proclaim the kingdom of God, and to perform healing."[13]

Obviously, in the Lord's mind authority went hand in hand with the proclamation of the kingdom. Authority authenticated the kingdom. How would it be possible to say there was a kingdom of God that was to supplant the kingdom of Satan unless it carried power and authority?

Those two words, "power" and "authority," have a significance of their own, too. First, the passage says, the Lord gave them "power," which is translated from the Greek word *dunamis*. It means "resident power." Dynamite, for example, has that kind of power. Christians who have the Holy Spirit operating in their lives also have it. It is the power to perform miracles.

But the Lord also gave them "authority." This is translated from the Greek word *exousia*. It, too, carries with it the idea of force and power, specifically in the sense of authority like that of a magistrate or potentate.

Quite simply, Jesus gave them power to perform miracles and authority to use that power over the devil and all creation.

At another time, speaking to seventy people who had gone out to minister, Jesus said: "'Behold, I have given you *authority* to tread upon serpents and scorpions, and *over all the power of the enemy....*'"[14]

With that, He was referring directly back to the Fall, for serpents are a remembrance not only of the deception in the Garden of Eden, but also of the curse that followed. Serpents and men have been at enmity ever since God said the seed of Eve would one day bruise the head of the serpent,[15] pointing to the triumph of Christ over the devil and his works.

So, in giving his followers such authority, Jesus was indeed saying, "I reestablish your authority over the one who robbed you of it in the garden. You can reassert your dominion."

Our problem in the twentieth century, as we perish for lack of knowledge, is that it does us no good to have this authority if we don't exercise it correctly. And most of us don't.

Yet we have tried so hard in many cases to take seriously the words Jesus spoke to His people before ascending to heaven to sit at the right hand of His Father. We must examine those words closely and with understanding: "And Jesus came up and spoke to them, saying, *'All authority has been given to Me in heaven and on earth. Go therefore....*'"[16]

Jesus had already "'accomplished the work which Thou hast given Me to do.'"[17] He had destroyed "the works of the devil,"[18] which especially included the robbery performed in the Garden of Eden. He, the King of the kingdom, had "all authority."

"Therefore," He declared, "go!"

His people could move out to accomplish their worldwide task because He had restored man's dominion under God.

Satan's Strategy

Satan, although defeated, is alive today, of course, and is as dangerous as we allow him to be. His primary weapon is deceit, and he uses it to prevent Christians from exercising the authority that is truly theirs in this world.

First, of course, he tries to entice us into sin, which can cloud or obstruct our view of the Lord and His will and, untended, can separate us from God.

He also tries to lead us into another form of sin, through unbelief. He tries to make us feel unworthy of the grace in which we stand. If he gets the upper hand in this, then we neglect the authority and the power given to us. They fall into disuse and, ultimately, vanish like the mist. The dominion that has been so awfully and awesomely won for us serves no purpose if it is not exercised.

We must combat this with all our strength and all our alertness. We must not be deceived.

We should recognize that we, in fact, *are* unworthy but that through the Lord Jesus we become worthy in the sight of God. We are sinners but, like Paul, who described himself as chief and foremost among sinners,[19] we "can do all things through Him who strengthens" us.[20]

Too many times, people fall into the devil's trap of believing that we can somehow earn our dominion. If we fall for that, we will never feel worthy, and we will never use the dominion given us. And we will never overcome the crises in the world.

If Satan can keep us in a state of timidity, discouragement, or embarrassment, he will nullify our authority and delay the manifestation of the kingdom of God on earth. I have been amazed in recent years by the success of this very simple maneuver. He has rendered Christians ever so slightly embarrassed about being Christians. The world, for example, sees nothing wrong with a person carrying a copy of *Playboy* or *Penthouse* magazine around under his arm on the street, in the bus or subway. The same with a bottle of whiskey or a carton of cigarettes, with all of its life-threatening ingredients. Yet vast numbers of Christians have been intimidated about carrying a Bible on the street or bus or subway. They're afraid of being categorized as religious freaks, or perhaps old-fashioned and out-of-step with the world. They are nervous about being discovered in prayer or other attitudes perceived as different. As for authority—whether it be over Satan or over the natural order—their timidity is overwhelming.

And yet, as we have noted before, the Bible says, "God has not given us a spirit of timidity, but of power and love and discipline."[21]

Neither Satan nor the world has the authority nor the power to do this to the Lord's people. They are flying directly in the face of God's desire. He wants us to assume our rightful authority and to hasten the coming of the kingdom on earth. Jesus emphasized this when He said: "'And this *gospel of the kingdom* shall be preached in the whole world for a witness to all the nations, and then the end shall come.'"[22]

You see, there are many signs of the times that we can watch for, but this one is most critical. The gospel of the kingdom in all its fullness and power, with all its authority, is to be carried to every nation. Timidity must vanish. There will be "signs and wonders"[23]—miracles and other evidences of the kingdom.

The Law of Dominion, properly exercised, will guarantee that.

It Must Be Voiced

In practical terms, the Law of Dominion works much like the Law of Miracles. It depends on the spoken word. We are to take authority by voicing it, whether it involves the devil or any part of the creation.

We should not argue with Satan. We merely tell him that he has to go, that he has no authority, that he must release this person or that situation. Quite bluntly, we say, "In the name of Jesus, I command you to get out of here, Satan!"

Also, reaching the mind of the Lord, we tell the storm to quiet, the crops to flourish, the floodwater to recede, the attacking dog to stop. We simple speak the word aloud.

Again, the central point is to "'have faith in God.'"[24] But we do not have to await a directive from Him in ordinary circumstances as to when to exercise the authority, assuming that we are walking in His will and yielded to His sovereignty. For He has already given us general guidelines: "'Be fruitful and multiply, and fill the earth, and *subdue it*; and *rule* over the fish of the sea and over the birds of the sky, and over every living thing that moves on the earth.'"[25]

This especially covers "every creeping thing that creeps on the earth," symbolizing the one described in Christ's time as "'the ruler of this world,'"[26] who has now been utterly defeated. Even though we still must struggle against those forces that willingly choose to ally themselves with Satan, that struggle has already been decided.

St. Paul described it this way: "For our struggle is not against flesh and blood, but against the rulers, against the powers, against the world forces of this darkness, against the spiritual forces of wickedness in the heavenly places."[27]

But since the authority for winning that struggle has been granted, St. Paul was confident that Christians will "stand firm" in "the evil day." The instrument for wielding that authority, he said, is the Word of God, which he described as the "sword of the Spirit."[28]

We simply are to speak forth our God-restored authority, preparing for an even more amazing era.

Study Guide

Key Scripture: Gen. 1:26–30; Matt. 24:14; Luke 9:1–2; 1 Cor. 3:5–9; Eph. 6:10–18; 2 Tim. 1:7; Heb. 2:6–15

Key Idea: Almighty God wants us to recapture the dominion man held in the beginning. He has gone to great lengths to make that possible, sending His own Son as the second Adam to restore what was lost in Eden" (p. 227).

1. "In one of the tragic ironies of all history, the Fall meant not only that man became a slave of Satan and his own base passions, but also that a sizable portion of mankind would become slaves of flowers, vegetables, and fruit" (p. 229). What are some of the "cruel taskmasters" to which many are addicted and by which they have been enslaved?

2. In contrast to that slavery, what could be our position on earth according to Genesis 1:26–27?

3. What are some of the symptoms of lack of dominion among Christians today?

The Key Concept

1. When a president from Georgia invites "unknown" Georgians into the White House as his aides, who is the source of their power in Washington? When a Californian peoples the White House with his friends from the West, to whom do they owe their power? By the same token, who was man responsible to, and what was Adam's role, in the Garden of Eden?

2. "But stewardship requires responsibility. And implicit in the grant was a requirement that man order the planet according to God's _____
and for God's _____"
(p. 228). What is the prerequisite for this happening?

3. What makes the exchange between the serpent and Eve so ironic in the light of God's role for Adam and Eve?

4. Indicate whether the following statements are true or false, based on the material on pages 228 and 229.

True   False

_____ _____ Eve took of the fruit because she felt God had not given her enough power.

_____ _____ Satan lost all power to have dominion over man as a result of deceiving Eve.

_____ _____ God took dominion away from man as the result of the Fall.

_____ _____ In general, man has taken good care of God's creation.

_____ _____ Man has violated the Law of Responsibility in respect to God's resources.

_____ _____ God wants Christians to reassert dominion over nature.

5. "Men outside the kingdom clutch their 'pleasures' to their bosoms as if they were good, holy, and sacred rights" (p. 230). What is the minimum cost in human life and medical bills, according to the authors?

6. What do the authors mean by "the tyranny of warped concensus of a sinful world?" (p. 230). How can man be freed from it? (See John 8:31–32; Heb. 2:14–15.)

7. What are some ways the authors believe we can reassert our dominion over nature?

The Believers' Position

1. What is the believers' role according to Mark 16:20, 1 Corinthians 3:9; 2 Corinthians 5:20; 6:1?

2. If we are to become God's servants and carry His message around the world, what do we need from God? (Compare Matt. 28:18–19; Luke 10:19.)

3. What had Jesus done to make this transfer of authority possible? (See 1 John 3:8.)

Satan's Strategy

1. Satan is as dangerous as we allow him to be, say the authors. What are three ways in which he approaches us?

   a.

   b.

   c.

2. "The dominion that has been so awfully and awesomely won for us serves no purpose if it is not exercised" (p. 234). What should encourage us to exercise it? (See Phil. 4:13.)

3. Write out one example when you let Satan keep you timid, discouraged, or embarrassed, thus nullifying your authority as a believer.

4. Write out 2 Timothy 1:7 and memorize it. Put it on a card and set it where you will often see it.

Making It Happen

1. Write out one specific area for each of the following where you need to exercise dominion in keeping with the Law of Dominion.

   a. Your personal life

   b. Your family

   c. Your community

   d. Nature and its resources (see Gen. 1:28)

2. Whom is our struggle against in exercising the Law of Dominion in the above areas? (See Eph. 6:12.)

3. What are specific steps we can take to exercise our authority as believers in these situations? (See pp. 235, 236.)

Wrap-Up

"We simply are to speak forth our God-restored authority, preparing for an even more amazing era" (p. 236).

Scripture References

1 Genesis 1:26,27, KJV
2 Matthew 16:18, KJV
3 Hosea 4:6, Jerusalem Bible
4 Genesis 1:26, KJV
5 Genesis 1:29
6 John 8:31, 32
7 Hebrews 2:14, 15
8 Mark 4:39, KJV
9 Mark 16:20
10 1 Corinthians 3:9
11 2 Corinthians 5:20, 6:1
12 2 Timothy 2:12
13 Luke 9:1, 2
14 Luke 10:19
15 See Genesis 3:15
16 Matthew 28:18, 19
17 John 17:4
18 1 John 3:8
19 See 1 Timothy 1:15
20 Philippians 4:13
21 2 Timothy 1:7
22 Matthew 24:14
23 Romans 15:19
24 Mark 11:22
25 Genesis 1:28
26 John 12:31
27 Ephesians 6:12
28 Ephesians 6:13, 17

15. The Coming King

Jesus said an astounding thing to His disciples: "'. . . To you it has been granted to know the mysteries of the kingdom of God. . . .'"[1]

Logic dictates that, if you are a disciple of His, you too have been permitted to know the mysteries of the kingdom. The reason is simple, but very important. He wants you to live in that realm right now, to master its principles so you will be ready for the new world order that appears to be rushing toward us. Why? Because you are to rule with Him in it,[2] and how can you rule if you aren't experienced in its laws?

If you are not a disciple, the mysteries are clouded, for flesh and blood cannot inherit the kingdom of God.[3] You must be born of the Spirit and receive access to that secret kingdom. That can occur this moment, merely by accepting Jesus into your life as your Lord and Savior. For God desires that you not miss out on anything; that is why He has been so patient these thousands of years.[4]

From the beginning of man's history, the Lord has been intent on establishing—through love, not fear—a kingdom of people who will voluntarily live under His sovereignty and enjoy His creation. That is the thrust of His entire

242

revelation made in what we call the Holy Bible. He is building a kingdom. And a new, major step in that building shows signs of being at hand. The invisible world may be ready to emerge into full visibility.

One can almost hear Jesus speaking to His church: "Beloved, be ready. I have shown you the laws of my kingdom, the way things truly work. Use them. Live them. They will work for good even now."

There's a new world coming. And we already know its principles! There's the Law of Reciprocity, the Law of Use, the Law of Perseverance, the Law of Responsibility, the Law of Greatness, the Law of Unity, the Law of Miracles, and the Law of Dominion. There are others, perhaps not as sweeping, but nonetheless vital. Having been stated in the Scripture, they are God-breathed.[5] They will change the world as we know it and prepare the way for the new one, even speeding its arrival. They, and they alone, can calm the crises choking the world and thwart the imminent slide into chaos and dictatorship of the right or the left. They pose a realistic alternative.

The Outlook

Here is what we can expect to happen in the days, months, and years ahead.

Having been regathered from the countries of the world, Israel, a unified nation living in relative security, will be invaded by a confederation from the north and the east. The prophet Ezekiel described this force as massive, coming like a storm, a cloud covering the land. He identified elements of it as "Gog of the land of Magog, the prince of Rosh, Meshech, and Tubal," joined by "Persia, Ethiopia, and Put," along with "Gomer," "Bethtogarmah from the remote parts of the north," and "many peoples."[6]

Various poeple have been viewed as Gog and Magog throughout history—the Goths, the Cretans, the Scythians—but indications are that this great power from the north may be the Soviet Union, for that nation occupies land specified by Ezekiel. Other present-day nations that we seem to identify in the confederation are Ethiopia, Iran as Persia, Somalia or Libya as Put, and Eastern Europe (probably Germany) as Gomer. It is noteworthy that Iran, at this writing, is mounting a crusade to "liberate" Jerusalem and is drawing near to the Soviet Union. Ethiopia is a Communist dictatorship; Libya tilts toward Moscow, and Somalia, although leaning toward the United States, has been Marxist. East Germany, a Soviet satellite, has positioned police forces in South Yemen and other parts of the Middle East. Thus, the various pieces of Ezekiel's prophecy appear to be easing into place.

When the forces move against Israel and its "unwalled villages"—"to capture spoil and to seize plunder"—it appears that questions will be raised by people identified as "Sheba, and Dedan, and the merchants of Tarshish, with all its villages [or young lions]."[7] Ezekiel did not say that these people would resist the invaders, but merely ask, "Why have you come here?"[8]

These questioners can probably be pinpointed as Yemen, Saudi Arabia, and the United States, which was once settled by people who could be identified as Tarshish merchants. Tarshish was probably a Phoenician settlement in Spain, near Cadiz, that sent ships to Ireland, possibly to England, and then to the New World, their passengers traveling all over what was to become the United States. *If* there is a reference in the Bible to America, that would seem to be one.

Whether these questioners will assist Israel is unclear. Regardless, God, who is even in control of the invading horde from the north, will intervene in Israel's behalf with a great shaking—earthquakes, volcanic activity, fire, confusion, and even fighting among the allied invaders. He also speaks of fire falling upon Magog, the homeland of the leaders of the force, and upon "those who inhabit the coastlands in safety." This could, of course, be a vision of nuclear bombing. But it may also be the direct, miraculous intervention of God, for the prophecy says the following very pointedly: "'And My holy name I shall make known in the midst of My people Israel; and I shall not let My holy name be profaned anymore. And *the nations will know that I am the Lord, the Holy One in Israel.'"9*

According to Ezekiel, this will be followed by seven years of Israeli ascendance as the nation grows strong in the Middle East and increases in knowledge of the Lord, climaxed by a nationwide outpouring of the Holy Spirit.

Revelation's Clues

At the same time, the Book of Revelation appears to point to a successor kingdom to the Roman Empire that could roughly parallel the current European Economic Community.10 It is a ten-nation confederation that has an eleventh nation added, along with a merger of two of the nations, apparently, and could be a forerunner of what is called the Antichrist. Presumably this group will make a league with Israel and then turn on her and begin to oppress her.

The leader of this confederation will be a spritual being who will become a counterfeit Christ and draw men's allegiance. Exploiting confused, chaotic conditions, he will turn the league into a dictatorship, thus poising two kingdoms— the kingdom of God and the counterfeit kingdom—for climactic conflict.

Revelation points to another development that will be instrumental in this period. A system of buying and selling that utilizes individual marks will make possible the economic control of the world's population. The tremendous explosions in computer technology have made this feasible. Even now in Brussels, the headquarters city of the European Economic Community, a giant computer system—an interbank transfer computer—makes it possible to give every person in the world a number and allocate credits and debits on the basis of that number. It could be implanted in the skin by means of a chip or a laser tattoo in the forehead, perhaps concealed in the hair fringe, or on the hand.

Banks could institute debit cards, with the capacity to debit accounts instantly, and eliminate the need for exchange of currency. Even now, private business and government agencies are experimenting with so-called smart cards, which contain a tiny microchip computer capable of adjusting debit and credit balances as the cards are used. A next logical stop would be the control of buying and selling through the embedment of such a microchip on the hand or the forehead, as indicated in Revelation.[11]

Thus, one scenario seems capable of fulfillment at almost any time: A major war erupts in the Middle East, with the Soviet Union leading a force into Israel. The force is destroyed. A catastrophic upheaval results, in which oil supplies to Europe and elsewhere are cut off. Europe is thrown into economic shambles, setting the stage for a strong-man dictator to move swiftly, with great charisma and verve, to establish a new economic order.

The Return of Jesus

In the meantime, the kingdom of God will move forward, its future never in doubt. Those who choose to live under its rule will do so and be continuously prepared for that time in history when Jesus Christ will return to earth. The Bible says He will come back to destroy this new economic leader and his "kingdom," setting up a reign of peace and justice forever.[12] The invisible kingdom will become a visible one. And the world—the principalities and powers, the angelic host—will see the way God intended for His universe and His society to function.

We need to understand that God will not abandon His world. He has from the beginning been concerned about the historic record and about His own justification. He does not act arbitrarily. It is as though he will send Jesus, then gather His archangels, the angels, the entire heavenly host and say, "Look, this is the way the world would have worked had man not sinned. This is what I desired."

God does not have to justify Himself. He merely does it because He is a God of love and order and justice.

But that will not be the end. It might almost be called a transition period, between the earth as it has been and the ultimate plan of God, in which evil and opposition to the Lord will be finally removed and paradise established.

The Bible says this transition period will cover a thousand years, hence the name "Millenium."[13] In it Christ will reign and there will be peace. He will hold everything together and His greatness will be manifest for all the world to see. He will be revealed in the fullness of what the Scripture has been proclaiming for centuries: He is altogether righteous and perfect; there is no failing in Him; His wisdom is absolute.

> For a child will be born to us, a son will be given to us;
> And the government will rest on His shoulders;
> And His name will be called Wonderful Counselor,
>   Mighty God,
> Eternal Father, Prince of Peace.
> There will be no end to the increase of His government or
>   of peace,
> On the throne of David and over his kingdom,
> To establish it and to uphold it with justice and righteousness
> From then on and forevermore.
> The zeal of the LORD of hosts will accomplish this.[14]

Speculation will not be necessary. The beauty of the Lord will be evident to all, no longer dependent upon the vision of John:

> And I saw heaven opened; and behold, a white horse, and He who sat upon it is called Faithful and True; and in righteousness He judges and wages war. And His eyes are a flame of fire, and upon His head are many diadems; and He has a name written upon Him which no one knows except Himself. And He is clothed with a robe dipped in blood; and His name is called The Word of God. And the armies which are in heaven, clothed in fine linen, white and clean, were following Him on white horses. And from His mouth comes a sharp sword, so that with it He may smite the nations; and He will rule them with a rod of iron; and He treads the wine press of the fierce wrath of God, the Almighty. And on His robe and on His thigh He has a name written, "King of Kings, and Lord of Lords."[15]

The laws of the kingdom will prevail, and His people will govern with Him. Food, water, and energy will be ample. No longer will trillions of dollars be spent on weaponry. It will go for parks and forests, for scientific advances as yet beyond imagination.

But, if His people are to govern with Him in these circumstances, they need answers to several big questions. How do you run a just government? How do you run a world? What principles work and what ones do not?

That's why Jesus talked so much about the kingdom. He let His apostles teach about the church. He, the King, talked about His own kingdom and the way it works. He wants us to master those principles so we will be able to serve with Him properly.

Remember, those who are great now will become the least, and those who are least will become great.[16] He will take the little people, His kingdom saints, and exalt them to positions of power. The wealthy, the arrogant, the oppressors—they will be diminished. Their authority will go to the saints, "the fullness of Him who fills all in all."[17]

The Removal of Evil

The Bible says that at the end of the transition period, Satan will be allowed to lead a revolt of those who have still refrained from voluntarily accepting the rule of Christ. Then, after a relatively short period, the Lord will remove Satan (all evil and opposition) and bring forth "a new heaven and a new earth,"[18] the ultimate and eternal kingdom.

Jesus spoke at some length about the removal of evil in a story that has come to be known as the parable of the tares.[19] It tells of a man who sowed good wheat seed in his field, but at night someone sowed tares—false wheat, weeds—in the same field. Both the wheat and the tares grew; and when the landowner was questioned, he said, "'An enemy has done this!'"[20] But he wouldn't allow his workers to root up the tares for fear of what damage would be done to the wheat. "Let them both grow," he said, "and at the time of harvest I'll tell the reapers to put the wheat in the barn but to gather the tares for burning."

Later, when Jesus was alone with His disciples, they asked Him the meaning of the parable.

> And He answered and said, "The one who sows the good seed is the Son of Man, and the field is the world; and as for the good seed, these are the sons of the kingdom; and the tares are the sons of the evil one; and the enemy who sowed them is the devil, and the harvest is the end of the age [the consummation]; and the reapers are angels. Therefore just as the tares are gathered up and burned with fire, so shall it be at the end of the age [the consummation]; and the reapers are angels. Therefore just as the tares are gathered up and burned with fire, so shall it be at the end of the age [the consummation]. The Son of Man will send forth His angels, and *they will gather out of His kingdom all stumbling blocks, and those who commit lawlessness,* and will cast them into the furnace of fire; in that place there shall be weeping and gnashing of teeth. Then the righteous will shine forth as the sun in the kingdom of their Father. . . ."[21]

Everything that is offensive will be removed from the kingdom of God, not by men or the church or military might, but by the angels. They will know the righteous from the evil, and they will know how to act.

At that point, the "sons of the kingdom" will be the only ones left, basking in the light of the Lord, living in ultimate reality and perfection.

Jesus reinforced this understanding for His disciples, following the parable of the tares with one about fish, for several of His close followers were fishermen. He compared the kingdom of heaven to a dragnet cast into the sea to gather fish of every kind. When it was hauled in, the good fish were sorted into containers, but the bad were thrown away. The explanation was the same as before: "So it will be at the end of the age [the consummation]; the angels shall come forth, and take out the wicked from among the righteous. . . ."[22]

At this moment, our minds can't comprehend the perfection that will exist then. We can't speak about it. Our ideas and words are still too limited.

But think of this: What would it be like if all the energies of men and all creation were founded 100 percent on love? Or consider it in reverse: What if there were not a single trace of hatred anywhere?

That is the world God created for us. No pride, no greed, no fear, no crime, no war, no disease, no hunger, no shortage.

The Final Step

The Bible speaks of a step in this progressive unfolding of God's perfect plan that would appear to come after all the other phases. It sets forth magnificently the unity and harmony of the Godhead and the ultimate unity and harmony of all creation.

The apostle Paul spoke of it in a complex passage on the sequences of the resurrection of the dead. The point we should see in our context is illuminated clearly:

> For as in Adam all die, so also in Christ all shall be made alive. But each in his own order: Christ in the first fruits, after that those who are Christ's at His coming, *then comes the end, when He delivers up the kingdom to the God and Father,* when He has abolished all rule and all authority and power. For He must reign until He has put all His enemies under His feet. The last enemy that will be abolished is death. For He has put all things in subjection under His feet. But when He says, "All things are put in subjection," it is evident that He is excepted who put all things in subjection to Him. And when all things are subjected to Him, then the Son Himself also will be subjected to the One who subjected all things to Him, that God may be all in all.[23]

Again, these plans exceed our capacity for thought. Jesus, the Son and King, in whom all things will be summed up and united in the fullness of time,[24] will present all to His Father for all eternity.

What Will Men Do?

So, then, here we stand. What will men do?

Will they continue to ignore the principles governing the way the world works? Or will they learn from the secret kingdom?

I appeal to people everywhere to lay hold of the truths of our world—the Bible's insights into the way it works—and to put them into action. There is still time.

—Give and it will be given to you. This principle will not fail. We simply must begin to execute it—individuals, families, companies, nations. Imagine what our times would be like if we treated others the way we wanted to be treated.

—Take what you already have and put it to use. Don't wait until you have everything you want. Use what you have. Multiply it exponentially, consistently, persistently. The wonders of the world will explode into fullness.

—Do not give up. Persevere. Endure. Keep on asking, keep on seeking, keep on knocking. The world will keep on responding.

—Be diligent to fulfill the responsibility required of you. If God and men have entrusted talent, possessions, money, or fame to you, they expect a certain level of performance. Don't let them down. If you do, you may lose everything.

—Resist society's inducements to success and greatness and dare to become a servant, even childlike. True leadership and greatness will follow. The one who serves will become the leader.

—Reject the dissension and negativism of the world. Choose harmony and unity at every level of life—unity centered on the will of God. Mankind flowing in unity will accomplish marvelous results in all endeavors.

—Be humble enough, yet bold enough, to expect and to do miracles fulfilling the purpose of the Lord. Once and for all, become aware of the power of your speech as you walk humbly and obediently. Most importantly, grasp and exercise the significance of the principles of forgiveness.

—As a follower of the Son of God, assume the authority, power, and dominion that God intends for men to exercise over the rest of creation. Recapture that which prevailed in the Garden of Eden before the Fall. Move with power and authority.

Obviously, there are additonal laws of the kingdom that the Lord wants us to learn, and He will reveal them if we seek Him. But we can, and should—indeed, we must—begin to adhere to those that are now plain before us.

All is not lost. True, "the axe is already laid at the root of the trees,"[25] as John the Baptist warned nearly two thousand years ago, and those things running contrary to God's purpose will be cut down. The process has presumably already begun. God's plans will not be circumvented. Yet the movement to ultimate fulfillment need not be one of terror and agony. The crises of the world can be relieved. Just in themselves, the laws of the kingdom can accomplish that. The world can be a far better place as it moves toward fulfillment.

At some point, however, the laws by themselves will not be enough. A choice will have to be made regarding the kingdom itself. The laws will not operate forever outside the kingdom. Relief will only go so far. There will be a final shaking by God; only the kingdom will survive.[26]

So, why wait? Why separate the laws of the kingdom from allegiance to the King? Choose Him this moment. It can all be ours right now!

"Do not be afraid, little flock, for your Father has chosen gladly to give you the kingdom."[27]

Study Guide

Key Scripture: Ezek. 38:1–39:8; Matt. 13:24–43; Luke 8:9–10; 1 Cor. 15:22–28; 48–50; Eph. 1:9–10; 2 Tim. 2:11–13; Heb. 12:25–29; Rev. 13:16–17; 19; 20:1–10; 21:1–5

Key Idea: "From the beginning of man's history, the Lord has been intent on establishing—through love, not fear—a kingdom of people who will voluntarily live under His sovereignty and enjoy His creation" (p. 242).

1. "He [God] wants you to live in the realm right now, to master its principles so you will be ready for the new world order that appears to be rushing toward us" (p. 242). In the thirteen weeks since you began this study, what laws of the kingdom have you implemented in your life so thoroughly you are beginning to see results?

2. If Jesus were to visibly appear to you and ask you to be a ruler in His kingdom, what would you say?

Looking Ahead

1. What do you fear most about the future?

2. Based on Ezekiel 38 and the analysis of modern equivalents by the authors, how would you feel if you were a Soviet believer in the armed forces?

3. What will God do to prevent the confederation of armed forces from wiping out Israel? (See Ezek. 38:21–22; 39:4–6.)

4. Will Israel get the credit for the defeat of their enemy? (See Ezek. 38:23; 39:7.)

5. In Revelation 13 the apostle John describes the leadership of forces conspiring to win over the confidence of the people of Israel. What is their inglorious ending? (See Rev. 19:20.)

Can Jesus Be Far Behind?

1. When will the invisible kingdom become the visible one according to the authors? (See p. 246.)

2. What is meant by the term "millenium"? (See p. 247.)

3. What are some of the characteristics of Jesus in Revelation 19:11–16 that impress you?

4. What is one of the motivations for learning to use the principles of the kingdom now? (See p. 248.)

5. What kind of world do we live in now, according to Matthew 13:37–43?

6. Who will be involved in the removal of the evil ones from the earth? (See Matt. 13:41–42.)

7. What will be Satan's double effort to upset God's timetable for His reign (and us with Him)? (Compare Rev. 19:19; 20:3, 7–10.)

8. What will be the last enemy abolished by God? (See 1 Cor. 15:22–28.)

Making It Happen

"The process has presumably already begun. God's plans will not be circumvented. Yet the movement to ultimate fulfillment need not be one of terror and agony. The crises of the world can be relieved" (p. 252). Reviewing what you have learned about the laws of the kingdom, what can you do during the next week to start relieving the crisis we are in today?

Scripture References

1 Luke 8:10
2 See 2 Timothy 2:12
3 See 1 Corinthians 15:50
4 See 2 Peter 3:9
5 See 2 Timothy 3:16
6 See Ezekiel 38:2, 6, 7, 9
7 Ezekiel 38:11, 12
8 Ezekiel 38:13 (paraphrased)
9 Ezekiel 39:6, 7
10 See Revelation 17:9–14
11 Revelation 13: 16, 17
12 See Revelation 19
13 See Revelation 20: 2, 4, 7
14 Isaiah 9:6, 7
15 Revelation 19:11–16
16 See Mark 10:31
17 Ephesians 1:23
18 Revelation 21:1
19 See Matthew 13:24–43
20 Matthew 13:28
21 See Matthew 13: 37–43
22 Matthew 13:49
23 1 Corinthians 15:22–28
24 Ephesians 1:9, 10
25 Matthew 3:10
26 See Hebrews 12:25–29
27 Luke 12:32

PAT ROBERTSON, president of the Christian Broadcasting Network, Inc., and the CBN Cable Network, has hosted the popular "700 Club" television magazine show since 1968. Robertson is founder and chancellor of CBN University in Virginia Beach, Va. He received his M.Div. from New York Theological Seminary and his J.D. from Yale University Law School. He has written *Shout It from the Housetops*, *Answers to 200 of Life's Most Probing Questions*, *Beyond Reason*, and *America's Dates with Destiny*.

BOB SLOSSER, a graduate of the University of Maine, is the author of a number of other books, including *Reagan Inside Out*, *Plain Bread* with Ben Kinchlow, *Child of Satan, Child of God*, and *Miracle in Darien*. He has served as assistant national editor of the *New York Times* and editor of the *National Courier*, and is a former executive vice president of CBN. He continues to serve as a member of the CBN Board of Directors and is now the president of CBN University.

ANSWERS

TO 200 OF LIFE'S
MOST PROBING
QUESTIONS

Pat Robertson

Contents

Chapter Six—The Holy Spirit 352

B. Christians and Government 442

Acknowledgments

I want to thank Danuta Soderman, my colleague and co-hostess on "The 700 Club" television program, for spending hours with me in the CBN audio taping room, asking questions and then probing the answers with more questions.

My thanks to Joyce Jackson and Cherry Smithson for a masterful job of transcribing hours of audio tape.

To David Wimbish, my thanks for his laborious work in editing and organizing the preliminary manuscript.

To Helen P. Bird I extend heartfelt thanks for verifying scripture references, for organizing countless footnotes, and for hours spent at the word processor, seeing the manuscript through various stages of development.

My appreciation to Dr. J. Rodman Williams, Dr. Herbert W. Titus, and Dr. Peter Prosser, distinguished professors at CBN University, for their verification of theological concepts.

My appreciation to Ralph Sitton and Robert Womack, our CBN audio men, for their help in recording my initial answers.

Finally, my thanks to my wife Dede for her patience during 6 A.M. and 10 P.M. writing sessions at our dining room table which remained unsightly—littered with books and papers—during the project.

270

Introduction

Suppose you were told that you could ask God any one question. What would you ask? And would your question be the same one most Americans would choose to ask? What, in fact, would most Americans ask God if they were granted a one-on-one interview? That was something we at the Christian Broadcasting Network (CBN) wanted to find out. To help us, we turned to the Gallup Poll organization. The Gallup polsters interviewed some fifteen hundred people all across the country. People of widely divergent occupations, backgrounds, and ages were asked what one question they would most like to ask God.

From their survey, the Gallup people then determined America's top ten questions. These, in turn, were used as the basis for the Christian Broadcasting Network's prime-time television special, "Don't Ask Me, Ask God." That show included appearances by Mother Teresa, Malcolm Muggeridge, Alvin Toffler, and General Willaim C. Westmoreland. Numerous other celebrities helped us present God's answers to America's top questions. Celebrity guests included Steve Allen, Ned Beatty, Ruth Buzzi, Tony Danza, Norman Fell, Anita Gillette, Dean Jones, Marvin Kaplan, Doug McClure, Jayne Meadows, Vincent Price, Ben Vereen, and others.

In the first chapter of this book, we will consider the top ten questions as gathered by the Gallup organization. Then, in the following chapters of the book, we will present biblical answers to one hundred and ninety questions that address the heart of the Christian faith and the vital concerns of people not only throughout this country but also in all the world.

We will look to the Bible for the answer to these questions because the Bible is the authoritative Word of God. And because the Bible is the Word of God, we know that what it says is always true. This is the key to answering all of the questions.

The Bible itself tells us that every scripture is *theopneustos,* "breathed" by God. This is an inspired book. Every writing, every scripture, from Genesis to Revelation, is inspired by God, and "is profitable for doctrine, for reproof, for correction, for instruction in righteousness" (2 Tim. 3:16).

The Bible is the only book that contains the story of holy history. It starts at the beginning of time and carries through to the end of time, showing God's intervention in the events that have helped shape our world. It is the only story that tells the way of salvation—the way to find God.

The Bible is internally consistent with itself, even though it was written over a period of fourteen to fifteen hundred years. It contains the story of a nation which, out of all the nations of the earth, came to be God's people and that discovered the secret of God's salvation.

The Bible is the story of God's coming to earth in the person of Jesus to bring us eternal life.

The Bible has passed the test of time. There is no other book like it, and there never will be. When you look at the holy books of other religions, you find fantasy and bizarre supernatural events that do not commend themselves to reasonable people. But the Bible is actually authenticated by history.

It is a book of prophecies that have come to pass. The odds against all the prophecies about the coming Messiah being fulfilled in one person are more than a billion to one, but they were fulfilled in Jesus. There are many other outstanding prophecies, such as those being fulfilled in modern-day Israel right now. The Bible is not only a book about an ancient people but also a book as current as today's newspaper headlines.

It is a book that was given to us by the Holy Spirit. It is our guidebook, telling us what we must do, leading us from the day we are born to the day we die, with instruction in righteousness, truth, and salvation.

The Bible was written in various times and places as the Holy Spirit moved upon godly men. It was written by Moses. It was written by historians. It was written by poets. It was written by a number of holy men called prophets. It was written by a physician named Luke, by a tax collector named Matthew, by a disciple of Peter named Mark, and by one of Jesus' disciples named John. It was written by the apostle Paul, who saw a revelation of Jesus. It was written by a fisherman named Peter and a half brother of the Lord named James.

Thirty-nine of the books of the Bible deal with events before the coming of Jesus. They center around the covenant of God with Israel and are called the Old Testament. The text accepted by the Christian church comes from the Jews and is called the Masoretic Text.

Twenty-seven books of the Bible were written after the coming of Jesus. They center around the new covenant of faith and are called the New Testament. Those books bearing the seal of the Holy Spirit and in circulation since apostolic days were recognized as holy Scripture by a church council in A.D. 397. The Old and New Testaments make up the sixty-six books of the Bible.

This is the Bible, the book which holds the answers to all of your questions, no matter what those questions might be. It is the authority for the answers given to the 200 questions in this book.

Answers to 200 of Life's Most Probing Questions is offered prayerfully, humbly, and with the hope that it will

help you better understand God's plan for your life—and
your place in His world.

Please understand that the limitations of space force
these answers to be brief. May they serve merely as a spring-
board to deeper study and adventures in faith.

Pat Robertson
Virginia Beach, Virginia

1. The Gallup Poll's Top Ten

1. Why is there suffering in the world?

Suffering touches everyone who lives on this planet. All you have to do is pick up a daily newspaper or listen to a news broadcast to know that a great many people are suffering. They suffer because of automobile accidents or because of terrible diseases or because of crime. Some suffer because they were born in poverty, others because they were born in countries ruled by dictators. There are many causes of suffering, and the list could go on for pages. But our question is not concerned with causes. We are looking for the *reasons* for suffering.

To say there is suffering because there is crime, or because there are auto accidents, is not nearly enough. Our question goes far beneath the surface, where it hits at the very roots of human pain and anguish.

The first thing to be said about suffering is that most of it comes about because of the activities of a powerful supernatural being called Satan, or the devil. He delights in hurting man and in trying to turn man away from God. Very often people blame God when they suffer, but is it God's fault? Satan takes great pride in seeing God gets the "credit" for his misdeeds.

Suffering is also caused by man's rebellion against God and by the evil in men's hearts. How much suffering has been caused in the modern world, for instance, by Communism, or by men hurting other men? Godless dictators hurt their own people, and they hurt the people of neighboring nations as well. Just consider how much suffering has been caused, in this century alone, by men such as Adolf Hitler, Josef Stalin, and Mao Tse-tung. As the result of godless dictatorships, there is suffering in the form of poverty and disease, and in every form of heartbreak.

You might say that suffering is a result of freedom. God has given *man* a certain amount of freedom. If man were merely a robot, an automaton, then God could always force him to do what is right. But God gives man the freedom either to love and obey Him or to rebel against Him. When man rebels against God, he hurts not only himself but also his fellow man.

Something else to remember about suffering is that God set up certain natural laws to govern the universe. If it were not for the law of gravity, we would all go floating off into space. But that same law is going to cause pain to people who jump from the tops of tall buildings!

Consider the hurricane, the earth's way of releasing pent-up heat and energy. Heat from the southern climates has to move north and be discharged from the earth. When that happens, it causes a violent wind to blow. That wind, in turn, stirs up huge waves when it passes over the ocean. The hurricane is not meant to cause suffering, but if people ignore the warnings of nature, they will be injured by hurricanes.

The same is true of faultlines, such as the San Andreas Fault. Faultlines are necessary to keep the earth from just breaking apart. But if people insist upon building houses on the San Andreas Fault—as they do—then they are going to suffer when an earthquake comes. Such suffering does not result from God's intentions, but comes rather from man's foolishness. We can either go along with natural forces and accommodate ourselves to them, or we can ignore them and be hurt by them.

Much sickness, too, is man-made. Some of it is because of improper nutrition. People do not eat the right things. God gives us natural sugar, but we bleach it and make it white. We eat white bread, when whole wheat is much better for us. God gives us naturally fibrous fruit and plants, but we boil the fiber away. We do the same thing with oranges, when we squeeze the juice out of them and throw away the pulp, which is a beneficial part. We also peel potatoes and eat only the inside. In doing so, we throw away the part that God made to help us stay healthy.

It is probable that 75 to 80 percent of the illnesses in the United States are psychosomatic. We have not learned to cast all our cares upon God, as we are advised to do in 1 Peter 5:7, and so we let our worried and harried minds make us sick.

We also make ourselves sick voluntarily through doing such things as smoking cigarettes, drinking alcohol, and ingesting drugs. Automobile accidents cause fifty-six thousand deaths in our country each year—and half of those involve drunken driving.

The technological state of our society contributes to suffering too. If there were no automobiles, there would be no deaths and injuries resulting from highway accidents. Our air would not be polluted with smoke from factories and automobile exhaust if there were no cars and factories. All of these things are part of the price we pay for our state of civilization. If we do not want to pay the price, we can go back to a more primitive society. In today's world, our life-style is a large contributor to sickness and disease.

To illustrate again how man contributes to his own suffering, consider what has happened in Africa. The northern plain of that continent was once a beautiful, fertile, wooded area. But over several centuries, people cut down all the trees. As a result, the topsoil eroded and there was nothing left but desert. Without the protective cover of the trees, temperatures in the region rose steadily. The people moved farther south, seeking fertile land. As they moved southward, they continued cutting the trees, and consequently the desert moved southward. Today there are three-and-a-half million square miles of desert in the northern part of Africa. In northern Africa and in many other areas of the world, men have disturbed the ecological balance in nature. As a result, poverty and hunger are worse and worse.

India has a similar problem. India was once one of the most fertile lands in the entire world. But the Indian people have embraced a philosophy that says rats and cows are sacred. So the cows eat up much of the vegetation, and the rats devour a good deal of the grain. Given a new understanding of nature, proper agricultural techniques, a forestation program, and a cleansing of rivers which are now polluted, India could be agriculturally self-sustaining.

The problem is not caused by an act of God, but it stems from man's foolishness over a period of years, perhaps centuries. And the problems are steadily compounded over successive generations.

There are other forms of suffering that men bring on themselves. Consider, for example, such diseases as genital herpes, syphilis, gonorrhea, and AIDS. These all result from a conscious lifestyle that is opposed to God's Word and breaks God's laws. God did not send herpes. It is a natural consequence of immorality. When it spreads, it becomes an incurable disease, affecting millions and millions of people.

Why does God allow this to happen? When we ask this question, it brings us back to the statement that God has created man as a free being—free even to the point of ruining much of God's creation. God has sent preachers, prophets, and other holy men to warn the people to change their ways but most will not listen. They would not listen to the prophets four thousand years ago, and most of them will not listen today.

It is true that the righteous often suffer, and this will continue as long as we live in a world of wickedness. If someone speaks out against wickedness, he is going to be involved in a struggle, and that struggle may result in pain and suffering. Jesus said, "If they persecuted Me, they will also persecute you."[1]

Jesus Christ was the only perfect man who ever lived, and people killed him. Why? Because He came into contact with evil and tried to do something about it. John the Baptist was beheaded because he told people they were breaking God's laws.[2] It has been true throughout the ages that those who are God's messengers are often set upon and hurt by the people they have tried to warn. That kind of suffering is virtually unavoidable as long as we live in a wicked world of superstition, hatred, and ignorance.

Suffering, if we allow it to, does have a way of purifying us. Many people have had to suffer in order to turn to God. Until they had their material things stripped from them, and often their health taken away, they had no desire for spiritual things.

Those who are suffering may be tempted to turn away from God. They should never allow this to happen. Instead, they should worship God and be blessed and benefitted, even in the midst of their suffering. Those who hurt must remember that it is not God's will for anyone to suffer.

They must remember, too, that He will intervene for those who diligently seek Him. Thousands of people can testify that God will intervene to relieve pain and suffering, but this depends on a closeness and an intimacy with Him. Should we, then, accept everything, and thank God for whatever happens to us—good and bad?

God answers this question specifically in the Bible. "And we know that all things work together for good to those who love God, to those who are the called according to His purpose" (Rom. 8:28).

It is important to understand that accepting things is not the same thing as being resigned to them. You must accept suffering without becoming bitter, and you *can* accept it without resigning yourself to it. It is not your "lot in life" to suffer. Those who do suffer should never quit seeking God's touch and asking Him to set them free. Jesus said, "Ask, and it will be given to you; seek, and you will find;

knock, and it will be opened to you. For everyone who asks receives, and he who seeks finds, and to him who knocks it will be opened."[3] The key is to keep on *asking*, *seeking*, and *knocking*.

One final word about suffering. There is a certain amount of pain involved whenever growth is taking place. When people are moving to a higher level of intellectual activity, there is a struggle that has to take place, and in that struggle there is pain. When people who are great athletes are pushing through the limits of endurance to get to new records, there is constant pain. There is pain when you are running a mile or two at top speed, when your lungs are gasping and your body wants to quit. But there is also the overwhelming joy that comes when you finally do break through into that new dimension.

This kind of pain is not the same thing as suffering. Some people do not recognize the difference between the suffering that is caused deliberately by evil and the pain that comes about through striving to reach a new plateau of experience. Such suffering merely marks the transition period of going from one level of accomplishment to a higher level.

All suffering is temporary. It will all pass away when Jesus Himself returns to the earth. Revelation 21:4 reads: "And God will wipe away every tear from their eyes; there shall be no more death, nor sorrow, nor crying; and there shall be no more pain, for the former things have passed away."

---

2. Will there ever be a cure for all diseases?

Remarkable advances in science have led to the cure of such dreaded diseases as polio and tuberculosis. But, because much of the disease and illness people experience is caused by sin and by ignoring principles of healthy living, there will never be a cure for *all* disease until Satan's power is done away with.

Our bodies are only a part of what makes us human beings. We also have souls and spirits.[4] The body is the physical part of our nature. The soul corresponds to the mind. The spirit is that part of us that set us apart from the animals, that stamps upon us the image of God. The spirit is the part of us that yearns for communion with God. If the spirit in us is not in tune with God, then you do not have access to the source of healing. If you lived in the perfect presence of God, there could be neither sickness nor death. There would not be infection or disease because such things cannot exist in the presence of God.

Some disease is caused directly by sin. Much sickness is the result of deep-rooted bitterness and uncontrolled stress. When people refuse to forgive or when they let themselves be "stressed out" by the pressures the world puts on them, that frequently leads to sickness.

Those who live harried and hurried lives frequently develop ulcers, arthritis, high blood pressure, asthma, and similar ailments. Alcohol and cigarettes are also great contributors to disease because they weaken the human body.

Another reason for disease is that much of the food we eat contains poison and unhealthy additives. Sugar and salt and white flour and other harmful substances weaken our bodies when used in excess. We do not get enough of the natural nutrients we should have. We try to milk too much out of our land, and, in doing so, we wind up damaging the crops we grow for food. When we eat what is contaminated, our bodies are harmed also.

There will never be a decrease in diseases until people learn to eat properly, exercise properly, treat their bodies properly, and stop ingesting chemicals and other foreign substances that hurt their bodies. Nor will disease decrease while people continue polluting the water and air with carcinogens and fighting wars that destroy vegetation, uproot whole nations, and bring about famine. All these things are contributors to disease—and disease, because of infection and contagion, has a way of growing.

Sickness and disease will be a part of life on this planet

until Jesus comes back. When He comes, He will set things properly in order, and there will be no more sickness and no more death.

That is the promise we have from God. In Revelation 22:2, we are told that the heavenly city of New Jerusalem will contain a tree whose leaves "were for the healing of the nations." We are reminded in Revelation 21:4 that when we dwell in the presence of God, "There will be no more death, nor sorrow, nor crying; and there shall be no more pain, for the former things have passed away."

Man, through his own efforts, will never find a cure for all diseases. But Jesus, when He returns to earth, will do away with disease and sickness forever.

---

3. Why is there evil in the world?

First of all, God does not cause evil. Evil is a result of two major forces: the first force is a being named *Satan*. There *is* a spiritual being who is the enemy of mankind. He is malevolent, very powerful, and he wants to destroy God, so he seeks to destroy men and women, who are made in the image of God.[5] Much of the trouble that is in the world is a direct result of the evil that Satan himself causes.

The second source of evil is the *human heart*. The old radio show "The Shadow" started out with this phrase: "Who knows what evil lurks in the hearts of men?" God knows that there is a great deal of evil lurking in men's hearts. Because of the evil in their hearts, they hurt one another; and we have war, crime, injustice, racism, and all sorts of pain and heartbreak.

There is evil, then, because of Satan and because of man's nature—and evil has a tendency to multiply itself. The more evil men there are, the more society as a whole begins to take on an evil nature. If God did not give men the chance to be evil, there would be no freedom. What would happen if every time a man cursed God his tongue rotted out? God could do that, but then He would be ruling the universe through fear. God is not a dictator. He wants men to choose to love and serve Him, and to do what is good. The other side of that choice is that men may decide not to serve God, and to do what is evil. Giving man the freedom to choose between good and evil has been God's policy since He created the first man, Adam.

Adam was what we call the "federal head" of mankind. Just as a decision by the president of our country can have an impact upon all the country's citizens, so the decision that Adam made affects all of humankind. We are all tainted by his original sin. When Adam disobeyed God, death came not only to humanity but also to the animals, the plants, and the earth as a whole. From that moment on, man has had to sweat and slave and strain to survive. The fall of Adam introduced pain and suffering into the world, as Genesis 3 details.

A few short generations after Adam, the Bible records that men had given themselves up almost entirely to evil.[6] That illustrates how fast evil spreads and how it progresses from generation to generation. The human race is linked together in such a way that we are able to draw upon the accumulated wisdom and blessings of those who have lived before us, but we also receive an inheritance from their curses and their evil.

In the beginning, Adam was morally in neutral. He was able to choose to sin—and he was able to choose not to sin. Adam's sin predisposed all of his descendants toward evil. Therefore, we all have a tendency that pulls us toward sin.

Although we have a predisposition toward sin and evil, we can turn away from sin and turn toward God. God wants us to resist evil. He is willing to help us in the battle. But it is a hard one. Even Jesus Christ Himself was genuinely tempted to sin.

It is indeed regrettable that there is evil in the world. The real news, though, is that there is a way to overcome evil. And that way is through the Son of God—Jesus Christ.

4. Will there ever be lasting world peace?

Absolutely! We will have lasting peace on earth when the Prince of Peace returns. Jesus Christ has told us, and the Bible assures us, that He will come back again. When He comes, several things are going to happen. First, the rebellion of man against God is going to be put down. For a thousand-year period, God will restrain the evil that is in man and will not allow nations to fight one another.[7] When that happens, men will take the tools of war and turn them into tools of peace. Isaiah 2:4 says that men will beat their swords into plowshares and their spears into pruning hooks, and that people will not learn war anymore. With Satan out of the way, and man restrained, there will finally be peace.

The Bible goes on to say:

> When the thousand years have expired, Satan will be released from his prison and will go out to deceive the nations which are in the four corners of the earth, Gog and Magog, to gather them together to battle, whose number is as the sand of the sea. They went up on the breadth of the earth and surrounded the camp of the saints and the beloved city. And fire came down from God out of heaven and devoured them.[8]

When this prophecy is fulfilled, when Satan's final rebellion is crushed, there will be permanent peace. God will put away, out of His kingdom forever, everything that offends. He will take Satan and his followers and put them permanently into a place of captivity. From that time forward, there will never again be war. Until the earthly reign of Jesus comes, however, men will continue to fight one another. Jesus said there will be "wars and rumors of wars" right up until the time of the end.[9]

There is no way that a United Nations, a League of Nations, peace treaties, disarmament treaties, or any other human instrument can bring about peace. Such things mean nothing when one nation desires the land and resources of another. A lasting peace will never be built upon man's efforts, because man is sinful, vicious, and wicked. Until men are changed and Satan's power is removed, there will not be peace on earth.

Until that day comes, all we can do is be strong enough to restrain the evil that is among us. To do anything other than that is utopian and based upon wishful thinking rather than upon reality.

---

5. Will man ever love his fellow man?

There will always be people who love their fellow man, people of good will who want to live in peace. Those who truly follow the Prince of Peace, Jesus Christ, always want to live in love and harmony with others.

Why, for instance, would any woman want to spend her life in the worst slums of India? Why would she want to devote herself to working among the poor, to giving them a home, and to making their lives easier to bear? Mother Teresa does all these things because she wants to follow Jesus Christ. She has His love in her heart, and that makes her want to reach out in love to the less fortunate.

There are hundreds and thousands of other examples, although Mother Teresa is probably the best known. When people allow Jesus to govern their actions, they stop fighting and start showing love for one another. That is the hope of the world.

Granted, there are people who are not Christian believers who strive for peace, and there are Christian believers still filled with selfishness and hate. But in the final analysis, outside of the love of Christ, there is no hope for true peace. Until those who make the world's decisions are followers of the Prince of Peace—and until Jesus Christ Himself returns to earth—there will never be true love among men. There will be rivalries, racial hatred, and difficulties of all kinds—and men will not love their fellow men as God would have them to do.

Remember, though, that Jesus Christ is coming back to reign on this earth. When He does come, assuming His rightful role as our king, men of every nation, race, and culture will be able to live side by side in perfect harmony. Not because they have been *forced* to do so, but because they have *accepted* Jesus Christ as their king and He has changed their hearts.

In Isaiah 11:6–9, we catch a glimpse of what the world will be like after Jesus returns:

> The wolf also shall dwell with the lamb, the leopard shall lie down with the young goat, the calf and the young lion and the fatling together; and a little child shall lead them. The cow and the bear shall graze; their young ones shall lie down together; and the lion shall eat straw like the ox. The nursing child shall play by the cobra's hole, and the weaned child shall put his hand in the viper's den. They shall not hurt nor destroy in all My holy mountain, for the earth shall be full of the knowledge of the LORD as the waters cover the sea.

In that day there not only will be lasting love and fellowship among the people of the earth but also, according to the prophet, among the animals as well!

---

6. When will the world end?

The Bible says that the time will come when God will create a new heaven and a new earth, where there will be no sin, no sorrow, no crime, no tears, no disease, no tragedy—none of the evils we know now.[10] This will be the beginning of a new order.

Before the new order comes, we must live out the present era. Before that age dawns, people from every nation must have had a chance to hear of the salvation offered through Jesus. Jesus said that "this gospel of the kingdom will be preached in all the world as a witness to all the nations, and then the end will come"[11]

As the end of the age nears, there will be an acceleration of evangelism and an increase in the numbers of those who are giving their lives to Jesus. At the same time, those who refuse to accept Christ will grow worse and worse in their wickedness. It will become increasingly difficult for the church and the world to coexist. But we will see the church grow enormously during this period.

Following this, God's judgment will come upon those who have rebelled against him. The Soviet leaders, for example, who have turned against Christians and Jews, and who have persecuted religious people for so many years, must receive God's judgment. People who have lied and robbed and cheated and stolen must pay for their evil deeds. Then, Jesus Christ will come back and establish His thousand-year reign of righteousness. This will be a transition period where we will see how this world would be if there had never been sin—if man had not fallen away from God and Satan had never gained a foothold in this world. We will see what it would be like if men lived together as brothers.

Even in the midst of Christ's reign, however, the seeds of rebellion will remain. Satan will still be able to find a foothold at the end of this thousand-year era of peace.[12] At this time, God will finally do away with the present earth to create a new heaven and a new earth.

Second Peter 3:10 says:

> the heavens will pass away with a great noise, and the elements will melt with fervent heat; both the earth and the works that are in it will be burned up.

Revelation 21:1 adds, "I saw a new heaven and a new earth, for the first heaven and the first earth had passed away."

God will cleanse the universe totally and take out of it everything that does wickedness and everything that rebels against Him, and from then on the righteous will shine like stars in the kingdom of their father forever.[13]

The question is still, "When will all this happen?" The answer is that the end of this world as we know it will be one thousand years after the present age comes to a conclusion with the return of Jesus Christ to earth. And I believe that Christ's return could be very soon. It could be in just twenty or thirty years.

We can never say for sure, because God has not allowed man to know the times and seasons.[14] We cannot say with absolute certainty that these are the last days of the age. But there are certain signs that have been given to us as a compass. The regathering of the people of Israel into a nation is probably the greatest prophetic sign. That has only been accomplished since 1948. Jesus said, "Jerusalem will be trampled by Gentiles until the times of the Gentiles are fulfilled."[15] This happened in 1967 when Israel obtained control over all of Jerusalem. With the fulfillment of that prophecy, it would seem that the end of this age is very close. The so-called "Gentile Age" is coming to its conclusion.

"The end of the age" does not refer to the world exploding or coming to an end. Someday the world will be destroyed, but that will not happen until after Christ has ruled on the earth for a thousand years.

Jesus told us that until He comes again to reign on earth, things will be just as they were in the days of Noah. He said:

> For as in the days before the flood, they were eating and drinking, marrying and giving in marriage, until the day that Noah entered the ark, and did not know until the flood came and took them all away, so also will the coming of the Son of Man be.[16]

In other words, human life as we know it is going to continue right up until the time Jesus Christ comes back again.

If we knew that Jesus were coming tonight or a thousand years from now, we should live our lives the same—as God's faithful servants. Jesus Himself warned us to "be ready, for the Son of Man is coming at an hour when you do not expect Him."[17]

7. What does the future hold for me and my family?

Your future depends on your relationship with God. For those who know Jesus Christ as Lord and Savior and who love God, the future looks very positive. First of all, there is going to be a tremendous spiritual awakening. It is described in Joel 2:28–32. It began on the day of Pentecost, but it will intensify as this present age draws to its conclusion. For people who are a part of this awakening, there will be prosperity and joy. God's people, Jews and Christians, will no longer be the butt of jokes by those who are in the world. For God's people, there is going to be security, peace, and tremendous prosperity.

For those who do not know the Lord, the future does not look very positive. The Bible speaks of a time of judgment on the ungodly. There will be wars, revolutions, economic failures—possibly even a terrible economic collapse in our worldwide monetary system. There will be an invasion of the nation of Israel by the Soviet Union, as described in Ezekiel 37–39.

We can expect wars in other parts of the world. Jesus said that there will be wars, rumors of wars, and earthquakes in many places.[18] There will be famines, and, sadly, many people will starve. Millions of people will be out of work, and there will be revolution and upheaval. None of this will lessen until God's final judgment comes.

The future depends on where you stand in relation to God. If you know the Lord and follow His principles, the future is very, very positive. If you do not know the Lord, the future looks very dangerous. To understand what it will be like, consider what happened in Egypt under the Pharaohs when Israel was being held in captivity. In that day, God sent a series of plagues upon Egypt. Even while the plagues were devastating Egypt, the land of Goshen—which was inhabited by God's people, the Israelites—was prosperous. The plagues did not affect the people of Israel, only the people of Egypt. When the first-born children of the Egyptians died, the Israelites were untouched.[19]

It is possible for one group of people to prosper while an entire society around them is literally being plagued with troubles. People who have forsaken God, who are rebelling against Him just as the Pharaoh of Egypt did, are going to be caught up in the plagues that God will send upon the world. The plagues are intended to bring about repentance, but if people will not repent, the plagues will destroy them. God said in Exodus 8:23 that He knew how to make a difference between His people and the rest of the world.

God will bless His people in whatever they do, as long as they understand and follow the biblically-based principles of the kingdom of God. They must be careful that they are not too closely linked up with the world's economic system. That is why people must be warned to avoid debt, because debt makes one's security as fragile as a house of cards. When an economy built upon consumer debt starts to fall, all those who are connected with it have a tendency to fall too. The go-go, debt-creating type of society that we have had for the last twenty-eight years is most fragile. Therefore, if people have things paid for and they are not in substantial debt, then when the world's house of cards begins to crumble, they do not have to worry about crumbling with it.

Christians must always be careful to follow God's leading, because what might be a superb opportunity today could turn into a terrible problem two years from now. If people are going to enjoy the prosperity that God sends them, they must be willing to obey Him and to be responsive to what His Spirit says.

The prosperity of God's people is already beginning. We see evidences of it all around the world. Every indication is that the world is on the brink of one of the greatest spiritual shiftings in history. The nations are getting ready, demonstrating a tremendous spiritual desire and hunger for God.

There are some who would withdraw from the world because they are afraid of the future or because they think the end of the world is near. No one should stop living because he is afraid of what might happen tomorrow. Young married couples may wonder if they should have children. Yes, there will be a place for your children in the world! Those who may be considering marriage may be frightened by what looks like a foreboding future. But there is no reason to be afraid to enter into a marriage relationship. At CBN we are training leaders for the future. We are looking for a happy future, and when we look at tomorrow, our attitude is that we assume the blessings of God and move ahead. Now, more than ever, in every move we make, we must have God's wisdom.

In summary, your future depends entirely upon your obedience to God. If you listen to the Lord, you can prosper. If you fail to listen to God and go your own stubborn way, then you are going to run into insurmountable problems.

It will be as described by the prophet Malachi. He says the day will come when:

> To you who fear My name the Sun of Righteousness shall arise with healing in His wings; and you shall go out and grow fat like stall-fed calves. You shall trample the wicked, for they shall be ashes under the soles of your feet.[20]

The best thing you can do, then, to prepare for the future, is to be sure you are in a proper relationship with God.

---

8. Is there life after death?

Yes! Emphatically, there is life after death for all people. How *you* will spend your life after death depends upon your relationship with God now. Jesus Christ said, "I am the resurrection and the life. He who believes in Me, though he may die, he shall live. And whoever lives and believes in Me shall never die."[21]

The whole message of Jesus Christ was that He broke the power of sin and death, because death was the consequence of sin. Jesus said, "Because I live, you will live also."[22]

That is hope of the world—the resurrection. The apostle Paul said:

> I also count all things loss for the excellence of the knowledge of Christ Jesus my Lord, for whom I have suffered the loss of all things, and count them as rubbish, that I may gain Christ . . . that I may know Him and the power of His resurrection . . . if, by any means, I may attain to the resurrection from the dead.[23]

Not only is there life after death, but God is going to give us new bodies, better than the ones we have now. We are not going to be disembodied spirits. Those who believe in Jesus are going to have bodies just like the resurrection body of Jesus.[24]

The Bible says that there will be a resurrection of the good and a resurrection of the evil. Some will arise to honor and some to shame.[25]

Those who have lived for God are going to have a body such as Jesus has—a glorious, wonderful body—and they will be with Him forever in glory. Those who have not lived for Him will be in a place of torment and punishment. Yes, there is life after death, but the quality of that life depends upon how we spend our days in this "life before life."

Often, the question arises whether a loving God could really send anyone to hell. Remember that God is always calling people to Himself. He sends signs such as the sun, the moon, the seasons, and harvest to show us that His love is there. He also sends out preachers, teachers, and evangelists to warn those who are living contrary to God's will and to encourage such people to come to Him. Remember, too, that for heaven to be heaven, those in heaven should not be forced to live with the fear of a second satanic rebellion and another cycle of pain, suffering, and death. The only way to eliminate that fear is to see that those who absolutely refuse God and who want no part of His kingdom are given their wishes. Such people do not want to be part of God's kingdom, and so God says, "Your will is to be apart from Me, and I am going to let you have it the way you want it."

Apart from God there is everlasting darkness. It is a horrible thing to contemplate, but it is not God's choice to send anyone out into that darkness. Instead, He reluctantly allows people to have what they have shown Him they want. The Bible talks about everlasting fire and eternal darkness when it describes hell.[26] Whether these are literal descriptions, or figures of speech describing the remorse and emotional pain the lost will suffer when they realize that they are separated from God forever, we don't know. We do know that hell is *real and forever!*

Over the last few years we have had many cases of people returning to life after being "clinically dead" for short periods. Many of them have seen heaven and some have been allowed to see hell. They have seen a living being whom they presume to be God. They have communicated with Jesus. Some have asked to come back to this life, and He has let them; others have asked to stay, and He has told them that they still have a work to do here in this life. For all of them, the experience has been a life-changing one, and this is a uniform testimony to the existence of life after death. Such experiences, of course, are not proof that there is life after death, but they stand as support to the Bible's statement that life continues beyond the grave.

The Bible is also clear in its teaching that we should not attempt to communicate with the dead. Leviticus 19:31 says: "Give no regard to mediums and familiar spirits; do not seek after them, to be defiled by them: I am the LORD your God." Isaiah 8:19 adds this: "And when they say to you, 'Seek those who are mediums and wizards, who whisper and mutter,' should not a people seek their God? Should they seek the dead on behalf of the living?"

When his baby son died, King David said, "I shall go to him, but he shall not return to me."[27] When we die we either go to heaven or hell. We will join those loved ones who have gone to the same place as we have. Until then, the living are forbidden to attempt contact with the dead. So-called ghosts, or spirits that speak through mediums, are really demons masquerading as the spirits of dead human beings.

If you let them, they will deceive you. They will try to lead you away from God, and—if they can gain a foothold in your life—they will do their very best to take control of you.

---

9. What is heaven like?

Heaven is where God is. He is the light of heaven, the joy of heaven. As you mature in your understanding of the Bible, you realize there is no material concept of heaven that will do it justice. The Bible talks about streets of gold as clear as crystal and walls made out of precious stones.[28] All sorts of images immediately come to mind when we mention heaven. More than anything else, heaven is a spiritual condition where one spiritual being is in touch with another spiritual being, and there is total communication and fellowship.

Whatever we consider to be a joy here on earth will be heightened millions of times beyond anything we can conceive when we get to heaven. The apostle Paul put it this way: "Eye has not seen, nor ear heard, nor have entered into the heart of man the things which God has prepared for those who love Him."[29]

In the Middle Ages philosophers talked about the "ultimate good." The ultimate good to them was being in the presence of God. That will be the greatest aspect of heaven. Those who are there will be in His immediate presence, in a way no one can possibly know this side of eternity.

Being in God's presence will bring an intensity of delight that will far exceed anything we could know here on earth. Furthermore, in heaven there will be neither death, nor sorrow, nor sickness, nor poverty.

> He will dwell with them, and they shall be His people, and God Himself will be with them and be their God. And God will wipe away every tear from their eyes; there shall be no more death, nor sorrow, nor crying; and there shall be no more pain, for the former things have passed away.[30]

The Bible also talks about crowns and thrones in heaven, so we do know that heaven is not just a huge democracy where there is no differentiation of function.[31] There will be different functions and different levels of responsibility assigned to different people. For there will still be levels of order and structure throughout God's universe.

The Bible says that those human beings who are fortunate enough to enter into heaven will actually judge angels.[32] The fallen angels—or demons—will come before us and we will decide their fates. Perhaps people will be assigned to watch over a planet or two. We do not know for certain what tasks we will be performing in heaven, but there will obviously be an ongoing, functioning universe. We will be God's messenger-agents in ordering and running it.

There are many things about heaven we do not really know. Will there be animals in heaven? The Bible says that Jesus will be riding on a white horse when He returns to reign on the earth, but we do not know if this is a literal horse.[33] A white horse represents purity and power, so this may be symbolic. We cannot say for sure if there will be animals of any kind in heaven, but I believe there will be.

We do know that we will be able to recognize our loved ones in heaven, and we will experience great joy over being reunited with them.[34] Your real self will live on in heaven, not some shadowy part of you. You will never feel so *alive* as when you enter into the heavenly city, the New Jerusalem God has prepared for the saints.

There is also going to be an extension of man's mind beyond anything we could begin to understand now. There will be an opening of understanding into the secrets and mysteries of the universe. Furthermore, in heaven there will be no fear of any kind of evil, and God will provide magnificently for His people.

What is heaven like? It is better than anything any human being could ever imagine when he tries to picture the best thing that could ever happen to him. Beyond that, there is not much else we could say!

10. How can I be a better person?

The only way we can truly be better people is to give our hearts to God, because every good work a man does by himself is tainted with pride and self-will. The Bible says, "There is none who does good, no, not one."[35] This seems to be a rather dismal view of humanity, but that is the way it is. Unconverted man may try to do better, but he is ultimately doomed to failure. Think, for instance, about how many people resolve every New Year's Day to turn over a new leaf.

The Bible says no one can become worthy of God's blessings through trying to be better, whether you try by going on religious pilgrimages, getting involved in social work or church work or doing any other type of good work for mankind. Ephesians 2:8–9 reads, "For by grace you have been saved through faith, and that not of yourselves; it is the gift of God, not of works, lest anyone should boast."

You can gloss over some of the evil tendencies in your heart by attempting to control them, but inside, the heart of man is "deceitful and desperately wicked."[36] If the heart is against God, there is only one way that a person can truly become better—and that is by surrendering the heart to Jesus.

If you want to be a better person, you must be joined to Jesus. You must have the attitude that "I am going to come to You, Lord, and I am going to accept Your salvation by faith. Not because I am better or have improved myself. But I am going to come to You in faith and let You be my Savior and wash me of all the things I've done that are wrong."

When that happens it is as if God says, "I am going to acquit you of all your sins. I am going to treat you as if you are absolutely perfect, because you have been forgiven by the sacrifice and death of Jesus. He has become your substitute." Galatians 2:16 says, "A man is not justified by the works of the law but by faith in Jesus Christ." And in

Romans 8:1, we find that "there is therefore now no condemnation to those who are in Christ Jesus."

When you turn your life over to Jesus, you are not just a better person, but you are identified with a perfect Person—One who never sinned. At that point, you ask Jesus to be the Lord of your life, so He is not just the Savior but the Lord too. When He comes in and begins to place His Spirit inside you, you will be transformed into a new creature.

Perhaps the change will not come rapidly, but it *will* come, as you are yielded to Jesus. This is the experience where, little by little, you begin to walk with Him, and you begin to do good to others because of Him. You truly have become a good person. Why? Because Jesus is living in and working through you. You have died to yourself, and you are allowing Jesus to live His life through you.[37]

When you have Jesus in your heart, He is living through you. That means that He is loving through you, keeping God's commandments through you, and perfecting you. In an ongoing process, you are becoming a better person. More than better, in fact; you are becoming a holy person, because Jesus Christ is forming Himself in you.

When you come to Jesus Christ, having settled the ultimate questions of sin and salvation, several things happen to you. First, you no longer have to compete against other people. You can begin to rest in God and love your fellow man because you are experiencing the love and forgiveness of God. Secondly, you begin to have hope. You know that you are now part of the family of God and that He is taking care of you. Since your hopes now rest on Him, you become freer to reach out and help other people. Instead of struggling for your own survival, you are filled with the benevolent instinct that the Lord has for the less fortunate. People who have this freedom from selfishness begin to be better citizens in their communities.

Another thing that has happened is that the tendency to break the law has been taken away. God has given you a new nature. The Bible says, "If anyone is in Christ, he is a new creation; old things have passed away; behold, all things have become new."[38]

You no longer have to drink, take drugs, or smoke cigarettes. You do not have to eat too much. You do not have to hurt your body or hurt anyone else. You are free from compulsions because the Lord has made you free.

There is also the whole area of fear, psychosomatic problems, hatred, and petty bitterness. The Lord will take those things away from us if we let Him. He is more than able to cleanse you of despair, depression, and discouragement. Things that weigh heavily on your heart can be swept away in the light of Christ's love if you will turn them over to Him. In this way, you can be a better person. You can be happier and more productive because you are not being chained down to things that will destroy you.

There are Christians, of course, who live far beneath their privileges. They do not realize what Christ has done for them. Consequently, they allow discouragement to overcome them.

The Lord does not say He is going to make us into little gods who are impervious to problems. What He does say is that He will give us the weapons and ammunition to overcome problems. The weapons will not do us a bit of good if we refuse to use them. Even Christians can be overcome by problems if they let it happen. You can give in to discouragement or jealousy or any other unwholesome emotion. But you no longer *have* to give in. It is up to you.

For proof that victory over life's troubles comes through Jesus Christ, just take a look around. Everywhere you look you will see Christian churches full of people talking openly about God's grace. Many of them have come out of literal prisons to serve the Lord. Others have come out of prisons of their own making—prisons of fear, anger, and depression—to serve Him.

The reality of God's salvation can be seen on their faces and read in the stories of their lives. Men and women who hated are filled with love. Those who were always afraid are now walking in courage. Other who were always depressed now radiate peace and joy.

There is still more evidence. Consider those who have undergone physical changes because of the Lord's touch.

Some were dying of cancer; some were told they would never walk again; others were suffering from a variety of painful and incapacitating illnesses. The Lord brought them salvation and much, much more.

The evidences are overwhelming. Jesus Christ is exactly who He said He is—the Son of God. He will do exactly what He said He would—reach out to you with His love, granting you assurance of life at its fullest, beginning now and lasting throughout eternity. The only way you will ever determine if all this is true is to find out for yourself. If you have not done so already, ask Jesus to take over your life. In your own words, just surrender control to Him and tell Him you are sorry for the sins you have committed. Tell Him that you resolve to do things His way from now on and that you will turn away from your sins with His help. Then commit yourself to following Him wherever He may lead you.

Once you try things His way, you will know the reality of His love and will understand that you have truly become a better person. Beyond that, you will know that all of your questions, whatever they may be, really have only one answer. That answer is the Person—Jesus Christ.

Scripture References

1 John 15:20
2 See Mark 6:25–28
3 Matthew 7:7–8
4 See 1 Thessalonians 5:23
5 See Genesis 1:26
6 See Genesis 6:5
7 See Revelation 20:3–6
8 Revelation 20:7–9
9 See Matthew 24:6
10 See Revelation 21:1–5
11 Matthew 24:14
12 See Revelation 20:7–10
13 See Daniel 12:3
14 See Matthew 24:36, Mark 13:32
15 Luke 21:24
16 Matthew 24:37–39
17 Matthew 24:44
18 See Matthew 24:6, Mark 13:7
19 See Exodus 12
20 Malachi 4:2–3
21 John 11:25–26
22 John 14:19
23 Philippians 3:8–11
24 See 1 Corinthians 15:35–49
25 See Daniel 12:2–3, Matthew 25:46, Revelation 20:11–15
26 See Matthew 8:12, 25:41
27 2 Samuel 12:23
28 See Revelation 21:18–21

29 1 Corinthians 2:9
30 Revelation 21:3–4
31 See Revelation 4:4–11
32 See 1 Corinthians 6:3
33 See Revelation 19:11
34 See Luke 23:42–43, Hebrews 12:22–23
35 Psalm 14:3
36 Jeremiah 17:9
37 See Galatians 2:20
38 2 Corinthians 5:17

2. The Nature of God

1. What is God Like?

Theologians have tried to describe God in many ways. He is the substance of all human virtues. He is all-wise and all-knowing. He can do anything and everything we cannot do, and He is everything good that we would like to be. So we say that He is *omnipotent* (all-powerful) or *omniscient* (all-knowing) or *omnipresent* (present everywhere).

On the other hand, we can describe God by contrasting Him with our human limitations. For example, we are mortal, but God is immortal. We are fallible, but God is infallible.

God is a Spirit: eternal and ever-living. He has no beginning or end. He is a Person who is totally self-aware—"I am"—totally moral—"I ought"—and totally self-assertive—"I will." He is the essence of love, and He is loving. He is also a righteous judge—totally fair and just.

God is the Father of all creation, the Creator of all. He is all powerful and sustains the universe. He exists outside the universe (Theologians call this *transcendence*.), yet He is present throughout the universe (Theologians say He is *immanent*.) and is its ruler. He exists in nature, but He is not nature, nor is He bound by the laws of nature as the pantheists assert. He is the source of all life and everything that is.[1]

The best description of God is the name that He gave for Himself to the early Israelites, *Yahweh*.[2] *Yahweh* is usually translated Jehovah or LORD. Scholars believe that this is the *hiphil* tense of the Hebrew verb "to be" and literally means "He who [causes everything] else to be."

---

2. Is Jesus God?

Yes. The Bible says that He is the image—the mirror likeness—of the invisible God.[3] The apostle John put it this way, "In the beginning was the Word, and the Word was with God, and the Word was God."[4] Jesus Christ is the second Person of the Triune God. He is the eternal Son of God who assumed human flesh in the womb of Mary and became man. But He is Himself God as well—at once fully God and fully man. He is eternal. He is omnipresent. He is omniscient. He has all the divine attributes of God the Father; yet He fully shared in our humanity, except for sin.

He is eternal. He is omnipresent. He is omniscient. He has all the attributes that God the Father and God the Holy Spirit have, and He Himself is God.

---

3. How can there be a Trinity, a three-in-one God?

The Trinity is one of the great theological mysteries. There are some who think that because we believe in monotheism, one God, we cannot accept the concept of the Trinity. Yet the Bible teaches that the Godhead consists of three divine Persons—Father, Son, and Holy Spirit—each fully God, each showing fully the divine nature.[5]

The Father is the fountainhead of the Trinity, the Creator, the first cause. He is the primary thought, the concept of all that has been and will be created. Jesus said, "My Father has been working until now, and I have been working."[6]

The Son is the "Logos" or expression of God—the "only begotten" of the Father. If you want to know what the Father is like, look at the Son. In John 14:9, Jesus said, "He that has seen me has seen the Father." The Son of God is the agent of creation and our redeemer.

The Holy Spirit, the third Person of the Trinity, proceeds from the Father and is worshiped and glorified together with the Father and Son.

The Father, as prime mover, brings forth the creative thought. The Son, as agent of creation, expresses that thought. The Spirit activates the creative word and relates it to that which is created. He inspired the Scriptures and empowers God's people. He takes the things of Jesus and brings them to our remembrance. John 16:8 tells us that He convicts the world "of sin, and of righteousness, and of judgment."

All three Persons of the Godhead are eternal. The Father exists and has existed forever. With Him always existed His expression, the Son. Always the Father loved the Son, and the Son loved and served the Father. From that relationship of love arose the Spirit of God, who is eternal and has existed forever. There was, therefore, not a time when there was only the Father, then later the Son, and still later the Spirit. They all three have existed from before there was anything that could begin—three distinct Persons all functioning as One.

There are trinities in nature. Light can be divided into three primary colors; yet light is one. A prism will reveal the individual colors separately that are unique yet unified. An example of a trinity in nature which is sometimes given erroneously to explain the Trinity is the transformation of water to steam or to ice. The problem with this illustration is that water becomes either steam or ice, but does not at the same time remain water. This type of thinking leads to a heresy called *modalistic monarchianism*, which maintains that the Father changes into the Son or into the Spirit—different modes of the same being but never the three beings at one time.

Upon the occasion of Jesus' baptism, however, all three persons in the Trinity were present and active. The Father spoke from heaven, the Son was fulfilling all righteousness, and the Spirit descended upon the Son like a dove.[7]

The existence of the Trinity is a mystery that one day we will understand clearly. For now, we know that the Bible teaches it and Jesus revealed it, and the Christian church from the beginning has confessed and safeguarded this precious truth.

---

4. If God is all-powerful, why doesn't He destroy Satan?

God's government rests on love. The moral foundation of the universe is based on reason, love, and justice. If God ever chose to act arbitrarily and exercise superior force, there would be a danger that He would have to rule by fear, rather than love. What He wants are people who love and serve Him voluntarily, not merely because they are afraid of Him. When God allows Satan a certain amount of leeway, He is permitting the exercise of free will on the part of one of His created beings. He is carrying forth a drama on earth that is cosmic in nature, whereby men and women, created in the image of God, freely choose to serve Him.

If God just reached out with His power and struck Satan, other created beings could say He did it because He could not win by love, and so He had to resort to force and fear.

God's plan for the triumph of love over hate is breathtaking. God placed on earth a being—man—who was made in God's image. Then He permitted Satan to tempt man, and man gave in to bring about his own downfall. Then before all of the angels in heaven, there unfolded the drama of redemption whereby God Himself sent His Son to die for fallen man. The church began to grow out of the multitudes who chose freely to follow God's love rather than to participate in Satan's rebellion.

The time will come when God has assembled a body of people who freely love Him, which will prove beyond any doubt that love is the most powerful force in the universe. With the triumph of love complete, God will then deal with Satan.

First, God will put Satan in a place where he cannot escape for a thousand years (see page 376).[8] Then God will demonstrate how beautiful the world would be without Satan. At the end of that time, Satan is going to be set free, will deceive the nations again, and will be defeated totally. Then God will cast him into eternal torment.

Satan is a tool of God's love in the sense that he forces us to see God's loving patience.[9] People would have a harder time understanding the love of God without the obvious evil and hatred of His enemy. But God did not cause Satan to rebel just so we could have a better picture of His love. Satan sinned willingly because of pride. He thought his wisdom exceeded that of God's.[10] We must always remember that the devil and God are not coequal.[11] The devil is a creation of God, and God can do with him whatever He pleases.[12]

---

5. How can I know that God is real?

People can know the reality of love, but science cannot prove love. People can know the reality of God, but not through scientific research.

But what can be known about God—His eternal power and deity—can be understood by everyone because God has revealed it within them.[13] In other words, God has given mankind the ability to learn about Him from His creation, and to some He has given a special revelation of Himself through apostles, prophets, and Jesus Christ Himself.

We can deduce clearly from all the created things that there has to be a Creator. Someone said that the chance of man's being an accident is 'about as reasonable as walking into a scrap-iron yard, finding a Boeing 747 jetliner, and saying, "Look how those pieces of iron flew accidentally together and formed that airplane." We are very, very complicated. For example, the neurons and nerve paths from each human eye to the human brain number some five hundred thousand. There is just no way that could happen by accident.

As we see the sunsets, the regularity of the seasons, the laws of nature, we are drawn to the fact that there has to be an intelligence behind all of it. The Bible goes on to say that people suppress the truth, because their deeds are evil.[14] They do not want to believe what is clearly shown to them.

God also reveals Himself through special revelation: the Bible. Prophets of God who have walked with Him have had special revelations. They have written these down over many years to form the book we call the Bible.

Finally, the supreme revelation of God is Jesus Christ Himself. Jesus was God come to earth. He came in fulfillment of two thousand years of Jewish history, and His coming was precisely as foretold by the prophets. He came among us and showed us what God is like, so we could know Him better. As He told His disciple Philip, "He who has seen Me has seen the Father."[15]

To sum things up, we can know God from the general revelation of creation, and we can know Him from the special revelation of those who have known Him—and especially from the life and words of Jesus Himself.

People who say there is no God must realize that atheism takes a great deal more faith than does belief in God. Faith in God simply makes more sense! When you consider scientific theories regarding the beginning of the cosmos, you are struck with the fact that there have been at least ten major "cosmogonies" during the last two hundred years. Man is continuously changing his theory of how it all came to be. As our knowledge expands, we shift and shift and shift. But so far, no one has ever come up with anything better than the biblical account that there is a creator God who, in the beginning, made all that is.

Scripture References

1 For biblical references on the character and nature of God, see Deuteronomy 7:6–8, Psalm 147:5, Isaiah 43:3, 66:1, Jeremiah 32:17, John 4:24,
   Hebrews 1:3, and 1 John 4:9
2 See Exodus 3:13–14
3 See Colossians 1:15
4 John 1:1
5 See Matthew 3:16–17
6 John 5:17
7 See Matthew 3:16–17, Mark 1:9–11, Luke 3:21–22
8 See Revelation 20:2–3
9 See 1 Timothy 1:18–20, 1 Corinthians 5:3–5
10 See Isaiah 14:12–15, 1 Timothy 3:6
11 See Ezekiel 28:13–19
12 See Revelation 20:7–10
13 See Romans 1:18–20, 2:14–15
14 See Romans 1:18–21
15 John 14:9

3. The Nature of Man

---

1. Where did man come from?

The Bible tells us that God Himself is man's Creator. God said, "Let Us make man in Our image."[1] This meant that He was going to create a spiritual being, for God is a spirit; that He would create a moral being, because God is a moral being; and that He would create a rational being—someone who had a mind and could think. That much we know. Just how the human body, for example, or the human brain images God, we do not yet know.

The Bible tells us that God took a handful of dust (which speaks of the earth), and He breathed life into it (which speaks of spirit), and "man became a living soul [*nephesh*]."[2] Thus, the merger of the spiritual with the physical elements of the earth created a human soul, made in the image of God.

Man is therefore the only creature we know of, other than the angels themselves, who has the ability to relate to God and to worship Him. You do not find horses and cattle

309

on their knees praying for wisdom and guidance! Yet man not only prays but builds churches and cathedrals in which to worship God. God gave that desire to man. We were made with the precious nature of God, in the image of God, by God Himself.

---

2. What is man like?

Man was created in God's image and has a spirit, which the Bible often speaks of as the heart.[3] He has a soul, which is essentially his sense of self, the center of which would be the mind. And he has a body, which holds it all together. Human beings are made up of body, soul, and spirit. God intended that the spirit of man be continuously in touch with the Spirit of God. The spirit, in turn, is supposed to radiate through the mind and the body to the outside world.

The problem we are facing today is that most people are directed instead by external stimuli that come to us through the bodily senses. So the body begins to be the controlling factor through gluttony, sex, pride, or whatever. Because the body controls the soul, the soul is able to conceive of schemes to make the body happy. And the end result is that the spirit of man is submerged by self-ishness.

The spirit of the first man was like a mirror, reflecting the glory of God. He had the *imago dei*, "the image of God," clearly within him. Because God was personally revealed to him, God's way was uppermost. But when man sinned, his inner mirror was clouded or darkened. He could no longer see God clearly. As a result, instead of being directed by God's Spirit, people are manipulated by their bodies or their minds toward evil. In Genesis we read, "The imagination of man's heart is evil from his youth."[4]

When man was created, he had the capacity to serve God, and doing that came naturally because he was in the presence of God.

As long as man's spirit functions as it should, serving God is natural, so man tends toward good. But once he is removed from God, self-preservation becomes more important; and man will kill, lie, cheat, and hurt others in order to preserve his self-esteem, his self-image, and his life. Humans have a tremendous capacity for good or evil because they are made in the image of God. Man can do more good, but also more damage, than any animal because man has a godlike capacity.

Theologians have a saying that Adam in the Garden of Eden was *posse non peccare* (able not to sin), and if he had continued in that, he would have come to the point where he was *non posse peccare* (not able to sin). He would have become so established in righteousness that he would not have been able to sin. From then on he would have been transformed to ever higher righteousness. But instead, he fell, and as a result became evil.

That is why Jesus said that every man or woman had to be born from above, or "born again," in order to see God's kingdom.[5]

Man's spirit has to be restored by being cleansed from sin by Jesus Christ, then created anew by operation of God's Spirit. With his own spirit under the control of God's Spirit, the remainder of man's being—soul and body—would be controlled from within instead of from without.

---

3. Were Adam and Eve real, or is the story of the Garden of Eden just a fairy tale?

I believe it is real. It is as good an explanation of what happened as there could be. The word *Adam* means "red" or "of the earth." It also is a generic term for *man*. It does not offend my reason to think there was one original couple that God made, and that from this couple came all the other people on the earth. Nor would my faith be shattered if one day I learned that this story was an allegorical description of God's creation of man.

These original humans were not subhuman or Neanderthal creatures. They were beautiful human beings, created in the image of God, with tremendous intelligence and ability. If man has gone away from that, he has gone down instead of up.

Some people may ask where the Garden of Eden was. The Bible says that it was to the east (of Israel) and mentions four rivers relative to it: the Pishon, the Gihon, the Tigris, and the Euphrates.[6] These meager references would place the garden somewhere around modern Iraq or possibly northern Syria.

Ancient Chinese culture may refer to Eden. The written Chinese language symbol for west means two people in a garden. This character dates back at least three thousand years. If a Chinese person were asked to explain the word *west*, he would have to say, "Well, that is where two people lived in a garden." The existence of this remarkable symbol would indicate a pre-Christian tradition that the people who populated China came from the west, perhaps someplace in the Tigris-Euphrates valley, and that the early Chinese ancestors were familiar with the story of the first couple living in a garden—possibly the Garden of Eden.

---

4. Where did all the races come from?

According to the book of Genesis, the races all came from Noah. The human race started with Adam and Eve and grew evil very quickly. Pretty soon, "Every intent of the thoughts of his heart was only evil continually."[7] When God looked at the earth He saw violence. The earth had become a terrible place to live, because lust for self-preservation had grown so strong that in order to eat and find a mate and protect their families, men were killing each other. So God said He was going to destroy all the people and start a new race with Noah and his sons.[8] God did this by bringing a great flood upon the earth. After the flood there were Noah and his wife and their three sons, Shem, Ham, and Japheth, and their wives.

Ham became the father of the Egyptians, the Ethiopians, and the other black races, as well as the Canaanites who once lived in the land now occupied by Israel.

Japheth was the father of the Greeks, the people who lived in the islands of the sea and who settled Europe and Russia.

Shem was the father of the Semitic people—the Jews, Arabs, and Persians.

---

5. What is original sin?

Original sin is a theological term that goes back to the fall of man. As I said before, man was created in God's image, righteous and free. He was a free moral agent, freely able to choose God or turn away from Him. By eating the fruit of the tree of the knowledge of good and evil, he did the one thing he was asked not to do. Breaking God's one commandment to him was sin. At that point he was driven from the Garden of Eden and cut off from the tree of life.[9]

From that moment on, the spirit of man was damaged. It is as if man is now born with a moral handicap. He is lame in the most important part of his being—his spirit.

That is original sin. The Bible says, "They go astray as soon as they are born, speaking lies."[10] There is a rebellious nature in most children. They just like to do whatever you tell them not to do. This natural rebellion stems from man's original sin. Instead of being morally free, man has a decided tendency toward sin—urged on toward evil by what is called "the world, the flesh, and the devil."

Only those who come to Jesus can be rid of this tendency. That is the whole concept of being born again. Our spirits are re-created. Our spirits are now joined with God's Spirit, and we have the ability to live a godly, holy life in Jesus Christ. On our own, we simply cannot do it. The apostle Paul says, "O wretched man that I am! Who will deliver me from this body of death?"[11] He says, the thing that I want to do, I cannot do. The good I would do, I cannot do, whereas evil lies close at hand.[12]

Paul struggled against his fallen nature until he realized that "There is therefore now no condemnation to those who are in Christ Jesus, who do not walk according to the flesh, but according to the Spirit" (Rom. 8:1). He also said, "The law of the Spirit of life in Christ Jesus has made me free from the law of sin and death."[13] The renewal and change in Jesus Christ can free people from the bondage of original sin.

We should keep in mind that original sin is a tendency to do evil, not an act of evil. Guilt comes when we commit acts of evil. There is no such thing as "original guilt." God does not punish people for tendencies, only for what they do in light of what they know. Therefore, little babies do not go to hell because of original sin, because babies have never committed any sinful acts.

---

6. How can I have free will if God knows everything in advance?

This is another question that theologians have wrestled with for years. The Bible tells us definitely that God knows everything. Furthermore we are told that God has planned (or predestined) certain things. We were chosen in Christ from the foundation of the earth.[14] So if God knows everything, and He also has the ability to control everything, then how, indeed, can we have free will? Doesn't God have to work it all out in advance? The answer to that is no.

His foreknowledge could be likened to a motion picture. If we watch a movie we see the frames in sequence, so it looks as if Act 2 follows Act 1 and Act 3 follows Act 2. We see what looks like consecutive action. But if you were to take that same piece of film and hang it up on the wall, you could see the end, the beginning, and the middle all at once. You really would not have to control the action in order to see what was going to happen. In an imperfect sense this illustrates how God's foreknowledge and our free will can coexist.

Yet there are dimensions of life that are beyond our understanding. The concept of predestination and fore-knowledge, as opposed to free will, makes up one of those dimensions. If we say, "Well, it is all up to man," then we err, because that is not the case. If, on the other hand, we say, "It does not matter what we do, because God has prearranged it all anyhow," we are wrong.

There seems to be a tension between two ostensibly irreconcilable points: the free will of man, and the fore-knowledge and predestination of God. Our theology is lop-sided if we fail to include the reality of free will and predes-tination together.

The way I like to look at it is as if you have a basketball game consisting of visible and invisible players. The ones who make the points are the visible players, and yet the invisible ones are there feeding the ball and strategy to the visible players. Assume that the invisible players could act and interact with the visible players, or at least they could whisper signals and directions over the shoulders of the visible players.

In this illustration, the invisible players would be con-trolling the action. But from all an onlooker could see, the visible players are in charge of the entire game. In this analogy, the visible players represent man's free will, while the invisible players represent God's Spirit, angels, and demons. Visible and invisible are working and interac-ting together. There is not some timeless, immutable de-cree from God that governs man, but constant, loving help and direction from Him as well as hindrance from the enemy.

We will understand the full mystery when we know God better.

7. What is predestination?

Predestination is a term that refers to God's determination in advance that something will happen in accordance with His fixed purpose. Although the noun *predestination* is never used in Scripture the verb *predestinate* is used four times (Romans 8:29, 30, Ephesians 1:5, 11) and refers to God's determination that the Christian will be blessed as a result of salvation. God's choice of individuals who would be saved is referred to by the word *election*.

Two seemingly opposite concepts are involved in the idea of predestination and election. First, God, who is sovereign in the universe, is in complete control of human events and the lives of individuals. If that were not so, He would not be sovereign, and, thus, would not be God. Second, God has given people a freedom of choice to do as they will. We are accountable for our own actions and nobody can say, "When I sinned, I just did what God wanted me to do, and so why is He holding me accountable for it?"

Scholars have struggled with these seemingly opposed concepts for centuries, and two major views of predestination have developed. Calvinism holds that God offers irresistible grace to those whom He elects to save. If you are among the elect, you cannot say "no" to God. Arminianism, on the other hand, holds that God's grace is the source of redemption, but it can be resisted. In Calvinism, God has chosen the believer; in Arminianism, the believer has chosen God.

The apostle Paul, in explaining the obstinate refusal of Israel to accept the gospel of Jesus Christ, could have given a synthesis of predestination and free will that appeals to human reason and fairness. Instead, he said, "God has mercy on whom He wants to have mercy, and He hardens whom He wants to harden" (Romans 9:18). Then he described Pharaoh, King of Egypt, about whom the Bible says, God hardened his heart.[15] We must remember, however, that sunlight hardens clay and melts wax. It all depends on the substance being dealt with. If Pharaoh's heart had been tender, God's power would have softened it, not hardened it. Therefore, the concept of predestination and election is never an excuse to sin; as the apostle concludes, "O the depth of the riches of the wisdom and knowledge of God! How unsearchable are His judgments and His paths beyond finding out" (Romans 11:33).

---

8. Does the Bible teach evolution?

To answer this question we must first define evolution. To the scientist the theory of evolution customarily means a process by which the whole universe came about through a progression of interrelated phenomena. In biology or zoology the theory of evolution supposes that existing animals and plants have their origins in simpler forms that have been progressively modified through successive generations over extended periods of time. Scientific evolution eliminates belief in God or special creation and ascribes the origins of all life to the action of random chemical and physical forces.

The Bible does not teach random evolution. The Bible does teach an act of creation by God of a universe out of a formless void, and then individual acts of creation in an ascending order from the simpler forms of aquatic life to the mammals and finally to a creature made in God's image—man.[16] Human beings did not evolve out of the primordial ooze. They are the special creation of an all-powerful God.[17]

Therefore, it can be said that the Bible teaches "creation in ascending order." When the scientists discover the ascending order of the plants and animals on earth, their factual observations are generally in harmony with the Bible. The scientists go wrong, however, when they attempt to draw theological theories of origins from their findings.

The ascending order of living creatures is an observable fact. Apart from the Bible or the revelation of God, the source of their origin is unknown and scientific speculation about their origin can only be theory—never fact.

However, one major empirical fact negates the theory of scientific evolution. There has never been one observable case of any creature shifting (or evolving) from one biological class to another or from one phylum to another. There is no case where we have remains or fossils of an animal that died during the evolutionary process. The reason is clear. The Bible says that God made each animal "after its kind" through a special act of creation for each one of them.

I think the great example of this truth is the mule. The mule is a cross between a donkey and a horse. Mules are born sterile. They are unable to reproduce themselves. In other words, the horse and the donkey were close enough in the biological ladder to interbreed with each other, but their offspring could not continue the breeding process. Even that close link could not reproduce. Certainly nobody has ever bred a bird with a snake or an ape with a man. There is no reproductive evidence to support evolution.

---

9. Where do people go when they die?

Their bodies usually go into the ground, and they go back to the dust from whence they came. The spirit of man, on the other hand, goes into an everlasting state, because spirits are immortal and cannot die. As I understand the Bible, at death those who are Christians go to be with the Lord, to a place of bliss called paradise. Those who are not Christians go to a place of suffering and torment called hell. They wait there for a final judgment, while those who are dead in Christ wait for their final rewards.

The Bible does not teach soul sleep. For example, Jesus told about a rich man and a beggar named Lazarus.[18] When he died, the beggar went to a place called Abraham's bosom, where he was comforted by the patriarch Abraham and other Old Testament saints. When the rich man died he went to hell, or Hades. He asked Lazarus to come over and give him just a few drops of water, saying he was tormented in the flames. In this story we note that both men were conscious. They knew their own identity, and they recognized other people as well.

There was also some kind of torment. Since fire does not hurt spirits, it is possible that the fire may be symbolic.[19] It could be the fire of remorse, of thinking what could have been, yet was missed. Hell is also pictured as outer darkness, where there is loneliness and weeping and gnashing of teeth.[20] There are other references to a lake of fire.[21] Whatever hell is, it consists of eternal and unending anguish apart from God and all that is good.

10. Is reincarnation taught in the Bible?

Definitely not.

Reincarnation is an Eastern concept that speaks of the transmigration of the human soul. In certain cultures it is believed that the souls of those who die come back as dung beetles, or as the rain or the dew. In Nepal they teach that evil men come back as dogs, so they beat the dogs unmercifully. In India cows, rats, and grasshoppers are viewed as people who have been reincarnated.

The overarching concept of reincarnation comes from the Hindu belief that life and death make up an eternal wheel. Each individual is attached to the wheel, and attached to each individual is a *karma*, or fate. People supposedly purge their karmas by successive incarnations. There is no end, only bad incarnations or possibly good incarnations. There is no understanding, no rules, no reason; just mindless fate and hopeless attempts at the cleansing of guilt.

The Bible does not teach this at all. The Bible says, "It is appointed for men to die once, but after this the judgment."[22] In the story of the rich man and Lazarus, when the rich man died, he went to Hades. When Lazarus died, he went to paradise, called by the Bible "Abraham's bosom." There was no thought of coming back.

When Jesus Christ was on the Mount of Transfiguration, He met with Moses and Elijah and He talked with them.[23] Moses had been dead for years, but he was still Moses. Moses did not come back as King Tut or Marie Antoinette. Moses was Moses. He never lost his identity. The Bible teaches that when you are born you have the identity you will have for all eternity.[24]

You are never going to lose that identity. You are absolutely accountable for what you do in this life. There is no second chance and no opportunity to come back and purge yourself of the sins and wrongs you have done. Reincarnation vitiates the major teachings of Christianity about responsibility and judgment.

There are those who claim that reincarnation is a Christian concept, but it is not. It is a Hindu concept that has been totally discredited. It gives people a false hope, a false expectation, or a false despair—false because thinking about what awaits you in the next life makes it very hard to bring about any kind of moral reformation in this one. When you have this concept of karma (The same thought is found in the Mohammedan concept of kismet.), then you say, "Well, these people are the lower classes and that is their karma." You do not have to worry about feeding them, educating them, uplifting them, because they have that karma. They are where they belong. You will never find social justice and social progress in countries where the doctrine of reincarnation has a strong hold.

In comparison, the Bible says we are responsible for our brothers. We must be kind and good to the poor and the needy. The Bible teaches that all people are beloved by God and that they all have an equal chance, but the chance lasts only during this lifetime.

11. What does the Bible say about how long people should live on earth?

The psalmist said that our days on earth "are seventy years; and if by reason of strength they are eighty years, yet their boast is only labor and sorrow."[25] So man, according to the Psalms, has seventy years, and sometimes by reason of strength, eighty years or more. Now that is the average for modern man. But if you go back to the days of the patriarchs in Israel, one hundred thirty, one hundred forty or one hundred fifty years was not uncommon. If you go all the way back to the days just following creation, men lived nine hundred years or more. I wonder if, when the Millennium comes and there is no more sin on earth, people will once again live two hundred or three hundred years, or even longer.

12. What is God's purpose for man?

If you go back to Genesis, you find God telling men to "be fruitful and multiply; fill the earth and subdue it; have dominion. . . ."[26] God wants man to be fruitful. That can mean reproduction in terms of having children, but it also means spiritual reproduction. It means bearing fruit for the Lord, producing love, joy, peace, longsuffering, kindness, goodness, faithfulness, gentleness, and self-control.[27]

God wants human beings to increase and grow. Artificial limits on growth are not biblical. The concept of zero growth, for example, is not biblical; and the concept of the socialist-type government, which puts arbitrary controls on a man's ability to make money or create or invent, is not biblical. God wants man to be a frutiful, creative, reproducing individual.

God also wants men to have dominion over Satan. He wants us, as His representatives, to subjugate Satan. Jesus Christ gave us that authority. He wants us to do away with the works of Satan—to take away poverty, to lift the yoke of oppression, and to take away ignorance and lack of faith. He wants us to bring a blessing to people and to liberate them from the forces that would destroy them.

Then, when we have taken dominion over the things that will hurt our fellow man, He wants us to take dominion over the earth. We are to have dominion over the streams and the air, and the fields and the birds, and the animals in our world. We are not supposed to pollute the streams and befoul the air and rip up the minerals in this earth just for personal gain. We are supposed to be intelligent stewards, under God, of all these things. God wants us to manage the world as His sons and daughters. He wants us to bring about righteousness in this world. Our main purpose for being on earth is to be stewards of God's creation, to grow in God, and to function as God's sons and daughters.

In the *Westminster Shorter Catechism*, the Presbyterians say that man's chief aim is to glorify God and enjoy Him forever. The mandate in Genesis to take dominion has no meaning apart from giving glory to God. We are to be subject to Him, to love Him, to walk with Him, and to have fellowship with Him.

The prophet Micah sums it up when he says, "And what does the Lord require of you but to do justly, to love mercy, and to walk humbly with your God?"[28]

Scripture References

1 Genesis 1:26, KJV
2 Genesis 2:7, KJV
3 See Romans 10:10
4 Genesis 8:21
5 See John 3:3
6 See Genesis 2:10–14
7 Genesis 6:5
8 See Genesis 6:7–8
9 See Genesis 3:2–24
10 Psalm 58:3
11 Romans 7:24
12 See Romans 7:15–20
13 Romans 8:2
14 See Ephesians 1:4
15 See Exodus 9:12
16 See Genesis 1:20–25
17 See Genesis 1:26–27
18 See Luke 16:19–31
19 See Daniel 3:25–27
20 See Matthew 8:12
21 See Revelation 20:14–15
22 Hebrews 9:27
23 See Matthew 17:1–3
24 See Matthew 17:1–8, Mark 9:2–8, Luke 9:28–36
25 Psalm 90:10
26 Genesis 1:28
27 See Galatians 5:22–23
28 Micah 6:8

4. The Nature of Christ

1. What is the virgin birth of Christ?

The Bible says in Isaiah that God would give us a sign: "The virgin shall conceive and bear a Son."[1] The word in Hebrew that we translate as "virgin" is *almah*, and it can mean "virgin" or "young woman." The word has been translated "virgin," however, because there is nothing unusual about a young woman giving birth, so that would be no sign at all.

But in the New Testament, the word that is used for the Greek translation of *almah* is *parthenos*, and that clearly means *virgin*. It has no other meaning except *virgin*. The Bible tells us that there was a young virgin named Mary. The angel of the Lord came to Mary and said, "The Holy Spirit will come upon you, and . . . overshadow you."[2] He went on to tell her that a child would be formed in her, and she would give birth to the Messiah.

This is the way God entered into humanity to bring a

324

second Adam. God the Son enfleshed Himself—the Holy Spirit bringing about conception, parthenogenesis, the virgin beginning—without the intervention of the normal reproductive cycle of man. That is why Jesus is called the Son of God. He was not the son of Joseph, and He was not the son of a Roman soldier. He was not the son of any human father. He was conceived by the Holy Spirit. God brought about virtually a second creation, a second man, without the original sin of the male line from Adam. Linking Jesus into the family tree of Mary, however, made Him a descendant of David and Abraham, which fulfilled the various promises that God had made to them. Further, it was from His mother, Mary, that the Lord received His human nature. So Jesus Christ was unique, conceived by the Holy Spirit, but of "the house and lineage of David."[3]

---

2. How could Jesus be God and man at the same time?

When we discussed the attributes of God (see page 302), we said that one way of discussing Him is to say that He is immortal. He is eternal. In other words, He does not have a beginning or an end. We also said that He is invisible, and then we said that He is described in terms of *omnis* ("all"). He is omnipresent, omniscient, and omnipotent. So the question is really, how can God, who is unlimited, infinite, and immortal, take upon Himself human nature which is finite, mortal, and limited?

One possible clue is to consider that when God created man in His image, there may have been more similarity to the second Person of the Trinity than we have realized. Perhaps the gap between God and sinless man was not as great as we have always imagined. The Bible does tell us in 1 John 3:2, "We shall be like Him, for we shall see Him as He is."

Jesus Christ, according to the Bible, is the very essence of God. Jesus is the express image of God, and the Bible says that "in Him all things consist."[4] But we are also told that He emptied Himself in order to become a man.[5] He did not empty Himself of His love, His goodness, His kindness, or His gentleness; for His divine nature was undiminished in the incarnation. But to become a human infant He did empty Himself of the eternal majesty that He shared in the presence of His heavenly Father. He went through the teenage years, grew up to be a man, died, and then came back to life again.

Jesus was a flesh-and-blood man, with all that entails, except for sin. When Jesus died on the cross, it was not an illusion. He really died. He suffered as men suffer. He became tired and hungry. He was not some superman, free from pain and discomfort. The Bible says that He was tempted in like manner as we are, yet was without sin.[6] He went through all the problems that man can go through; yet He always possessed His divine nature and His awareness of the presence of the Father and the Holy Spirit.

There are some people who say, "Well, He became God when the Holy Spirit came upon Him." But that is not what the Bible teaches. The Bible teaches that He was truly God from the moment of His conception by the Holy Spirit. But at the same time He was fully human.[7]

---

3. How is Jesus different from Confucius, Buddha, and Mohammed?

Jesus claimed to be God, and he allowed Himself to be worshiped as God. After His resurrection, one of His disciples fell on his knees and said, "My Lord and my God!"[8] To a good Jew, this would have been blasphemy, but Jesus received it approvingly. Jesus also said, "You will see the Son of Man sitting at the right hand of the Power, and coming on the clouds of heaven."[9] He identified Himself as the Son of God.[10] In His lifetime, He said things about Himself that, if they were not true, would have been the words of a madman.

Jesus said, "I am the light of the world. He who follows Me shall not walk in darkness."[11] He said, "I am the bread of life."[12] He told people, "Unless you eat the flesh of the Son of Man and drink His blood, you have no life in you."[13] He made a series of claims about His own divine nature. When people challenged Him on it, He said, in effect, if I denied my deity I would become a liar, as you are.[14]

Mohammed believed that he was a prophet. Buddha felt that he was a seeker after truth. Confucius never claimed to be anything but a wise teacher. Only Jesus has made claim to be the eternal Son of God. He is God and He proved His deity.

Jesus Christ was dead and buried, but rose again from the dead.[15] He was seen by about five hundred people after His resurrection.[16] He had the ability to walk through doors,[17] to travel vast distances in an instant,[18] and to ascend into heaven.[19] He had taken on a completely spiritual resurrection body. He reached heaven and sent the Holy Spirit to indwell and empower His disciples. This, as the apostle Peter affirmed, proved that He actually arrived in heaven.[20]

---

4. What makes Jesus' teachings unique?

It has been said that if Jesus is not God, then we should worship the man who thought Him up, because never did any man speak that way before or since.

The teachings that I have discovered, especially about the kingdom, have truth that is self-validating. They resonate with the experience of people throughout all the ages. When these principles are put into practice, they lead invariably to peace, harmony, victory, and love. This does not mean that the teachings of Jesus will not bring conflict. Because when someone accepts the teachings of God, there will be conflict with those who wish to continue in evil.

Jesus' words pulsate with wisdom. For example, His concept about civil government: "Render therefore to Caesar the things that are Caesar's, and to God the things that are God's."[21] The concept of God as a Spirit: "Those who worship Him must worship in spirit and truth."[22] The Sermon on the Mount: "Love your enemies, bless those who curse you, do good to those who hate you."[23] The greatest commandment: "Love the Lord your God with all your heart, with all your soul and with all your mind . . . love your neighbor as yourself. On these two commandments hang all the Law and the Prophets."[24]

Jesus' understanding of the sweep of history was absolutely superb. There has never been anyone in history who has even come close to Him. Above all else, Jesus rose from the dead, appeared to people, sent His Spirit to people, and has transformed the lives of millions. Wherever you find the gospel, you find progress, freedom, liberty, and family loyalty—all the things that human beings acknowledge as the desires of their hearts. It is not coincidental that the nations that have been characterized as "Christian" have surpassed the rest of the world for centuries in almost every measure of achievement.

It is true that there have been many crimes perpetrated upon humanity in the name of Christianity, but those who did such things did not really know Christ or His teachings. Christ did not lead people to persecute and torture Jews and "heretics." Many so-called "heretics" were actually ones who knew the Lord, and *they* were being persecuted by zealots who did not know Him.

What happens in religion is that one generation finds Jesus and lives for Him. The next generation learns His teaching by rote. The third generation does not really know it at all, but decides to use religion as a justification for holding on to temporal power. Such people launched the crusades and conducted the Inquisition. They were using religion, but they did not know Jesus. Wherever you find political power and worldly ambition using Christianity, you will often find the absence of New Testament truth. Then there may be sinful excesses done in the name of religion. Neither Jesus nor His teachings should be blamed for sinful excesses committed under cover of His name.

5. When Jesus died on the cross, did He also die spiritually?

A controversy has arisen recently on this point because of a few well-known teachers who erroneously assert that Jesus Christ on the cross died not only physically but spiritually as well. They say that this shows how great His love for us is and how much power He released because He gave up so much for us. Well, that is an interesting thought, but it is an impossibility, a contradiction in terms. By definition, a spirit cannot die. A spirit is an immortal being.

Of course God cannot die either. If God died, the universe would fall apart. And Jesus is God. If the Spirit of Jesus died, then God himself would have died, and the whole universe would have collapsed.

These teachers say that they mean by "death" a separation from God. According to them, in order for a person's spirit to be redeemed, Jesus' Spirit had to die. However, for Jesus to be separated from God, He would have had to be a sinner. But a sinner could not have been the "lamb without blemish and without spot" offered for the sins of the world.[25] If Jesus—the Son of God and second Person of the Trinity— were truly separated in spirit from the Father, then God Himself would be torn asunder and would cease to be— another impossibility.

The book of Hebrews states:

> Therefore, when He came into the world, He said: "Sacrifice and offering You did not desire, but a body You have prepared for Me. In burnt offerings and sacrifices for sin You had no pleasure. Then I said, 'Behold, I have come—in the volume of the book it is written of Me—to do Your will, O God.'" Previously saying, "Sacrifice and offering, burnt offerings, and offerings for sin You did not desire, nor had pleasure in them" (which are offered according to the law), then He said,

"Behold, I have come to do Your will, O God." He takes away the first that He may establish the second. By that will we have been sanctified through the offering of the body of Jesus Christ once for all.[26]

The Bible clearly states, "We have been sanctified through the *offering of the body of Jesus Christ* once for all." It is His physical death in obedience to the will of the Father that sanctifies us. Jesus' humanity, which knew no sin, tasted the horror of the sin of all humanity. He was offered as a sacrifical lamb before God to pay the price for all of our sins.

After his physical death and before His resurrection, Jesus' Spirit descended into hell and preached to all those who were there, leading "captivity captive."[27] His Spirit was neither dead nor separated from God. Instead, He was continuing to please and serve the Father, as He is at this moment.

Scripture References

1 Isaiah 7:14
2 Luke 1:35
3 Luke 2:4
4 Colossians 1:17
5 See Philippians 2:5–8
6 See Hebrews 4:15
7 See Philippians 2:5–8, Hebrews 2:14–18, 4:14–16
8 John 20:28
9 Matthew 26:64
10 See John 3:16–18
11 John 8:12
12 John 6:35
13 John 6:53
14 See John 8:55
15 See Matthew 28:7, Acts 13:30–31
16 See 1 Corinthians 15:4–8
17 See John 20:19, 26
18 See John 6:21
19 See Luke 24:51, Acts 1:9–11
20 See Acts 2:33
21 Matthew 22:21
22 John 4:24
23 Matthew 5:44
24 Matthew 22:37–40
25 1 Peter 1:19
26 Hebrews 10:5–10
27 See 1 Peter 3:18–20

5. Salvation

---

1. What is God's law, and how did I break it?

God's law is first of all, the spiritual law that we have in the New Testament. Second, it is the covenant between God and Israel. Third, it is the law God gave to mankind at the very beginning of human life on earth.

The law we have today can be summed up in a few words: We are to love God with all our hearts and minds and strength, and we're to love one another, even as Chirst loved us. The apostle Paul said, "He who loves another has fulfilled the law."[1]

There are two objects, then, of our love. First, we love *God* with every bit of our being. Second, we must love *our fellow man* as much as we love ourselves. That encompasses all the law. In Jesus' words, "On these two commandments hang all the Law and the Prophets."[2]

In the law given at Sinai, on the other hand, there were specific rules and regulations, beginning with the Ten Commandments. The first four commandments have to do with devotion to God. The fifth commandment has to do with obedience to someone who stands in the role of God, namely our parents. The remaining five have to do with the way we treat our fellow man. Don't steal his wife. Don't steal his possessions. Don't lie about him. Don't murder him. Don't hurt him. If you do to him as you do to yourself, if you love him the way you love yourself, you have followed those commandments.

So in the final analysis, God's law is that we should put God first in our lives. He wants us to function under Him as loving, obedient sons and daughters. We must listen to Him, obey Him, and be prepared to do His bidding, whatever it is. That is the ultimate in God's law, and it is the law of the Spirit of life in Christ Jesus.[3]

The written law, which was given by God at Mount Sinai, had many dietary rules and contained other provisions, but this law was given essentially to Israel. The Bible says that this law was a shadow of good things that were to come.[4] The fulfillment of the law is in Christ. Christ enters into us, and we live out in our lives the righteous commandments of the written law. The Spirit of Christ within us helps us to do naturally what the law attempted to force us to do.

Law, when you see it in today's world, is essentially a restraint on people who do not live in love toward others. There are traffic lights, pollution controls, laws against murder, kidnapping, theft, fraud, and a host of other things. All these laws seek to prevent conduct that will hurt someone else. But for those who walk in love, law doesn't really need to exist—no law to burden or bind them, because they naturally and voluntarily fulfill through the Spirit all the righteous demands of the written law.

Since the law is based on loving God and our fellow man, we break God's law whenever we fail to love Him or whenever we harm our fellow man. Since harm to another— be it theft, adultery, murder, or false witness—usually begins in our inner being, God added to the law a prohibition against coveting—a mental sin. Jesus expanded the concept by saying that lustful thoughts are the equivalent of the act of adultery, and that anger, along with demeaning insults, is the equivalent of murder.[5]

2. What is sin?

Sin is falling short of the glory of God. We sin when we do not do what God wants us to do, or when we do what He does not want us to do. The word *sin* in Greek is *hamartia*, and it means "to go apart from a mark." If you were to shoot an arrow at a target, and you missed the bull's-eye, you would be missing the mark.

The mark of God is perfection—total perfection. Anything that falls short of His perfection and holiness is sin.

There are two other words which refer to specific kinds of sins. The first is *iniquity*. Iniquity means *twistedness* or *crookedness*. It is a perverseness, a twisted desire to do something contrary to an established norm. If Jesus Christ is our standard, then repeated conduct deviating from His example, would be iniquity. The second word is *transgression*. Transgression means the deliberate breaking of a known law or standard. You know what God wants you to do at a particular point, but you deliberately go against His will. Iniquity bends and distorts God's will for our lives. Transgression deliberately cuts across it and breaks it.

There is one final definition of sin. The apostle Paul said that "whatever is not from faith is sin."[6] In other words, when in doubt, don't. There are many areas where we have to ask ourselves if what we are doing is right or wrong. To one person something may be all right, while to someone else, it might not be.

For example, if someone is a long-distance runner, eating a piece of cake the night before a race could be a good idea. He is getting some extra carbohydrates into his body— a process called carbohydrate loading—and that is a smart thing for a highly trained athlete to do before a long race. On the other hand, if the man is a diabetic, he has no business eating that cake. Eating it could result in great harm to him. So there are different nutritional standards for different people, and this is true in spiritual service as well.

If someone is going to the mission field, he may have to

give up material things because it will be necessary for him to live in a poorer culture, and many possessions would hurt his relationship with the people he wants to reach. On the other hand, if a person is a business executive, then he has to function among his fellow executives. If he lives in a grass hut and wears overalls, then he will neither be able to have a proper relationship with his colleagues nor be able to share his faith with them.

To the one man, living in an expensive home might be sin; to the other it might be a sin not to. It depends on the circumstance, because God has a special plan for each of us. Therefore, the standard for the undefined areas of our life is faith itself. "Whatever is not from faith is sin" (Romans 14:23).

We should copy Jesus and not necessarily one another. The Bible says, "There is none who does good, no, not one."[7] "All have sinned and fall short of the glory of God."[8] "They go astray as soon as they are born, speaking lies."[9] But in Jesus Christ there is perfection. It is only in Christ that we can hit the mark. Jesus is the only sinless man, and there will never be another.

When we trust in Christ, we take His sinlessness upon ourselves. That is the only way we can enter into heaven—without any sin. The Bible says, "If we walk in the light as He is in the light, we have fellowship with one another, and the blood of Jesus Christ His Son cleanses us from all sin."[10] As we are walking with Jesus, whatever sins we commit by our contact with the world are being continuously forgiven by the blood of Jesus as we confess them.

---

3. How does Jesus save me?

He saves us by His death from all our sins: past, present, and future. We all have broken God's law, and the wages of sin is death.[11] Jesus Christ never sinned, so as a sinless "second Adam," He was able to die as a substitute for all human sinners. Therefore God was able to preserve His righteous law and government by punishing the breaking of the law while offering a pardon to those who had broken it.

The apostle Paul said that Jesus redeemed us from the curse of the law.[12] The word *redeemed* means to buy back a slave in the marketplace. Mankind was in bondage to the curse of the law, which is death. Under this analogy, the death of Jesus was the "ransom" needed to set us free from the bondage of the law, sin, and death.

So in one sense, Jesus is our substitute; in another, our ransom. In yet another, He is our *hilasterion* (translated "propitiation") or mercy seat, a reference to the lid or covering over the ark of the covenant. When the mercy seat was covered with the blood of a sacrifice, the law's condemnation against the people was shut out before God. Jesus Christ is our complete and only covering.

Our salvation has three parts. First, at the moment we receive Christ in faith, His death cancels completely all of our sins. This is called "justification by faith."[13] In Christ our position before God is sinless. We are totally absolved from all past sins, just as if we had never sinned. This is salvation of our spirit.

Then as we walk with Jesus day after day, we have present salvation, and we grow in holiness. We enter into the state of *sanctification*, where we become freer from sin and more like Jesus. Paul said that we change from one degree of glory into another, even as by the Spirit of the Lord.[14] The goal of the Christian is to grow up into Christ. This is our ongoing salvation.

The third part of salvation is future, where we will lose these bodies which are always being pulled by sin, and we will get brand new bodies.[15] This salvation is also called *glorification*. So salvation is total. It is a matter of the past, present, and future.

---

4. What is faith?

In the book of Hebrews, the Bible defines faith as "the assurance (the confirmation, the title deed) of the things [we] hope for, being the proof of things [we] do not see and the conviction of their reality."[16] We are hoping to reach heaven, a world we cannot see, and faith gives substance to our expectations.

Faith can be a title deed to things we cannot see. For example, suppose there is a lot in a Florida resort, which you have never seen. A salesman comes to you and says, "I have a lot in this plat, and if you will give me $10,000, I will give you a deed to it." So you give him the money, and he gives you the deed. The moment the deed transfers, you own the property. You might not see it for many years, but you know it is yours, because the title deed has conferred all ownership privileges upon you. From that moment on, you can begin to enjoy it.

That is faith. It is the title deed to things we cannot see. Faith is an attribute given by the Spirit of God that enables us to reach into God's invisible world and take possession of that which we cannot see.

Faith is one of the fruits of the Spirit, and this means that it grows naturally for those who belong to God.[17] The Bible says the testing of faith produces patience, which means we can develop a stronger faith by working on it.[18] If we exercise faith, just as we would exercise a muscle, it will grow. The more we walk in faith and appropriate things by faith, the more our faith grows. We get to a point where we say, "If God can do what I have experienced, then surely He can do something more." Our faith will grow as we use it, whether it is faith for healing or for family unity or for finances or even for the conduct of national affairs.

There is also what is called a manifestation, or a gift of faith.[19] This is a supernatural enablement of faith that God gives when it is especially needed.

This supernatural faith is the kind of faith that can move mountains, provide divine protection from danger, or provide for an unusual financial need. Faith can be something that is continuously growing through use, or it can be something that comes instantaneously as a gift from God.

5. What is justification by faith?

Justification by faith is the forgiveness of sins because of faith. Faith in what? In the work of Jesus Christ. The apostle Paul said, "By grace you have been saved through faith, and that not of yourselves; it is the gift of God, not of works, lest anyone should boast."[20]

We are justified because of the unmerited favor of God. That is what grace is—favor we did not work for. We have faith in the fact that Jesus Christ died for us, that He rose again, and that He offers us eternal life through believing in Him. When we do believe this, Jesus comes into us, lives in us; and we become identified with Him through His sacrifice. Then, when God looks at us, He does not see our sin; He sees the blood of Jesus. And He says, in effect, about each one of us, "This person has not done anything wrong. He is covered by the blood of Jesus. Therefore, I pronounce him righteous." That is justification by faith.

6. What is being born again? Do I have to be born again in order to be a Christian?

Yes, you have to be born again in order to be saved. Unless you are saved, you are not Christian, regardless of which denomination you belong to or whatever you happen to call yourself.

What is being born again? The Bible tells us that there was a member of the Sanhedrin named Nicodemus, who came to Jesus by night. He said, "Rabbi, we know that You are a teacher come from God." What he was really saying was, "Teach me how I can find God." Jesus cut through the discussion and said, "Unless one is born again, he cannot see the kingdom of God." Nicodemus did not understand that and asked, what is this "born again"? Do you want me to go back into my mother's womb and be born all over again? Jesus responded by saying, "Unless one is born of water and the Spirit, he cannot enter the kingdom of God." Then Jesus referred to the wind. He said, "The wind blows where it wishes, and you hear the sound of it, but cannot tell where it comes from and where it goes. So is everyone who is born of the Spirit. . . . Are you the teacher of Israel, and do not know these things?"[21]

Jesus was telling Nicodemus that he had to be born from above, by the Spirit of God, and by water, which I presume is the water of baptism (although there are others who think it may be the bursting of the waters at initial birth, or the Word as referred to in Ephesians 5:26: "the washing of water by the word"). There is a transformation by the Spirit of God of our lives that is tantamount to a second birth.

God said through the prophet Jeremiah that He was going to write His laws on the hearts of His people.[22] This is one result of being born again. Suddenly the law of God is no longer something on tablets of stone, but is something written upon the heart. One is motivated from within as the Spirit of God begins to lead in obedience to the righteousness of God.

First, God says, "You are righteous by faith," then He gives you the Holy Spirit so you can live righteously. Once you have been born again, you live the righteous demands of the law by the leading of the Holy Spirit. This is the process of regeneration that turns a sinner into a saint, fit for God's kingdom: "Unless one is born again, he cannot see the kingdom of God."[23]

---

7. What do I have to do to be saved?

To be saved you must turn away from sin, believe in the death and resurrection of Jesus, and receive Him as Lord and Savior of your life.

Here is the step-by-step process. First, you must consider your life and then turn away from everything in it that is contrary to what God wants. This turning away from selfishness and toward God is called *repentance*.[24]

Second, you must acknowledge that Jesus Christ died on the cross to forgive you of sin. You take Him as your Savior to cleanse you from sin—as the substitute who paid the price due you for your sin.[25]

And third, you must ask Him to be Lord of your life, acknowledging openly and verbally that Jesus is not only your Savior but your Lord.

The Bible says that as many as received Him were given the power to become the sons of God.[26] So when you open your heart and receive Him, He comes into your heart, your inner person, through His Holy Spirit, and begins to live His life in you. From that point it is a question of confessing what God has done. "If you confess with your mouth the Lord Jesus and believe in your heart that God has raised Him from the dead, you will be saved."[27]

8. If I sin, will I lose my salvation?

An act of sin does not cost you your salvation. There are people who teach that if you sin once after you have accepted Jesus, you must be saved again. But that is not what the Bible teaches.

Can you conceive of somebody adopting a child and then telling the child that if he walks on the floor with muddy shoes he will be thrown out in the street? We would not do that to a child, and God will not do it to us, either. When you are saved, you are adopted into the family of God. You must, out of love on one hand and godly fear on the other, try to live a life that is pleasing to Him. But the idea that one act of sin would cause someone to be thrown out of God's family is just not in agreement with the Bible. The

Bible says, "If we walk in the light as He is in the light, we have fellowship with one another, and the blood of Jesus Christ His Son cleanses us from all sin."[28]

And we are told in the little book of 1 John, "If we confess our sins, He is faithful and just to forgive us our sins and to cleanse us from all unrighteousness."[29]

Acts of sin or rebellion will take away the joy of your salvation. When David committed adultery with Bathsheba and had her husband killed, he lost the joy of his salvation. When he wrote Psalm 51 about it, he said, "Restore to me the joy of Your salvation."[30] He had no joy, because he had rebelled against God. Then he said, "Do not take Your Holy Spirit from me."[31] Even though he had committed adultery and had been responsible for an innocent man's death, by his clear statement he still had the Holy Spirit. But, David did not get away without being punished. He had a rebellion in his own household and actually lost his throne for a time.[32] Nevertheless, God forgave and loved him because David was repentant before the Lord.

If you continue in a course of known sin, you will lose the assurance of your salvation, however. You will not know if the Holy Spirit is with you because you will be at odds with God. I am not referring here to an actual loss of your salvation or to the Holy Spirit, only to your awareness and assurance of salvation and the Holy Spirit. The Bible says, "Anyone born of God does not continue to sin."[33] It does not say that a Christian never commits an act of sin, but that he does not continue in a course of sin, refusing to confess and repent of his sins. So if someone has been born of the Spirit of God, there will be something inside of him drawing him back to repentance every time he sins.

Beyond that, we can gather from reading in the book of Hebrews that if somebody actually says the blood of Jesus Christ is a despised thing and renounces the salvation he has received, then that person may have lost it all. But then the Bible immediately says, "But, beloved, we are confident of better things concerning you."[34] It is very hard to believe that someone who has been born again will turn that far away from God.

But you might ask, if we are new creatures in Christ, why do we even have the capacity still to sin? The answer is that perfection for the Christian awaits us in heaven: "When this corruptible has put on incorruption, and this mortal has put on immortality, then shall be brought to pass the saying that is written: 'Death is swallowed up in victory.'"[35]

We are united with Jesus at salvation, but we are being progressively transformed into His nature.

The Bible says, "We all, with unveiled face, beholding as in a mirror the glory of the Lord, are being transformed into the same image from glory to glory."[36] We are being changed throughout our lives, but there is no instantaneous moment, short of death, when the believer becomes sinlessly perfect. The apostle John said, "If we say that we have no sin, we deceive ourselves, and the truth is not in us."[37]

---

9. Does the Bible teach that once I am saved, I am always saved?

The phrase "once saved, always saved" is not found in the Bible. Our salvation is past, present, and future. That implies a continuous relationship and an unfolding process rather than a fixed state. The person who has given himself or herself to Jesus Christ and has truly repented from sin can find repeated assurances of the eternal covenant given to His people by a God who cannot lie. The Bible tells us that the gifts and calling of God are without repentance (see Romans 11:29). The work of Jesus Christ is eternal. It will never be revoked. Apart from the Bible, the greatest assurance any Christian has of eternal security is the day-by-day witness of the Holy Spirit in his life that he is a child of God and the fact that day-by-day he is becoming more like Jesus.

The Bible teaches security in the Holy Spirit and in the things of God. Jesus said, "My Father, who has given them to Me, is greater than all; and no one is able to snatch them out of My Father's hand."[38] So we are secure in the hand of God, and we are to rest secure in the Lord. God has put His Spirit within us; He has given His Word to us. Jesus Christ is at the right hand of God, constantly making intercession on our behalf;[39] and God has sent angels to watch over us.[40] In other words, we are surrounded by tremendous helps. We should constantly remind ourselves that we are secure, that God loves us, and that we belong to Him.

The reason we are saved is not because we are holy or do good works, but because of the blood of Jesus. Salvation comes through faith, and it stays because of faith. So we should have a feeling of security. But, at the same time, there should be a healthy fear of falling. We should not presume on God and say, "I am saved, so I can do anything I want to." Paul condemned people who were teaching that a person could sin boldly so that God's grace could abound.[41] If we truly are dead to sin, then we are not going to live in sin any longer, but we will aim to serve God.

We should walk with reverence, because God is a consuming fire, a very awesome Being.[42] I would not counsel anybody to presume on God because of a doctrine of eternal security. Anybody who says, "I believe that once I am saved, I am always saved, so I am going to go out and commit adultery and steal and lie and cheat and rob," is being very foolish. If somebody really loves God, those things would not be present in his life.

I have walked with God for nearly thirty years, and for the last twenty-five years or so, I have never even thought about the possibility of losing my salvation. It just is not a reality for me at all. The reason is that I live for the Lord. The thought of doing otherwise just does not occur to me. Do I commit acts of sin? Yes. Do I fail God? Yes. Are there things I should do that I do not do? Yes. I need the cleansing forgiveness of the Lord constantly. My concern is that I realize God's purpose for my life and that I do not fall short of what He intends for me. But as far as losing my salvation, it just does not come up for me, nor should it for any sincere Christian.

---

10. What part does the Virgin Mary play in my salvation?

There are some who teach that the Virgin Mary is a co-redemptress, that she assists people in attaining salvation because she has special access to her Son. These are very well-meaning people, but the Bible differs with that view.

The Bible teaches, in the writings of the apostle Paul, that there is one mediator, or go-between, between God and man—the man Christ Jesus.[43] We do not need a mediator or buffer between Jesus and us.

When Jesus was on earth, He was in a house teaching the people and ministering to them. There was such a large crowd outside that it was impossible for Mary and Jesus' brothers to get in. Word was sent to Him, "Look, Your mother and Your brothers are standing outside, seeking to speak with You." Jesus then pointed to His disciples and said, "Here are My mother and My brothers! For whoever does the will of My Father in heaven is My brother and sister and mother."[44] In this statement He elevates all who love Him to the status of being in His "immediate family." He was laying claim to a larger family than merely His earthly family, including His mother.

Mary is blessed among all women, because she gave birth to our Lord Jesus.[45] But He has ascended and reigns over His church, together with the Father and the Holy Spirit. We are called upon to honor Mary, for the Scriptures teach that all generations will call her blessed. But there is nothing in the Bible to indicate that this wonderful woman has any special claim on Him or any role in our salvation.

11. How can God send people who have never heard of Christ to hell?

God does not send people to hell because they never heard of Christ. He sends people to hell because they have sinned. The judgment for sin will be in relationship to how much they knew. To phrase it another way, it is action in light of privilege. A person living in America has maximum spiritual privilege. Therefore the spiritual standard for America would be the gospel of Jesus and everything in the Old and New Testaments. But someone who grew up in an uncivilized jungle might be held to account for the fact that something in his conscience told him there is a Creator worthy of his worship. The Bible says his conscience will either accuse him or excuse him on the day of Jesus Christ.[46] God is not going to condemn people if their own consciences excuse them. Regretfully, every human being has sinned against his or her own conscience.

God does not judge people for failure to believe in Jesus, but because they are sinners. The problem is that "all have sinned and fall short of the glory of God."[47] For those who have received Jesus Christ as Savior, there will be forgiveness and mercy.

12. Will babies who die without being baptized go to hell?

Babies who are not baptized will not go to hell because they are not guilty of anything. God will judge people on the basis of what they did in light of what they knew. Babies have not done anything wrong because they do not know the difference between right and wrong. And so they have not sinned. Furthermore, Jesus said, "Their angels always see the face of My Father who is in heaven."[48]

Remember also, original sin is a tendency to sin, not an act of sin. Original sin is not original guilt. To be guilty before God, a child has to understand that what he or she is doing is wrong.

---

13. What is the age of accountability?

This is a term that is not in the Bible but that some religious groups use to refer to the time when a child becomes accountable to God for his actions. That time comes whenever he or she is old enough to understand the difference between right and wrong and good and evil.

It may be at a very early age. Some children who are four or five years old are old enough to know Jesus Christ and be saved, because they are old enough to know the difference between right and wrong. We have to be careful with little children. We should not cause them to build up an unnatural sense of guilt and make them feel guilty for things that are not really sin at all. If we teach them the major moral rules, that God Himself has set forth, then they will learn properly and naturally.

Children do reach an age where they are old enough to be held responsible for what they do. When that time comes, they will be judged by the same standards as everyone else.

---

14. What is the difference between heaven, paradise, and purgatory?

When Jesus was hanging on the cross between two thieves, one of the thieves railed at Him and made fun of Him. The other thief admitted they deserved to be punished, but said Jesus had done nothing wrong. Then he turned to Jesus and said, "Lord, remember me when You come into Your kingdom." Jesus said to him, "Today you will be with me in Paradise."[49] So paradise must be where Jesus is, because the thief was going to be there with Him. It also must be a place that those who have faith in the Lord will enter immediately upon death. Paradise is a place of bliss and happiness. But it would seem to be an intermediate place, as opposed to the final establishment of a new heaven and a new earth which we have referred to elsewhere.[50]

In certain instances heaven refers to the place where God rules. Heaven also refers to the final place where the spirits of the righteous dead will spend eternity after they have been joined with their resurrection bodies. Also, heaven can mean the space above the earth.

The wicked dead, as in the story of the rich man and Lazarus, go immediately to a place called Hades.[51] They are waiting for a final judgment when they will be cast into the lake of fire with the devil and his angels.[52] So in a sense there is an intermediate heaven and an intermediate hell.

The concept of purgatory is not biblical. Purgatory is supposed to be a transition period of indefinite duration intended for the perfecting of those people who die in Christ. It is taught that they experience suffering to pay for the sins they committed in this life until they are ready to enter into heaven. The Bible does not teach that. The apostle Paul said, "I am hard pressed between the two, having a desire to depart and be with Christ, which is far better. Nevertheless to remain in the flesh is more needful for you."[53]

Paul knew only of two states of being. Either he was going to stay on earth, or he was going to be with Jesus. The concept of purgatory seems to have been unknown to the apostles and does not seem to have any biblical basis at all. The Bible teaches that there are levels of heaven, but there is no mention of a place of purging and torment that would bring us up to a point of being acceptable to God after death.[54]

---

15. Why aren't the wicked punished for what they do?

David addressed this question in one of his psalms: "I have seen the wicked in great power, and spreading himself like a native green tree."[55] He also observed:

> For I was envious of the boastful, when I saw the prosperity of the wicked. For there are no pangs in their death, but their strength is firm. They are not in trouble as other men, nor are they plagued like other men. . . . When I thought how to understand this, it was too painful for me—until I went into the sanctuary of God; then I understood their end. Surely You set them in slippery places; You cast them down to destruction.[56]

The only thing I can add to what David said is that God permits a period when the wicked have the chance to repent. God's patience is meant to lead them to repentance.[57] But instead, they often presume on God and say, "He does not know what we are doing. We are getting away with it." And this seems to be true, for a time. But they will spend eternity in hell. Eternity is so long, and life is so short!

It is often true, too, that their own evil catches up with them. There is a statement in the common parlance, "What goes around comes around." If you deal out evil to people, it will come back to you.

Can you imagine anything more horrible than the latter years of a Mafia don, waiting for someone to do to him what he has done to someone else: always in fear for his life, always in torment that someone will hurt him, just as he has hurt other people? Not having anyone to trust or count on; not knowing when the assassin's bullet is going to come?

This is true of so many of the wicked. They will usually

be punished on earth while they live, even if it is not obvious to the rest of us. It may be nervous problems, or disease, or a child who disgraces them, or a wife who torments them. Rest assured, no one gets away with evil. Judgment always comes. Only the timing is uncertain.

Scripture References

1 Romans 1:8
2 Matthew 22:40
3 See Romans 8:2
4 See Colossians 2:16–17
5 See Matthew 5:21–28
6 Romans 14:23
7 Psalm 14:3
8 Romans 3:23
9 Psalm 58:3
10 1 John 1:7
11 See Romans 6:23
12 See Galatians 3:13
13 See Romans 3:24–30, Galatians 2:15–21
14 See 2 Corinthians 3:18
15 See 1 Corinthians 15:42–44
16 Hebrews 11:1, AMPLIFIED
17 See Galatians 5:22
18 See James 1:3
19 See 1 Corinthians 12:7–9
20 Ephesians 2:8–9
21 John 3:1–18
22 See Jeremiah 31:33
23 John 3:3
24 See Matthew 3:7–10, Acts 3:19
25 See Romans 5:9–10, Titus 2:14
26 See John 1:12
27 Romans 10:9
28 1 John 1:7

29 1 John 1:9
30 Psalm 51:12
31 Psalm 51:11
32 See 2 Samuel 15:18
33 1 John 5:18 NIV
34 Hebrews 6:1–9
35 1 Corinthians 15:54
36 2 Corinthians 3:18
37 1 John 1:8
38 John 10:29
39 See Hebrews 7:25
40 See Hebrews 1:14
41 See Romans 6:1–2
42 See Hebrews 12:29
43 See 1 Timothy 2:5
44 Matthew 12:46–50
45 See Luke 2:42–45
46 See Romans 2:14–16
47 Romans 3:23
48 Matthew 18:10
49 Luke 23:39–43
50 See 2 Peter 3:10–13, Revelation 21:1–7
51 See Luke 16:20–25
52 See Revelation 20:11–15
53 Philippians 1:23–24
54 See 2 Corinthians 12:2
55 Psalm 37:35
56 Psalm 73:3–5, 16–18
57 See Romans 2:5–7

6. The Holy Spirit

1. Can I live a holy life?

If it were not possible to live a holy life, God would not have commanded it. He said, "You shall be holy, for I the Lord your God am holy."[1] To be holy means to be separated to God. Something about God's nature itself speaks of holiness. Being set apart to God makes us holy.

We are *not* made holy by doing good things. We *are* made holy by faith in Christ, just as we are saved by faith. Little by little, as we grow and live with the Lord, we will become more like Him. Paul said, "We all, with unveiled face, beholding as in a mirror the glory of the Lord, are being transformed into the same image from glory to glory, just as by the Spirit of the Lord."[2]

As we look at Jesus, think about Jesus, study about Jesus, pray to Jesus, and seek to follow His example, we become like Him. We begin to think like Him and act like Him. We become like Him because we are set apart to Him. This is true holiness.

If you are a Christian, ten years from now your life should be considerably different from what it is now. Your

352

motives and desires, as you get closer to Him, should be continuously more holy.

Jesus said, "Blessed are the pure in heart, for they shall see God."[3] We can achieve a degree of purity in this life. It comes from God, as we grow closer to Him and are more like Him. Although perfection is not totally attainable in this life, it is something we should constantly strive toward and aim for.

---

2. What is Christian maturity?

Christian maturity is being a responsible son or daughter of God. I think the mature in Christ are people who have stopped being concerned about their own needs and pursuits and have entered into the global vision of their Father so that they may transform a hurting world. The mature go out as His agents in order to accomplish the aims of the Lord's Prayer, "Your kingdom come. Your will be done on earth as it is in heaven."[4] It's like a son who is being brought into the family business. Instead of racing fast cars and running around with girls, he finally buckles down and says, "Dad, I'm part of it. It's my business, too, and I'm going to work hard and undertake the burden of this work." That is real maturity. We undertake the burden of God in the way Jesus Christ would do it. Not in the energy and heat of our own flesh, striving to do something ourselves, but in the anointing of the Spirit of God, by the power of the Holy Spirit.

---

3 What is the indwelling Spirit?

When you come to Jesus Christ, you receive Christ into your heart. Jesus does not physically enter into your chest cavity and live there, but the Spirit of God comes and joins with the spirit of the believer. This is what is meant by the term "the indwelling Spirit." His function is to reproduce the life of Jesus in the believer. He will manifest the fruit of the Spirit in the believer's life. The nine attributes of Jesus that develop in the life of someone who has been born again and who has been indwelt by the Holy Spirit are love, joy, peace, long-suffering, kindness, goodness, faithfulness, gentleness, and self-control.[5]

In Romans 8:14 the apostle Paul tells us that those who are led by the Spirit are sons of God. We could transpose those words and say that the sons and daughters of God can expect the leading of the blessed Holy Spirit.

You might ask then, *where does the constant struggle in the life of some Christians come from?* Many Christians run into problems when they do not cooperate with the Spirit. We have a choice. The Spirit does not force Himself on us. For example, in the first century the apostles and elders in Jerusalem were debating a matter of doctrine. After they heard much discussion, they responded to the believers in Antioch, saying, "It seemed good to the Holy Spirit, and to us, to lay upon you no greater burden than these necessary things."[6] That was an awesome statement for those men to make. They were saying, in effect, that their opinion was equal to the opinion of the Holy Spirit. They said, "It seemed good to the Holy Spirit, and to us." You might ask yourself, *if it seemed good to the Holy Spirit, who cares what the apostles thought about it?* They were acknowledging a God-given partnership. They could choose whether or not to cooperate with the Holy Spirit. They can hold back and fail to acknowledge Him, or they can accept His leading to do what He wants them to do. They have that freedom, but they eventually have to deal with the blessings or problems resulting from their free decisions.

John the Baptist can be our role model. He said, "He must increase, but I must decrease."[7] Our wills and our egocentric natures have to decrease, whereas the Spirit of Jesus within us has to increase. This is a continuing process. Little by little, Christ is being made bigger, and we are being made smaller. If you fight that process and say, "I am going to assert myself and have my own way, but I will go to church on Sunday, acknowledge Christ, and take His bene-

fits," you are going to be a defeated, immature Christian.
The struggle will go on as long as you give your flesh, the
world, and the devil a place in your life.

---

4. What is the fruit of the Spirit?

The fruit of the Spirit consists of nine characteristics of
Jesus mentioned in Galatians. Remember, fruit takes
time to grow as it develops on a healthy plant. This
fruit grows in spiritually healthy Christians and centers
around the three major virtues of faith, hope, and love. As
noted in Galatians 5:22–23, "The fruit of the Spirit is love,
joy, peace, long-suffering, kindness, goodness, faithfulness,
gentleness, self-control."

Those who belong to Jesus and who live for Him become more like Him. It is as if Jesus were sitting for a
portrait and the Holy Spirit were painting that portrait
inside us. The manifestation of the fruit of the Spirit in our
lives is the tangible evidence that we are being changed into
the nature of Jesus Christ.

Contrasted with the fruit of the Spirit are the works of
sinful, uncrucified flesh: immorality, impurity, debauchery,
idolatry, witchcraft, hatred, discord, jealousy, envy, and the
like. These evils war against the Spirit and must be put to
death in the life of each believer.[8]

---

5. What is the baptism in the Holy Spirit?

The baptism in the Holy Spirit is the empowering for
service that takes place in the life of the Christian. It
can take place at the moment of faith in Christ as in
the case of the first Gentile convert, Cornelius; but tradi-
tionally and experientially it follows repentance, saving
faith, and baptism (see Hebrews 6:1–2). It enables a believer

to witness to the Lord's salvation and to demonstrate one or more of the nine gifts, or manifestations, of the Holy Spirit.[9] Just as the indwelling Spirit reproduces the life of Jesus, the outpoured, or baptizing, Spirit reproduces the ministry of Jesus.

To illustrate, if I had a glass of water and took a swallow, then the water would be inside me. If, on the other hand, I went down to the beach and stepped into the ocean, then I would be in the water. We receive, as it were, a drink of the Spirit when we are saved, but when we are baptized in the Spirit, it is as if that initial drink becomes an ocean that completely surrounds us.

When we give ourselves to Jesus, the Holy Spirit comes to live within us. The Holy Spirit places us into Jesus. In turn Jesus immerses us in the power of the Holy Spirit, and from this experience comes the ability to reproduce the works of Jesus, including miracles and healings.[10] Just as there are nine attributes of the fruit of the Spirit, there are nine gifts of the Spirit. Before He ascended into heaven, Jesus said, "John truly baptized with water, but you shall be baptized with the Holy Spirit."[11] He also said, "You shall receive power when the Holy Spirit has come upon you: and you shall be witnesses to Me."[12] When the day of Pentecost came, Jesus' apostles were all together in the same house. There was the sound of a mighty wind, and then tongues of fire sat upon them. They "began to speak with other tongues, as the Spirit gave them utterance."[13]

In subsequent instances, when this experience came upon the people, it seemed as if the Spirit of God activated their speech. First of all, this showed that they had been empowered to witness for the Lord. Second, their higher speech centers had been brought under the control of Jesus Christ. As James said, "If anyone does not stumble in word, he is a perfect man."[14] The tongues of these people had been brought under the Lord's control. Finally, by the words they spoke, they were able to do miracles. That is because the spoken word brings about healings, miracles, and the works of power that Jesus did. All of this is encompassed in the baptism in the Holy Spirit.

6. Does a person have to speak in tongues in order to be saved?

The work of the Lord Jesus Christ and the mercy of God bring salvation and the indwelling Spirit, and that does not involve speaking in tongues. Speaking in tongues, from all indications in the New Testament, is the consequence of the baptism in the Holy Spirit. It happened to Cornelius. It happened on the day of Pentecost and in other recorded instances.[15] There was an initial utterance in tongues, bearing witness that the tongue had been sanctified and empowered by God for His use. But speaking in tongues was not necessary for the salvation of those people.

7. How do I receive the baptism in the Holy Spirit?

You need to do a number of things in order to receive this blessing.

First, you need to be born again. The person who is going to be filled with the Spirit must have the indwelling Spirit and must belong to Jesus.

The second thing you have to do is to ask. The Bible says, "Ask, and it will be given to you."[16]

The third thing you have to do is surrender. The apostle Paul made this need clear in the book of Romans when he said, "Present your bodies a living sacrifice."[17]

Fourth, you must be willing to obey the Spirit. God does not give this power to someone and then say, "You can take the part you like and leave the part you do not like." If you want to be immersed in the Spirit, you need to be prepared to obey the Spirit.

Fifth, you need to believe. The apostle Paul, speaking to the Galatians, said, "Did you receive the Spirit by the works of the law, or by the hearing of faith?"[18] The answer, obviously, is faith. You have to believe that if you ask, you will receive.

Finally, you have to exercise what God has given you. Having asked, having received, having been willing to obey, and having believed, you need to respond in a biblical fashion. The Bible says those baptized with the Holy Spirit on the day of Pentecost "began to speak with other tongues, as the Spirit gave them utterance."[19] This means they spoke the words that the Spirit gave them. The Holy Spirit gave the words, but the apostles and disciples voluntarily responded. There was action based on faith, not merely passive acceptance of the blessing.

For example, suppose someone came to me and asked, "Could you let me have a dollar?" and I said, "Certainly." Then I reached into my pocket and handed him a dollar. What if he just looked at me and said, "You don't understand. I'm terribly desperate. May I please have a dollar?" I would offer the dollar again and say, "Here's the dollar." But what if, instead of taking it, he said, "Oh, please, don't you see I'm starving? Let me have a dollar." We could keep that up forever! The person would go without, and my arm would grow tired of handing him the dollar. He would never receive it, and I would never give it. But the minute he said, "Thank you," took the dollar, and put it in his pocket, that would be the moment the blessing was received.

That is the way it is with God. God is offering the baptism in the Holy Spirit to people who need only to reach out and take it and then enjoy the blessing.

---

8. Could you explain the gifts of the Spirit?

In 1 Corinthians 12, Paul speaks of nine *charismata*, which we call gifts, or enablements, of the Spirit. All of these come about by the Holy Spirit, who manifests

Himself in the lives of those who have confessed Jesus Christ as Lord and have received the baptism in the Holy Spirit.

An analogy would be a house wired for 200 amps of electricity, which could run an iron, a stove, a heater, a hot water heater, a woodworking shop, and any number of other electrical appliances. They all draw from the same power source. In the believer, the Holy Spirit is the source of power, and He can manifest Himself in healings, miracles, revelations, or utterances.

There are nine manifestations, or gifts, of the Spirit, which can be divided into three groups of three.

The first group consists of the manifestations of revelation. The *word of wisdom* has to do with knowing about the future or having supernatural wisdom regarding a present situation, such as in Luke 12:11–12 and Acts 6:8–10. The *word of knowledge* is discerning something that is not available to the senses. The third gift in the group is the *discerning of spirits*, which has to do with seeing the invisible world of human spirits, angels, devils, and the appearance of Jesus Himself.

The second group involves works of power, including *miracles*, gifts of *healing*, and the working of *faith*. The gift of miracles includes doing such things as stilling storms, restoring limbs, and raising the dead. The gifts of healing are for the healing of various diseases. The working of faith is essentially for defense and protection or for the accomplishment of some extraordinary task far beyond the ability of an individual.

The third group has to do with utterance, which includes bringing messages in *tongues* in an assembly, being able to *interpret* those messages, and proclaiming *prophecy*. Prophecy is for exhortation, edification, and comfort; people speak a direct word from God, such as, "Thus says the Lord, 'I am in your midst to help you and encourage you.'"

These, then, are the nine gifts of the Spirit, and they are all available to those who have been baptized in the Holy Spirit.

9. Didn't miracles stop when the last apostle died?

Many people teach that miracles stopped at the end of the first century when the last apostle died. Those people misinterpret 1 Corinthians 13:8 which says, "Whether there are prophecies, they will fail; whether there are tongues, they will cease; whether there is knowledge, it will vanish away." The chapter goes on to say that when the perfect has come, the imperfect will be taken away. Some say "the perfect" is the Bible.

There is only one that is perfect, Jesus Christ. So, 1 Corinthians 13:8 is not referring to the Bible but the return of Jesus to earth. When that happens tongues will cease because we will be in His presence. We will not need prophecy and knowledge, because He will reveal all things to us. The things that are imperfect will be done away with when we see the perfection that will come in Jesus Christ.

Until He comes, we need to have His life and His weapons for bringing His rule on earth.[20] Perhaps we need His power more today than the church did nineteen hundred years ago, because today we are faced with powerful forces of unbelief and satanic power

As we draw closer to the return of the Lord, spiritual warfare will intensify.[21] Those who oppose God will be stronger and more malevolent than ever before, and those who serve Him will experience an intensification of God's miraculous power as never before.

10. Are healings caused by the power of suggestion?

It is possible that some people are healed of psychosomatic illnesses by suggestion. I do not question that this occurs. But that is not to suggest that *all* healings take place because of suggestion. There are many examples of healings that could not be explained in these terms. Here is just one.

At age nineteen, Barbara Cummiskey was diagnosed as having multiple sclerosis. By the time she was thirty-one, the MS had helped cause a slowly paralyzing diaphragm, bouts of pneumonia and asthma, a collapsed lung, and tumors on her hands. She was technically blind and confined to her bed. These were well-diagnosed medical problems, and she was operated on more than once. But on June 7, 1981, she heard a voice say, "My child, get up and walk." She did just that and was healed! Barbara's legs had atrophied from lack of exercise. When she first got out of bed, however, her legs had muscle tone. Her mother shouted, "Calves! you have calves!"

Similarly, I have come across instances where people were not near a television set when "The 700 Club" was used by God to heal them. One man went to bed blind, but a prayer request came in to our television program for him, and when he woke up, he could see.

I know of instances where little children have been healed. The power of suggestion could not have been responsible for these healings.

---

11. Should Christians consult with doctors and take medicine?

I believe medical science is a gift from God. The skill that doctors have is, without question, a blessing that God has given us for our good. However, we must understand that all healing comes from God.[22] Medicines can help, but they only speed up the natural process of healing. Ambroise Paré, the sixteenth-century father of modern surgery, often said, "I dressed his wounds; God healed him."

I believe God heals through prayer, through rest and nutrition, through medicine, and through doctors. It is God's will that those who are sick be made whole, just as it is His desire that all might come to know Him. Regrettably, as long as people are as they are and the world is as it is, all will not come to know God and all will not be healed.

---

12. Can healings and other miracles be lost after they are received?

It is possible to lose a healing. I remember I prayed for one girl who had terrible vision. She was virtually blind. After prayer, her sight improved dramatically. But as she looked around, she thought, *I can see, but I am not supposed to see!* Her healing went away. There was no way we could get it back. It just left.

When Peter saw the Lord walking on the water, he wanted to walk on the water as he saw Jesus doing. Jesus said, "Come on out." So Peter got on the side of the boat, put his feet on the water, and started walking. But then Peter looked around and became frightened. He thought, *I am not supposed to be walking on water!* The minute he started to think that, he started to sink.[23] Today, some people receive a healing and then think, *I am not supposed to have this*, and they lose it. The devil has a way of coming to people and saying, "You are not really healed. You still have that disease, and you had better go back and take your medicine and put your braces on."

I remember one instance involving an acquaintance who was healed of multiple sclerosis. The doctors said he had a remission, but he knew it was a healing in answer to prayer. For a year, he had no evidence of the disease. Then one weekend, the entire force of multiple sclerosis began to come upon him. All the symptoms started to come back, and for an entire weekend he wrestled against it, saying, "Satan, I will not accept this." In the name of Jesus, he continually proclaimed that he was well. When that weekend of struggle was over, the symptoms left him. He has not been troubled since then. But if he had given in to those symptoms, he would have once again had multiple sclerosis, and he probably would have died from it.

---

13. What is prayer?

Prayer is communion with God. It is the closest, most intimate relationship with the Creator you can have.

Prayer is not playing magic games, spinning prayer wheels, reading off a list, or asking for things to be done. It is a communion. "Deep calls unto deep," the Bible says.[24] In prayer the depths of your spirit are in communion with the depths of the Spirit of God. Out of this can come instruction, guidance, or a burden to pray for certain things.

The apostle Paul said, "For we do not know what we should pray for as we ought, but the Spirit Himself makes intercession for us with groanings which cannot be uttered."[25] There are times when we can emit only wordless groanings because we don't know how to pray about a specific situation.

We can learn much from the Lord's Prayer, the model prayer.[26] The first is that if we are to structure prayer, we should begin with an acknowledgment of the One we are talking to—God, our Father. We should also include adoration, "Hallowed be Your name." We are to glorify and worship His name, His very Being.

Next, we must be concerned about the extension of His kingdom. We ask that men should come to know Him and submit to Him. "Your kingdom come. Your will be done on earth as it is in heaven." Next to the name and the person of God Himself, the most important thing in prayer is the extension of God's kingdom.

After that, we ask God for our daily bread—whatever we need to carry out His work. It may be money, a car, food, clothing, a house, or a $20 million budget for a Christian organization. It may be money to feed the poor. It may be a lot of things. We ask Him to give us, day by day, bread that is sufficient for us. That is the petition part of prayer. The first part of prayer is *praise*, the second is *intercession* for others, and the third is *petition*, when we ask for our needs to be met.

Finally, we seek God's protection that we might not be led into temptation and that God will keep us from evil. We ask Him to keep us walking in His way, so that we might be covered by His power and anointing and not be susceptible to Satan's influences.

We must remember that prayer is rooted in forgiveness. "Forgive us our debts, as we forgive our debtors." The relationship of God's people to Him comes about because of continuous forgiveness. If we are going to see miracles in our lives, we have to be willing to forgive other people, even as God is willing to forgive us.

Christians should always be in an attitude of communion with God. Prayer can take place in every circumstance.[27] In my life, as events pass by, I may find myself talking to Him, wanting to know something, asking for advice and counsel, or for favor and blessing. The Christian's life should be filled with prayer. In addition, we should set aside specific times, at least once a day, for prayer and for reading the Bible.

As we read the Bible, we should pray, worship God, speak to Him about our needs, and listen to His answers. This should be a time of communication between two spirits that sets the order of events for each day.

---

14. What does it mean to pray in the name of Jesus?

Jesus once made a statement that sounds rather sweeping: "And whatever you ask in My name, that I will do, that the Father may be glorified in the Son. If you ask anything in My name, I will do it."[28] That is a fantastic promise, but it must be understood properly, because simply adding "in Jesus' name" to the end of every prayer does not guarantee success.

In our legal system, we have what is called the grant of

a power of attorney. This means that an individual who owns property, money, or some right gives control over it to someone else, and that person acts *in the owner's name*. In whatever he or she does regarding the thing under control, the action is done with the owner's authority. It is as if the owner himself were acting. Likewise, in the promise above, Jesus gives us His authority to make requests of the Father. When we ask in His name, it is as though Jesus Himself were making the request. In that name there is absolutely awesome power.

For this authority to be exercised properly, however, the attorney must be a faithful agent of the owner. That is, his actions must be in accord with the owner's wishes. To do otherwise is to abuse the power of attorney. We see that this is true also of God: "Now this is the confidence that we have in Him, that if we ask anything *according to His will*, He hears us."[29] So when we prepare to ask something of God in Jesus' name, we need to be sure that our request reflects His will, not ours.

Then, too, God answers prayers offered in Jesus' name "that the Father may be glorified in the Son." The result of such prayer should be that God is honored and glorified, for that is its whole purpose.

Jesus has given us the power to ask in His name, and it is a wonderful privilege of which we should take full advantage. But to misuse that power is presumption.

---

15. How do I pray for a miracle?

When we are faced with a great need, either for ourselves or others, we should begin by humbly seeking to know what God's will is in the matter.[30] "Father, what do You want to do in this situation?" Jesus said, "My Father has been working until now, and I have been working."[31] He listened to the voice of the Father, and He watched Him. Be careful not to start or end a prayer by saying blindly, "If it be Thy will." Rather, you should seek to know God's will in the situation and then to base your prayer upon it. Say, "Father, in advance, tell me what Your will is and what You are doing." Then you can ask Him to perform the miracle that you know He wants to bring about.

Most people ask God for a miracle, but many omit a key requirement—the spoken word. God has given us authority over disease, demons, sickness, storms, and finances.[32] We continue to ask God to act, when, in fact, He has given us the authority to act with divinely empowered speech. We are to declare that authority in Jesus' name. We are to command the money to come to us, command the storm to be stilled, command the demon to come out, command the leg to grow, command the cancer to leave.

Jesus said, "Whoever says to this mountain, 'Be removed and be cast into the sea, and does not doubt in his heart, but believes that those things he says will come to pass, he will have whatever he says.'"[33] Believe in your heart that it has already happened! With the anointing of faith that God gives you, you speak it forth.

---

16. Is it permissible to pray more than once for something?

Some people teach that if we pray once, that is sufficient, and any prayer beyond that one is evidence of a lack of faith. This is not in accordance with biblical teaching. Jesus instructed His disciples about prayer. The original New Testament text of His instructions used the Greek present tense which implies continuous action. Jesus told His disciples to "Ask and keep on asking, and it shall be given you; seek and keep on seeking, and you shall find; knock and keep on knocking, and the door shall be opened to you."[34] This is not one prayer but continuous prayer.

Jesus told a parable about a man who was at home in bed.[35] It was at midnight when he heard frantic knocking on his door. A neighbor needed some bread to feed a guest who had arrived unexpectedly. At first the man said, "I cannot gct up, I will not do it." But the neighbor kept on knocking, and the householder finally walked downstairs, shoved a couple of loaves of bread out the door, and went back to bed. The man who was petitioning got his request only because of his persistence—not because he was a neighbor or a friend, but because he kept on knocking. Therefore, the concept that you must pray only once about something is clearly not biblical.

There is one exception—when God says yes. If you ask God for $1,000 and God says, "Yes, I am sending it," you should praise and thank Him for it. If you continue to ask Him, then you act as if you do not have a relationship with Him. You need to know His voice and be able to hear Him, especially when He says yes or no.

---

17. How can I know God's will?

The best way to know God's will is to be familiar with the Bible. That is because virtually everything you need to know concerning the will of God is in the Bible. If you are totally familiar with the Bible, can interpret it, and understand it clearly, you can know the will of God.

Another way you can know the will of God is through prayer, when you commune with God and learn what pleases Him. The Bible says, "Let the peace of God rule in your hearts."[36] This means that the peace of God is like a regulator, so that when you violate the will of God, His peace leaves you and you have inner turmoil. You then know immediately that you are going against God's will. I would say emphatically that the Bible and the peace that comes about through a continuous relationship with God are the best ways of knowing His will.

It is true that God will show us His will through a number of other means. He will show us His will through godly counselors. We can know His will in part through circumstances. We can also know the will of God through the inner voice of the Spirit as God speaks to us.

Sometimes God will send us visions or dreams. He may send us angels or even appear to us Himself. God is infinite, and He can reveal His will to us in many ways.

The key is to be sure that we are submitted to Him and are willing to do whatever He shows us. If we purpose to do His will, we will know His leading.

Finally, for people who seemingly are unable to discern God's positive directions, I recommend "negative" guidance. Say, "Father, I want Your will above all else. Please do not let me miss Your plan and purpose for my life." As the writer of Proverbs put it, "Trust in the Lord with all your heart, and lean not on your own understanding; in all your ways acknowledge Him, and He shall direct your paths."[37]

18. What is the unpardonable sin?

The concept of an unpardonable sin has been a source of difficulty for many because it seems to go against the Bible's teachings about grace. We understand that God's grace forgives every sin, but our Lord mentioned one sin that cannot be forgiven.

Let us put it in its biblical context. The religious leaders had come out to hear Him, but they opposed virtually everything He said. As He was doing miracles and casting out devils, they said, "This fellow does not cast out demons except by Beelzebub, the ruler of the demons."[38]

Those people were so blind spiritually that they were attributing the work of the Holy Spirit to Satan. Not only were they doing this, but they were also rejecting the Holy Spirit's work in their own lives. The Holy Spirit was saying, "This is the Son of God. This is God." And they were saying, "He is not God! He is Satan's agent." Then Jesus said, "Every sin and blasphemy will be forgiven men, but the blasphemy against the Spirit will not be forgiven men. . . . whoever speaks against the Holy Spirit, it will not be forgiven him, either in this age or in the age to come."[39]

Obviously, the unpardonable sin is not merely saying

an unkind thing about the Holy Spirit. The religious leaders involved had turned totally against the revelation of God. They were so far into their own wickedness that they rejected not only Jesus Christ but also the Holy Spirit. They were saying that good was evil and evil was good. They called the Spirit of God, Satan!

They had rejected spiritual understanding and so could never come to Jesus, the one source of forgiveness. If a person does not accept Jesus, he cannot have forgiveness. If he rejects the Holy Spirit and turns away from Jesus Christ, he can receive no forgiveness. That is what these so-called "religious leaders" had done.

If you want to obey God but are concerned that you may have committed the unpardonable sin, you have not committed it. If anyone today has committed this sin, it would be one who is hard-hearted, who has turned against Jesus, reviled Him, and become so depraved that he would claim that God's Spirit is Satan.

Scripture References

1 Leviticus 19:2
2 2 Corinthians 3:18
3 Matthew 5:8
4 Matthew 6:10
5 Galatians 5:22–23
6 Acts 15:28
7 John 3:30
8 See Galatians 5:17–21
9 See 1 Corinthians 12:7–10
10 See John 14:12–16, Acts 1:5, 8
11 Acts 1:5
12 Acts 1:8
13 Acts 2:4
14 James 3:2
15 See Acts 2:4, 10:44–46
16 Luke 11:9
17 Romans 12:1
18 Galatians 3:2
19 Acts 2:4
20 See 2 Corinthians 10:3–6
21 See Ephesians 6:12
22 See Psalms 103:2–3, Isaiah 53:4–5
23 See Matthew 14:28–30
24 Psalm 42:7
25 Romans 8:26
26 See Matthew 6:9–13
27 See 2 Chronicles 70:3, Psalms 4:4, 5:3, Daniel 6:10, Acts 21:5, 1 Thessalonians 5:17

28 John 14:13–14
29 1 John 5:14
30 See 1 John 5:14–15, Romans 12:1–2, 8:26–27
31 John 5:17
32 See Matthew 10:1, Luke 10:19
33 Mark 11:23
34 Luke 11:9, AMPLIFIED
35 Luke 11:5–8
36 Colossians 3:15
37 Proverbs 3:5–6
38 Matthew 12:24
39 Matthew 12:31–32

7. Angels and Demons

1. What are angels?

Angels are spiritual beings created by God to serve Him. They are very powerful beings who function as God's messengers. Many times in the Bible they appeared to people and said, "I have come as a messenger from the Lord."

The New Testament tells us they are also ministering spirits sent to look after human beings who are the heirs of salvation.[1] Jesus seemed to indicate that little children have angels assigned to them, for He said their angels always behold the face of God.[2] So the concept of guardian angels has its basis in the Bible.

In addition to the worker angels, there are archangels— angel princes such as Michael.[3] Scripture seems to indicate that he represented an entire nation.[4]

Although we do not know for sure what angels look like, the Bible mentions some angelic features. The first chapter of Ezekiel tells of a vision in which the prophet saw

372

a group of angels who were so holy that they appeared as flames of fire. These creatures seemed to be like men, yet they had four wings and multiple faces.[5] They responded instantly to God's Spirit. The book of Isaiah mentions angels called "seraphim" who have six wings.[6] Another group of angels is called "cherubim." Seemingly, cherubim were present to cover the very holiness of God Himself, and on the lid of the ark of the covenant their wings formed the throne for the presence of the Lord.[7]

Angels are magnificent creatures, not at all like the tiny, childlike cherubs that we see in some Renaissance art. Their power is so great that just one angel was able to destroy 185,000 Assyrian soldiers in one night.[8] Their presence is so awesome that those who see them have known to fall unconscious on the ground or to voluntarily prostrate themselves.[9]

---

2. What is a demon?

A demon is a fallen angel. When Satan, who was the very highest angel, rebelled against God, he took a large number of the angels with him in rebellion. When their rebellion failed, they were cast out of heaven. Those angels are now demons.[10] In the same way that angels can reach the very heights of spirituality, demons have the ability to reach down into great depths of hatred, bitterness, and perversion. Demons seem to be interested in tormenting people, possessing them, and leading them away from God and His truth.

Although lust, homosexuality, drunkenness, gluttony, and witchcraft are expressions of sinful flesh, these things can also be expressions of demonic activity in the lives of people. I am persuaded that many grossly perverted sexual practices, such as sadomasochism and pedophilia (sexual preference for children), have demonic roots. In a similar manner, schizophrenia (split personality) can be a mental disease, but it can also be caused by demon possession. I believe that Adolf Hitler and Karl Marx were both demonized.

Just as the angels have archangels and higher powers, the demons have what are called "principalities and powers." It is possible that a demon prince is in charge of New York, Detroit, St. Louis, or any other city. Particular sins are prevalent in certain cities. One city might have rampant homosexuality, while another might be troubled by excessive lust. In another, it may be witchcraft or spiritism. Nations, as well as cities, can be gripped by demon power. This could explain the willingness of the German people to tolerate the attempt of Adolf Hitler and the Nazi SS to exterminate all of the Jews in Europe.

There is conflict in the invisible world between God's loyal messengers and demonic hosts. Somehow in God's wonderful order, He uses the prayers of His people to restrain demonic activity and to direct the action of angelic powers to control demons. The book of Daniel tells of a struggle between the archangel Michael and the demonic "Prince of Persia."[11]

The Bible says, "He who is in you is greater than he who is in the world."[12] The Christian believer, by having the Holy Spirit within him, has power over all demons. When Jesus Christ sent His apostles out on their mission, He said He was giving them authority (*exousia*) over all the power (*dunamis*) of the enemy.[13] Jesus' authority is greater than satanic power. When the disciples returned, they told of casting out demons. The Lord said, "Nevertheless do not rejoice in this, that the spirits are subject to you, but rather rejoice because your names are written in heaven."[14] The Christian believer has unlimited authority over demons in the name of Jesus, but that authority is nothing compared to the glory and authority we will know in heaven.

3. How powerful is Satan?

In a message addressed to the king of Tyre, but obviously meant for Satan, we have these words, "You were the seal of perfection, full of wisdom and perfect in beauty. . . . You were the anointed cherub who covers; I established you; you were on the holy mountain of God. . . . You were perfect in your ways from the day you were created, till iniquity was found in you."[15]

And in Isaiah, "How you are fallen from heaven, O Lucifer, son of the morning! . . . For you have said in your heart: 'I will ascend into heaven, I will exalt my throne above the stars of God . . . *I will be like the Most High.*'"[16]

Satan was the highest of the created beings. As such, he is extraordinarily powerful. He is also subtle, deceitful, vile, and hateful beyond imagination. Jesus called him the "prince of this earth" and the "father of lies."[17]

His name Lucifer means "the light one." His name Satan means the "adversary." His name Beelzebub, according to some, means the "lord of the flies" or the "restless lord." His name Apollyon means "destroyer."[18] The apostle Peter said that he is like a roaring lion going to and fro seeking whom he may devour.[19]

Christians must remember that Satan appears as "an angel of light"—very beautiful, very seductive, very appealing.[20] His initial appearance is not that of some hideously deformed creature. That view comes later. Satan's guile and power notwithstanding, every Christian has the power, in the name of Jesus, to resist him and to overcome him. Jesus gave His disciples authority over all the power of the enemy![21]

---

4. What is going to happen to Satan?

Several things will happen to Satan. The Bible says that he comes to earth, knowing that he has a short time.[22] Because he knows that his days are short, he will be filled with wrath. We are going to see manifestations of Satan in this world that will be frightening to those who do not know Jesus. We have already seen some hideous manifestations of demonic power.

For example, I think that Adolf Hitler was demon possessed and that the terrible crimes he committed against humanity were satanic manifestations. I also believe that Karl Marx was a satanist priest and that his hideous philosophy, which has resulted in the massacre of tens of millions of people, is clearly based on satanism. The persecutions of innocent people in the gulags of the Soviet Union and other Communist countries are manifestations of supernatural inhumanity. In the future we may see a flood of evil that will attempt to destroy all human witness to God on earth.

Another thing that will happen to Satan is that he will possess a human being who is known as "the beast," or "the Antichrist," who will become a worldwide dictator.

This individual will exercise power in the name of Satan for at least three-and-a-half years.[23] There will be an attempt to set up a satanic kingdom on earth, with all manner of lying signs and wonders to back up the authority of the Antichrist. Finally, the people will be told to worship this creature. At that point, there will be a revolt against God and an attempt to destroy Israel. But when this happens, Jesus Christ will come back to earth and destroy the Antichrist. The devil will then be bound for one thousand years.[24]

During that time, we will have a period of peace on earth. Men will no longer be under demonic oppression. It will be a time of love, brotherhood, and no more war; even the animals will be at peace. But at the end of this time, after man has seen the paradise that results when God's will is done on earth, the devil will be set free one final time. He will lead one final assault on God. But he will lose, and he will be cast into a lake of fire. He and his angels will be there for the rest of eternity with no possibility of escape.[25]

5. What is demon possession?

Demon possession is the seizure of a human being by a demonic being to such a degree that the individual is controlled in whole or in part by the demon.[26]

The person who is demon possessed can manifest demonic qualities one minute and then be back in his right mind the next. The disease known as schizophrenia could, in certain individuals, be demon possession. This could be the case in instances where the person may speak in different voices and act in bizarre ways. One minute he could be a nice, calm, normal individual, and the next minute he could rage, foam at the mouth, and speak in an entirely different voice, blaspheming God.

In certain instances, demon-possessed individuals hear voices—voices that tell them to kill somebody, commit suicide, or undertake various kinds of sins. Such people may have an uncontrollable lust. They may have an uncontrollable desire to have harm done to themselves. Masochism and sadism and other perverted sex practices are, in many instances, the result of demon possession.

Demon possession can be manifested in many ways. But the goal of demons is to debase, defile, and ultimately destroy a human being who is made in the image of God. That is what Satan wants to do: attack God by destroying people who are precious in God's sight. However, people who serve Satan—the satanists and devil worshipers—will eventually be destroyed by that which they worship.

It is interesting to note that those who volunteer to serve Satan—the fortune-tellers, spiritists, witches, warlocks, and satanists—are themselves consumed by Satan. Not only will they share Satan's ultimate punishment by God, but they will be tormented and debased by Satan himself prior to final judgment.

6. Can a Christian be demon possessed?

People disagree over whether or not a Christian can be demon possessed.

I recall an incident from my own life when I was staying in a motel near Seattle, Washington. One morning, when I was in that stage between sleep and waking, an awful depression seized me. I felt that everyone was against me, that people around me were failing, and that everything I was doing was falling to pieces. Discouragement overwhelmed me like a dark cloud.

As I struggled to wake up, I realized I was under demonic attack. I immediately took control over it and said, "Satan, in the name of Jesus, I cast you forth." The minute I said that, my mind was free and my despair was gone. I realized later that the Seattle-Tacoma area led the nation in suicides. The spirit that was coming upon me was a suicidal spirit, the sort of influence that would lead to such depression that a person would wish to kill himself. I was in an area where many had been gripped by this kind of demon.

Had I not recognized what I was dealing with, I could have gone into a very deep depression that would have been hard to get out of. Even Spirit-filled Christians are subject to this kind of demonic influence upon their minds or in their bodies.[27]

However, I believe that if our spirits are joined to Jesus Christ, there is no way a demon can possess them. We have given our spirits to the Holy Spirit who keeps them safe. He is stronger than demons.[28] So I believe it would be impossible for a Christian to be possessed in his spirit by a demon.

---

7. What is the gift of the "discerning of spirits"?

In 1 Corinthians 12, the apostle Paul lists nine enablements, or manifestations, of the Holy Spirit. One of these is the "discerning of spirits." It is the ability to see into the spirit world, to see angels, demons, and, when He permits, even the Lord Himself. This can be frightening because with the operation of discerning of spirits, a person can see not only angels and demons but also the spirits of people. It is a glimpse behind the scenes into the invisible world.

For example, Jesus looked at Nathanael and said, "Behold an Israelite indeed, in whom is no guile!"[29] How did He know that? Through the discerning of spirits. Jesus also knew when He was dealing with demons. He saw them and recognized them, for example, in the Gadarene countryside.

Before casting them out, He recognized and spoke to one or more of a legion of demons occupying a demon-possessed man there. This manifestation of the Holy Spirit is extremely valuable, but it is often hard to handle.

---

8. What is exorcism? How can a demon be cast out?

Exorcism is commanding, in the name of Jesus, a demon to come out of an individual, a house, or wherever the demon happens to be. Exorcism is accomplished by the spoken word, in the name of Jesus, through the power of the Holy Spirit, and it is done simply and quickly.[30]

The person who is doing the exorcism should be filled with God's Spirit. He should not have any unsurrendered sin in his life, because the demon will take advantage of any weakness.[31] So, this person has to be pure of ulterior motives, sexual impurities, greed, and any other things that might lay him open to some charge by the devil, who is the accuser of the brethren

Another word of caution: People should not go out looking for demons or make up demons where they do not exist. A believer should be prepared to confront demons when the need arises, but he or she should not go out looking for this kind of encounter.

---

9. Does Satan know what I am thinking?

We do not know precisely how much Satan knows or does not know of what we are thinking. Scientists have shown that electrical current is generated by the human brain. According to at least one source I read, this current takes on the transmission qualities of radio signals. This explains, in some measure, why people who are very close often know what each other is thinking without spoken words being exchange. For this reason, it is possible that Satan knows at least a little bit about what we are thinking.

It would seem, also, that satanic forces are aware of blessings and opportunities that lie before believers. It seems that demonic forces do everything they can to discourage the Christian just at the moment of blessing. That has happened repeatedly in my life. Just before some great blessing comes, a time of maximum attack or discouragement seems to occur.

We do not know how well-informed, intelligent, or powerful Satan and his demons are. We understand something of their abilities, but we cannot be too definitive. What we do know is that as believers, we have authority over Satan and his entire army. We also learn that God has placed a hedge of protection around us.[32] We have the ability to attack and defeat Satan while being defended by God against Satan.

---

10. Do seances, Ouija boards, and fortune-telling lead to demonic possession?

Undoubtedly, various types of occult involvement are the prelude to demon possession. Little children are not aware, when they begin to play with these games, that a demonic reality is behind them. The current game called "Dungeons and Dragons" is based in large measure upon demonic symbols and types. When people begin to visualize these beings in their minds, they are giving an invitation to demons. When people become involved in transcendental meditation, the mantras they use are names of Hindu gods. If a person goes to an Ouija board to ask for direction, there is the possibility of deception by a demon. A visit to a fortune-teller will open a person to the ministration of a person who has a familiar spirit.[33]

All of these things are sins against God, forbidden by the Bible. They are also potential sources of demon possession.

Scripture References

1 See Hebrews 1:14
2 See Matthew 18:10
3 See Jude 9
4 See Daniel 10:13
5 See Ezekiel 1:5–6
6 See Isaiah 6:2, 6
7 See Exodus 25:18–22
8 See 2 Kings 19:35
9 See Daniel 10:9
10 See Isaiah 14:12–15, Ezekiel 28:12–19, Luke 10:18, Revelation 12:3–9, Matthew 12:43, 45, Matthew 25:41, 2 Peter 2:4, Ephesians 6:12, Jude 6
11 See Daniel 10:12–13, 20
12 1 John 4:4
13 See Luke 10:10
14 Luke 10:20
15 Ezekiel 28:12–15
16 Isaiah 14:12–14
17 See John 8:44
18 *Unger's Bible Handbook* (Chicago: Moody Press, 1966), 520–21.
19 See 1 Peter 5:8
20 2 Corinthians 11:14
21 See Luke 10:19, 1 John 3:8, James 4:7
22 See Revelation 12:12
23 See Revelation 13:4–8
24 See Revelation 20:1–3
25 See Revelation 20:7–10
26 See Matthew 8:28–32, Mark 1:23–27, 7:24–30, Luke 9:37–42
27 See 1 Thessalonians 5:23

28 See 1 John 4:4, Revelation 12:11
29 See John 1:47
30 See Acts 16:16–18
31 See Acts 19:13–16
32 See Job 1:10
33 See Leviticus 20:6

8. The Church

---

1. What is the one true church?

The one true church is the universal body of believers everywhere who have given their hearts to Jesus Christ as Savior and Lord. That is the only true church.[1]

The Bible teaches us that we must maintain the unity of the Spirit[2] until we come into unity of faith.[3] In other words, spiritual unity is something that all Christians can have. Complete unity of knowledge is something for the future.

The fact that there are many different denominations reflects a lack of knowledge in the church. In many instances, it also reflects pride. People are unwilling to meet together with others and submit their concepts to the body of Christ. And many denominations have come about because of doctrinal error. What begins as a beautiful and fresh revelation of God often degenerates into lukewarmness and then into fighting what God is doing.

Many times those who *claim* to know God persecute those who really do. It becomes necessary for the Lord Himself to come back with a fresh revelation to break through the solidification of the orthodox believers. This happened in Israel. Israel had lost sight of the Lawgiver in their exaltation of the law. They killed Jesus, who was the manifestation of God, in the name of their law.

In the Middle Ages, when the church had gained political as well as religious power, it began to grow corrupt. Then a reform movement came about through Martin Luther and others, who were persecuted severely by the church. Later on, Lutherans began to persecute Calvinists. Then Calvinists began to persecute Anabaptists, who brought out truth from God on baptism.

Still later, Baptists persecuted Pentecostals, who brought out a different truth about the baptism in the Holy Spirit. There have been succeeding waves of truth that God wants to restore to the church. These revelations of truth have been the seed for some of the major denominations which many times began as despised and persecuted sects.

The new Christian needs to find a fellowship of believers who love the Lord and who believe the Bible. There are Episcopal priests who love God with all their hearts, who are filled with the Holy Spirit, who serve Jesus, and whose churches are beautiful places of worship. In some Catholic churches born-again Christians could feel at home. There are Baptist churches where the members love God, Presbyterian churches where the members love God, as well as Methodist, Assemblies of God, Nazarene, and Holiness churches and many others where the members love God.

When you are looking for a church home, the first thing to do is to ask the Lord to guide you. Ask Him where He wants you. Find a church that is true to the Bible, one where the people love Jesus Christ and serve Him as Lord. Are the doctrine, teaching, and practice of that church in accordance with the Word of God? Do the members try to live out the doctrine they profess? If you find those characteristics and a warm fellowship, the church may be for you.

2. What are the chief differences between Roman Catholics and Protestants?

I believe the major difference between Roman Catholics and Protestants is the place given to the Bible. Although Roman Catholics believe that the holy Scriptures are inspired of God, they also believe that, along with the Bible, the tradition of the church through history, brought about by church councils, is to be given weight in matters of faith and doctrine. Protestants believe that the sole rule of faith and practice should be the holy Scriptures, and therefore, they do not accept certain Catholic practices that are primarily justified by appealing to tradition. They do not accept the authority of the pope. They do not accept the practice of praying to the Virgin Mary, and they do not accept other rituals practiced in Roman Catholicism.

At the time of the Reformation, a Roman Catholic monk named Martin Luther rediscovered the doctrine of justification by faith set out by the apostle Paul in the book of Romans.[4] If a man is justified from his sin by faith alone, Luther reasoned, then what is the need for pilgrimages, penance, indulgences, purgatory, and the last rites? Since Luther's findings were interpreted to undercut Roman Catholic tradition, he was excommunicated. However, large numbers of Germans flocked to hear him, and there arose what came to be the Lutheran church.

Then other theologians such as John Calvin challenged Roman Catholic teaching, and Calvinistic churches known as Reformed churches emerged. These churches, arising out of a "protest" to reform Roman Catholicism, were called Protestant churches. That period of history, approximately from 1500 to 1650, is called the Protestant Reformation.

3. According to the Bible, what must a person do to become a saint?

The traditional view of sainthood gives special recognition to people who have lived godly, holy lives. This is not the biblical view. According to the Bible, when someone meets Jesus Christ as Savior and is born again, that person becomes a saint not by virtue of a holy life but because of a relationship to Jesus Christ.

When the apostle Paul wrote to one of the other New Testament cities, he addressed his letter to the "saints" of God in that city. He was talking to every church member. Anyone who has been made holy in Jesus is a saint. Unless we belong to Jesus, our accomplishments do not mean anything in God's sight.

Obviously, if God is fair, and He is, He will not ignore the labors of Christians in this life. There will be rewards in heaven. Having done everything we can do, we still must realize that we are only doing what we should and that our righteousness—our sainthood—comes from Jesus, not from our works.

4. Does being a church member ensure that I will go to heaven?

Many people believe that joining a church, being baptized in a church, or going through some ritual in a church guarantees them heaven. That is not true. The Bible says that unless you are born again, you cannot enter the Kingdom of God.[5] It takes more than being a church member to get into heaven. If you *are* born again, you are part of the body of Christ and you are a member of the universal church. Merely putting your name on a church roll does not bring you salvation.

---

5. Do I have to go to chuch to be saved?

No. However, Christianity is not a solitary religion. We are a communal people, and the Bible tells us not to forsake the assembling of ourselves together.[6]

We need fellowship, we need encouragement from one another, and we need to have our views and concepts balanced and checked by other Christians. Jesus said that it takes two or more gathered together for Him to be in their midst.[7] That means a family can have the Lord in their midst. But even there, one person acts as a counterbalance on another. You do not have some person who goes off and sits on a high mountain all by himself and comes up with a new religion.

You do not have to be in the church to be saved, but to continue effectively in the things of God, you must be in some type of fellowship with other Christian people, and churches meet that need.

---

6. Should babies or adults be baptized, and how should it be done?

The Bible teaches the baptism of believers.[8] And in the early centuries, Christian baptism was by immersion. The concept of infant baptism is not specifically found in the Bible.

The early church began baptizing infants because of the idea that children are born in sin and need immediate baptism to ensure their salvation. At the time of the Reformation, though, Martin Luther rediscovered the biblical truth that spiritual regeneration and justification are by faith. A baby cannot exercise faith. Nevertheless, because so many of those who became his followers had already been baptized as infants in the Roman Catholic Church, Luther did not require them to be baptized again. In fact, he continued to baptize children of believers.

When John Calvin came on the scene in Geneva, he taught what is known as "covenant theology." According to covenant theology, if the parents have entered a covenant relationship with God, then their children are part of the covenant, too, and are proper candidates for baptism as infants.

In churches that practice infant baptism there is usually some type of confirmation rite in which a child of ten, eleven, or twelve reaffirms the parental faith expressed at his or her baptism.

Some Reformation theologians strongly disagreed with infant baptism. They maintained that people should be baptized only as believers, because baptism is a symbol of the death, burial, and resurrection of Jesus.[9] Baptism to them was the end of the old life and the beginning of a new life in Christ. Since a baby does not have an old life to deal with, they maintained, if someone has been baptized as an infant, he needs to be baptized again as an adult believer. These people were called "Anabaptists," which means "rebaptizers."

Today there is still disagreement about the proper form of baptism. But, more and more, Methodist, Presbyterian, and some other churches that have historically practiced infant baptism are looking anew at both the qualification of a candidate for baptism and the mode of baptism. A number of people, even though they may have been baptized as infants, are being rebaptized by immersion as adult believers.

---

7. What form of church government is the best?

The New Testament church had a central governing body of "apostles and elders" in Jerusalem, possibly modeled after the seventy-member Jewish Sanhedrin, whose primary task was the preservation of doctrine and practice. Churches were established by apostles chosen by God and recognized by the body of believers. The apostle Paul, and others of the apostles, ordained *presbyters* (elders) to preside over the church in each city or region.

Many scholars feel that the presbyter or teaching elder was the same as the *episkopos* (overseer or bishop). In the Jerusalem church and in the other churches, men were chosen who were "full of the Holy Spirit and wisdom," called deacons, who were placed by the apostles over the financial and other temporal concerns of the church in order to free the apostles for the ministry of the Word and prayer. Spiritual authority flowed from God, through the apostles, to the local bishops or elders, then to the people.

Spiritually, the early church was a theocracy, but in matters concerning money and property, the local assemblies appeared to be autonomous and more democratic, acting as they wished upon the advice and counsel of spiritual leaders.

Among the better known denominations today, the church government I feel most closely paralleling that of the New Testament is the Presbyterian. On the local level is the "session" consisting of the pastor, or teaching elder, and the ruling elders.[10] These elders or presbyters are responsible for the spiritual life of the church. Along with them is the board of deacons. The deacons[11] govern the temporal affairs of the church, including ministry to the poor, the needy, and the shut-ins.[12] The local congregation is self-governing; yet a regional group of elders from the local churches called "the presbytery" oversees the qualifications of ministers and serves as an appeals board for the local churches. On a national basis, the General Assembly deals with major issues and questions of creeds and doctrines, and it coordinates missionary, educational, and publishing programs.[13]

Often lacking in this system, in practice if not in theory, are the offices established by Christ: apostle, prophet, teacher, pastor, and evangelist.[14] Nevertheless, this governmental form usually has an excellent balance between the autonomy of the local congregation and the supervision of denominational officials.

Other denominations, notably Baptists and most independent churches, have a congregational system of government. All authority is vested in the membership of the local congregation which, by democratic process, elects a governing body of deacons, calls a pastor, and usually has trustees to hold titles to property.

Although this form of church government gives maximum freedom to the members of a local congregation, it is handicapped by the absence of an effective appeals procedure in case of doctrinal disputes, financial disputes, or problems arising in pastoral relations. As a result, congregations can dominate the pastor, who should be God's servant. On the other hand, the people can either be dominated by a strong pastor or stuck with an unsatisfactory one. Without a true spirit of prayer and humility, the only remedy left in such a situation is a power struggle, a suit in a secular court, or a messy church split.

Another form of church government is the Episcopal, governed by an archbishop or presiding bishop and council of bishops. In the Roman church the papal system has developed in which great power is given to a pope who, in turn, appoints other church officials such as cardinals, archbishops, and bishops. These more autocratic forms of church government have the advantage of a great sense of historic continuity, plus the ability to mobilize coordinated resources and to control both purity of doctrine and the practice of the clergy. Because of concentration of power, the functioning of hierarchical forms of church government depends in large measure on the quality of their leaders. These churches can be led to great spiritual heights by the proper leaders, or they can be more easily corrupted by the wrong leaders.

---

8. Should I pay my tithe to the local church?

In the Old Testament, the Jews were told to take their tithes to the storehouse.[15] In Israel, the storehouse was the temple, the center of religion for the entire country. All the people paid their tithes by taking them to the storehouse.

Prior to the time of the temple, however, Abraham met an unusual man named Melchizedek, who was the king of Salem (modern day Jerusalem.)[16] The word *Melchizedek* means "king of righteousness." He was a king of righteousness and peace, and he was a type of Christ. When Melchizedek blessed Abraham, after Abraham had won a battle, the patriarch gave Melchizedek one-tenth of everything he had won. The lesson we learn is that the spiritual authority which brings blessing is entitled to a tithe.

Today there is not one central storehouse. The body of Christ has various manifestations. It has colleges, local churches, television ministries, overseas missions, evangelists, hospitals, relief agencies, and orphanages. All of these make up the storehouse of God. People can give their tithes to any spiritual authority that is ordained of God.

One final word, though. When you commit yourself to be a member of a local church, then that church should be honored with your financial support. You should do this not because it is an absolute obligation of scripture but because you have entered into a covenant of membership entailing both privileges and responsibilities.

9. How do I recognize a cult?

Practically every cult has certain characteristics that can tell the careful observer that something is wrong. For instance, what does a group think about Jesus? Jesus Christ is God, Lord of all, the only source of salvation. Invariably, a cult will put something else on an equal footing with Christ. It will have a ritual that is equal to Christ, or it will have a doctrine equal to Christ, or it will have a leader who is equal to Christ. In other words, even if it acknowledges Christ as Savior, it will say that you need something else before you can get into heaven. Cults teach that salvation comes through Christ, *plus* their little unique way. Some cults do not acknowledge Christ at all. They may make Him coequal with their religious teachers or with certain great men of history. The quickest way to recognize a cult is by its treatment of Jesus.

Second, cults frequently attempt to instill fear into their followers. The followers are taught constantly that salvation comes only through the cult. "If you leave us, you will lose your salvation," they say.

The third area has to do with the exaltation of the leader of the cult. Cults often center around a man or woman who is trying to gain power, money, or influence from manipulating people. This appears to be the case in the Unification church with Sun Myung Moon. In the Children of God, Moses David Berg is an autocratic leader. In the People's Temple, Jim Jones drew attention to himself and asked his followers to die with him. A true leader who serves Jesus Christ has one goal, and that is to exalt and manifest Jesus. When someone says he has unique insight into God or is the special one that God has anointed to reach the world, you are dealing with cultic behavior.

A final mark of a cult is the unwillingness of the leaders to let the people grow up. A true shepherd will do everything he can to bring Christian people to maturity as quickly as he can. He will not seek to avoid necessary teaching, nor will he try to keep people from maturity. Many cults perpetuate spiritual dependence so that their followers lose the ability to make independent, rational decisions. Often techniques of brainwashing are used to create robotlike behavior.

Although there are other marks of cultic behavior, these seem to be the ones that stand out.

---

10. What do Mormons believe?

Mormons are some of the most exemplary human beings, especially in regard to their behavior patterns and their adherence to the fundamental values of our society. But their religious beliefs are, to put it simply, wrong. They believe that an angel named Moroni left some gold tablets in upstate New York and that these tablets were discovered by a man named Joseph Smith. From these tablets, Joseph Smith "translated" the *Book of Mormon*, which is the foundation upon which Mormonism is built. Mormons also consider two other books, *Doctrine and Covenants* and *The Pearl of Great Price*, to be divinely inspired.

Mormonism differs from biblical Christianity in several areas. Mormons do not believe, for example, that salvation comes through faith in Jesus Christ. Mormons must work their way to heaven.[17]

Mormonism teaches that God is not the *only* deity and that we all have the potential of becoming gods.[18] (Remember that Satan's fall came about because he wanted to be like God.) God, according to Mormons, is not just Spirit but has "a body of flesh and bones as tangible as a man's."[19] They teach, "As we are, he was. As he is, we shall become."[20] There has been constant revision of Mormon doctrine over the years, as church leaders have changed their minds on a number of subjects, including polygamy, which was once sanctioned by the church.

In summary, the Mormon church is a prosperous, growing organization that has produced many people of exemplary character. But when it comes to spiritual matters, the Mormons are far from the truth.

---

11. What do Jehovah's Witnesses believe?

Jehovah's Witnesses believe, essentially, that to gain salvation you must witness for Jehovah; you must go out on the streets and proclaim salvation in Jehovah. They are different from Christians in that they believe Jesus Christ is only one of many gods and that He is a created being. They translate John 1:1 as, "In the beginning was the word . . . and the word was *a* god." The Greek says, instead, "And the word was God."[21]

Because Jehovah's Witnesses give allegiance only to

Jehovah, they do not pledge allegiance to the flag, they do not vote, they do not serve in armed forces, and they do not hold public office. They do not celebrate holidays or birthdays. Another unique teaching prohibits them from taking blood transfusions.

Jehovah's Witnesses originally taught that the world would end in 1914. It obviously did not. They also taught that there were only 144,000 people who were going to be saved by going to heaven. When Jehovah's Witnesses membership went past 144,000, they said they were the meek and were going to inherit the earth.

A major problem with the tenets of Jehovah's Witnesses is that there is never an assurance of salvation. In Christianity, a person can know that he is saved by trusting in Jesus. Jehovah's Witnesses believe that salvation comes through good works, so they must work continuously, without ever really knowing whether they will be saved. Many of their other doctrines are not biblical either.

---

12. What do Unitarians believe?

Unitarians do not believe in the trinity and they do not believe that Jesus is divine. They say they worship God only and are attempting to demonstrate a "genuinely religious" community without doctrinal conformity. They believe in rationalism, social action, and the inherent goodness of humans. Because they do not believe in salvation through Jesus Christ, who would have to be divine in order to save us, they have developed a humanistic type of religion that makes salvation dependent upon ethical good works.

The beliefs of one member of this society were clearly summarized a few years ago in an advertisement:

> Do Unitarians Believe in Anything?
> We believe in brotherhood; . . . in Civil Rights; in the United Nations; in upgrading our educational system; in an

attack on the problems of poverty; in the nuclear test ban treaty. . . . Many of us even believe in God.

In 1961, the Unitarians merged with a group called The Universalists who, during the 19th century held that salvation was ultimately for everyone, regardless of repentance in this life. The Universalist teaching acknowledges that Jesus is God, but takes away any human responsibility in salvation. Because the Unitarians do not believe Jesus is God, it is hard to understand how these two groups could have gotten together, but they did.

Today it is difficult to distinguish the statements of Unitarians from humanists and atheists.

---

13. What does the Unification Church teach?

The Unification Church centers around the Reverend Sun Myung Moon, who developed the church in Korea and moved its headquarters to the United States in 1972. Since then it has grown rapidly in size and respectability. Reverend Moon believes that there is a political solution to the world's problems and that he should be the world's leader.

The teachings of the Unification Church are found in *The Divine Principle*, which is supposedly made up of revelations from God to Moon. According to Moon, three Adams comprise God's plan for the earth. The first Adam and his wife Eve were supposed to establish the kingdom of heaven on earth through their offspring. But they sinned and their fall thwarted God's plans. The second Adam—Jesus Christ—was supposed to get married to the perfect mate and take political power away from the Roman Empire. Instead, says Moon, Satan invaded Christ's body, He was killed, and God's plans were thwarted again. Moon says that Jesus is not God but merely a man who perfectly understood what God wanted. Moon rejects the bodily resurrection of Christ and belief in the Trinity.

The third Adam—what Moon calls the Lord of the Second Advent—will marry the perfect mate, found the perfect family, and bring physical as well as spiritual salvation. The Lord of the Second Advent will take Jesus' place and all nations will unite under him. Although Moon has not said explicitly that he is the Lord of the Second Advent, everything he tells his followers appears to lead them to believe that to be so.

A good part of what the church teaches is secret. In fact Moon's followers are encouraged to practice "Heavenly Deception," deceiving people by telling them anything to get donations. However, their tactics and techniques are well known. Former members of the Unification Church— "Moonies"—say the church uses oriental deprivation techniques to brainwash their young adherents who are often picked up on the street. Once the young people are "loved" into the church, they are taken to houses where church members live together in community. Former Moonies have said prospective members are permitted no sleep for hours, and are harangued over and over again until they are insensible. They acknowledge and accept the church's doctrines not so much of their own free will but through brainwashing. After the brainwashing, they are then sent out on the streets to solicit money for the Unification Church. It is said that adherents get meager amounts of food, live in spartan surroundings, and are deprived of contact with the outside world. They do not even have time to reflect upon the lies they are being told.

The Unification Church has been extraordinarily successful financially, and this has enabled it to pour a lot of money into its evangelistic efforts. It owns many companies in Korea including Il Wha Pharmaceutical Company and Tong Wat Titanium Company. In the United States it has bought a number of companies: the Diplomat National Bank, the New Yorker Hotel, and the *Washington Times* newspaper.

14. What is Hare Krishna?

Hare Krishna (the International Society for Krishna Consciousness) is a Hindu cult that worships Krishna as the supreme deity. Hinduism has many gods, but the most important three are Brahma (god of creation), Shiva (god of destruction), and Vishnu (god of preservation). Vishnu, it is believed, had many incarnations on earth, the most popular one of which is Krishna. In the 1930s a follower of a cult of Krishna in India was commissioned to spread the cult's teaching to the West. He was given the name Swami Prabhupada. He came to the United States in 1965 and started Hare Krishna in New York City.

Like most Hindu cults, Hare Krishna teaches that we somehow make up part of a universal consciousness and that we are part of god. Also like most Hindu cults, Hare Krishnas believe in reincarnation. Hare Krishnas, however, teach that Krishna is the same as the God of Judaism, the God of Christianity, and the god of Islam. Other religions, Hare Krishnas say, just don't recognize his true name: Krishna. Salvation comes through Krishna consciousness. And since Krishna is the same as his name, chanting his name is tasting him and giving an offering to him.

Followers of Swami Prabhupada therefore chant and dance before Hindu deities daily. They exercise sixty-four items of devotional service prescribed by Prabhupada. They wear a distinctive saffron dress, and the men have shaved heads except for a pigtail. Food is important to Hare Krishnas—who are vegetarian—because each meal is seen as communion with Krishna.

The Hare Krishnas, who frequently appear in airports and other public places begging or selling literature or flowers, are just one manifestation of the various Hindu groups that have come to America in the last twenty-five years. Bagwan Shree Rajneesh in Rajneeshpurim, Oregon, is a more recent example.

Significantly, the land of their origin—India—has horrible poverty. It also has desperate problems of overpopulation, illiteracy, hunger, mismanagement, and suffering. So it seems strange that religions which have brought such trouble to India would be imported to America where we have flourished and prospered under Christianity for several centuries.

---

15. What are the principal beliefs of mind control, spiritism, Edgar Cayce, and Hinduism?

In one way or another each of these cults focuses on the "universal consciousness" concept that human beings—

- are part of a vast, timeless consciousness,
- are ultimately divine,
- will live forever in various forms,
- can communicate with the dead or various spirits in the universe through reincarnation,
- and can receive power through psychic and, in some instances, bodily exercises to transcend nature, understand mysteries, and affect their own destinies or the lives of those around them.

These groups, in the name of "research and enlightenment," "psychic research," "transcendental meditation," "yoga," etc., are actually not in touch with some great "God consciousness" or psychic power but Satan and demons.

The Greek word *psuche* is translated "soul," and from that we get the term *psychic*. Most of these things deal with psychic, or soulish, phenomena. When people touch the true God, they do so through the human spirit. God does not work on the soul of man but the spirit.

The apostle Paul, writing to the Corinthians, said the *psuchikos* man, the soulish man, will not receive the things of the Spirit of God, for they are foolishness to him.[22] Mind control, the Edgar Cayce teachings, and the new age movement all appeal to the soulish man, because they do not require repentance. They do not require being born again. A concept in most of these cults is that if a person gains sufficient knowledge, he can dominate and control the events of the world because he is part of god. He can manipulate god, because he *is* god. He is part of the universal consciousness, and as he opens himself up to progressive revelations, he in turn is lifted to higher and higher levels of understanding. As he advances, they teach, he gains authority over himself, his body, and those around him.

We must remember that the soulish realm is the realm of demons. Demons can and often do enter into this psychic area. The people who are in touch with the dead, in touch with "the other world," are not tapping into some universal consciousness. They are in touch with demons. Demons lurk behind the Hindu and other oriental religions, as well as behind the mind control teachings. As people try to exercise their soulish powers and manipulate others, they are trying to project themselves into this world of demonic power. They are not asking for a savior. They are not asking for forgiveness. Instead, they are asking for human power, for expansion of human psychic potential, and therein is their downfall. Those who stay with these beliefs long enough get deeper and deeper into them. They will sooner or later be in touch with, and perhaps even possessed by, demons.

The Bible does not tell us to get involved in sharpening our psychic powers. Such things are not of God. God will give people the wisdom they need through the Bible. And through the Holy Spirit, He will give them the power they need to live the life they are supposed to live. This inordinate seeking of knowledge about the future, the inordinate seeking of power over other people, the inordinate seeking of enhancement of human potential, is dangerous. Just entering into such activity is bad. I have heard of people who have started to levitate, and some who have had horrible faces appear to them in the night. All such things are symbols and signs that these people are in touch with demons.

16. What is the greatest problem facing the church today?

From my point of view, the greatest problem facing the church is lack of unity. When Jesus Christ was getting ready to leave this earth, He prayed for His disciples and asked especially that they would be united.[23] He said that whenever His followers acted in unity, the world would know that the Father had sent Him.[24] However, it is extremely difficult in this world to achieve the kind of unity, love, and concern for one another that Jesus Christ shared with His disciples.

I am not advocating unity at the expense of purity or at the expense of doctrinal truth. We cannot throw out the Bible in order to have unity. We cannot embrace any strange doctrine just to have superficial unity. But we must have unity where those who truly love Jesus Christ will love each other and try to work together. Even though they may differ over techniques and other superficial things, Christians must work together and emphasize areas of agreement. When this happens, the church will become a supernaturally powerful force. According to the book of Genesis, upon the occasion of the building of the tower of Babel, God saw that the poeple had one language and were of one accord. Because of this, He said that nothing they wanted to do would have been impossible for them.[25] If the church could achieve unity, it could change the political and social structure of society with no trouble at all. The world would be a beautiful place to live in if the church would get together. Regrettably, we do not. We have a divisive party spirit . . . we have jealousy . . . we fight . . . we are suspicious of one another. I am not talking about those who do not really believe in God. I am talking about the ones who are believers, who have been born again. If people will truly follow after the Spirit of God, they can operate in unity, because the Spirit of God will give them unity.

Unity begins to break down when man's selfishness enters the picture. For unity we have to have mutual respect and a mutual willingness to give and to surrender, not to the other person so much, but to Jesus. We can truly have unity when we all want God's will to be done.

---

17. Is Saturday or Sunday the true Sabbath?

I think the true Sabbath is a day of rest—one out of seven days. Jesus said, "The Sabbath was made for man, and not man for the Sabbath."[26] By that He meant that God has set up a cyclical type of existence for us, where it is absolutely imperative that we take a break in our work to rest, to be refreshed, to think of things of the Spirit, and to worship Him. Moslems celebrate Friday, Jews Saturday, and Christians Sunday. It is hard to say that one day has any benefit over another. The apostle Paul says in Colossians that we are not to be bound by any days. He tells us that we are not saved through the observance of Sabbath days or various feast days, because such things are just a shadow of the truth and the truth is Jesus Christ.[27] So in a sense we have a Sabbath rest in Jesus Christ all the time.

From a practical standpoint, I believe that people should read Isaiah 58 and see what it says about keeping the Sabbath. We should dedicate a day to the Lord, a day when we do not think our own thoughts or spend time in business or worldly pleasure but when we rest and meditate on Him. God says, in Isaiah 58, that if we do that, we will receive the heritage of Jacob and we will ride on the high places of the earth. That is a wonderful promise.

I have found that in my own life, taking a day off, which for me is Sunday, is a most welcome time. It is a time when I am not watching television or going to ball games or running around. Instead, I am seeking God. I am praying, I am studying, I am reading the Word, I am talking to the Lord, and I am being refreshed with rest. Setting aside one day a week for your Sabbath can make a tremendous difference in your life.

The reason Christians worship on Sunday instead of Saturday is that Sunday is the day of the Resurrection. Jesus rose from the grave on Sunday, and the Christian church celebrates that day. The early Jewish believers probably also kept Saturday as a rest day. Remember, however, that those who would be legalistic in this affair of literal Sabbath-keeping should stop work at sundown on Friday, observe complete rest, and not work again until sundown on Saturday. Frankly, I do not believe that Christians have to keep Jewish customs in order to please God. Jesus has fulfilled all the demands of the law so that His followers might live under grace.[28]

---

18. What are tithes?

A tithe is a tenth. In the Bible we are told to bring tithes and offerings to the Lord.[29] A tithe is one tenth of your income. An offering is anything beyond the tenth. As I study the Old Testament, I find there were three tithes: (1) a tithe given to the church, or to the temple, for the work of the Levites and the priests; (2) a tithe to be distributed to the poor in the land; and (3) a praise tithe of the produce, which was to be either eaten before the Lord or exchanged for money.[30]

Thinking about this causes me to speculate on an ideal taxation system. It would be wonderful if 10 percent of everyone's income would go toward religious instruction, teaching, and worship so that the whole population could be instructed in the Word of God. Then, a second 10 percent could go for welfare, roads, harbors, various social projects, old age relief, and any other social needs. Then, another 5 percent or so could be spent on personal vacations. Not vacations that were orgies of lust and personal pleasure, but vacations where people rested, worshiped and enjoyed God, thanking Him for what He had done. This would be a time when people could go to the pleasant places and eat good food. They could relax, praise the Lord, and acknowledge that He is in their midst.

This plan would require 25 percent of our national income. I believe that if we adopted the first 10 percent for religious training, our needs for welfare would be reduced dramatically as people began to look after their own elderly and their own sick, thereby reducing the burden on government.

In determining a giving pattern, the Christian should consider 10 percent as an irreducible minimum. We belong to the Lord and so do all our possessions. Therefore, what we give should be determined by God's leading in our lives. Some may give 25 percent, others 50 percent. Some might use 10 percent to live on and give away 90 percent.

We give as God has blessed us. I believe there is also merit in the concept of anticipatory tithing. Consider the income that you anticipate receiving, and tithe as if you already had it.

---

19. What does the Bible teach about the Jewish people and the nation of Israel?

The nation of Israel is unique in the role God chose for it. In the creation there was Adam, and then there was Noah who survived the Flood. From Noah's child, Shem, came a family out of which was born a man named Abram (Abraham). He was called by God to journey to a foreign land, which is now Palestine. God said to him, "In you all the families of the earth shall be blessed."[31] From Abraham came Isaac and then Jacob, later called "Israel." From Jacob came twelve sons whose families became the twelve tribes comprising the nation of Israel.

To this nation was given the revelation of God, His nature, His laws, and His history. Israel was entrusted with the Bible, and because of these people all the nations of the earth have been blessed.

But the greatest blessing by far that was entrusted to Israel was the bringing forth of the Messiah who would die for the sins of mankind, to restore man to the fellowship with God that he lost at the Fall. For two thousand years the children of Abraham were sheltered, set apart from the nations, and instructed in the ways of God. Then in what the Bible calls "the fullness of time," God sent to the Jewish people Jesus of Nazareth, who was the Messiah or "anointed one"—the Christ.[32] The message of His coming, His death, and His resurrection has been the true means whereby all the nations of the world have been blessed.

The people of Israel are still precious to God. The Old Testament promised that the nation of Israel would be restored in the last times.[33] This prophecy was fulfilled in 1948. Even though Israel was destroyed and its people scattered abroad because of their unbelief, God said He would rebuild the nation just prior to the end of the age. At the climax of history the Israelis will turn to God, and the nation will once again become a center of God's revelation to all mankind.[34] The law will go forth from Jerusalem, and all the nations will come to Jerusalem to learn the law of the Lord.[35] At that time, the natural sons of Abraham will be exalted, along with those who, through faith in Jesus Christ, have become sons of Abraham after the Spirit. So in the last days the Jews and the church will share a wonderful glory.[36]

The nation of Israel as a whole did not accept Jesus when He was on earth. The apostle Paul said that even their unbelief became a blessing to the rest of the world, because they were temporarily cut off from God's salvation and the Gentiles took their place. When the Jews refused to believe, the rest of us were offered a chance. But when they return to faith it will be equivalent to the resurrection of the dead.[37] Some people think that a certain sign of the return of Jesus Christ to earth will be the restoration of the Jewish people to an understanding of God's full revelation in Christ.

Scripture References

1 See Ephesians 1:22–23, Colossians 1:18
2 See Ephesians 4:3
3 See Ephesians 4:13
4 See Romans 3:24–30
5 See John 3:3
6 See Hebrews 10:25
7 See Matthew 18:20
8 See Mark 16:16, Acts 8:36–37
9 See Romans 6:4, Colossians 2:12
10 See 1 Timothy 3:1–7, Titus 1:6–9, 1 Peter 5:2
11 See 1 Timothy 3:8–13
12 See Acts 6:1–4
13 See Acts 15:5–29
14 See Ephesians 4:11–12
15 See Malachi 3:10
16 See Genesis 14:18
17 B. R. McConkie, *Mormon Doctrine* (Salt Lake City: 1958), p. 191
18 Ibid., p. 576
19 *Doctrine and Covenants*, 130:22
20 Joseph Smith, "The King Follett Discourse," p. 9
21 John 1:1
22 See 1 Corinthians 2:14
23 See John 17:20–21
24 See John 17:23
25 See Genesis 11:6
26 Mark 2:27
27 See Colossians 2:16–17
28 See Romans 6:15, Galatians 4:4–7

29 See Malachi 3:10
30 See Deuteronomy 14:22–29, Numbers 18:28
31 Genesis 12:3
32 See Galatians 4:4
33 See Ezekiel 11:17
34 See Zechariah 12:10
35 See Isaiah 2:2–3
36 See Romans 11:25–26
37 See Romans 11:1–32

9. Last Things

1. When is Jesus Christ coming again?

Nobody can say with any degree of certainty when Jesus is coming again, because He said clearly that even the angels in heaven do not know that day.[1] No man knows that day, and the Son of God, when He was on the earth, did not know either. This knowledge, the Lord Jesus said, was strictly reserved for the Father.

We can see certain signs, or clues,[2] that His coming is approaching. Jesus said there would be wars and rumors of wars, revolutions, widespread famine, disease, and earthquakes in many different places.[3] There would be an increase of lawlessness and anarchy. The apostle Paul said, "That day will not come unless the falling away comes first, and the man of sin is revealed, the son of perdition, who opposes and exalts himself above all that is called God."[4] Along with the "man of sin" will come what is called an apostasy, or a falling away. Many of the believing people will grow cold in their faith.[5] There will be persecution of Christians and a time of general trouble.

I think all these things are happening with increasing frequency.

Another event that had to happen before Jesus could return was the re-establishment of the state of Israel. The original Israel disappeared from the globe hundreds of years ago. In 1948 a new state of Israel was established. The regathering of Jews to Israel is a clear sign, in both the Old and New Testaments, that our age is just about over. Jesus said, "Jerusalem will be trampled by Gentiles until the times of the Gentiles are fulfilled."[6] On June 6, 1967, the Jews, for the first time since Jerusalem was captured by Nebuchadnezzar in 586 B.C., took over control of the entire city of Jerusalem, thus signaling the approaching end of Gentile world power.

Jesus said, however, that the one major thing which would herald His coming would be the proclamation of the gospel. He said, "This gospel of the kingdom will be preached in all the world as a witness to all the nations, and then the end will come."[7]

These are signs of the times. We are to hold ourselves always ready for our Lord's return. But nobody knows the day and hour when that will be.

---

2. What else must happen before Christ returns?

Some people teach that Jesus could come at any time because Jesus warned His disciples always to be watchful. While it is true that we do not know exactly when He will come, certain signs of His coming were discussed in my last answer. Jesus said the coming of the Son of Man will be just like the days of Noah.[8] The thing that strikes me about the days of Noah is that even in the midst of terrible apostasy, evil, violence, and rebellion against God, the people went ahead with their normal lives. They planted fields, they harvested crops, they built houses, they got married, and they had children. They went about business as usual, until the very day that Noah entered the ark, and then destruction came and took them all away.

That is how it will be when Jesus comes again. Business will go on pretty much as usual until the dreadful wrath of God and the Tribulation fall upon the earth. Then it will be too late to turn to God. At that point Jesus will come back again.

He *could* come back tonight, but it is my personal feeling that some of the signs of His coming—especially the revelation of the "man of sin"[9]—have not yet occurred.

---

3. Are these the last days?

The Bible says that in the last days many scoffers will say, "Where is the promise of His coming? For since the fathers fell asleep, all things continue as they were from the beginning of creation."[10] On my birthday, when I was fifty-four years old, the producer of "The 700 Club" television program gave me a front page of the *New York Times* for the day I was born in 1930. The similarity between those days and these days is striking. There are the same kinds of trouble in the world, the same kinds of international tension, and the same kinds of money problems. So these days are not far different from those days. Yet, by now, we have seen the occurrences of some very significant events that convince me that these are the last days.

First of all, the nation of Israel was reborn in 1948. That nation will complete a generation of forty years in 1988. Second, the Jews now control all of Jerusalem and have since 1967. That is very significant as I have noted in previous answers. Third, we have the ability, with nuclear weapons, to obliterate all life, or to kill, as Revelation puts it, at least one third of all people in a single war.[11]

Another thing that we have today is an incredible explosion of knowledge.[12] Our knowledge doubles every six years. We have unlocked the atom and the secrets of the gene. We have come close to the heart of life itself, and in the process we have grown callous toward our fellow men and toward the Creator of life.

We are expanding our knowledge in many areas which

could benefit all people by making their lives healthier and easier. But this same knowledge has dreadful potential for misuse. Those who work in the field of genetic engineering, for instance, are not too far from being able to clone human beings by taking parts out of embryos in order to create some kind of master race. Other scientists are working to create computers that appear to reason like men. These could open up vistas of great blessing, but they could also bring about horrors if placed in the hands of the wrong people. Add to this the ability of computers to monitor the behavior of populations and to control all of the world's money. These developments are fulfilling biblical prophecies. This tells me that we are getting very close to the time when God is going to say that the human race has gone far enough. He may be ready to step in to terminate this phase of human activity and to start another one.

That is why I firmly expect to be alive when Jesus Christ comes back to earth.

---

4. Who or what is the Antichrist?

In the book of Revelation we are told that a dictator will arise from the revived Roman Empire. He will be endued with the power of Satan himself and will take unto himself the prerogatives of God.[13] The apostle Paul said there would be someone who would stand in the temple of God, claiming that he was God.[14] Revelation amplifies this subject when it speaks of a false prophet who will stand in front of this dictator and do signs in his name, and also cause a statue of this dictator to perform miraculous signs.[15]

We do know that the book of Revelation was written during a time when Christians were being persecuted in the Roman Empire. We also know that the Roman emperors liked to think of themselves as gods. They even made statues of themselves and asked people to fall down and worship them. There is always the possibility that the Antichrist is already in the world. I believe those earlier dictators were merely representations of the final world dictator. This man will appear as a great leader, speaking great words of wisdom, and will draw all of the non-Christian people to worship him. To them he will be the sum of wisdom, with the answers to all their problems.[16]

For an antichrist figure to come into the modern world, there must be a breakdown of the world system as we know it now. There would have to be breakdowns in currency, in law and order, and in the power structures of national states.

A financial panic could help pave the way for him. So could a nuclear war. Such disasters could leave people crying out for a man of peace, who will be Satan's counterfeit to Jesus Christ. This man will seem to be like Jesus, until such time as he is ready to show his true self. Then he will be incredibly cruel. He will be like a combination of Adolf Hitler, Joseph Stalin, Genghis Khan, Mao Tse-tung, and other dictators who have butchered millions of people. The Antichrist will be the most hideous example of dictatorial power that the world has ever known.

Remember that the antichrist spirit is in anybody who tries to draw people away from Jesus, saying, "Worship me." The antichrist spirit is present now in the worship and veneration we give to governments, dictators, military leaders, and various other human figures. The humanism that is being taught in our schools, media, and intellectual circles will ultimately lead people to the Antichrist, because he will be the consummate figure of humanism.

---

5. Will Christians have to go through the Great Tribulation?

When we use the term *Great Tribulation*, we are referring to a period of suffering that the world will be exposed to in the last days coinciding with the judgment of God upon the Antichrist and his government.[17] Some theologians think that the Tribulation has already taken place. There was a great persecution of Christians and Jews during the Roman Empire. It is true, too, that some theologians believe that the Tribulation refers only to Israel or the Jewish people, and not to Christians or the rest of the world. If we assume that the Tribulation will be a future worldwide time of persecution, then I must say that Christians will indeed go through it. I do not find in the Bible the teaching that Christians will be "raptured" prior to the Tribulation.

The Bible teaches two comings of Jesus—one, His birth; the second, His coming again in triumph. There is no third coming for a secret rapture. The book of Matthew specifically says, "Immediately *after the tribulation* of those days. ... Then the sign of the Son of Man will appear in heaven ... and He will send His angels ... and they will gather together His elect from the four winds, from one end of heaven to the other."[18]

This is just one of many references that indicate we will be going through a time of tribulation until Jesus Christ comes back.[19]

I do believe that Christians will be protected in the midst of tribulation, however. After all, the Israelites were protected when the plagues fell upon Egypt. God knows how to make a distinction between His people and those who are not His people. He allowed sorrow and suffering to rain upon the ungodly in Egypt while He caused the children of Israel to prosper.

But we must recognize also that the devil and his emissaries despise Christians. There has always been a struggle between the people of God and those who serve Satan. Throughout history there have been successive martyrdoms of Christians, and it is the height of arrogance to assume that only twentieth-century Christians in the United States of America will be spared any kind of persecution. That goes against the flow of history for the last two thousand years. The book of Revelation speaks of Tribulation martyrs—those who were slain for the witness of Christ—standing near the great throne of God and crying out, "How long ... until You judge and avenge our blood on those who dwell on the earth?"[20] So there will be people during the Tribulation who love Jesus, and who will give their lives for Him.

Jesus said, "He who endures to the end shall be saved."[21] Persecution is simply part of living as a Christian in this world. The saints in China, Russia, and other Communist countries have been tortured, have suffered privation, have had their jobs and their families taken away from them. Many of them have already died because of their witness for Jesus. It is hard to contemplate much worse tribulation than these great men and women of faith have already endured.

---

6. What is the mark of the Beast?

In the book of Revelation there is reference to the number of the Antichrist, which is 666.[22] *Six*, in biblical numerology, is just short of perfection, represented by the number *seven*. *Six* is the number of man, whereas *seven* is the number of perfection. So 666 may refer to the quintessential humanist. Revelation tells us that the number 666, or the mark of the Antichrist, is going to be stamped upon the hand and the forehead of every person in the world during the reign of the Antichrist.

The forehead represents our wills, our volition; while the hand represents our activities. Somehow the Antichrist will get his imprint on people everywhere, causing them, through their wills and their actions, to serve him. We already have techniques whereby an imprint can be made on the hands and foreheads of human beings. This imprint can be read by lasers and can contain all the credit information on an individual, and his blood type, his city of residence, and other vital information.

Computer technology can be used to control population, credit, and the movement of people. So-called "smart cards," which have tiny microchips in them that contain biographical data and revisable credit information, can be implanted under the skin. Every time a person makes a purchase, the "smart card" can deduct the amount from a credit balance, and every time the person deposits money, it can be added to the credit balance. Everyone's records can then be stored in a giant interconnected computer system.

It is not too far-fetched to think that the Antichrist could impose population control by the same kind of a mark. In the words of the book of Revelation, "And he causes all, both small and great, rich and poor, free and slave, to receive a mark on their right hand or on their foreheads, and that no one may buy or sell except one who has the mark or the name of the beast, or the number of his name."[23]

The Bible warns us that if we have the mark of the Beast, we will then share the terrible fate of the Beast.[24] If we regard the forehead as the center of the will and the hand as being symbolic of what we do, it seems that the mark is more than just some computer laser imprint. What we are really talking about here is who gets our allegiance. Will we give the Antichrist our minds and our work? If our allegiance is to God, we will not serve the Antichrist, and we will not take his mark upon us.

---

7. When will the Rapture of the church take place?

The word *rapio* is a Latin word meaning "seized." As far as I can tell, the word *rapture* does not appear in the Bible. It is a term people use to describe the catching up of Christians when Jesus comes back. Paul said that we will be caught up to meet the Lord in the air.[25] That is what we call the Rapture of the church. It will happen at the end of this age when Jesus Christ comes back to earth again. As He comes from heaven, we will be caught up to meet Him in the air, and then we will be forever with the Lord.

I believe it will happen after the Tribulation and before the thousand-year reign of Christ on earth called the Millennium.

---

8. What is the resurrection of the dead, and who will be resurrected first?

The resurrection spoken of in the Bible is the uniting of man's spirit, which is immortal and leaves his body at physical death, with a new spiritual body. The spiritual body will become immortal and will have incredible powers, such as being able to move through physical objects like walls and doors and travel great distances instantaneously. These will be the bodies that Christians will have forever.

There is confusion regarding the word *resurrection*. Jesus raised Lazarus from the grave, but this was a resuscitation, not a resurrection.[26] Lazarus came back in his original body that was still subject to death. Some years later Lazarus died again and stayed dead.

When Jesus Christ comes back again, He will resurrect those who have been born again. They will then be joined with the spiritual bodies that have been prepared for their spirits.

The apostle Paul says that those who are alive will not be resurrected ahead of those who sleep.[27] So those who are dead will rise first, followed by those who remain alive when Christ comes back. Those who are still alive will be changed in a moment. These mortal bodies will be transformed into bodies like the one Jesus had after His resurrection. These bodies will be eternal and have the same qualities that Jesus Christ had, for the Bible declares, "We shall be like Him, for we shall see Him as He is."[28]

There also will be a second resurrection, which will come at the end of the thousand-year reign of Christ. At that time there will be a great resurrection of all people. Those who have done evil will be sent to hell. Forever. But those who have lived in accordance with the righteous teachings of the Lord will live forever with God.[29]

---

9. What is the Millennium?

A millennium is one thousand years. The biblical Millennium will be a period of peace, love, and brotherhood when all nature lives in the harmony that was intended in the Garden of Eden.[30] The book of Isaiah speaks of a time when the wild animals will live at peace with domestic animals, when the serpents will no longer bite. A little child will be able to play by a cobra's den or lead wild beasts around and not be harmed. Military schools will close, and implements of war will no longer be manufactured. The money and resources that now go into warfare will then be devoted to peaceful pursuits. When this day comes, every person will have his own plot of ground, his own home. All will live in harmony with their neighbors. No one will be afraid that someone will try to steal his belongings. There will be universal peace, for the knowledge of the Lord will cover the earth as the waters cover the sea.[31]

I believe the Millennium is a transition period, when Jesus Christ comes back to earth to show mankind what it would have been like if sin had never entered the world. It will be a time when Jesus Christ will reign as king, and the Kingdom of God will be established on earth. There will be a one-world government under the leadership of Jesus with nation-states subject to Him.

The Bible says representatives of the nations of the earth will come to Jerusalem each year.[32] Apparently all governments will be subject to godly people and, at that time, Israel will be the key nation on earth.

10. What is hell like?

There are two descriptions of hell in the Bible. One is of a burning fire. Jesus often used the word *Gehenna* to describe hell. Gehenna was the refuse dump outside Jerusalem that was always on fire. Jesus said hell was a place of worms, maggots, fire, and trouble. From that we get the image of a lake of fire and the concept of perpetual burning. The evil ones there are full of remorse and torment.[33]

Jesus also said that hell would be "outer darkness." He said that some in His day "will be cast out into outer darkness. There will be weeping and gnashing of teeth."[34] Here the image is one of terrible loneliness. There will be separation from God and man. Those who are consigned to hell will be put out into the inky blackness of eternity, with nobody to turn to, nobody to talk to, and they will be constantly alone. They will suffer the remorse of knowing they had the opportunity to come into heaven with God but turned it down.

The Bible speaks of a lake of fire reserved for the devil and his angels.[35] Human beings were never intended to go into hell. But the ones who choose to reject God will one day follow Satan right into hell.

There will be no exit from hell, no way out, no second chance. That is why it is so important in this life to receive the pardon that God extends to all men through the cross of Jesus Christ.

11. Can I ever lose my place in heaven?

Heaven is forever.[36] In order for heaven to be heaven, there can never be the nagging possibility of a revolt which would cause us to lose the glory of it again. There will be no doubt, no confusion, and no fear in heaven.

God will remove from the scene the cause of all rebellion—Satan and sin.

Consequently, God cannot allow people who rebel against Him to enter heaven. Everyone must be born again before he or she can enter heaven. Anyone who has not been transformed in his spirit would be a source of spiritual contagion, contamination, or rebellion in heaven. A little tendency to sin today could grow into a hideously dangerous nature in, say, a million years. Therefore, the seed of rebellion will never be allowed to enter heaven.

12. Will I have my family in heaven?

I see no reason to suppose that there could not be families in heaven. However, all Christians are part of God's family now, and the bonds that draw human families together probably will not be necessary in heaven. There, we will all be part of one enormous family, and we will all feel a deep love for everyone else. There will not be the idea that "I am here with my wife and the two of us are separate from everyone else." We will all be one in Christ.

Having said that we will probably have families in heaven, however, let me add two things. First, your husband or wife or child or parent will be in heaven with you—if you are a Christian—only if they have been born again by the Spirit of God. If you are saved, your closeness to God will not save the members of your family. They must have their own personal relationships with Jesus Christ.

We should understand that there will no longer be human procreation in heaven. The necessity of mating and child nurture will cease. Jesus said of the resurrection, "They neither marry nor are given in marriage, but are like angels in heaven."[37]

13. What Is the Great White Throne Judgment?

The Great White Throne Judgment,[38] according to the book of Revelation, will take place at the end of the Millennium, prior to the time when God will "make all things new."[39] This will be the final and irreversible judgment of Satan and his angels and of all the unredeemed. According to the Bible, the great books recording the deeds of all mankind will be opened. Those people whose names were not recorded in the "book of life" will be cast into the lake of fire reserved for the devil and his angels. This experience is called "the second death" to distinguish it from mere physical death.

However, Jesus taught that anyone who believes in Him "shall not come into judgment, but has passed from death into life."[40] We therefore must conclude that those who have been "born again" by receiving Jesus Christ as Lord and Savior will be transformed into a heavenly state when Jesus Christ comes back again. All of these people, according to the apostle Paul, will answer for their Christian service and stewardship at the "judgment seat of Christ" at that time.[41] None of these true believers, however, will face eternal condemnation at the Great White Throne, because Jesus Christ has already paid for their sins at Calvary.

Everyone else will have to come before God and account for the way he or she has lived. It will be an awesome day of judgment. Some people think there may be those who lived before Christ, or who never had a chance to hear of Christ, who will be judged worthy of heaven. This is extremely doubtful, because the Bible says none has lived righteously.[42] But God, who is the judge of all the world, is going to judge by the standard of righteousness. He will allow each person to come before Him and present his case. In each case, the accuser or excuser of the individual will be his or her own conscience.[43] What did each one do in relationship to what he or she knew to be right or wrong according to the revelation they had of God's will?

Scripture References

1 See Mark 13:32
2 See Matthew 24:3, Luke 21:7
3 See Matthew 24:6-7, Luke 21:10-11
4 2 Thessalonian 2:3-4
5 See Matthew 24:12
6 Luke 21:24
7 Matthew 24:14
8 Matthew 24:37-39
9 See 2 Thessalonians 2:3
10 2 Peter 3:4
11 See Revelation 9:18
12 See Daniel 12:4
13 See Revelation 13:1-18
14 See 2 Thessalonians 2:4
15 See Revelation 13:13-15, 19:20
16 See Revelation 13:18
17 See Revelation 6:1-17
18 Matthew 24:29-31
19 See John 16:33, Romans 8:35, Revelation 7:13-14
20 Revelation 6:9-10
21 Matthew 24:13
22 See Revelation 18:18
23 Revelation 13:16-17
24 See Revelation 14:11
25 See 1 Thessalonians 4:17
26 See John 11:43-44
27 See 1 Thessalonians 4:16-17
28 1 John 3:2

29 See Revelation 20:11–15
30 See Revelation 20:6
31 See Isaiah 11:6–9
32 See Isaiah 2:2–4, Zechariah 14:16
33 See Mark 9:43–48
34 Matthew 8:12 (see also Matthew 22:13)
35 See Matthew 25:41
36 See Revelation 22:5
37 Mark 12:25
38 See Revelation 20:11–15
39 Revelation 21:5
40 See John 5:24
41 See Romans 14:10, 2 Corinthians 5:10
42 See Romans 3:10
43 See Romans 2:15

10. Christian Life and Practice

A. SEX AND MARRIAGE

---

1. What obligations do marriage partners have to each other?

The apostle Paul, writing to the church at Ephesus, laid down some very good guidelines for husbands and wives. To the men he said, "Husbands, love your wives, just as Christ also loved the church and gave Himself for it."[1] To the women he said, "Wives, submit to your own husbands, as to the Lord."[2] That kind of relationship brings about a lack of tension in marriage.

The husband should be willing to sacrifice himself for the wife's good. If he loves her enough that he is willing to give himself for her, even as Jesus did for the church, then the wife will be willing to submit to his leadership. She will know that he is always looking out for her good and always willing to put her interests ahead of his.

By the same token, a wife has the ability to make her husband the head of the household by uring him to take his proper role as priest in the home. She should encourage him to seek God, to find out what God is telling the family to do. She can build her husband up and, by being willing to submit, give him a sense of responsibility so that he will assume his proper role.

The one who always insists on "rights" will destroy the marriage relationship. If the husband says to the wife, "You must obey me because the Bible says so," he is going to alienate her. At the same time, the wife who refuses to submit to the husband and fights him all the time will make him apprehensive about following the Lord. He will start thinking, *What if I get a message from God? All I am going to get is opposition from my wife, so I might as well just follow my own desires and let her follow hers.* Such attitudes will pull couples apart, whereas God's standards should draw them together.

The husband who departs from God's laws, and insists that his wife do the same thing, has lost his mandate of authority. God did not give the husband a mandate to break His law, to abuse his wife, to become involved in bizarre sex practices, or to lead his wife into stealing or lying or cheating or drunkenness. But as long as the husband is following the mandate of the Lord, the wife should submit to his leadership, even though she may disagree with it.

God's standard is true, yet in many marriages, the wife is more able than her husband. Regretfully, a woman with great abilities sometimes marries a man who does not have much ability. This wife must resist the temptation to dominate her husband. Her husband will sometimes make decisions that the wife feels are wrong. She must either gently persuade her husband that he is wrong, or else pray that God will change her husband's mind. A woman has voluntarily surrendered a portion of her autonomy to her husband when she marries. She must trust God that His way will work out. However, a husband who wants his wife to deny God, to engage in group sex, or to commit an act that is obviously against God's law has lost his authority. The wife's first allegiance is to Jesus Christ and she must follow Him. She cannot submit to what is unlawful or unnatural.

It is important to remember that husbands and wives are partners. Someone has rightly pointed out that woman was taken from the side of man, not from his head or foot. She is not to dominate her husband, nor is she to be supine and let him walk over her as if she were a doormat. A husband and wife are to be partners in life and are to share a living relationship that acknowledges that the man is the head of the family as long as he is submitted to Christ.

___

2. What does the Bible say about divorce and remarriage?

The Bible is explicit about divorce and remarriage. In the Old Testament, Moses permitted a man to obtain a divorce on just about any grounds.[3] Later on, in the New Testament, when Jesus was asked about divorce, He replied that Moses gave permission to divorce because of the hardness of their hearts. He said that in the beginning it was not this way. Jesus continued, "Have you not read that He who made them at the beginning 'made them male and female,' and said, 'For this reason a man shall leave his father and mother and be joined to his wife, and the two shall become one flesh'? So then, they are no longer two but one flesh. Therefore what God has joined together, let no man separate."[4]

Before God, marriage is a lifetime relationship that should never be severed by human action. In the book of Malachi, God says that He hates divorce (see Malachi 2:16). God's perfect will is the preservation of society and future generations by the preservation of marriages. God will give anyone great help in sustaining a marriage relationship or in the reconciliation of estranged marriage partners. In extreme cases, there are only two grounds for divorce and remarriage.

When adultery has taken place, a divorce can be obtained, because adultery has already severed the marriage relationship and divorce is a formal acknowledgment of what has already taken place.

The apostle Paul added to the teachings of Jesus what is called the "Pauline privilege." According to this concept, Paul taught that if an unbelieving spouse leaves a believer, the believer is not bound to the marriage relationship, but is free to remarry.[5] And some people recognize such a thing as a "constructive desertion," which would be when a husband so brutalizes his wife that it is impossible to live with him any longer; or when a wife has so harassed or brutalized her husband that it becomes impossible for him to stay with her. When that happens, whether or not the person actually moves out, the situation is the equivalent of desertion, and divorce and remarriage are permissible.

Except for these reasons, there is no justification given in the Bible for divorce. No grounds exist for divorce on the basis of incompatibility, lack of love, or differing career goals. Frankly, it seems impossible that two born-again Christians who are dedicated to serving Jesus Christ can find any grounds for divorce.

Obviously, when a person who does not have biblical grounds for divorce remarries, he or she is technically committing adultery. For an elaboration, read my answer to the next question.

---

3. What should I say to two believers who divorced, remarried, and are now aware of what the Bible says about divorce?

Divorce is rampant in the United States, and it is rampant among Christians and non-Christians alike. There are some instances where people have married not once or twice, but three, four, five, or six times. They have had a succession of mates, a succession of children, and a succession of problems.

God is on the side of people. He loves people, and He

understands what has happened in such situations. But it is impossible for me to say that this conduct is all right. A minister of God must teach what is in the Bible; yet the teaching must be tempered with the biblical understanding of God's love. It is very difficult to make hard and fast rules.

Does one, for example, tell a three-times-divorced man to go back to his previous mate? What if the previous mate is now remarried? Is it right to ask the remarried couple to make a second divorce and break up a second home? The basic rule is that divorce and remarriage are not permitted, except for adultery or desertion, and that is the rule the church should stick to. Young people should be made aware that marriage is for life—for keeps—and not something to be entered into and then gotten out of whenever one feels like it.

However, given the appalling state of marriage in the modern world, I feel that the church should use its power of "binding and loosing"[6] to provide guidance in the way of forgiveness to divorced and remarried couples who have received Jesus Christ after their divorce. In other words, the church should (and I personally would) say that what happened in your past life is covered by the blood of Christ. Enjoy your present marriage and live in it to the glory of God without recrimination. However, for Christians who have divorced (after being born again) for reasons other than adultery or desertion, I believe they should either be reconciled to their Christian mates or remain unmarried.

Finally, in these complex personal matters, I recommend prayer, study of the Bible, and that you counsel with a wise and godly pastor in your own community.

---

4. Should a Christian marry an unbeliever?

Absolutely not. The Bible says, "Do not be unequally yoked together with unbelievers . . . what accord has Christ with Belial?"[7]

Billy Graham put it very succinctly a few years ago when he said that if you take an unbeliever for a mate you also get the devil for your father-in-law. Much heartache results when Christians marry unbelievers.

Some Christians go ahead and marry unbelievers, thinking that they can convert them after marriage. But if God has really chosen that man or woman for you, He is perfectly capable of bringing that person to Himself *before* the marriage. If He does not do it, it is a good enough sign that this marriage is not what He wants for you. Christians need to learn to wait on the Lord, to wait for what is right. Anything short of that can prove to be a dreadful mistake.

5. If I am married to an unbeliever, should I stay or leave the marriage?

If you are married to an unbeliever and he or she wants you to stay, then you should stay. By your conduct, attempt to bring that loved one to the Lord. However, if you have just become a Christian, the change in your lifestyle may be so drastic that the unbeliever may want to leave. If your sincere attempts to preserve your marriage fail, and if your unbelieving spouse refuses to live with you, you have no choice but to let him (or her) leave. You are not bound in that case, and you may get married again if you want to, but only to someone in the Lord.

6. Is cruelty grounds for divorce?

It depends. I do not think mental cruelty is grounds for divorce if mental cruelty concerns the way a mate twists the toothpaste tube or hangs stockings in the bathroom. That type of mental cruelty has been defined in so many different contexts it has no meaning.

However, I do think physical brutality and abuse, and mental abuse of a nature that endangers the person's mind or body, are clearly grounds for divorce. The Pauline privilege,[8] which I mentioned earlier, permits divorce on the grounds of desertion by an unbelieving spouse. For mental cruelty to be grounds for divorce, it must involve conduct which makes it impossible to live with the spouse without endangering oneself.

The sort of cruelty I have in mind would not spring from a criticism of a soufflé or a brother-in-law. Minor irritations need loving attention, but should not be allowed to rupture a holy relationship.

Obviously, a couple composed of two born-again Christians does not fall under the Pauline privilege. Divorce and remarriage for any reason are truly unthinkable for two people who sincerely love God and are trying to serve Him.

---

7. What is the difference between adultery and fornication?

Sexual intercourse between a married person and someone who is not his or her mate is adultery.

The Ten Commandments contain the prohibition against adultery: "You shall not commit adultery."[9] The reason is simple: marriage is the foundation of society, and with it comes the responsibility of child rearing. Casual sex outside marriage not only imperils marriage but also destroys the paternal or maternal feeling for the children of the marriage, and blurs the lines of inheritance and family, clan and tribal relationships.

Fornication is sex between two unmarried people. The apostle Paul said this is a sin against the body. He commands Christians to flee fornication as a sin against self and God, for the believer's body is the temple of the Holy Spirit.[10] Paul says that if a believer takes his body and joins it to a harlot (or someone who is immoral), he is joining Jesus Christ to that person.[11]

It is very important to understand that neither fornicators nor adulterers will enter the kingdom of heaven.[12] In today's world, the term *fornication* is rarely used and immorality between unmarried people is commonly accepted as a lifestyle. But immorality, however commonplace, is a sin that will keep millions of people out of heaven, unless they repent.

---

8. Is oral sex okay?

Oral sex is a type of sexual practice without the possibility of reproduction, and is one of the kinds of activity engaged in by homosexuals. Paul, in his letter to the Romans, speaks of women's exchanging "the natural use for what is against nature."[13] My personal feeling is that oral sex is "against nature" in that the sex act should be based on reproductive possibility and on a shared partnership. Neither partner should become an "object" for the gratification of the other.

However, the Bible is not explicit on sex practices between married people. Although it says that the marriage bed is to be undefiled, it does not say what it means by this.[14] There are a number of practices of love and sexuality in marriages on which the Bible is silent. Therefore, it is difficult to pontificate and say, "Well, this is right and this is wrong."

In undefined matters such as this, there is a biblical rule: "Whatever is not from faith is sin."[15] If one feels that oral sex is not from faith, then he should not do it. God has called us to holiness, not to sensuality. But the expression of physical and sexual love in marriage is good, holy, and God-given. Therefore, do not be afraid to ask God to direct you to those expressions of sexuality that are acceptable in His sight.

---

9. Does the Bible allow sex for pleasure?

There are some religious people who feel that the only reason for sex is reproduction. Others believe that there are higher reasons for sex: the ultimate joining together of a man and woman—the joining together of two spirits; the joining together of two minds; and the joining together of two bodies. In the Old Testament the term for sexual intercourse was "to know" (a husband or wife). The most intimate knowledge of marriage partners comes about through these three joinings in a Christian marriage. This is why Christians can have a much more stimulating sex life than non-Christians. Non-Christians cannot join together in the spirit. They lack that extra dimension.

The Bible says that marriage partners should offer their bodies to each other in marriage and should not deny each other except for a short season for fasting.[16] God made men and women sexual beings. He made our nervous systems capable of receiving pleasure from the sex act. Sex in marriage is good and holy and ordained of God.

10. Are interracial dating and marriage all right

In the Old Testament, God told the people of Israel not to intermarry with the nations that surrounded them. The reason for this was not the color of the skin; it was the condition of the heart. These people were idol worshipers who engaged in all manner of filthy practices, sexual and otherwise, that would have corrupted Israel.

This prohibition against the godly marrying the godless is still in effect today. God's children should not marry Satan's children. But this has nothing to do with the color of skin or country of origin.

However, young people need to be aware of the unfortunate truth that prejudice still exists. There are people who take offense at a racially mixed couple. Children from such a marriage are often scorned by both racial communities. From a sociological standpoint, couples who enter into interracial marriages will face prejudice and rejection. There is nothing spiritual about it, but it is a fact of life.

Since the pressures upon them can be enormous, a couple contemplating an interracial marriage must be absolutely sure of each other, their own motives, and especially God's will in the matter.

---

11. What does the Bible say about homosexuality?

The Bible says that it is an abomination for a man to lie with a man as with a woman, or a woman to lie with a woman as with a man.[17] The Bible says that because of certain abominations such as homosexuality, a land will vomit out its inhabitants.[18] The apostle Paul called it "shameful," the result of being given up by God to "vile passions."[19]

In the Old Testament, those who practiced these things were removed from the congregation of Israel by execution. We are told in the New Testament that those who practice homosexuality will not enter the Kingdom of God.[20] The apostle Paul, in the book of Romans, indicates that homosexuality is the result of the final rebellion of people against God. He says that when people exchange the truth of God for a lie, and begin to worship the creature instead of the Creator, they are given up to evil. At a moment in society when values are turned upside down and moral anarchy appears, men burn with lust for other men and women burn for women, and they will receive in their own bodies the punishment for their actions.[21]

From a biblical standpoint, the rise of homosexuality is a sign that a society is in the last stages of decay.

---

12. Should a Christian divorce a spouse who is homosexual?

Terrible heartache is being visited upon homes by the spread of homosexuality. Imagine the feelings of a wife who knows she is sharing her husband with one or more male lovers. Imagine the feelings of a husband who is contending for the affection of his wife with one or more female lovers.

In addition to heartache, given the known proclivity of homosexuals for multiple sex partners, the possibility of contracting venereal disease from a homosexual spouse is very high.

But God is always redemptive. In this situation, I would advise the heterosexual spouse to use every means possible to get the mate delivered from homosexual bondage. Homosexuals can be set free and begin very satisfactory heterosexual relationships. They will never be delivered without love, understanding, and forgiveness. Very perceptive spiritual counselors are needed because many homosexual mates have so deceived themselves that they turn into remarkably convincing liars to cover up their conduct.

Finally, if all else fails, divorce from a homosexual mate is both wise and proper. Children should not be subjected to that type of influence. Whatever happens, the husband or wife should not feel guilty—wondering, "How have I failed?" Let Jesus Christ give you a new start for your life.

---

13. Is abortion wrong?

Abortion is definitely wrong. It is the taking of a human life. It is my feeling that abortion is tantamount to murder. We read in the psalms that God fashions us while we are in our mothers' wombs.[22] We also read of a prophet named Jeremiah who was called by God before he was born.[23] The apostle Paul believed that he was called to serve God from his mother's womb.[24] We are told that John the Baptist leaped in his mother's womb when the voice of Mary, the mother of the Lord, was heard.[25] Obviously children in the womb have spiritual identity.

From a biological standpoint, there is absolutely no basis for believing that human life begins at any time other than conception. From the moment of conception there is a progression of development that continues through adulthood. The flow of life never stops. It is a continuing process.

Abortionists claim that a person becomes fully human at the moment of birth, but a five- or six-month fetus may be delivered by Caesarean section and have its life maintained outside the womb.

Abortion is terribly wrong. God condemned the Israel-ites who were offering their children as sacrifices to the heathen god Molech. Such children were burned up in the fires of sacrifice.[26] But we are offering our children to a god of pleasure and sensuality and convenience. By doing so we are saying that human beings are not worth anything. This is a terrible sin and a blot on our society.

The Bible is not more specific on the matter of abortion because such a practice would have been unthinkable to the people of God. For instance, when Israel was in Egypt, a cruel Pharaoh forced the Israelites to kill their newborn babies. In the Bible this was looked upon as the height of cruel oppression.

The thought that the Hebrews would kill their own children would have been anathema to them. All through the Old Testament, women yearned for children. Children were considered a gift from God. Women prayed not to be barren. How could a righteous woman have turned against her own children to destroy them?

Mother Teresa of Calcutta said she fears for America because the women of America are killing their own babies. She believes society is doomed when women become so heartless that they will kill their own young. Abortion is not only unthinkable, it is also the height of pagan barbarity.

---

14. What training should I give my children?

The Bible says that we are to bring up our children in "the training and admonition of the Lord."[27] It also says that "foolishness is bound up in the heart of a child, but the rod of correction will drive it far from him."[28] More than anything else, a child needs to know love, because a child's relationship with a loving father will teach him the love of

God. Parents must show their children loving concern, fairness, and stability.

But along with love must be a measure of physical punishment to teach right and wrong, good and evil. That is what God gives us. He gives us love, fairness, and stability, but He also punishes us if we go wrong beause He loves us.

Children cannot be allowed to be subject to their own biological or emotional needs at the expense of everybody else. A loving parent will set certain guidelines for his children, and let them know in a kind but firm fashion that these limits must be observed.

Then, as they get older, they may be given more freedom and responsibility. They must depend less on their parents and rely more and more on God. The goal of child rearing is to produce mature, responsible adults whose lives are governed by the Bible and centered in Christ.

---

15. Is physical punishment of children allowed in the Bible?

Yes. The saying, "Spare the rod and spoil the child," has a biblical basis.[29]

Sexual and physical abuse of children is unlawful, immoral, and deplorable. Loving discipline, however, is absolutely necessary to produce mature, well-rounded adults who can handle the give-and-take of marriage, child rearing, and a competitive world. A self-willed, undisciplined child who grows up to be a husband or wife is a danger to society.

When a child flies into a rage, or breaks something, or displays behavior that is obviously malicious and wrong, there is nothing wrong with smacking him sharply once or twice on his bottom. That is much better than berating him for an hour verbally. It is much better to administer punishment and get the matter out of the way than to let the thing fester or to let the child think he can get away with doing something wrong.

We face a great danger in society from those who abuse children sexually or physically. But an even worse danger could come from public officials who, in overreacting to abuse, might forbid intelligent parental discipline—giving us a generation of youthful tyrants and emotionally stunted adults.[30] We forget that indifference also is a form of child abuse.

---

16. Does God have a perfect mate for everyone?

Marriage is not for everyone, but for those who should be married, I believe God will lead you to the mate best suited to you, although possibly not a "perfect" mate. Here is why.

Each person has a unique personality made up of hundreds—probably thousands—of intangible spiritual, mental, and environmental characteristics. Each person has a genetic code made up of millions of physical characteristics. To find a "perfect" mate would involve a special act of creation of another person by God with millions of characteristics, each of which would exactly complement your own characteristics. God does not form each human being by a special act of creation, but by natural biological processes.

What God will do, however, if you ask Him, is lead you to the person who best complements your personality, background, and desires, and whose genetic makeup, when joined to yours, can produce offspring pleasing to God, to you and your spouse, and to your fellow man. Since the variables involved in this are mathematically staggering, it behooves us to seek God's infinite wisdom in the choice of our mates. The secret of knowing His leading is expressed in Proverbs 3:4–5.

That does not mean people who are looking for a husband or wife should sit at home and wait for God to send someone to knock on their doors. It is certainly appropriate to ask God to lead you to various places where there are single people to meet, whether it is a social gathering at church, an educational opportunity, or some other place where there are people of like interests and beliefs. There are many places that provide opportunities to meet a prospective mate. God will bring us the right person if we will let Him.

Remember only a mate who has Jesus Christ living within can ever be considered "perfect" or suitable for you.

---

17. Does the Bible permit artificial insemination and *in vitro* fertilization?

We cannot give a categorical answer from the Bible of yes or no to this question, but we can draw inferences that would strongly suggest a biblical prohibition against experimental tampering with human life and its genetic structure.

These new scientific techniques open up a Pandora's box of problems that can lead to incredible abuses. Such methods of fertilization are already in use in the beef industry. A prize cow is implanted with frozen semen from a prize bull. Then the little embryo is removed from the prize cow and put into another cow who will act as host until birth. Then, two or three months later, that same prize cow is again implanted by a prize bull and another top-quality embryo is created. In this way, one prize cow can have three or four calves a year, and the quality of the cattle can be greatly improved.

Now these techniques are being transferred to human beings. But one cannot regard a human being made in the image of God in the same way that one regards a cow. We have the ability to worship, to create great works of art, to build cathedrals, to rise to the very heights in Jesus Christ.

Some scientists view human beings as no better than cattle. If an embryo transplant in a top-grade cow is deformed, it will be killed. If there is some accident of birth because of the implant procedure, the top-grade cow can be destroyed without remorse, because it is an animal. But what happens when human babies are frozen for periods of time and then later implanted into the wombs of mothers? What happens when wealthy women begin to hire poor women to bear their children for them?

What happens when human embryos are left in test tubes so they can be used as organ repositories? What happens when we learn how to clone human beings, so that we can take bits of cell tissue from one human and make somebody almost like him to function as a subhuman servant? The things that are being developed by our scientists seem benevolent, but they have the possibility of absolute horror in the wrong hands.

The Bible tells us that we should not mix different kinds. For example, we should not plow with an ox and a donkey linked up together.[31] We should not wear linen and flax mixed together.[32] These prohibitions may have been placed in the Bible as a guideline for us in other matters as well as the ones they directly relate to. The most serious danger today of mixing various species comes from the technique that we call recombinant DNA. Scientists can actually enter the genetic code, which organizes the development of the cell structure of living beings, and begin to manipulate and change it. The problem is that there are millions of variables. We might set out to create some kind of superrace and end up with people who have no resistance to disease. Or, we might come up with a new life form that could destroy us all. We are entering into God's province— an area where we do not belong; an area of potential danger to mankind greater than the atomic bomb.

Was God thinking of these developments when He forbade the intertwining of different types of animals and plants?

Despite the good things that have come about through plant engineering, there could be dangers ahead. Suppose, for example, that we have developed a strain of wheat that yields much more abundantly. What would happen if that same wheat, after we came to depend on it for most of our acreage, turned out to be absolutely unable to survive in a time of cold or lack of moisture? It could be that the hearty, resistant plants we had before, which did not yield quite so much grain, might have been the thing that would have saved humanity during a prolonged drought or cold spell. The new hybrids we have created might totally fail and leave us in desperate straits.

We simply do not have the ability to determine which characteristics best equip nations, or individuals, or animals to survive the extreme changes that occur periodically in our world. We simply do not know what God knows. When we begin to enter into God's marvelous world of genetic engineering, we are asking for trouble. Any thinking person has cause to fear what might emerge from this Pandora's box of technology, just as we fear the spectre of nuclear annihilation that the scientists of World War II gave us.

---

18. Should grown children continue to honor their parents according to the biblical commandment?

The Bible teaches, "Honor your father and your mother, that your days may be long upon the land which the Lord your God is giving you."[33] Since the relationship of parent to child endures until death, so does the honor due parents from children.

Jesus condemned the Pharisees for breaking this commandment. They did so by saying to their parents, "Whatever profit you might have received from me is *Corban*," which means dedicated to God.[34] They did not give the money to God; they merely dedicated it to the temple for a future time and thereby avoided their obligation to their parents. People today need to understand that grown children owe their parents the duty of material financial support as a part of honor and respect. The apostle Paul said that if a believer will not take care of his own, "He has denied the faith and is worse than an unbeliever."[35]

The Bible also teaches that in marriage "a man shall leave his father and mother and be joined to his wife, and the two shall become one flesh."[36] At that point the husband and wife are responsible before God for the conduct of their marriage. Despite their position in life or their marital responsibilities, they still owe honor and respect to their respective parents.

The Bedouins of Saudi Arabia in 1925 bore some resemblance to the early Hebrew nomads of the Bible. To illustrate true honor for parents on the part of these people, we have only to consider the late King Abdul al-Aziz ibn Saud who so honored his father that, even after he had conquered most of what is now Saudi Arabia, he knelt on the ground before his father so that the old man could dismount from his horse or camel by stepping on his son's back. It is a wise parent, however, who avoids presenting a grown child with a conflict between marital responsibilities and the honor due the parent. That should not occur if the relationship between parent and child is right.

Scripture References

1 Ephesians 5:25
2 Ephesians 5:22
3 See Deuteronomy 24:1–4
4 Matthew 19:4–6
5 See 1 Corinthians 7:15
6 See Matthew 16:19
7 2 Corinthians 6:14–15
8 See 1 Corinthians 7:15
9 Exodus 20:14
10 See 1 Corinthians 6:18–19
11 See 1 Corinthians 6:15–16
12 See 1 Corinthians 6:9–10
13 Romans 1:26
14 See Herbrews 13:4
15 Romans 14:23
16 See 1 Corinthians 7:5
17 See Leviticus 18:22, 20:13
18 See Leviticus 18:25
19 See Romans 1:24–27
20 See 1 Corinthians 6:9–10
21 See Romans 1:22–27
22 See Psalm 139:13
23 See Jeremiah 1:5
24 See Galatians 1:15
25 See Luke 1:44
26 See Leviticus 20:2
27 Ephesians 6:4
28 Proverb 22:15

440

29 See Proverb 13:24
30 See Isaiah 3:12
31 See Deuteronomy 22:10
32 See Deuteronomy 22:11
33 Exodus 20:12
34 Mark 7:11
35 1 Timothy 5:8
36 Matthew 19:5

B. CHRISTIANS AND GOVERNMENT

1. What is the purpose of government?

Government was instituted by God to bring His laws to people and to carry out His will and purposes. In the Old Testament, government maintained the place of worship, provided judges to decide civil cases between the people, restrained and punished lawbreakers, and mobilized the nation for action against external enemies.

The first government was a theocracy, where God dealt directly with the people. When God was in charge of things, no other government was necessary. He worked through the family, clan, or tribe. The father or patriarch acted as the agent of God for the rest of the family.

During the period of the judges the people became rebellious, and clear direction from God was lacking. Both religious and civil life became confused, and "everyone did what was right in his own eyes."[1] At the close of the period of the judges, God raised up Samuel, who was both a prophet and a judge. At that time, the formal religious life of the country was under the direction of the high priest. During Samuel's administration, the people asked for a king, and God gave them a monarchy which rose to its height during the reign of David and his son Solomon.[2]

When the perfect government is established during the Millennium, Jesus Christ will combine in Himself the offices of prophet, priest, and king. This will be a perfect theocracy, made possible because the perfect law of God will be universally accepted by all mankind, and "the earth shall be full of knowledge of the Lord as the waters cover the sea."[3]

Perfect government comes from God and is controlled by God. Short of that, the next best government is a limited

442

democracy in which the people acknowledge rights given by God but voluntarily grant government limited power to do those things the people cannot do individually. Contrast these forms of government with Communism, which maintains that the dictatorship of the proletariat is supreme and an essential evolution of history; that God does not exist; and that citizens have only those privileges granted by the state.

---

2. What duty do I owe the government, and what duty do I owe God?

That question was asked of Jesus: "Is it lawful to pay taxes to Caesar, or not?" He said, "Show Me the tax money." They gave Him the denarius, on which was a picture of Caesar. Then He asked, "Whose image and inscription is this?" They said "Caesar's." He answered, "Render therefore to Caesar the things that are Caesar's, and to God the things that are God's."[4] And that has become the standard for what we owe the government.

We owe the payment of taxes for the necessary services government renders to us. We owe a law-abiding and honest type of personal life.[5] Especially, we owe government informed, active citizenship.

We do not owe the government the allegiance we owe God. To God we owe our worship and our loyalty. We must remember that government exists only as long as God gives it the ability and the power.

When any civil government steps outside the mandate authorized by God Almighty, then that government does not have any further claim over its citizens. When the apostles came before the government of their day, they were commanded not to speak about Jesus. They told the authorities that they could not help speaking of the things they had seen and heard.[6] Even though they were threatened with jail, beatings, and other reprisals, they continued to proclaim their faith to the people. The apostles obviously considered the government's power to be at an end when it began to restrict their freedom to worship God and to proclaim their faith in Jesus.

In the United States, we believe that our government derives its powers from the consent of the governed. We believe that God has given certain inalienable rights, vested in humanity itself. The people give their support to the government so it can do such things as build roads, highways, and harbors; train armies; establish courts of law and maintain currency; establish uniform standards; and do other things that individuals cannot do for themselves.

In our society, Caesar is all the people. When we are told to render to Caesar what belongs to Caesar, that means we ourselves should be responsible for government. Therefore, we owe the obligation of serving in public office, of being informed citizens, of voting, and of being active in politics at all levels. That is part of the duty we render to Caesar.

We give God the spiritual allegiance that is His. We give Him our tithes, our offerings, our love, our worship, and our testimony in praise. To the government we give good citizenship, knowledge of the affairs of the day, and taxes that are due. We also give the government our services as political figures, as statemen, as public servants in every level of government.

Some might ask: "But what are rights under a dictatorship or a Communist government?" People have the same rights everywhere. Every man should have the right to his own personal life, his property, his freedom of movement, and his freedom of conscience. But there are some governments, such as those controlled by the Communists, that do not give those rights to the people. There is a totally different mindset in the Communist world.

That does not change the order that God established. Those under Communist domination must sometimes disobey the government. They must continue to speak and testify to their faith in God, even though this is very costly. Many of them go to prison. Many are tortured and beaten and deprived. When they get out of prison, they go right back to testifying and preaching again. We in America do not have any idea what those people have to go through in order to practice their faith in God.

Still, we must recognize that the apostle Paul was living under tyrannical Roman emperors when he wrote, in the book of Romans, that Christians are supposed to pay taxes to whom taxes are due, and that the civil government is not supposed to be a terror to those who do well, but to evil-doers.[7] He also said Christians are supposed to pray for those in authority over them, so that they might live a quiet and godly life. This is so that the Word of God might go forth freely to the end that all should come to the knowledge of the truth.[8] This kind of praying even should be done for bad rulers and governments.

---

3. Should a Christian pay taxes?

There is no question that Christians should pay taxes. However, in a country such as America, when there is waste of mammoth proportions, and when money is being used for programs that are abhorrent to Christians, the Christian should do everything he can to bring about change and reform. He must help to curtail the excessive spending of government, the growth of government, the profligate nature of government; and he must protest the improper use of his money.

The Bible does tell us to pay taxes to whom taxes are due and as good citizens we must pay our taxes.[9] We cannot cheat. There is a significant difference between tax evasion and tax avoidance. Tax evasion is an illegal activity in which an individual fails to declare certain income or overstates certain deductions. Tax avoidance is the use of legal methods to minimize the amount of taxes to be paid. The Christian is free to take advantage of all the legal deductions he can find, the greatest of which is legal permission to deduct from taxable income up to 50 percent of adjusted gross income if that 50 percent is given to Christian or charitable causes.

4. Should a Christian be involved in police work or military service?

There are some who do not believe that Christians can be soldiers or policemen. The apostle Paul said, "Rulers are not a terror to good works, but to evil. Do you want to be unafraid of the authority? Do what is good, and you will have praise from the same. For he is God's minister to you for good. But if you do evil, be afraid; for he does not bear the sword in vain; for he is God's minister, an avenger to execute wrath on him who practices evil."[10] The purpose of this minister of God is to restrain evil. The police, as God's ministers, provide an essential service to society. As long as there are sinful people, we will need policemen. As long as men and women will not submit voluntarily to the righteous commands of God, force will be necessary to keep them from murdering, raping, kidnapping, stealing—from victimizing innocent people. Thus, it is proper for a Christian to be involved in police work or in military service. There have to be law and order, for no one is safe when there is anarchy.

In both ancient and modern times, governments have been taken over by selfish, dictatorial people who have used police power to oppress the innocent. Christians never have a Godgiven duty to serve oppressors. A corrupt government cannot be in alliance with God.

On the international scene, given the sin of mankind, there must be armed forces. Unless there are strong, righteous nations to restrain the adventurism of a Hitler, a Stalin, or a Mao Tse-tung, then all freedoms of all people everywhere will be compromised. There will be nothing but conformity to the will of the dictator, and many innocent people will be killed as that dictator takes power. So it is necessary for the family of nations to raise up an international police force to restrain evil.

There are those who, because of sincere religious beliefs, feel that they could never kill another human being, even in war. Society must accommodate the views of such people. During World War II, for instance, conscientious objectors were given the job of fighting forest fires in the Pacific Northwest by parachuting into remote areas. They performed a very useful duty in a dangerous, quasimilitary environment. However, they were doing what they considered to be good for mankind instead of evil.

I must reiterate that when Jesus Christ establishes His reign on earth, there will be no more war and killing. The Bible says that men will not even study war anymore.[11] The great military establishment that has been built up at such an incredible price is going to be dismantled. We should all work toward this end, but it will never happen until Satan is bound and all men acknowledge God's reign in their lives.

But in the present time, with aggressors such as the Soviet Union, Cuba, North Vietnam, and other bellicose powers that are anxious to subjugate their neighbors, Christians cannot sit idly by and say, "Well, we don't believe in war. We will disarm and let those people take over the world." Doing so would be foolish and unbiblical.

---

5. Does the Bible teach pacifism?

The Bible teaches that when Jesus Christ comes back again there will be no more war. Imagine what a wonderful world it could be if the $600 or $700 billion the world spends on arms every year were devoted to peaceful pursuits. We could use that money to build roads, harbors, dams, and bridges, and to irrigate fields, and to provide cultural pleasures and things of beauty for the world, and to alleviate human suffering and need. War is hell. Only madmen would wish it continued.

But we live in a time when evil is increasing instead of diminishing, when some men seem to be controlled by selfishness and madness, when some men are bent on the subjugation of other men. As long as such attitudes exist, righteous men must stand against evil. I know there are some Christians who believe that war and their participation in it are morally wrong. While I respect their views and must allow them to follow their consciences, I do not believe the Bible teaches pacifism. The Bible teaches us that we are to lift the yoke of oppression from those who are downtrodden and oppressed. The yoke of oppression is not lifted by prayer alone. Action is necessary.

Sometimes we can bring change peacefully, through democratic processes. At other times freedom must be won through the use of military force. I do not know where this world would be if the United States had failed to respond to the challenge of Adolf Hitler during World War II. Fortunately, history records many examples of countries that have come to the rescue of other, weaker nations in times of distress.

People should think of what pacifism might mean on a personal level. If your sister, mother, or wife were being attacked by a gang of thugs, you would want someone to come to her aid. If such an attack happened and people just stood and watched, without helping, the indifference would be as bad as the crime itself. As citizens we demand effective protection from attacks against our persons. What is true on an individual scale is also true on an international scale.

We should also note that battles have been won by the strength of prayer and praise. Jehoshaphat won a war by sending people to sing and praise the Lord. As they did, the huge army that had assembled against him began to crumble in confusion.[12] Nevertheless, Jehoshaphat had the army gathered anyway. The soldiers were there, even though they did not have to use their weapons.

When Joshua went to Jericho, he had an army prepared. They did not have to use their weapons because God fought for them.[13] In many instances when Israel went into battle, its soldiers did not have to fight because the enemy fled. But they were ready to fight all the same. God is able to defend a nation without any use of arms. Prayer can be used of God to win wars even today. However, secular nations such as the United States can establish their foreign policy based on the miraculous intervention of God only if their people and policies reflect obedience to His will.

---

6. What rights does the state have over a Christian and his children?

The family-state relationship has become a battleground. In general it is conceded that the state under its so-called "police power" has the authority to prevent one citizen's injuring another. For example, the state has the authority to make sure that a family is not a source of contagious disease. The government could quarantine someone who has chicken pox or diphtheria or some other contagious disease. The state has the right to make sure that someone's home does not become a festering ground of rats and garbage to the detriment of the neighborhood. If someone's children are running around the street, delinquent and neglected, the state has the right to intervene and insist on proper care and control of the children.

The state has a stake in general literacy, so it can establish educational standards, public schools, and truancy laws. In time of war, the state has the right to enlist the young for service in the armed forces. As we have seen, the state has the right to collect taxes in various forms from its citizens to pay for the legitimate costs of government.

The problems we face today, however, go much deeper than this. The state is attempting to assert control over the thought life of children. For instance, the federal government published a course called MACOS, "Man, a Course of Study," that attempted to indoctrinate young children into the teachings of humanism. The federal and state governments also have been at the forefront of liberal experimentations with amoral sex education. Humanist values are being taught in the schools through such methods as "values clarification." All of these things constitute an attempt to wean children away from biblical Christianity.

Another subtle encroachment of the state into family life deals with the discipline of children. We have a severe problem with child abuse in our country, and the state obviously has a role in protecting children from unfit parents. However, state social welfare agencies have been known to attempt to prohibit Christian parents from disciplining their children in accordance with biblical precepts. But loving discipline is a fundamental part of child-parent relationships. Children need it and parents must give it if they love their children.[14] To characterize normal parenting as "abusive" is itself an abuse of state power.

In one instance, a state attempted to take a daughter away from a divorced woman because she made her daughter attend church and forbade the girl to smoke marijuana or attend rock music concerts. A state social worker termed this conduct mental abuse. When things like this happen, the state is exceeding its proper bounds. More and more there is a tendency for humanistic or irreligious educators or social workers to intrude on the relationship between Christian parents and their children, thereby destroying the trust between them.

To Christians, children belong to God and have been entrusted to their parents. To Communists and many humanists, there is no God, and children ultimately belong to the state. Christians believe that parents, not the state, must have primary control over children. This is where opposing values come into conflict. Some battles deal with whether the state can force a child to be brought up by a homosexual parent, whether two lesbian women can adopt children, or whether two homosexual men can raise children.

Such cases are being taken into court, and judges and sociologists are making decisions which are totally contrary to the Bible. We are going to see more and more of this during the next ten or fifteen years, unless there is a dramatic spiritual revival and a return to biblical values.

Unless America repents and regains a proper respect for God's law and God's moral order, the time will come when God will punish us. I think we are suffering now, in the sense that more than one million children run away from home every year. For every two new marriages formed one marriage ends in divorce. A shockingly high rate! One quarter of all American children suffer sexual abuse. Just look at the number of teen-age pregnancies, the millions of young people on alcohol and drugs, and the pervasiveness of violence and juvenile delinquency. Regrettably, as our traditional Christian family values break down, the government will step into the vacuum and will use secular solutions to the problems. These "solutions" will only exacerbate the nation's decline.

---

7. Can one be both Christian and Marxist?

There is no way that one can hold simultaneously to philosophies from God and the enemy of God. Marxism, at its base, is an atheistic system that has a view of history based solely on materialism. Marxism is in itself a religion, and it demands the allegiance of people everywhere. The Leninist model of Marxism demands allegiance at the point of a gun and the violent overthrow of legitimate governments.

It is ludicrous to think that Christianity can be believed along with a system that calls religion "the opium of the people" and a falsehood. In every instance where Marxists have taken control, they have suppressed the church. They have outlawed the Bible, forbidden the instruction of the young in religious values, and persecuted believers. Communists are always enemies of Christianity. Why the Western governments and many people still cannot see that, after all these years, is a mystery to me.

"You cannot serve God and mammon."[15] You cannot serve Christ and Belial, and there is no way a Christian can serve Jesus Christ and Karl Marx.

8. Is capitalism right or wrong?

Although capitalism can be abused and abusive, it is the economic system most conducive to freedom, most in accord with human nature, and most closely related to the Bible. The unfettered *laissez-faire* concept of Adam Smith led to the free-booting robber barons of the nineteenth century. The story of the Rockefellers, the Vanderbilts, and other monopolistic capitalists, who built up the industrial base of our nation but who did so at the expense of their competitors, is not a pretty one.

However, the basis of free enterprise is very biblical. We read in the Old Testament that in the millennial time, everyone will sit under his own vine and under his own fig tree on his own property.[16] There we have an idealized concept of the private ownership of property.

In the early days of our country, the Massachusetts Bay Colony attempted a primitive form of socialism. Land was owned jointly, everyone was to work together, and then the produce was to be divided to each according to his need. This experiment failed miserably. The people began to starve to death because there was not enough incentive to work. It was only after the land was divided into acre plots and given to individual families that the people began to prosper. That was because they were now working for enlightened self-interest and giving to one another out of their increase.

God has given each human being a healthy personal self-interest. Jesus said, "You shall love your neighbor as yourself."[17] This is something we all can relate to. There are few so altruistic that they will give up all they have produced for the good of other people. A person may love others as well as he loves himself, but he will not love them to the exclusion of himself.

Communism, on the other hand, demands that everyone work for the state; that everyone be controlled by the state; and that the means of production be in the hands of the state. There should be no profit motive, because Communists say the profit motive is evil.

But the profit motive is *not* evil; it is a creative force. It is based on self-interest, to be sure, but from this has come technology, creativity, the tremendous explosion of the scientific method, and other things that have made our world a better place in which to live. The profit motive has also produced tremendous social initiatives that have provided millions of dollars to help the poor, to care for the sick and needy, and to build hospitals, schools, and charitable institutions.

Yes, unbridled capitalism must be restrained, or people will get too much money and too much power and will use it to oppress others. But at the same time, government must allow people the freedom to create, to own property, and to develop the potential God has placed within them.

And the Bible contains a solution to the problem of excess accumulation of wealth and power. It is the year of Jubilee.[18] Under Old Testament law, every fifty years there was a cancellation of all debts. All the slaves were set free, and those who were in economic bondage also were set free. All the money was redistributed and the means of production was placed back in the hands of the original families. Personal property and city land that had been accumulated could be kept, but wealth resting on debt was cancelled.

I believe that free enterprise is much closer to the biblical model than any other form of economic system. But wealth contains great spiritual danger. Just as the coercive utopianism of Communist materialism is not of God, neither is a capitalist materialism—based on the amassing of riches for personal gain, with disregard for the afflicted and the needy—right.

Just remember that Jesus said, "You cannot serve God and mammon."[19] If money becomes your god, you cannot serve Jesus Christ. Gain is not godliness. A man's life does not consist of the abundance of things he possesses.[20] The rich man was called a "fool" for not being rich toward God.[21] A rich young ruler was told to sell all he had and give it to the poor.[22] Jesus told His disciples that it was easier for a camel to pass through the eye of a needle than for a rich man to enter the Kingdom of God.[23] The apostle Paul taught that the love of money is the root of all sorts of evil.[24] The apostle James pronounced woe upon rich men who oppressed their workers.[25]

In short, economic freedom and the private ownership of property are the biblical model. But wealth contains great spiritual danger; and no system based on materialism, in whole or in large part, can claim to be Christian.

9. When should a Christian disobey the civil government?

When a civil government refuses people the liberty to worship and obey God freely, it has lost its mandate of authority from God. Then the Christian should feel justified in disobeying.

Thomas Jefferson believed in the right to revolt against tyranny. He believed that when a government began to be tyrannical, it was the right and even the *duty* of the citizens to rebel against the government. Our forefathers rebelled primarily because they were being unfairly taxed by a foreign parliament. They felt that taxation without representation was tyranny. The Christian is called to bear with his government wherever possible. Jesus did not call for revolution against Rome, even though it was an oppressive conqueror of Israel. On the other hand, the apostles refused to obey an order not to preach and teach in Jesus' name.[26] Whenever the civil government forbids the practice of things that God has commanded us to do, or tells us to do things He has commanded us not to do, then we are on solid ground in disobeying the government and rebelling against it.

Several years ago, a group of people was tested concerning how much authority they would accept without question. They were seated at a set of controls behind a glass, while on the other side of the glass a man was strapped to a machine which administered electrical shocks. A person in a white coat directed these citizens to inflict pain on the subject. They started moving the dials as the man strapped to the machine screamed in pain. The person in the white coat, who was the authority figure, kept telling the people to push the lever higher, and they continued to do so until the subject seemed to be either in a state of collapse or dead. Though the subject gave every evidence of being in excruciating pain, people obeyed orders to hurt him, simply because those orders came from an authority figure. Only a few people resisted orders to inflict pain. The rest of them did whatever they were told to do.

It is this kind of blind obedience to government that we all need to fight. However difficult or costly it may be, we all must reserve the right to say no to things that we consider oppressive or immoral.

---

10. Is capital punishment wrong?

Capital punishment is unfortunately a necessary corrective to violent crime.

In ancient Israel, there were no prisons. A thief was commanded to pay back four or five times what he had stolen or damaged.[27] Public whippings were also administered to criminals.

In ancient Israel, it was believed that blood shed in murder would defile the land and that shedding the blood of a killer was restitution to the land.

Those who were considered incorrigible, who had committed unseemly acts that turned Israel against God or destroyed the fabric of society, had only one alternative—capital punishment.[28] Through capital punishment, society was rid of that offense, and the land was cleansed of evil.

In the Ten Commandments there is the prohibition, "You shall not murder."[29] Righteously administered judicial executions were not considered murder and therefore not prohibited by the Ten Commandments. In fact, the same law that included the Ten Commandments also had clear provision for capital punishment for specific offenses.

Capital punishment, if administered surely and swiftly, is a great deterrent to crime. It is no deterrent whatsoever if it is uncertain and continually delayed. But if those who scoff at society, and who constantly prey on innocent victims, were aware that death would be the penalty for their actions, we would see a dramatic drop in our crime rate.

Today we place criminals in penitentiaries—places of confinement in which the offender is supposed to become penitent or sorry for his sins. In truth, these places are breeding grounds for crime. In even the best of them, 85 percent of the inmates will be incarcerated again.

Society must pay for the anguish suffered by the victims of crime, then pay again each year to hold the criminal in prison, a cost equivalent to an Ivy League college education. The biblical model is far wiser. The perpetrator of lesser crimes was returned to society where he was made to make restitution to his victim. The hard-core, habitual criminal was permanently removed from society through capital punishment. In neither case was society doubly victimized as we are today.

Scripture References

1 Judges 17:6, 21:25
2 See 1 Samuel 8:4–5, 19–20, 1 Kings 9:3–5, 10:23
3 Isaiah 11:9
4 See Matthew 22:17–21
5 See Romans 13:1–7
6 See Acts 4:18–20
7 See Romans 13:1–7
8 See 1 Timothy 2:1–4
9 See Romans 13:7
10 See Romans 13:2–5
11 See Isaiah 2:4, Micah 4:3
12 See 2 Chronicles 20:20–23
13 See Joshua 6:15–21
14 See Proverbs 13:24, 23:13–14
15 See Matthew 6:24, Luke 16:13
16 See Micah 4:4
17 Matthew 19:19
18 See Leviticus 25:8–17, 27:17–24
19 Matthew 6:24, Luke 16:13
20 See Luke 12:15
21 See Luke 12:20
22 See Luke 18:18–23
23 See Matthew 19:24, Mark 10:25, Luke 18:25
24 See 1 Timothy 6:10
25 See James 5:1–4
26 See Acts 5:27–29
27 See Exodus 22:1
28 See Leviticus 20
29 Exodus 20:13

C. CHRISTIANS AND ETHICS

1. What is the great commandment?

There are three parts to the great commandment. The first part is: "You shall love the Lord your God with all your heart." The real you, the deepest part of your being, should love God. The next part of the commandment is, "with all your soul, with all your mind." This includes your ego—the mental processes that focus toward mankind, yet are in touch with your spirit. And then, the third part is to love God "with all your strength." That has to do with your body. Your physical being must reflect your love of God too.[1]

In summary, a person must dedicate the totality of his being to a self-giving love for God. Every aspect of his nature must focus on loving God. To illustrate, a person would break the great commandment if his spirit was partially centered on making money to the exclusion of God; or his mind was centered on high fashion, pride, or revenue; or his body was centered on gluttony, alcohol, or nicotine. God demands every bit of all of us!

This is why no human being can satisfy the demands of God merely by going to church or observing external religious ceremonies. No one can say, "I am a good person." In fact, keeping God's commandments is impossible unless you have the Holy Spirit dwelling within through a personal relationship with Jesus Christ. Jesus Christ fulfilled the great commandment perfectly, and He is the only human being ever to do so. Through His blood and His Spirit within us, we can live in a way that pleases God. On our own it is impossible.

458

2. What virtues and vices survive death?

People usually think of virtue or vice in relation to sexual behavior, alcohol, money, or food. But when we die, gluttony, lust, greed, and other fleshly sins will die with those of us who are Christians. We will not carry these things into heaven.

The things we will take into heaven have to do with the values of the human spirit. The apostle Paul wrote, "And now abide faith, hope, love, these three; but the greatest of these is love."[2] The love we have for each other and for God will survive the grave. The hope we have in God will survive the grave. The faith we have in God will survive the grave. These three inner qualities of the spirit of man will go into heaven.

On the other hand, people will take spiritual characteristics to hell with them too—things like pride, rebellion, envy, pettiness, and self-seeking. Hell goes on forever, so what starts out at forty or fifty years of age as a manageable tendency could be increased and magnified at the age of one million to an absolutely hideous characteristic. Imagine what pride, selfishness, cruelty, envy, or anger would be like if they were allowed to multiply for one million years!

This is why heaven must be reserved for those whose spiritual tendencies have been reborn and why rebellious sinners cannot be allowed to enter the place that God has prepared for those who serve Him.

3. What do employers and employees owe each other?

An employee owes his employers the duty of behaving as if he were working for Jesus Christ. The Bible says, "Whether you eat or drink, or whatever you do, do all to the glory of God."[3] It also tells us that we are not to seek to please men but to serve the Lord Jesus Christ.[4] Wherever you work—in an office, as a union member, in a factory, as a salesman, or in any other place—you are to act as if you are working for Jesus.[5] Remember that our reward will come from Him. Whatever the nature of the person you are working for, you should love that person, be loyal to him, and serve him with all your heart.

An employer, on the other hand, is to be gentle and tender with his employees, especially if the employees are Christians. Such employees are to be treated as brothers in the Lord. The book of Philemon consists of a letter that Paul wrote about a runaway slave. Paul told Philemon that his runaway slave had become a Christian. Because of this, Onesimus was no longer just a slave, but was now a brother in Christ and should be treated as such. Modern employers must see their employees as precious creatures made in the image of God. They are not just numbers, or nameless faces on an assembly line. They are people for whom Christ died!

Together, employers and employees should respect each other, work in harmony, and remember the basic commandment of Jesus: "Whatever you want men to do to you, do also to them."[6] This golden rule should underlie all labor relationships. If you would not want to be put in a dust-filled room with poor light and no toilet facilities, and allowed only a fifteen-minute break for lunch, do not put your employees under those conditions.

Conversely, if you, as an employee, do not appreciate shoddy workmanship, constant bickering, and lack of respect for your personal property, remember that your employer has the same dislikes.

In short, employers and employees should acknowledge the claim of God on both, the God-given dignity of both, and the mutual consideration that each would want if roles were reversed.

4. Do people have to be poor in order to be holy?

It has been taught for many years that holiness and poverty go hand in hand. The apostle Paul said, "I know how to be abased, and I know how to abound." Then he added, "I can do all things through Christ who strengthens me."[7]

You can be just as holy when you are financially comfortable as you can be when you are poor. Perhaps it is easier to cry out to God for help when you are in need. But if Christians sanctify God in their hearts ahead of material concern, they should be able to live above their circumstances whether that includes prosperity or poverty.

Poverty is a curse, not a blessing. It is certainly not equated with righteousness. It comes sometimes because of the horrors of war, sometimes because of unjust or unwise government, sometimes because of oppression by the greedy and the ruthless, sometimes because of disobedience to God's commandments, and sometimes because of lack of knowledge of God's principles of blessing. Sometimes a transition from one of God's destinations to another brings temporary poverty. Sometimes temporary poverty follows a satanic attack or a serious and unexplainable calamity. Whatever its cause, poverty is not equated with holiness.

Some voluntarily take a vow of poverty so that they can give themselves totally to God. In that situation, poverty becomes a blessing for those people, because they have given up material riches for God. However, simply being poor is not a sign of holiness. Of course, neither is being wealthy. Godly people are those who are content wherever God has placed them and are serving Him to the best of their abilities, irrespective of material circumstances.

5. Is money the root of all evil?

Money is not the root of all evil. The Bible says, "The *love* of money is a root of all kinds of evil, for which some have strayed from the faith in their greediness, and pierced themselves through with many sorrows."[8] The *use* of money can be very worthwhile. It can be used to build orphanages and hospitals, to feed the poor, to preach the gospel, to build universities, to educate people in righteousness, to establish churches, and to broadcast the gospel. It takes money to print Bibles, to publish religious books, and to advertise evangelistic meetings. There is nothing intrinsically wrong with money.

The question is, what is money being used for? Is it being used for God's glory, or is it being used only for pleasure? Is it being used for pride, to support dictators, and for the purchase of arms with which to kill people, or is it being used for a higher purpose?

The love of money is a root of evil, because some people love money more than they love God. Jesus said a man cannot serve God and Mammon (the false god of riches and avarice).[9]

The wage earner must earn money to stay alive. We call it "earning a living." In earlier societies, if a man had no wages he faced literal starvation and death. A supply of food insulated him from the fear of death by starvation. Later, money became the substitute for supplies of food and clothing. Soon, those who had more forgot the reason they had accumulated so much wealth. The pursuit of money became an end in itself—a status symbol—a measure of achievement. The question, "How much is he worth?" almost always refers to money—not musical ability, athletic ability, or spirituality.

The rich man begins to feel superior to those who have to earn a living. He can enjoy a life of luxury that is not available to the average person. He is also given tremendous power and can use his money to control and dominate other people. Money has become so important that men will lie, cheat, bribe, defame, and kill to get it. The love of money becomes the ultimate idolatry. This is why Paul said, "The love of money is a root of all kinds of evil."

6. How do I forgive my enemies?

The first step in forgiveness is to recognize your resentment against an enemy. You must understand who the enemy is and what he has done to hurt you. Then you must consciously say, "I forgive that person for the following wrongs against me." Then repent of your feelings against your enemy and ask God to forgive you, even as "we also forgive everyone who is indebted to us."[10]

After that, begin to pray actively for your enemy's good. Jesus told us to pray for our enemies and that doing this will help to fill us with love for them.

When you pray for your enemies, asking God to meet their needs and manifest Himself to them, you are overcoming evil with good. Instead of fighting negative thoughts in your mind, you are filling your mind with positive thoughts. You are now on the side of your enemy; you have a spiritual stake in his well-being. If God answers your prayer, which you want Him to do, the person prayed for will be blessed, and you will learn about redemption—the ultimate form of forgiveness.

Keep in mind that if you ask God to bless somebody, God will bring that person to a condition where blessing is possible. God will not bless an evildoer until he or she repents of sin, provides restitution where necessary, and gets right with God. So if you ask God to bless someone who has wronged you, the result may well be a repentant sinner and a new brother or sister in the Lord!

7. What does the Bible mean when it says, "Do not be overcome with evil, but overcome evil with good?

There is only one way that evil can overcome a Christian, and that is if the Christian returns evil for evil. If someone insults you and snarls at you, you are not overcome. You are overcome if you begin to snarl right back. Then the unpleasant person has become your role model. You are copying evil and evil is overcoming you. If someone hates you and you hate him back, then evil is getting the victory. If someone strikes you and you strike back, then you have become like the evil one.

The Bible says, "Do not be overcome by evil, but overcome evil with good."[11] If someone reviles you, you are to smile back and say, "God bless you." The person will not know how to react to that, and you have overcome him. You have won. That person has not changed you, but you have gone on the offensive with the most powerful weapon in the world—love! If someone strikes you on the cheek, Jesus said you should turn the other cheek.[12] And that will leave your adversary totally confused! And then on top of that you should say, "I love you."

If someone forces you to go one mile, go two miles. If someone takes your coat, give him your shirt as well.[13] Do so graciously, cheerfully, even assertively. God has given you the spiritual weapons to discern who your enemies are and then to conquer them by making them your friends. (Of course, as long as there are vicious criminals and international tyrants in the world, there must be a system of restraint through local or international police. In Romans 13, police and legitimate armies are considered by the apostle Paul as "ministers of God" to bring vengeance on lawbreakers.)

8. What is lying? Are "little white lies" wrong?

Lying is a deliberate attempt to deceive by use of any form of untruth. By words, gestures, circumstances, or silence an attempt may be made to convince another that there is a reality different from what we know to be true.

The book of James tells us, "Let your 'Yes,' be 'Yes,' and your 'No,' 'No,' lest you fall into judgment."[14] Our word should be our bond. A person who feigns illness to avoid work is lying. A person who has his secretary say he is out, when he is in, is lying and forcing her to lie too. A person who fails to declare his income accurately on his tax return is lying. A person who falsifies his achievements or age is lying. A person who covers up or exaggerates facts is lying. A person who misrepresents merchandise is lying. A person who bears false witness against another breaks the ninth commandment by lying, and one who does so in court is guilty of the crime of perjury.

A woman came to evangelist Billy Sunday on one occasion and asked, "Reverend Sunday, how can I stop exaggerating?" He looked at her and said, "Call it lying." It is the same way with the "little white lies." There is no such thing as "a little white lie." Lies are lies.

Yet lying is a part of society. We train our children to lie. For example, suppose you go to someone's house for dinner, and they give you a delicious meal. If you say, "That was delicious," you have told the truth and everything is fine. But what if you go to someone's house and they serve you something that is absolutely terrible, and you say, "That was the most delicious meal I have ever had"? You are lying. You may have done it for a good reason—a white lie— but you still lied. Honestly praise something, or be silent; but do not lie! The Bible tells us that by "speaking the truth in love, [wc] may grow up in all things into Him who is the head—Christ."[15]

People take little children to visit a relative and, by telling them to say certain things that they do not mean, teach them to lie. People go to church and sing hymns to God they do not mean. We sing a song called "A Mighty Fortress Is Our God." One stanza reads, "Let goods and kindred go, this mortal life also." This song was written by a man facing excommunication and possible death for his faith. Yet how many communicants in the church he founded—or in any other—are willing to make such a commitment? So we sing lies to God.

We must begin to be truthful to God and to one another. There is no way that the Holy Spirit can operate in someone's life if there is a lack of truth. The Spirit of God is the spirit of truth. Jesus Christ is "the way, *the truth*, and the life."[16] It is a dreadful condemnation on us as evangelicals that the term *evangelistically speaking* means the exaggeration of attendance figures. We only honor God when we exhibit truth and integrity in everything we do.

---

9. Is it possible to steal without knowing it?

The Bible says, "You shall not steal."[17] Stealing is taking without permission what belongs to somebody else. It can involve tangible and intangible things. Stealing would include thefts from households, shoplifting, pilfering, industrial espionage, embezzlement, and similar acts.

Dishonesty of all sorts, including stealing, has reached epidemic levels in society. Many Christians are involved in stealing without knowing it. It is possible, for instance, even to steal time. In most businesses the payroll is the biggest expense. Yet studies have shown that the average worker gives perhaps thirty-two to thirty-three hours a week instead of forty. When long lunch hours or time spent at the coffee machine, gazing out the window, or visiting with neighbors are added up, the amount is staggering.

It is true, too, that people are careless with the use of company stamps, stationery, paper clips, tools, and parts.

This is stealing. In one factory, where many hand tools were disappearing, management decided to have a search of the employees as they left for home at end of the work day. When this announcement was made, as the workers were preparing to exit, there was the sound of metal dropping all over the yard. Because the workers did not want to get caught, they just dropped stolen wrenches, hammers, and screwdrivers, leaving the yard littered with tools.

People do not pay their bills on time, denying interest to the companies they owe. People take merchandise home and use it and then return it as if it had never been used. People borrow books and tools and never return them.

Not correcting clerks when they undercharge one for goods purchased is stealing. Claiming credit for someone else's work or achievement is a form of stealing. Company officers who divert corporate opportunities to their own personal gain are stealing. God desires complete honesty from His people. Any form of stealing should be forsaken as not worthy of God's children.

---

10. What does it mean to bear false witness?

The ninth commandment says, "You shall not bear false witness against your neighbor."[18] Two or three witnesses were needed in ancient Hebrew law to establish a claim under civil law or a crime under criminal law. A false witness could lie under oath during judicial proceedings in order to establish guilt in a criminal case, or fault in a civil case. Since judgment based on false testimony could destroy the life or property of innocent human beings and discredit a country's system of justice, the penalty for perjury was very severe.

But the commandment against bearing false witness has a much broader application. Outside the context of the courts, it is termed *slander*. It is possible to bear false witness or slander by spreading rumors. For example, a well-known gospel singer was picked up in Los Angeles because of his careless driving. A search of his car revealed some white powder, and he was booked on a drug charge. It turned out that the white powder was a diet mix, and so the singer was discharged from his arrest and confinement.

It was too late to stop the false rumors that this man was involved in drug dealing. These rumors hurt the man's career and reputation. Those who spread them were guilty of bearing false witness.

Frequently people say untrue things about others. Marriages are broken up because of false rumors that someone has spread. Reputations of honest and honorable people are damaged. I can think of several times when rumors have started about me. Christian people not only believe falsehoods but also pass these stories on without even stopping to investigate. Starting lies about someone or spreading them is bearing false witness, a terrible offense in the sight of God.

A Christian might not be involved in drug addiction, drunkenness, fornication, adultery, or homosexuality, but a Christian may be big on slander and backbiting. I can think of no practice—other than deep-seated hatred and lack of forgiveness—that will so quickly cut off the blessing and power of God in a Christian's life.

---

11. What is coveting?

Coveting is an inordinate desire to have something that someone else has, whether it is an automobile, house, employee, wife, husband, or anything else. Coveting is a condition of the heart—an inner condition which ultimately leads to an outer offense. If someone covets something that someone else has, it can lead to lying, to bearing false witness, to committing murder, to stealing, or to any number of other crimes, even war between nations.

There are a finite number of houses, lands, automobiles, wives, and husbands in this world, so we are not permitted to desire what already belongs to someone else.

Coveting is followed ultimately by a clash of wills, painful unhappiness, or open conflict. But God Himself is infinite, and His supply for His people is infinite. We need not covet what belongs to another. Instead, we can ask God to supply, peaceably and freely, the desires of our hearts.

We are permitted, however, to covet God Himself, to long for Him, because there is enough of Him for everyone. God is not diminished if one person "takes" a great share of Him. An equally great share is available for you and for everyone else in the world. So you can let all your desire for fulfillment be devoted toward desiring God. As Jesus put it, "Seek first the kingdom of God and His righteousness, and all these things shall be added to you."[19]

We must also guard against wanting to *be* another person. For instance, Billy Graham is a great man. But I am not Billy Graham and I cannot be. God did not choose me to do what Billy Graham does, nor did He choose Billy Graham to do what I do. I can do things he cannot do, and he can do things I cannot do. But if I desire to be him, and he wants to be me, then we both have serious trouble.

Some people are successful entertainers, some are businessmen, some are politicians, some are athletes, some are craftsmen. God gives talents, abilities, and situations that are suitable for each individual. We need to seek His perfect will for each one of us, not the career achievement of another.

To attempt to be someone else can set a person upon a false course which can lead to heartbreak, frustration, and even destruction.

---

12. How can I tell whether or not something is sinful?

The best way to know whether or not something is sinful is to know the Bible. You need to be immersed in the Word of God. That means you need to spend hours carefully studying the Bible, memorizing verses, and meditating upon them. The psalmist said, "Your word I have hidden in my heart, that I might not sin against you."[20] If we do that, the Word will take care of the questionable situations that arise. To know what the Bible says is the best way of knowing what is right and what is wrong.

There is another helpful guide. The apostle Paul said, "Let the peace (soul harmony which comes) from Christ rule (act as umpire continually) in your hearts."[21] An umpire announces, "You are safe," or "You are out." When that peace inside your heart disappears, you know "you are out." Your heart is saying, "This course of conduct is wrong." When you begin to feel troubled within yourself, you know that what you are doing is ill-advised, improper, or sinful.

Paul made it even clearer when he said, "Whatever is not from faith is sin."[22] This principle covers gray areas of conduct. To the person who lives in France, a glass of wine with dinner may be perfectly in order. That may be his lifestyle. Besides, the water may be impure and the wine helps his digestion, so there is no spiritual problem.[23] In America, where there is a high incidence of alcoholism and where many Christians have taken a strong stance against drinking any alcoholic beverage, a glass of wine might cause the downfall of someone for whom Christ died.[24] When the Bible does not speak explicitly about something, whether it is sin depends, in many instances, on culture, on the person's status, and on the level of maturity in the Lord. In areas where there are no definite rules as to what is sinful, it is a question of faith. If you feel that something is wrong, if you have a question in your mind about it, and you cannot do it freely without regret or pangs of conscience, then do not do it. To you it is sinful.

---

13. Are organ transplants permissible?

Surgical techniques to transplant a cornea, a kidney, a heart, or some other organ from a live or recently deceased donor to a needy recipient are of very recent origin. These techniques were not known in Bible days.

Jesus Christ said, "Greater love has no one than this, than to lay down one's life for his friends."[25] A donation of an organ to give life or better health or sight to another is like laying down a part of your life. It is an act of love.

For this reason I believe it is entirely proper for a person to will selected organs, such as the cornea of the eyes, to a donor organ bank for use in organ transplants, so that after the death of the donor, someone now blind may see, or someone sick may become well.

Scripture References

1 Mark 12:30
2 1 Corinthians 13:13
3 1 Corinthians 10:31
4 See Galatians 1:10, 1 Thessalonians 2:4
5 See 1 Corinthians 10:31
6 Matthew 7:12
7 Philippians 4:12–13
8 1 Timothy 6:10
9 See Matthew 6:24
10 Luke 11:4
11 Romans 12:21
12 See Matthew 5:39, Luke 6:29
13 See Matthew 5:40–41
14 James 5:12
15 Ephesians 4:15
16 John 14:6
17 Exodus 20:15
18 Exodus 20:16
19 Matthew 6:33
20 Psalm 119:11
21 Colossians 3:15, AMPLIFIED
22 Romans 14:23
23 See 1 Timothy 5:23
24 See 1 Corinthians 8:8–13
25 John 15:13

D. PERSONAL GROWTH AND DEVELOPMENT

1. Is all pride sinful?

Pride was the first great sin. Satan had been created a beautiful creature. After considering his own splendor and wisdom, he came to the conclusion that he knew more about running the universe than God did.[1] Satan's attitude was called pride. It was the beginning of sin in the universe. We are exhibiting pride in its worst aspect when we feel that we can do a better job of things than the Creator. In the Bible it resulted in the statement, "I will exalt myself."

The sin of pride conveys a sense of inordinate self-esteem, arrogance, and haughtiness. One of the Hebrew root words translated "pride" or "proud" means to lift up or be high. We use the term *high and mighty* to describe a proud person. This attitude of heart is deeply wrong—thoroughly repulsive, in fact—before the Lord.

However, we also use the word *pride* to mean a sense of accomplishment or a desire to do well. For instance, you may be proud that your child makes a straight-A average in school. That does not mean you are trying to put yourself above somebody else; it means you are pleased with this achievement.

I think satisfaction in a completed job well done is proper, even though Jesus had a corrective for that attitude if it went too far. He said that when we have done all, we are to remember that we are "unprofitable servants. We have done what was our duty to do."[2]

Pride, as a sin, must be guarded against. The best way to eliminate pride is to look at yourself, your family, and your achievements as objectively as possible. However, knowing what you can do well is certainly not pride. For example, a world class runner would lie with false humility if he said, "I'm just an old slowpoke." He should say, rather, "God has given me the ability to run very fast, and I use it for His glory and praise Him for it." If somebody is a wonderful architect or artist, he should say, "I thank the Lord for the talent He has given me."

Many times, God will give me a teaching that I did not know before. I can sit back, look at it, and say, "Well, isn't that interesting? I have never heard that before, and the Lord just revealed it to me!" I admire it because it is something that God gave me. It should not be a source of pride to build me up, but a source of satisfaction to know that the Lord has done it. The danger comes if I think, *I am more exalted than others because God gave me something that others do not have.*

You must make an honest appraisal of who you are. This is proper and glorifies the Lord. But when you begin to compare yourself to other people, you begin to get into trouble. "I can build a better house than he can. I am faster than he is. I am smarter than she is. We are richer than they are." That sort of thinking leads to pride that is unhealthy and sinful. The psalmist said, "In God we boast all day long."[3] We are proud of the Lord. I boast about Jesus because He is wonderful. That kind of pride is certainly all right.

---

2. How does God guide people?

God's primary means for giving us guidance is the Bible.[4] The Bible is our rulebook of faith and practice. If we know and understand the scriptures, we will be well on our way to having His guidance. He never guides His people contrary to the clear principles of His written Word.

Second, guidance comes from a knowledge of God Himself. We need to know what pleases Him and what displeases Him. There is no substitute for walking with God, sharing with Him, and talking to Him daily.[5] When you do that, you will experience His direction and His correction. You will come to know what His desire is.[6] This relationship develops over a long period of time, not instantaneously. Through constant use, your senses become sharpened so that you know good from evil.[7] Spiritual maturity forms a basis for guidance.

A third key to God's guidance is found in the book of Proverbs, where we read: "Trust in the Lord with all your heart, and lean not on your own understanding: in all your ways acknowledge Him, and He shall direct your paths."[8] This means that you are not only to know God, but to trust Him implicitly. Every aspect of your life is to reflect His sovereignty over you. "In all your ways acknowledge Him" means in your work, in your family, in your personal life, in your thought life, in your recreation, in everything you do, you acknowledge that God is in control of you. Then, lean *not* on your own understanding. If you think you know all the answers, if you have everything all figured out, then you are leaning on your own understanding. If you trust God, acknowledge Him in the way that you live, and do not lean on your overconfidence or past experience. Let Him guide you.

You must have knowledge of the scriptures, a personal knowledge of God, and the knowledge that you are living each day in tune with Him, expecting His guidance. Finally, to have His guidance, you need to be filled with His Spirit. The Bible says, "As many as are led by the Spirit of God, these are the sons of God."[9] Jesus said that the Holy Spirit will lead you into all truth.[10] In the book of Acts, there are recorded instances where the Holy Spirit gave personal guidance. He said to do this or not to do that. He gave revelations. And He still does all these things! He guides by means of specific scriptures that suddenly come alive for you. He guides by bringing people to you providentially to give you advice and counsel. He guides through circumstances. But you must be filled with the Spirit.

There are many other ways that God can guide you. If

your heart and life are centered on God, His Word, and His Holy Spirit, you can rest assured that He will direct your path.

---

3. How do I know I am hearing a word from God?

There is no way of knowing for certain that someone is hearing from God, unless that person has been listening to God over a long period of time and then testing what he or she has heard. Such people have become accustomed to discerning God's voice.[11] There are many others, however, who think they are hearing from God when maybe they are not. How annoying are the superspiritual who always say, "God told me this—God told me that—God told me this other." It seems that *their* every thought is a revelation from God. God does not customarily operate that way. He speaks to us, but He does not chatter away, day in and day out, the way some people claim He does. This has been my experience, and it is the concept that is in accordance with the biblical record.

The Bible says that we can tell if someone is a prophet by seeing if what he has said comes to pass.[12] That is a very pragmatic test, and it works.

A friend who purported to hear from God told me, "My second child is going to be a boy. God told me." His second child was a girl. He said, "Well, God told me that it was not the second child who was going to be a boy, but the third child." His third child was a girl too. At that point I determined, *That brother isn't hearing from God.* It was clear: he made a statement, supposedly from God, that did not come to pass.

There is no shortcut to spiritual understanding. You have to learn to walk with God and to know His voice; otherwise, you will mistake your own voice for His. You even may be fooled by the voice of Satan, or you may hear the clamoring voice of the world. It is so easy to get these voices mixed up. Usually, God speaks to us in a still, small, quiet voice.[13] It takes time, prayer, and waiting on God to hear His voice.

Nor does God scatter His pearls around recklessly. He said, "You will find Him if you seek Him with all your heart and with all your soul."[14] God does not reveal Himself to every casual onlooker who would take sacred things and play with them like toys. I have known some adults who treated the gifts of God as if they were just little baubles to play with. To please God and to receive counsel from Him, people must be both determined and serious.

How do we succeed in hearing God's voice? By spending time with God. The ultimate is not merely to get direction from God; the ultimate is to *know* God. God can make it difficult for us to get into His presence, because He wants to see if we truly will expend the spiritual energy and exercise necessary to do so. Will we stop certain sins? Will we get rid of things that hinder us? Will we truly seek Him will all of our hearts?

Some people only want a quick fix. "God, tell me how to make money on this business deal, please. See you next time!" And then that is the end of it. But God wants to be treated with the reverence and deference that His nature warrants. He wants to change us, not merely give us quick answers to difficult problems. We will never be changed unless we come into His presence, spend time with Him, and allow Him to purify us from our sinful nature.

---

4. What is the secret of happiness?

The secret of happiness has been defined by someone as the progressive accomplishing of worthwhile goals. Ancient theologians used the term *summum bonum*, which means "the greatest good." They believed that the greatest good was the "beatific vision"—seeing God—the attainment of that condition of spirit and soul which would allow them to come into the presence of God, to talk to

Him, to see Him, and to be with Him. That was the ultimate good and the ultimate happiness.

Happiness is not a warm puppy or a fire on a cold night. It is not the beach at dawn or the other things that people say would make them happy. The deep, deep happiness that transcends all else comes from knowing God and, in turn, from being known by Him. Happiness is a communing with Him, hearing His voice, and knowing that the work you accomplish in life, whatever it is, is in fulfillment of His desire for you. When you know and do these things, then you will begin to know perfect happiness.[15]

---

5. What makes people happy?

People are, by and large, happy when they are giving up themselves for something bigger than they are. Jesus spoke about such happiness in the beatitudes: Blessed are the poor in spirit, for theirs is the Kingdom of God. Blessed are they that mourn, for they will be comforted. Blessed are the peacemakers, for they will be called the sons of God.[16]

There are many degrees of happiness, but the greatest happiness comes from serving God, knowing Him, and knowing for certain that your life is contributing, in a positive fashion, to His ultimate purposes. I think that is the greatest happiness a person can have.

People who do not know God will never find lasting happiness. They may achieve a transitory type of happiness, but it will be shattered whenever unpleasant events come. A man may say, "I am very happy, because I have a lovely wife, healthy children, a nice home, and a good job." But what happens if he loses his job, his house is repossessed by the finance company, his wife leaves him, or one of his children becomes sick? What becomes of his happiness then?

If you are fellowshiping with God and serving Him, peace and happiness will be there despite the circumstances. You can be happy in the midst of problems.

6. What is success?

The world defines success as the obtaining of power and/ or the accumulation of wealth and fame. In the Kingdom of God, the successful person learns the principles of the kingdom and applies them for the good of mankind and for the honor and glory of God.[17] The *Westminster Shorter Catechism* says that man's chief end is to glorify God and to enjoy Him forever. Anyone who has learned to glorify and enjoy God can be considered truly successful.

To the Christian, the ultimate success, according to Jesus, is not to have devils subject to you or to do mighty works or great deeds, but to have your name written in the Book of Life.[18] Primarily, success for us should mean being saved and knowing we will go to heaven. Beyond that, success means to learn and to apply heavenly principles here on earth.

There is nothing wrong with being successful financially, but you must be careful not to make riches and honor your god. The Bible tells us, "By humility and the fear of the Lord are riches and honor and life."[19] If a man is humble before God and learns to fear the Lord, he will be granted riches, honor, and life as a result. Jesus Christ said, "But seek first the kingdom of God and His righteousness, and all these things shall be added to you."[20] In God's eyes, the successful person is the one who lives within the kingdom and by its rules. Worldly possessions are of secondary importance.

7. How can I lose weight?

Have you ever said to yourself, "I have tried every diet there is and I just cannot lose weight"? One person confessed to me, "I must have lost two thousand pounds on various diets, but the weight always came back." It is amazing that Americans have to spend so much time trying to lose weight, when about one-fourth of the people in the world are suffering from malnutrition and starvation.

The Bible says that our bodies are fearfully and wonderfully made.[21] They need proper care. There is not any type of a gimmick diet that will really help us. We need to eat sensibly, perform regular exercise, and get appropriate amounts of rest.

God has put in our world certain very significant families of food for our benefit. The fibrous, complex carbohydrates are the best things for us to eat. I am speaking of vegetables (such as potatoes, carrots, and turnips), various types of grain (such as whole wheat, whole corn, beans, and brown rice), and various fruits. This type of food should make up 60 to 70 percent of our total caloric intake.

We should avoid simple carbohydrates, because these are the ones that give calories without beneficial fiber. These are fruit juices, white breads, white sugar and various types of sweets, snacks, sugared dishes, and so-called "junk food." We should almost totally avoid processed sweets. The sugar we get should come in the form of melons, grapes, bananas, apples, peaches, and other fruits.

And we should cut down on the eating of fat. Fat breeds fat. Butter, cream, whole milk, and cheeses contain an enormous amount of animal fat, but we should try to restrict the intake of fat to no more than 15 percent of the calories we consume. Meat protein, such as beef, should be restricted, too, because beef has so much fat in it. We should spend more of our available protein calories on fish and poultry which are less fattening.

With that kind of wise diet, you can eat just about anything you want. Your weight will automatically begin to go down because you will not be pumping in calories that fail to satisfy your appetite.

Still, diet alone may not be enough. You may have to exercise to stimulate the burning of the calories. Some people jog, some swim, others ride bicycles, and some only walk. You should spend at least thirty minutes a day walking, at least five or six days a week at a minimum. That much walking can take away thirty, forty, or fifty pounds in a year. Eating wisely, coupled with exercise, will balance out your metabolism and will give you a very easy weight loss regimen.

However, some people are controlled by gluttony. They have eaten so much fat-producing food they are obsessed with it. They are as addicted to sweets as some people are to alcohol. To such a person, food has become a means of psychological gratification. It is a means of retreat from the demands of the world, a crutch one can lean on in place of normal human relationships. The more a person eats, the harder it becomes for him to function in normal relationships. He is in a vicious cycle, from which escape seems impossible. Somewhere in the cycle, he or she may have become actually obsessed by a demonic spirit of eating.

Such people need prayer for deliverance. They need to have a spirit of gluttony cast from them. Then they must begin to adjust their thinking. They must understand that food is neither a reward for good behavior nor a solace for grief.

If they start substituting foods I have already mentioned for the type of fattening food they normally eat, they will find themselves losing weight. In fact, if a man eats three or four backed potatoes a day, he will not ingest as many calories as are in one piece of pie, as long as he leaves off the butter and sour cream. But he will be full! He will not have room for sweets or fatty foods! And if he starts moderate exercise, he will most certainly be able to achieve a long-range solution to his weight problem.

But for certain people there needs to be a definite prayer of deliverance to overcome the craving for food.

---

8. Is drinking alcohol a sin?

The Bible says that "wine is a mocker, intoxicating drink arouses brawling."[22] The Bible also says, "Woe to him who gives drink to his neighbor, pressing him to your bottle, even to make him drunk."[23] Yet the Bible does not say that drinking a glass of wine or beer, or a cocktail with dinner, is a sin. Drunkenness is a sin, forbidden by the Bible, but having one drink may not be wrong.

Is drinking alcohol wrong? I do not drink alcoholic beverages for one major reason: my conduct might cause someone else, who is weak, to stumble. The apostle Paul established a rule of conduct that I think is very good. He said he would not eat meat or drink wine or do anything else which would cause a weaker brother to stumble.[24]

In a country where there are at least twenty million problem drinkers, and millions of others who use alcohol to excess, Christians just cannot stand by and say, "I can drink alcoholic beverages because the Bible does not say not to." My conduct should be governed by the law of love. If I love my brother, I will not cause him to stumble and be offended. I personally refrain from drinking alcohol for that reason.

There is another reason for not drinking. The believer's body is the temple of the Holy Spirit. It is hard to think that we could pour liquor into the temple of God without defiling it. Liquor destroys blood vessels and brain cells. Long-term consumption of alcoholic beverages can cause cirrhosis of the liver, lead to *delirium tremens*, and make for habitual alcoholism.

It is also very difficult to think that anyone could worship God with his mind befogged by drinking. Even one ounce of liquor can begin to bring on intoxication. Two or three ounces can make a person legally drunk. Half of all the traffic deaths in the United States are caused by people who have had at least one drink prior to driving.

To take our money, our lives, and our bodies, all of which belong to Jesus, and subject them to a state of intoxication can hardly be said to glorify the Lord or be an act of faith.

Some would raise the issue of what Jesus did when He changed water into wine. In ancient Israel there was almost no alcoholism, and there is little problem with it in Israel today. But in Jesus' day, wine was used at meals and in ceremonial functions or for special parties. As a national matter, wine was not a problem for them. Their wine was probably a low-alcohol-content grape derivative, and it was more of a refreshing beverage than it was an intoxicant. Jesus lived in a society in which alcoholism was not the problem that it is in our day. So, for Him, in the context of that culture, wine was all right. But for us in America today, alcohol is not all right.

---

9. How can I quit drinking or depending on drugs?

In both of these instances a person has to make up his mind to quit. I do not believe in gradually tapering off of cigarettes, narcotics, or alcohol. You need to make a total break. That means you should get rid of anything you have that might tempt you.

In my case, when I found Jesus, I poured some valuable Scotch down the drain, to the consternation of my wife, who had not yet made the same commitment. That was a definite break for me. From that moment on, I was not going to drink any more. I believe this is the case with any habit a person regards as sinful. He or she must say, "That's it. That's the last one. No more." And from that moment on, ask God to help you.

You must confess that you have been doing something you consider wrong, and that you have been defiling the temple of God. You must tell God that you want and need His forgiveness and deliverance. You must renounce your habit and cast the spirit of alcohol, the spirit of narcotics, or the spirit of nicotine from your body. Command it to leave you and resolve that, with God's help, you will never again smoke another cigarette, another joint of marijuana, or whatever it may be that you are giving up, again.

After that, do not consort with those who helped to get you into trouble or who would soon have you back where you used to be. It may be hard to do that, but it is necessary. Instead, you should try to find some others, preferably Christians, who have given up the same habit themselves, to support you during the first days of quitting. Alcoholics Anonymous is one such group that is very helpful.

It takes about thirty days to establish a habit. You have to get into the habit of not smoking or not drinking. It will take about the same length of time for your body to clean out the poisons and the chemical dependency. After that time period, the craving should be over, and in the case of cigarettes, you may discover that the smell of cigarettes and cigarette butts will actually become repugnant to you.

---

10. Is there anything wrong with gambling?

In the Bible, the sacred lot was cast as a means of determining the mind of God.[25] In ancient Israel it was assumed that God was in control of the dice and that He would speak to His people this way. Although there is no such thing as luck and God is in control of everything, when somebody takes money that belongs to God (because everything we have belongs to God) and bets it on the turn of a roulette wheel, that person is, in a sense, saying "God, I am forcing You now to show Yourself. You must make that ball go into the hole I bet on, because I am a Christian." When you act like that, you are putting the Lord to the test. You are tempting God and that is a sin.[26]

When somebody pushes a stack of chips onto a poker table to bet God's money on whether the next card will be red, or a ten, or whatever, he is asking for trouble. He is saying by his acts, "God, I am risking Your money and my faith on the fact that You are going to permit me certain cards." Tempting God like that is wrong and Christians should know better.

Gambling can even destroy a person, becoming an obsession and a compulsion just like alcoholism. The habitual gambler ruins his family and his life. And many people steal from banks and businesses in order to get money for gambling. It becomes a disease that has destroyed literally tens of thousands of people.

Pervasive gambling teaches people that fame, success, and fortune are available without work or struggle. A roll of the dice, a turn of a card, the spin of a wheel, the run of a horse, the drawing of a lottery number are held out as the way to riches. The virtues of industry, thrift, careful investment, and patience are all undermined by this vice. In their place come human greed, lust, avarice, sloth, and a live-for-the-moment mentality. How tragic to see the legislatures of sovereign states linking their budgetary futures to legalized gambling and lotteries that will undermine the very virtues their citizens need for true long-range growth and prosperity!

---

11. How do I get over depression?

Webster's dictionary defines *depression* as "a psychoneurotic or psychotic disorder marked by sadness, inactivity, and feelings of dejection." I believe that one of the principal causes of depression is a sense of failure and frustration caused by unwillingness to do what should be done or to stop doing what should not be done. A person becomes ashamed and begins a process of self-depreciation. Then, along with personal shame, comes a loss of fellowship with God, either real or imagined.

Some years ago I knew a woman who was living with a man outside of wedlock. She was a born-again Christian, active in religious matters. She knew that cohabitation outside of marriage was wrong. She knew she was living a lie, that she was in a relationship that was wrong; yet she did not have the power to break it. She began to hate herself. You can imagine the depression that came about because of this sense of failure.

As a result, she had overdosed on drugs and was in a hospital in a near-death situation when I saw her. She had become so depressed that she had tried to commit suicide, which is what happens in the last stage of depression. Somewhere down inside her there was a voice saying, "I have failed myself and failed God." She wanted God, but she was too weak to break with sin. So she took what seemed the "easy" way out.

Depression can also be caused by a dietary deficiency. If you are lacking iron and certain of the B-complex vitamins in your diet, you can become seriously depressed. This type of depression needs to be corrected by wholesome nutrition along with massive doses of vitamins and minerals. Junk food and excess caffeine should be avoided, and you should exercise vigorously.

The worst thing about depression is that it makes its victims withdraw and lapse into inactivity. A person has to get going again and begin to help other people, going to church, going to work, or doing anything other than sitting around feeling sorry for himself. Becoming active is a key remedy for depression.

Also, a terrible tragedy or personal loss can shock the system, bringing on a feeling of hopelessness and despair. Many times these feelings are compounded by a failure to eat well and a failure to exercise or get out among other people. As the withdrawal begins, a downward spiral takes hold that needs to be broken.

But our question is: how do you get over the depression? You have to recognize what is causing it. If it is sin, you have to go to the root of the failure and do whatever it takes to get your life right with God. If it is merely a sense of failure, examine your expectations. If they are too high, change them to a more realistic level. If indeed there is a real failure to perform, then grasp the task and do it.

If the depression has to do with diet and exercise, begin to eat nutritious foods, take heavy doses of therapeutic vitamins and minerals, and begin vigorous walking or other exercises. In the case of someone who has suffered an emotional trauma, that person needs to reach out for the help and support of friends. Be frank about your problem; say, "I am terribly depressed. Will you please come and be with me? Will you pray with me? Will you help me?" Try to open up to other people and draw them in. It always helps to pray and read the Bible, which is the source of comfort and the source of life.[27]

Above all else, stop feeling sorry for yourself. Instead, reach out a hand of compassion to someone whose grief and tragedy exceed your own.

---

12. How do I get free from fear?

The apostle John wrote, "Perfect love casts out fear, for fear has torment."[28] The main cause of fear is an excessive concern about one's self: self-preservation, self-image, what the future holds for one's self. Those feelings may not be on the surface, but they are the real cause of fear. If a person is filled with love for someone else, then the focus is away from self and on the other person. The perfect love that comes from Christ should fill our lives. As it does, it crowds out all fear.

There are many kinds of fear. We have different scientific names for them. Some people fear the dark. Some are afraid to go outside. Some fear other people. Others are afraid to be shut up in closed spaces. Some fear heights. Some people have a fear of tunnels. Some are afraid of snakes. Some fear is submerged in the subconscious and manifests itself in psychosomatic illness, ulcers, headaches, depression, or even paralysis.

Knowledge and experience can help us overcome fear. We fear the unknown and are comfortable with the familiar. Therefore, people who fear should be gradually exposed in a nonthreatening context to the object of their fear.

Even as fear tends to inhibit action and bring paralysis, in like manner, action tends to dispel fear. The psalmist discovered one great weapon against fear when he wrote, "The Lord is my shepherd . . . I will fear no evil."[29] We should remind ourselves over and over that God is all-powerful and that His protection is sufficient for any need.

Some fear is healthy. We should fear—or at least respect—fire, electricity, lightning, bullets, bankruptcy, and especially God Himself. God placed within man a beneficial mobilization technique triggered by fear that marshals his responses in times of danger or need.

On the other hand, we should recognize that some extremes of fear are totally false and may be induced by demons. In these cases, spirits of fear need to be commanded to depart in the name of Jesus.

Perfect love casts out fear. The Word of God sets people free. The person who is victimized by fear should focus on Jesus, on His love, on His power, and should memorize and recite the Word of God, zeroing in on those promises that deal with the hope Christians have in Christ.[30] The victim should shout these promises out loud, using them to praise the Lord.

Praising the Lord is an excellent antidote to fear. Not only does this rebuke the spirit of fear and Satan who brings it, but it also brings the Christian into the direct presence of God. The psalmist tells us that God inhabits the praises of His people.[31] We can bind Satan's power by praise. Out of praise, we will find deliverance from all our fears.

---

13. How can I be stable and mature spiritually, and eliminate the ups and downs in my Christian life?

If a person ate only one meal a week, he would be very malnourished. He would also have physical and emotional peaks and valleys caused by the malnutrition.

Although we understand the principles of nutrition, some Christians seem to think that one hour a week of spiritual food is sufficient for the nourishment of their spirits. Then they wonder why they don't have stability.[32] The food for our spirits and souls is God's Word and prayer, and we need that food every bit as much as we need physical food. If we have to eat daily to nourish our bodies, we should have daily nourishment for our spirits and souls.

Everyone who knows God should set aside a specific time every day to spend alone with Him.[33] This should be a time to read the Bible, to meditate on the precepts of God, to recite His promises, to talk to Him, and to listen to Him.[34] It should be a time to cleanse the heart of sins and to receive God's forgiveness. The Bible says, "If we walk in the light as He is in the light, we have fellowship with one another, and the blood of Jesus Christ His Son cleanses us from all sin."[35] But the Bible goes on to say that when we sin, "If we confess our sins, He is faithful and just to forgive us our sins and to cleanse us from all unrighteousness."[36] Continuous forgiveness and fellowship with the Father are the keys to spiritual stability.

At the same time, there needs to be a continuous building of our spirits through reading the Word of God, meditating upon it, and letting it become a part of us so that we begin to think and act like Jesus. That's how we grow.

Once we have a solid relationship with the Father and the Lord Jesus Christ, we can begin to reach out to others, to be His hand extended to the world. As we reach out to others, we will find Jesus being more actively manifested in our lives, and we will begin to grow personally and be more stable in the Lord. If, on the other hand, we constantly feed our spirits and souls without sharing with others, our spiritual life will stagnate.

Jesus gave His followers a special means of growth—the baptism in the Holy Spirit (see pp. 355–356). A manifestation of that experience can be speaking in tongues. The apostle Paul said, "He who speaks in a tongue edifies himself."[37] Paul's own exercise of this gift undoubtedly built up his spirit to enable him to accomplish his mission.

Finally, Christians need to get together with other Christians. Christianity is a communal religion. It is necessary to have the support and encouragement of other Christians. We must share with them, encourage them, and be encouraged by them. If we do that, we will grow together in the things of the Lord.

14. How do I get out of poverty and debt?

Poverty is a lack of money or material possessions. Poverty is usually accompanied by debt obligations to others. Debt, whether or not associated with poverty, is a form of slavery. Following God's principles will break the hold of both poverty and debt.

First of all, you must commit yourself, your finances, your family, and your life to Jesus Christ. Agree to live by God's principles and seek to know what He has to say to you in your situation. Be absolutely honest about the faults and mistakes in your life, past or present, that may have caused your problem of debt. To escape trouble, you must know what put you there.

Second, do everything you can to understand God's principles. The Bible says, "My people are destroyed for lack of knowledge."[38] There are many Christians who have no concept whatsoever of the principles of God's kingdom. They understand neither God's laws dealing with material prosperity nor their own privileges as children of God. So, for lack of knowledge, they suffer.

People in debt or in poverty especially need to understand a rule of God's kingdom that I call the Law of Reciprocity. This is a law of cause and effect, of action and reaction. In the area of money, the law is simple: "Give, and it will be given to you: good measure, pressed down, shaken together, and running over will be put into your bosom. For with the same measure that you use, it will be measured back to you."[39] When a person begins to give to God's work and to the poor and less fortunate, God begins to give back to him. Regardless of the debt burden, a person should give a very minimum of 10 percent of his income to the Lord. Even if you are at a poverty-level income, you have something you can give to God. Start where you are. Reach out in compassion to those less fortunate than yourself. As a first priority, get into a position to give love, time, energy, and money to other people even if it is only a little bit.

Next, set up a realistic budget. Most people do not have budgets, and their spending has neither plan nor control. Whatever your income level, you should set up a budget that includes one or more tithes (see pp. 402–403) plus offerings to the Lord, which may be in the form of aid to those who are less fortunate.[40] After setting aside your tithe, establish a realistic plan to pay off your debts. Go to your creditors and obtain an agreement that they will accept your payment schedule. Make it understood that you cannot pay any more than a certain amount, and they will almost always accept your plan.

Once you have done that, you have to resolve in your mind that there will be no more accumulation of debt. You cannot go back to living beyond your means. Make a vow to God that you will not buy anything on credit, and that your lifestyle will be curtailed to fit your income. This takes a definite mental and spiritual commitment. It may take a year, or two years, or five years, but you are going to get out of debt.

It has been suggested by a very wise businessman that part of any budget should go for recreation. There should be some time each month when the family can get away from the pressures of life. Maybe it can be a picnic in the park, a fishing trip, or possibly a night away from home in a motel or resort. Recreation includes anything to get away from the constant pressure and to allow your mind to be recreated in God.

Along with recreation, I recommend a Sabbath rest. You cannot work seven days a week. There must be one day a week that is dedicated to God, to thinking about Him, praying to Him, studying the Bible, and resting. All of these things are necessary to prepare your mind and spirit to win the battle.

Then, with all of these things going for you, you need a renewed faith in God. He is the source. As you give to Him and trust Him, God will begin to take you from bondage to debt into His blessings. He will open doors for you and will give you concepts and ideas to help you overcome your situation. You must believe this and expectantly look for His answer rather than to some other person as your source. *God* is your source.

Every day, speak words of confidence. Say out loud that you are going to be free from debt and that God is going to put you in a different position. Memorize scripture verses where God says things such as, "He raises the poor from the dust/And lifts the beggar from the ash heap./To set them among princes."[41] Speak these words over and over again, confidently, knowing that God can do all things and do them well.

With that frame of mind, you should be on your way. It may take a year to pay off your debts. In the instances that I know of, the average was about eighteen months. But it may take three, four, or even five years. You will win the battle if you use the weapons that God has made available to you! You *can* be debt free!

---

15. Should Christians have a will?

Everyone should have a will. Even the penniless Bowery bum should have a will because he might be hit by a bus and his estate might have a claim against the bus company.

The prophet Isaiah told King Hezekiah, "Set your house in order, for you shall die."[42] Any person, wealthy or not, male or female, has the privilege under law and custom dating back to Bible times of determining the guardians for his or her children, as well as the privileges they shall enjoy if the maker of the will dies while the children are young. Wills can provide for the care of the wife or husband, and gifts to religious organizations and other charities.

Without a will, the state might apply a rigid set of rules to give the wife only a percentage of an estate, usually one-third, and the children would get the remainder. If there is no surviving husband, wife, or children, the possessions of a lifetime may be given to brothers, sisters, or nieces and nephews. Usually, nothing goes to a charity unless it is designated in a will.

A will is a very simple document to write and to execute. For maximum protection against challenges in any state, a will should be signed and declared to be a last will and testament in the presence of two or three witnesses who are assembled at the signing and who are not beneficiaries under the will.

Without question, a valid will and a thorough estate plan are a vital part of stewardship for every Christian. Wills can be rewritten and re-executed as circumstances change. To write a will does not mean that death will soon follow, as many superstitiously fear.

Scripture References

1 See Ezekiel 28:14–19
2 Luke 17:10
3 Psalm 44:8
4 See John 16:13
5 See Isaiah 58:11
6 See Psalms 25:9, 32:8, Proverbs 11:3
7 See Hebrews 5:14
8 Proverb 3:5
9 Romans 8:14
10 See John 16:13
11 See John 10:27
12 See Deuteronomy 18:22
13 See 1 Kings 19:11–13
14 Deuteronomy 4:29
15 See Isaiah 26:3–4, Philippians 4:7, Proverbs 28:14, John 13:17
16 See Matthew 5:3–12
17 See Proverbs 2:10–11, 4:7, 9:10, 22:1
18 See Luke 10:20
19 Proverb 22:4
20 Matthew 6:33
21 See Psalm 139:14
22 Proverb 20:1
23 Habakkuk 2:15
24 See Romans 14:14–21
25 See Leviticus 16:7–10, Jonah 1:7, Acts 1:24–26
26 See Deuteronomy 6:16
27 See Isaiah 41:10, Jeremiah 29:11–13, Hebrews 4:15–16
28 See 1 John 4:18

29 Psalm 23:1, 4
30 See Matthew 28:20, Mark 11:24, 1 Corinthians 6:11, 2 Thessalonians
    3:3, 1 John 2:25, Revelation 21:4
31 See Psalm 22:3
32 See Psalm 66:18, John 9:31, 15:7
33 See Mark 1:35, Luke 5:16, 6:12
34 See Psalm 19:12–14, Ephesians 3:14–21, 1 Peter 1:3–10, 4:7
35 1 John 1:7
36 1 John 1:9
37 1 Corinthians 14:4
38 Hosea 4:6
39 Luke 6:38
40 See Malachi 3:10
41 1 Samuel 2:8
42 2 Kings 20:1

11. Bafflers from the Bible

---

1. Who was Cain's wife?

This is one of the most common questions posed by people who want to dispute the Bible. Cain and Abel were the first two boys born to Adam and Eve, the first people. At maturity they fought, and Cain killed Abel. Later on, the Bible tells us that Cain was married.[1] The question is, where did his wife come from?

The only conclusion we can draw from the scant record given in scripture is that Adam and Eve had daughters as well as sons, and that Cain married his sister. In the early days of the human race, there would not have been a prohibition against incest; otherwise, there would have been no way for mankind to replenish the earth.

Later on, incest became a societal taboo for various good reasons, especially genetic ones. I do not believe that Cain's marriage to a sister would have presented genetic problems, because they would have had almost a pure genetic strain from which to produce offspring. Inbreeding and

496

intermarriage bring out defective recessive genes today; but presumably, Adam and Eve and their children had no defective genes to begin with, since they were created perfect.

We really do not have any record, one way or the other, about Cain's wife, and so any answer has to be conjectural.

---

2. Why isn't everyone healed?

Jesus Christ was the perfect expression of God's will. During His recorded lifetime He never refused anyone who asked for healing. Therefore, we may assume that it is God's perfect will to heal everyone. To understand more about those today who are not healed we must consider *how* Jesus healed.

First of all, He had the gift of discerning spirits.[2] He knew whether a sickness was caused by a demon, a disease, unconfessed sin, or if it was a psychosomatic disorder. If it was a disease, He would speak to the disease; if it was a demon, He would cast out the demon; if it was sin, He would forgive the sin. He always knew exactly what was called for.

Jesus also had complete access to the Father.[3] He had no sin to cloud His understanding. When He spoke, it was with pure power. And He had an absolute understanding of how to use His power; therefore, there was no sickness or disease that could stand in His way.

Today, those of us who minister in His name seldom exercise true spiritual discernment. Our access to power is clouded by sin and unbelief, or earthly cares, all of which prevent us from having complete access to God.[4] Consequently, our prayers are not as effective for healing as His. Beyond this, many people have been taught that God does not heal today, so neither they nor their spiritual leaders take the necessary steps to bring about spiritual healing.

I should add that there are some people who enjoy being sick. They use sickness as an excuse not to face up to life. Some people are tired of life and consciously or unconsciously want to die. They are not healed for the simple reason that they do not want to be. There are some people who harbor unconfessed sin. They may seem holy and righteous on the surface, but, deep down inside, they are filled with resentment. There are others who are sick because of demonic activity. Prayer for healing will not work for them, because the demon has to be addressed and cast out, usually by someone else.

In certain cases a healing does not take place until the individual's spirit and mind are in a condition where he or she can be receptive to what God has to offer. The healing in such cases is not instantaneous, but gradual, because the person being healed needs to come to an appreciation of the promises and the truth of God. Others are so overcome by shock or grief or pain or medical treatments or contagion that it is virtually impossible to focus their spiritual energies on the healing powers of God.

These are just some of the reasons, and there are many more. Remember that Jesus Christ showed us what is possible. His life and ministry were not intended to add to our suffering by pointing out our failings but to give us an attainable goal to strive for. In searching for answers we must ask, "What is it in this situation that is blocking or preventing the healing?" Once we have discovered the problem, the healing may take place.

---

3. Should women teach men?

The apostle Paul wrote, "I do not permit a woman to teach or to have authority over a man."[5]

In the New Testament, there were deaconesses who had key roles in the church and women prophets who had the gift of being able to prophesy and speak forth God's Word. In the Old Testament, the woman Deborah was a leader and judge of Israel. She led her people safely through a time of danger.[6]

However, nowhere in the Bible is there an example of a woman pastor who actually directed the spiritual lives of a congregation of believers. That is what Paul said he did not permit.

God has established a pattern. He is the head of the man, and the man is to be the head of the woman, and together they are to be the head of the children. God sets this divine order in the church. This does not mean that a woman cannot be a business executive or a politician or a lawyer, but in the government of the family and the church, men are to be the leaders. These two institutions are a type of God's universal fatherhood that must be adhered to.

---

4. Are suicide victims forgiven?

The American judicial system presumes that a person who commits suicide is insane. In many instances, this is undoubtedly true. If someone does not know right from wrong, and does not realize what he is doing, he cannot deliberately sin and thus be held accountable for his actions. He therefore has no guilt for what he has done.

However, some people know precisely what they are doing when they take their own lives. They are not crazy. They calmly decide that they are going to take matters into their own hands, and in so doing, they kill a life that belongs to God.

The Bible is not clear about what happens to a suicide victim in relation to eternal salvation, but we do know that unless the person is insane, suicide is a sin. It is an unconfessed, unforgiven sin at the moment it takes place. A suicidal person is taking an extreme risk in gambling with eternal destiny merely to get out of a difficult situation on earth.

There is absolutely no guarantee that I can give to a person who is determined to commit suicide, or to someone who has lost a loved one through suicide, that a suicide victim would go to be with Jesus forever. We know that God's mercies are very great, but I hesitate to presume upon them.

5. If God is love, how can He send anyone to hell?

Christians need to understand the nature of ultimate evil and ultimate good. In heaven, there has to be freedom from fear. The righteous in heaven must be assured that they will not have to go through the cycle of sin, rebellion, restoration, and fall all over again. For heaven to be heaven, there can be no rebellion against God—no sin, no sickness, no death, and no war. There has to come a time when all those things are finished, where the righteous can say, "We are now in another world where we can enjoy freedom forever."

If there were someone in heaven who was a rebel against God, and who was essentially evil, he would not get better over the years, but worse. Ultimately, that individual would threaten the security of everyone else in heaven. That sort of person must be kept apart from those who willingly serve God. God doesn't send people to hell so much as they send themselves away from heaven.

God says to all of us, "Will you accept Me now? Will you please take My will and be Mine? Will you do what is necessary to enter heaven?" But some people answer Him, "Not Thy will, but mine be done." So when they die, God says, "You asked for your will to be done, so I will let you have it your way. You would not take My will on earth, so I am going to let you have your will in eternity." For all eternity, those people will be alone, apart from God, shut out of heaven by their own desire.[7]

God is just; He has given them what they asked for. Even as a good ruler on earth must lock up criminals so that innocent citizens can be free of fear, even so a loving God must one day shut off rebellion so that His universe can be free from fear and filled only with creative love.

6. Should I go into debt now?

The Bible says that the debtor is the servant of the lender.[8] This has always been true. It is a great tragedy to have to borrow money to pay for current expenses, to live beyond your means and constantly try to make $100 do the work of $200.

I believe that those who do not live within their means and who borrow to meet day-to-day expenses wind up being the slaves of those who lend to them. They do not have peace, and very often their marriages are torn apart. Some marriage counselors and financial consultants assert that 80 percent of marriage failure is caused by money pressure and that money problems account for about 50 percent of the impotence in married men. Living beyond your means, which results in debt, can be devastating.

There are some types of debt that are not always damaging, however. For example, a business may need to borrow to purchase productive assets; the servicing of interest and principal payments make up a business expense that is included in the operating budget. Modest debt can allow a business to buy equipment, buildings, and land, and to expand in an appropriate fashion. The same justification applies to the debt-financed purchase of a house. Mortgage payments are not considered by some as debt but as a monthly budgeted expense.

Of course, the happiest people in this regard are those who have no debt on anything, who have paid cash for their cars, their furniture, and their houses, and who have funded their businesses out of either equity or cashflow. These people are better off in times of recession or even in times of rampant inflation. Especially in today's world, when in the next ten, fifteen, or twenty years I believe we are going to be faced with increasing deflationary pressures, the paying of debt is going to be extremely difficult, because we will pay off debt with more and more expensive dollars. It will be a terrible situation. A time of deflation is a debtor's hell.

The present economic environment is the worst possible time to incur debt for anything. If at all possible, do not go into debt now.

---

7. Is cremation right or wrong?

In Leviticus 20 and 21, the Lord commanded that certain types of sinners were to be burned with fire. In the case of King Saul and his sons, whose bodies had been mutilated, their flesh was burned but their bones were buried.[9] Other than these extraordinary cases, the only honorable or proper disposition of the dead in the Old Testament was by burial, which was also the New Testament practice and that of the early church.

Both the Jews of the Bible, and subsequently Christians, believed that the body would one day rise from the dead. We are therefore to preserve the body and honor it. The body is the temple of the loved one's spirit that is now gone but that will one day be reunited with a glorified body. Therefore, in the Judeo-Christian tradition, cremation has generally not been practiced.

The Bible speaks of the tombs of Abraham, Isaac, Jacob, and David, and of the burial place of Jesus Himself, and of the graves of other of the saints and heroes of the Old and New Testaments. All were buried in traditional fashion.

Many religions practice cremation. The Hindus and the ancient Vikings cremated people. In the Shinto faith of Japan ancestors are cremated and their ashes put into little household shrines as objects of veneration.

There are some, of course, who cremate from a very practical standpoint. Some countries encourage cremation because they cannot afford the space for burials and expensive funerals.

Although there is no specific prohibition of cremation in the Bible, it was not practiced in those days, and I believe it should not be practiced now because of our belief in the resurrection.

8. Are credit cards associated with the mark of the Beast?

I n the book of Revelation, there is a discussion of an individual who will become a world dictator, ruler of a domain that looks very similar to the old Roman Empire. This individual is called the "living creature," or the "beast." The Bible tells us he has a number: 666.[10]

Six is the biblical number of humanity. It is one less than perfection. The man whose number is 666 will lead humanity's revolt against God. There are some who feel that Nero could have been that man whose number is 666, and various other names have also been put forward as that person. But Revelation says that, when he comes onto the scene, he will have such dominance that no one can buy or sell without taking his mark, either on the forehead—which indicates will—or on the hand—which indicates action.

So, how will that mark come to be accepted? There are a couple of possibilities. Today we have developed devices called smart cards. These are tiny credit cards that have a microchip implanted in them. They can be put through a card reader at a store that will reveal a person's entire credit history, including the amount of his bank account. The person's transaction in the store can be sent back to a central bank and one master account can then be kept in a computer.

Now there is also the SWIFT system, which means Society of World-wide Interfunds Transfers, headquartered in Brussels, Belgium. It ties together about seven hundred major banking systems around the world. Every day, hundreds of billions of dollars in bank transactions are processed by this vast world-wide computer network. Clearly, mankind now has the technology to link up virtually all the credit in the entire civilized world from the local retail outlet right through to the international banking center.

So, it would not be too difficult, technologically, to move from the smart card to a microchip implanted in the hand. This could be read by a laser-type device that would in turn be connected to a master computer. This could lead to a time when there would be no need for cash or checks: everything would be done by computer. With these developments, it becomes easy to see how the world may be controlled.

Banks are moving in the direction of ever more efficiency with the advent of so-called "transaction cards." These are not charge cards, but they debit an account immediately. As a charge is made, they immediately subtract the money from the bank account. This entire electronic funds transfer system is gaining momentum in the drive toward a checkless, cashless society. This society will not necessarily occur, but it certainly is technologically possible, and could easily fulfill what Revelation says: that people could not buy or sell without the mark of the Beast.

Of course, with all our discussion of technology, we should never lose sight of the deeper implications of the "mark of the beast." The forehead signifies volition, while the hand signifies action. Together, they indicate a willing spiritual acceptance of a satanic being (or system) that has been put forward against God and in place of Jesus Christ. Nothing short of this would lead a just God to send these people to be "tormented with fire and brimstone" as we are warned by Revelation 14:9–11.

---

9. What do you think of long hair for a man?

Many people have raised this question. A few years ago, when hippies were common, respectable society felt that long hair for men was a disgrace.

The apostle Paul wrote about excessively long hair for men. He said that for women, long hair was their glory, and yet it was a shame for men to have very long hair.[11] At the same time, every painting I have ever seen of Jesus, Moses,

Abraham, or of the patriarchs, except for a painting by Salvador Dali, showed them with long hair, and often with a long, full beard. They did not have barber shops around every corner in those days, and Hebrew men especially did not have closely shaven faces and closely cropped hair. The Nazarites, for example, were even forbidden to shave their heads![12]

In view of this, I really do not think there is any problem with long hair. I think the reaction against it was really a reaction to a group of people who were taking drugs and living a lifestyle that was outside the bounds of accepted morality. Their unkempt appearance, long hair, and beards were symbols of their revolt against society. The issue was their lifestyle, not the length of their hair.

10. How is it that Christians sometimes lose the joy of their salvation?

When a person comes to Jesus Christ, his sins are forgiven; he comes into a relationship with the Father; and he is filled with the love of the Lord, having what the book of Revelation describes as his "first love" for God.[13] In that state, there is great joy—joy in being forgiven, joy in having a relationship with the Lord, and joy in life itself.

Some Christians then begin to be careless: they speak a word of slander about a friend; they use a curse word from their old vocabulary; or maybe they take a drink when they do not think they should. Perhaps an immoral affair begins, or perhaps they just get involved with the cares of this life. They get wrapped up in their businesses and their families, and they lose sight of God. He no longer is their first love.

When someone loses his joy, there is a terrible sense of loss. He feels a great emptiness and will not be satisfied by the things of the world. That which pleased him before he knew Christ cannot satisfy him now. God will have taken from that person the ability to be happy apart from Himself.

God has recreated us in Christ to breathe the air of heaven and dwell in mansions of glory. Once we have tasted this life, we are miserable anywhere else.

Such persons can continue in indifference and sin until they lose their assurance of salvation. They will not feel saved, and they will begin to question whether God really did anything for them because their lives no longer reflect salvation.

The Holy Spirit will continue to give a witness in a person's heart. Then, like land that has been repeatedly rained upon and then baked by the sun, that heart will become callous and will no longer be sensitive to the wooing of the Holy Spirit. Such people will be barely distinguishable from non-Christians, with the possible exception that they may refuse to engage in the grosser acts of sin and immorality. They may still maintain a certain moral standard, but inwardly they will have neither joy nor assurance of salvation.

The Old Testament prophet warns us to "break up your fallow ground" so the Lord may come and rain righteousness on us.[14] A Christian in this condition needs to repent and seek forgiveness for being careless and indifferent, for not loving God, for doing and saying things that offended Him, and for not studying the Bible and praying. That person needs to rid himself of the weeds—the cares of this life and the deceitfulness of riches—that have choked the Word in his life and made it unfruitful.[15] He needs to seek cleansing and forgiveness from Jesus, and he needs to re-establish his love affair with the Lord.

This is what Jesus meant when He spoke to the church of Ephesus, saying, "You have left your first love."[16] When that love affair is back in bloom, there will come joy, assurance of salvation, and effectiveness in the Kingdom of God. The choice is ours: God gives us freedom, but He is continuously wooing us to Himself that we might be His willing servants.

God will not violate our free will. He is tender, like a dove, for otherwise we would be His slaves. What He wants from us is voluntary, loving obedience, not the cowed, cringing subservience of a whipped slave. He wants us to be free and loving. He wants the voluntary, joyous devotion of sons and daughters who are destined to share eternity with Him in glory.

11. Did Jesus have brothers and sisters?

According to Matthew 12, when Jesus was teaching a group inside a house, with quite a crowd at the door, some people came to Him and said, "Look, Your mother and Your brothers are standing outside, seeking to speak with You." Jesus replied, "Who is My mother and who are My brothers?" He continued, "Whoever does the will of My Father in heaven is My brother and sister and mother."[17]

By this statement, He moved beyond His earthly family relationship to a new spiritual family based on obedience to God's will. This and other Bible references clearly establish the fact that Jesus had a mother, a father, and siblings.

In fact, the apostle James was one of the Lord's brothers. The apostle Paul confirmed this fact when he wrote, "I saw none of the other apostles except James, the Lord's brother."[18]

Some teach that James was really Christ's cousin, because they believe in the perpetual virginity of Mary. But the Bible tells us that Joseph took his wife Mary and did not know her, or have sexual relations with her, until such time as her child was born.[19] But the clear assumption is that they lived together normally as husband and wife from that time on, and that they had other children besides Jesus. Other statements to the contrary lack any biblical basis.

12. Could you explain the ten virgins in Matthew's gospel?

In Matthew 25, Jesus told three stories—two parables, and a discussion of what He will do at the end of the age. The first parable has to do with ten virgins—five of whom were foolish, and five of whom were wise. The five wise virgins bought oil for their lamps prior to a wedding feast. The five foolish ones put off buying the oil. After the bridegroom had delayed his coming for a while, they all dozed off to sleep. Then at an unexpected hour—say one o'clock in the morning—there was a great shout. The bridegroom was coming! It was time for the wedding.

The wise virgins trimmed their lamps and got ready to go with the procession. The foolish virgins wanted to borrow oil because they did not have any. The wise virgins said they could not share it, because they then would not have enough, and told those without to go buy their own oil. The foolish virgins frantically ran away to get oil, but when they came back, they found that the door was shut against them. The joyous wedding feast was in progress and they were excluded.

What does that mean? Some feel that it relates to the baptism in the Holy Spirit. Some think it concerns salvation. In the context, I believe Jesus was warning about personal godliness and integrity.

In the preceding chapter, Matthew 24, Jesus had told His servants to watch until He comes back, to look after His household until He comes, however long it takes. In the watching process, the top priority should be our personal lives. We are to guard our personal integrity, our truthfulness, our honor, and our righteousness before God. We must manifest love for others as well as love for Jesus. We must pray, study the Bible, be born again, and be filled with the Spirit. All of these things are part of what we must be doing as we await His coming.

Jesus is saying that there is no way a person can borrow personal morality in a moment of crisis. If you have been dishonest, you cannot go to someone else and say, lend me a portion of godliness. You either have it or do not have it. No one can lend a share of his honesty or decency to someone else; nor can he share his salvation or the baptism of the Holy Spirit. The Lord is telling us, in effect, "Always be prepared."

There will be times when we let down. We cannot be awake twenty-four hours a day in the physical realm nor in the spiritual realm. But our personal godliness, righteousness, and honesty are with us all the time. These are not things that we pick up and lay down, that we get rid of or we use up. They have to be accumulated by personal initiative, effort, and zeal. They have to be kept up continuously. They become a part of you.

You have to maintain integrity. You have to be moral *this* week. You have to be truthful *this* week. You have to be honest and loving *this* week. You have to be prayerful and full of the truth of God's Word *this* week. You have to be saved *this* week. You have to be filled with God's Spirit *this* week. Then, when a crisis comes—or the Lord returns—your personal life will be intact. This is the meaning of the parable of the ten virgins.

---

13. Are prayer cloths proper?

We read in Acts that even handkerchiefs and aprons that had touched the apostle Paul were taken to sick people, and the sick people were made well when they received them.[20] The characterization of this by Luke, who wrote the book of Acts, was that God did extraordinary miracles through the hands of Paul. This was an example of something extraordinary.

There is certainly nothing improper about prayer cloths. It is possible to bless a piece of cloth or paper, send it to somebody else and, on account of the prayer attached to it, see healing take place. That type of miracle has happened in the past and happens today.

However, this also can be a device for charlatans, who sell magic amulets and such. In the Middle Ages, mountebanks sold objects of veneration such as milk from the Virgin Mary and splinters from the true cross. They reportedly sold enough splinters from the true cross to build a church!

This sort of thing still goes on. I have personally heard a radio preacher selling Moses' anointing oil. There are others who sell "holy" water from the Jordan River, special bath tubs, and on and on. Prayer cloths can come into that category as a device to deceive and fleece innocent people. The concept, in itself, is certainly biblical; but there must be integrity behind the prayer cloths, and there must be the anointing of the Holy Spirit.

---

14. Is acupuncture wrong?

Acupuncture as a medical technique may have some validity. However, it definitely has non-Christian roots. At its source is the Taoist concept of Yin and Yang, which are the opposing energy forces in the universe: good and evil, male and female, health and disease. (The Korean flag contains the symbol of Yin and Yang.) The acupuncturist seeks a balanced flow of these life forces in the body to relieve pain and bring about healing.

The acupuncturists claim that there are certain nerve junctures in the body that can be activated and made to release energy at another point in the body. Through this process, pain can be alleviated and diseased members receive healing energy.

It is true that medical science has recently found a substance called endorphins, or beta endorphins, which are manufactured by the human brain, and are natural pain killers. I have been present at acupuncture centers in Communist China, where the most unbelievable conditions of dirt and lack of antisepsis were present. Nevertheless, sick people were put into a state where they felt no pain. There apparently are certain places in our bodies that can be touched and made to release endorphins to deaden pain.

When joggers receive what is called a "jogger's high," it is said to be caused by a release of endorphins. When someone runs to the point of near exhaustion, suddenly he feels a tremendous sense of well-being. The body fights the agonizing pain by releasing natural pain killers to inhibit pain centers in the brain.

Whether or not people can be healed of various ills by the manipulation, pressure, or puncture of parts of their body, I am not really able to say. I do believe that some practices of acupuncture and acupressure are based on valid medical principles. However, I feel that the religious or metaphysical justification given for acupuncture by the Chinese and Koreans is not in accord with the Bible and is, in my opinion, wrong.

---

15. Is hypnosis wrong?

I believe that any time a person allows his subconscious mind to be taken over by someone other than himself, he is asking for trouble.

Hypnosis, basically, is nothing more than expanding one's susceptibility to suggestion. The suggestion can be made that the subject is feeling sleepy. If he accepts that suggestion and becomes drowsy, then the hypnotist makes another suggestion. Soon, the hypnotist has the power to implant other thoughts into the subconscious of the hypnotized person. The conscious mind has, in essence, been put to sleep, and the subconscious mind has been surrendered to the hypnotist.

That makes hypnosis extremely dangerous, because almost anything can be implanted in the subconscious. What is called post-hypnotic suggestion can be like a time bomb. A preset cue may cause a certain inexplicable reaction on the part of the hypnotized person.

After hypnosis, the subject becomes more susceptible to future hypnosis. Any cue—a word, or the snap of the fingers—can put him back in a submissive trance. My frank belief is that no human being should submit his deepest self to anyone other than God the Father, Jesus Christ, and the Holy Spirit. Any other type of submission is inviting trouble and danger.[21]

16. Why are some people closer to God than others?

Some people are wiser than others, some more learned than others, other more diligent than others, and some work harder than others. The Bible says that those who seek God with all their hearts will find Him.[22] Some people are willing to spend more time, energy, and effort to seek God. They are willing to fast and to pray. They are willing to spend days talking to God. They are willing to make the sacrifices it takes to be God's person. Many others, like Esau in the Old Testament, have no interest in spiritual things.[23] Others want to be closer to God, but they refuse to expend the effort to achieve the relationship.

There are people who have been chosen by God to accomplish special tasks. Samuel was one such person. God began to speak to Samuel when he was just a little boy, maybe eleven or twelve years old, and to reveal deep truths to him.[24] God's Spirit was present in John the Baptist, the Bible says, "from his mother's womb."[25] The apostle Paul also felt that he had been chosen from his mother's womb.[26]

Some people have a godly ancestry, as I do. I have many people of God in my family tree. I was dedicated to God by a great-aunt when I was a little baby. She believed that I would be a servant of the Lord. In that way the blessings of God last from one generation to another. Therefore, there is a call of God on some people's lives from birth that is not present in others.

There are some people whose parents are involved in the occult, witchcraft, and similar activities. These people are closer to the realm of Satan than those who have a great Christian heritage and have more to overcome when they decide to follow Christ.

In any case, the same individual can feel very close to God at some times, but a little farther away at other times. I do not think God leaves us. The privileges and benefits of

God remain constant, but our perception changes such as in a time of revival, when there seems to be a heightening of God's presence. Such an occurrence happened on the day of Pentecost, when God visited His people with an extraordinary burst of power, and they were supernaturally filled with spiritual power.

Even when He may seem far away, God has not left you. The Bible says, "He will not leave you nor forsake you."[27] The original language reinforces this concept with a succession of negatives—"I will *no, not never* leave you."

---

17. Does God play favorites?

God does not show partiality.[28] He does not respect one man over another. He does not respect one race over another. However, He does have callings on people's lives for service, and He will equip people for various functions that are different.

For example, I am persuaded that in the year 1980 Ronald Reagan was God's choice as president of the United States. He was chosen for that office. I am also persuaded that King David was chosen by God to be the ruler of Israel at a particular point, as was his son, Solomon, who followed him. I believe that the Jews were chosen by God to be the bearers of the Bible, and to be the ones through whom the Messiah was born. That does not mean that all of these people are God's favorites, but they are people called to do a job. God equips people to do work for Him, not because He is playing favorites but because He needs a job done. He gives certain people special tools to get the job done.

For example, if I want a building constructed, I will give some construction workers cranes to lift steel, bulldozers to grade land, trucks to haul supplies; and I will give them the steel, concrete, bricks, and mortar. The architects will receive none of these things. They have drawing pencils, easels, special lights, and computer equipment instead. The builders are not favored over the architects, nor the architects over the builders. Both have a task to perform, and the tools they receive reflect the demands of the task.

Hudson Taylor, founder of the old China Inland Mission, which is now Overseas Missionary Fellowship, was asked why God chose him. Taylor replied, "He looked until He found someone small enough to do the job." The Bible says God is not impressed with the strength of a horse or the legs of a man.[29] He said that, "on this one will I look: on him who is poor and of a contrite spirit, and who trembles at My word."[30] What impresses God most is a person who will listen to His voice, be humbled before Him, and carry out His program.

Over the centuries, God has called some rather remarkable people. Moses was an extraordinary individual. He was mighty in word and deed in Egypt and was a powerful figure in Pharaoh's courts.[31] The apostle Paul sat at the feet of the great teacher Gamaliel.[32] He was heading toward being a leader in Judaism. Billy Graham is obviously a very gifted individual. He could have been a success in any field he chose. He was a top salesman before devoting his life to the ministry.

God takes skills that He has already put in someone's possession and then strengthens them for His glory. Humility, more than natural ability, qualifies a person for God's service. Moses spent forty years in the palace of Pharaoh. He needed forty years of humiliation on the "back side of the desert" before he was ready to lead God's people.[33] Saul of Tarsus was a leader of Israel, but it required time in the desert, in prison, and in countless tribulations, to form the apostle Paul.[34]

If you would be favored by God, seek humility, seek obedience, seek a broken and contrite heart. These things He will not despise.[35]

Scripture References

1 See Genesis 4:1–17
2 See 1 Corinthians 12:10
3 See John 11:41–44, 14:9–11
4 See Psalm 66:18, John 9:31, 1 Peter 3:7
5 1 Timothy 2:12
6 See Judges 4:1–24
7 See Luke 14:16–24, 1 John 2:15–18
8 See Proverbs 22:7
9 See 1 Samuel 31:12–13
10 See Revelation 13:11–18
11 See 1 Corinthians 11:14–15
12 See Numbers 6:1–5, Judges 13:5, 16:15–22
13 See Revelation 2:4
14 Jeremiah 4:3
15 See Matthew 13:22, Mark 4:19, Luke 8:14
16 Revelation 2:4
17 Matthew 12:46–50
18 Galatians 1:19
19 See Matthew 1:25
20 See Acts 19:11–12
21 See Deuteronomy 18:10–13, 1 Corinthians 2:16, 2 Corinthians 10:3–5,
   1 Peter 1:13
22 See Deuteronomy 4:29
23 See Genesis 25:34
24 See 1 Samuel 3:1–14
25 Luke 1:15
26 See Galatians 1:15
27 Deuteronomy 31:6–8

28 See Acts 10:34
29 See Psalm 147:10
30 Isaiah 66:2
31 See Acts 7:22
32 See Acts 22:3
33 See Exodus 3:1
34 See 2 Corinthians 6:4–10, 11:22–33
35 See Psalm 51:17

12. Twenty Questions About the Kingdom of God

1. What is the Kingdom of God?

A kingdom is a place where a king rules. The Kingdom of God is wherever God reigns over the lives of His subjects. The Kingdom of God is not visible because God is not visible. It is a spiritual kingdom, not a visible one. Jesus Christ said, "The kingdom of God is within you."[1]

Jesus gave us, in the Lord's Prayer, a petition to God: "Your kingdom come. Your will be done on earth as it is in heaven."[2] This prayer shows the priority Jesus gave to the Kingdom of God. Can we not say that the Kingdom of God will come on earth when the will of God is as respected here as it is in heaven, when the visible world totally reflects the invisible world? I think we can. In the Kingdom of God, everything is subject to God's power, instantly, with no question. In the visible world, there is resistance to God's will.

The Kingdom of God is eternal. It is the place where all Christians ultimately will dwell. At the present time, it is an invisible kingdom here in our midst. Wherever there are those who honor the king, and wherever the Spirit of the king is, there is the Kingdom of God.

---

2. How does one enter the kingdom?

A ruler of the Jews named Nicodemus came to Jesus by night. He was looking for teaching that would enable him to discover God. Nicodemus was a righteous Jew, a godly man, and yet he sensed a need in his life. He wanted to enter the Kingdom of God.

Jesus answered him, "Unless one is born again, he cannot see the kingdom of God."[3] There ensued a discussion with Nicodemus about what "born again" meant. Nicodemus wanted to know how an elderly man could go back into his mother's womb and be born again. Jesus was not talking about a rebirth of flesh. He said, "Unless one is born of water and the Spirit, he cannot enter the kingdom of God."[4]

When a human being is born the first time, it is a natural birth, springing from a sexual relationship between a man and woman. The second birth occurs when the individual voluntarily submits his or her life to God. It comes about when someone receives Jesus' sacrificial death to cleanse from sin, makes Jesus the Lord of his spirit, and receives the indwelling Holy Spirit. This experience is so profound that it is equivalent to a second birth. With the new birth, the spirit of man is re-created and joined with God's Spirit, thereby enabling the individual to have the spiritual vision necessary to see and enter the Kingdom of God.

When Adam and Eve were created, they had within themselves the spiritual equivalent of a reflecting mirror that reflected the image of God. Therefore, they could see the kingdom and could know spiritual things naturally. With the onset of sin, that mirror, the image of God within man, became darkened.

When a person is born again, that mirror is polished and brightened, and the individual can once again see God and His kingdom. That person can enter the Kingdom of God and be a part of it. But God's kingdom is only for spiritual beings: it is not for those who are carnal or fleshly or natural. The apostle Paul said, "The natural man [or the soulish man] does not receive the things of the Spirit of God, for they are foolishness to him; nor can he know them, because they are spiritually discerned."[5]

So, access to this kingdom is gained only through the new birth by the Spirit of God.

---

3. What is the greatest virtue in the kingdom?

If pride is the greatest sin—and it is—then humility must be the greatest virtue.[6] It is humility that allows me to acknowledge that God has a claim on my life, that I am a fallible, mortal creature, and that God is the Master of the universe. It is humility that says, "I am a sinner, and I need to be saved." Humility is the beginning of wisdom.[7] The truths of the kingdom are only perceived by those who are humble. No one who is proud will ever gain anything from God, because "God resists the proud, but gives grace to the humble."[8]

Those who are humble receive the grace of God and are given the secrets of the kingdom, because they come as beggars. Jesus Christ said, "Blessed are the poor in spirit, for theirs is the kingdom of heaven."[9] The real meaning, in Greek, is, "Blessed are spiritual beggars, for theirs is the kingdom of God." A spiritual beggar is not proud or rich. He has his hands out, saying, "I am poor. I am needy. I need help." This is the one who receives from the Lord.

4. What is the greatest sin in the kingdom?

The greatest sin is pride—for a number of reasons.[10] First, pride was the fundamental sin of Satan when he first sinned. Pride says, "I can do it better than God," and Satan thought he could do a better job of running the universe than God could! Second, pride inevitably leads to the sin of rebellion. By proudly carrying on our plan for our lives and those around us, we necessarily come into conflict with God's plan. That is why the Bible says, "God resists the proud, but gives grace to the humble."[11]

There is no way of being neutral in the kingdom. You are either for Jesus or against Him. If you are proud, you are automatically against Him, because your life will not be yielded to Him and to what He wants to accomplish. You will be fighting Him every step of the way.

Finally, pride leads to a sense of self-sufficiency where we are unwilling to learn or receive from God or man. Jesus said, "Unless you are converted and become as little children, you will by no means enter the kingdom of heaven."[12] Children are trusting and they are teachable. Children ask questions all the time. "Daddy, why is the grass green? Why is the sky blue? Why do dogs bark?" They always want to learn.

But once a person becomes proud, he says, "I am supposed to know this. Do not tell me." A person who thinks he knows everything cannot possibly learn anything. But the good things of the Kingdom of God are given only to those who ask; if you do not ask, you do not receive. God's name reveals this truth. He is "I AM."[13] I am what? The answer—I am the supply of your need. I am healing, wisdom, sanctification, provision, victory, and salvation. His great power extends to His people like a blank check. We are to fill in the blank according to our need. It is only when you realize that you are needy that you can truly experience God. God reveals part of Himself to us each time that He meets our urgent needs.

If we feel that we have no needs, if we are totally self-sufficient, then we have closed God out of our lives. That is why pride cuts off all of the blessings of the kingdom. By pride we sin against God and against ourselves.

---

5. What law of the kingdom underlies all personal and corporate development?

I call this law the "law of use." The gospel of Matthew records a teaching of Jesus called the parable of the talents (a talent was a piece of currency).[14] He told about a rich man who was going away on a trip. Prior to his trip, he gathered his servants to him and gave one of them five talents, one of them two talents, and another one received only one talent, each according to his abilities. Then he said, "Occupy with these until I come back."

The man who had the five talents went out and traded. He bought and sold. He took chances. He invested into ten talents. The man with the two talents did exactly the same thing. He took risks, traded, invested, bought, sold, and he doubled his lord's money.

However, the man who received one talent was suspicious. He knew that his master was a hard man, and he was not sure whether he would be rewarded if he worked hard or not. He was not only distrustful but also selfish and lazy. For safety and ease, he took the one talent and buried it in the ground.

When the master came back, he called his servants to him and asked for an account of the way they had used their talents. The first two were praised and rewarded for their diligence.

Then the one came who had the single talent. He said, in essence, "I have not lost anything. Here is your money back." His master was furious. "Wicked and slothful servant!

You knew I reap where I have not sown and gather where I have not scattered. Therefore, you ought to have deposited my money with the bankers, and at my coming I would have received back my own with interest." So he took the money away from him and gave it to the man who had ten talents.

When Jesus told this story, there was a great gasp in the crowd, because the ending seemed so unfair—taking away the one and giving to the man with ten. Jesus firmly announced this law of the kingdom: "To everyone who has, more will be given . . . but from him who does not have, even what he has will be taken away."[15] In other words, if you use what is given to you, you will gain more. If you fail to use what is given to you, you will lose even what you think you have.

The physical realm illustrates this truth. If you exercise a muscle regularly, that muscle will grow. You will get more muscles, more stamina, and more ability. This works in running, swimming, weight lifting, football, in any physical activity. Each level of activity opens up new vistas of opportunity for you. Likewise, if you tie your arm to your side for five or six months, it will get so that you cannot even use it. The muscle will not function, and you will hardly be able to life a cup of coffee with it.

The law of use applies in intellectual pursuits as well. One level of knowledge opens up another. As knowledge is used, more becomes available. The biology student becomes the medical student. The medical student becomes the intern. The intern becomes the resident. The resident becomes the specialist. The specialist may become world famous as he uses his growing skills.

In finance, money invested at interest multiplies of an awesome rate. A business which grows at 30 percent annually will double in less than three years. Just think, a $1 million company will grow to a $128 million company is less than twenty-one years at 30 percent increase per year. Yet during inflationary times, money that is idle will lose much of its value in a short time because it is not used.

The law of use underlies all personal growth and development. Whatever is given you, however small it is, use it.

Use it diligently and use it on an ever-increasing scale. Set a goal to increase whatever you do by a certain percentage, whether it is 10, 20, 30, or 40 percent. Before long, the amount of your achievement or the opportunity available to you will become absolutely awesome. This is the secret of the kingdom which guarantees success to any Christian who applies it.

---

6. What is the year of Jubilee?

The law of use, in terms of money, is an awesome principle. Money, compounded, grows of an astonishing rate. Baron Rothschild called compound interest the "eighth wonder of the world." If a person takes $100 and doubles it every year for twenty years, he will have $50 million. If he continues doubling it for thirty more years, he will have $12.8 quadrillion, which is more money than there is in the entire world! Such is the power of compound interest.

But God is not unaware of the law of compound interest. After all, this is His basic law of personal growth in the kingdom. Therefore He wisely made a provision in Israel to counterbalance the effects of compounding, the year of Jubilee.[16]

Every fifty years during the year of Jubilee the people had to do three basic things. First, they had to cancel debts. Every debt outstanding, by every debtor, was cancelled. Second, they had to release slaves, because slavery is a form of indebtedness. Every person had to be given his freedom, unless he voluntarily and freely acknowledged that he wanted to remain a slave. Third, all agricultural land, what we would term today the means of production, was to be returned to the families who had originally owned it.

There was, every fifty years, a redistribution of wealth through the cancellation of debt and a reassignment of land. Then another fifty-year cycle began. For the next fifty years, the people were permitted to accumulate as much as they wanted to without any arbitrary limits. At the end of that time, there was another year of Jubilee. Debts were cancelled, slaves were freed, and the basic means of production redistributed.

In our capitalistic Western society we have a redistribution mechanism called a depression. Every fifty to fifty-six years, the accumulation of debt becomes insupportable, and in the normal free market mechanisms fail to function. Over-capacity develops, prices fall, and we have a crash. During that time, banks fail and debtors go into bankruptcy. As debtors are released one way or the other, credit is contracted, the accumulation of debt is diminished, and many of the means of production are put into new hands.

There is a new, fresh vitality that comes about in society. Society, in a sense, starts over again. Our way of doing it is very painful. The biblical year of Jubilee is something that our society ought to learn. Otherwise, we will be faced very shortly with a major crash and a depression.

7. What law of the kingdom is at the heart of all relationships?

Jesus Christ gave a law that is so profound that it should be adopted by every society. It is the law of reciprocity. I use the term *law* because it is a universal principle: "Whatever you want men to do to you, do also to them."[17] How profound an effect this "golden rule" would have if applied at every level in our world!

You would not want a neighbor to steal your tools, so do not take his. You would not like to be struck by a reckless driver, so do not drive recklessly. You would want a helping hand in time of need, so help others in need.

We would not want the person upstream from us polluting the river, so we should not do it to the person downstream from us. We would not want to breathe chemically polluted air, so we should not pollute someone else's air. We would not want someone to squander our money, so we should not squander money that is entrusted to us. We would not want outrageous taxes taking money away from us; therefore, if we are in government, we should not confiscate the money of others. We would not want automobiles that would fall apart when they are driven, so, if we are carmakers, we should not make that kind of car. We would not want to be oppressed in the workplace, so we should not oppress our employees.

Think of the effects this kingdom law would have on the world if it were applied. We would not need any armies; we would not need any jails or prisons; our traffic problems would be relieved tremendously, because there would not be any speeding or drunken driving. If practiced, the law of reciprocity would minimize the burden of government, while freeing the productive energies of all the people.

"Do unto others as you would have them do unto you," if put into practice, would revolutionize our society. This is the kingdom foundation for all social relationships.

---

8. Is it unreasonable to think that all men should follow the law of reciprocity?

The law of reciprocity should govern the affairs of born-again people *now*. We should hold to it as our standard. There is no reason we cannot. Do unto others what you would have them do unto you. It is a simple thing to put into effect.

The only thing that keeps it from happening on a worldwide basis is the selfishness of most people. Thus, I do not expect that the law can be universally adhered to in an unconverted world.[18] But we as Christians can help to change this world for the better. Demonstrating the excellence of the law of reciprocity is one way to help bring about that change!

9. What is the secret of financial prosperity?

The laws of reciprocity and use, put together, can greatly enhance your financial prosperity. The Bible says, "Give, and it will be given to you."[19] If you give good service, you will get back good service. If you give an honest, intelligent day's work, you should receive a promotion and better pay. If you give kindness and mercy to people, you will get kindness and mercy back.

If you give to God, He gives back thirty-, sixty-, and one hundredfold.[20] Regarding tithes, He said in the Old Testament, "Prove Me now in this" and see "if I will not open for you the windows of heaven and pour out for you such blessing that there will not be room enough to receive it."[21] So, we are looking at a measure of prosperity that exceeds what we could imagine! God is saying, "If you want My blessing, give to My work and to other people." If you want to succeed as a worker, a businessman, or in any field, give generously of yourself, your time, and your energy. If you are generous, open-handed, and open-hearted, you will get back more. That is the law of reciprocity.

The law of use, coupled with reciprocity, makes an unbeatable combination. Whatever talent God has entrusted to you, use with all your might. To illustrate, some years ago I talked one Sunday night to a volunteer receptionist who was completely upset. She was partially disabled, but under revised guidelines she no longer qualified to receive welfare assistance. Her world had collapsed around her. I knew that despite her physical disability, she was uniquely gifted in making exquisite Christmas ornaments with religious scenes. I challenged her to use her talents. In fact, I offered modest financial backing to get her started in her own business. The backing was never called for, because her creations were an instant success. Not only did her new income considerably exceed her previous welfare payment, she was able to employ four people to assist her.

Perhaps you have a small amount of money. Why not use it to make more money? If you can begin an investment program where you can set aside $100 or $200, and then $400, pretty soon, you will have $800. After a while, the money will begin to work for you. The law of use and the law of compounding interest will begin to build up an enormous amount of money. If a person could simply double $100 every year for twenty years, it would become $50 million!

As you give, God will begin to pour His blessing upon you. As you use your talents, under His direction, and allow your resources time to grow, His blessing will multiply beyond anything you can now imagine.

---

10. What law of the kingdom is necessary for the laws of reciprocity and use to work?

Jesus said to keep on asking, to keep on seeking, and to keep on knocking.[22] The reason we say keep on asking, seeking, and knocking is that the Greek present tense used here means continuous action. Jesus was not saying knock once and stop, but keep on knocking until the door is opened. God, in His wonderful wisdom, has built the world in such a fashion that only those who are diligent and who persevere win the highest prizes. The person who is determined to achieve his God-given goal, despite all obstacles, will wind up a winner. Those who are faint-hearted and faltering, whose minds are not made up about something, will always lose.

God makes us reach high for the better things. Only a few will strive hard enough to win them. Those who keep going in spite of problems, pain, and difficulty will eventually overcome them.

It is necessary to keep at something long enough to let the laws of use and reciprocity work for you. If you give someone $1 and expect to get back $100 by tomorrow, that is just magic. If you invest $100 at interest, and when you get $110 back you spend it, you will never see the marvel of compounding. If you begin a course of running, weight lifting, or dieting, then quit after two weeks, you will accomplish nothing. The apostle Paul proudly declared, "I have fought the good fight, I have finished the race, I have kept the faith."[23] He wrote to the Galatians, "Let us not grow weary while doing good, for in due season we shall reap if we do not lose heart."[24] In whatever task God places you, do not quit, but stay the course.

---

11. What kingdom law accompanies prosperity?

Jesus Christ said, "Everyone to whom much is given, from him will much he required."[25] there is a saying, *noblesse oblige* (nobility obligates). If a person is diligent in the kingdom and applies the laws of use and reciprocity, he will have the type of success that brings honor, recognition of some nature, power, authority, or increased scope of responsibility. To such an individual, the Lord says that when you are given much, much is going to be required of you.

With every increase of your station in life, more demands will be made of you and higher performance will be expected. Someone who is a student, just learning medicine, can be excused certain errors in his judgment and in his knowledge of biology. If he becomes a neurosurgeon, he cannot be excused any errors when he is cutting into someone's brain. The person who handles $100 may or may not make a profit with it. He might make $5 or $10, which might be considered a good performance. If one day he happens to be the president of General Motors, however, he cannot offer an annual profit of just $100. His trust involves the stewardship of tens of billions of dollars. Performance is expected to be commensurate with his opportunity.

The person who is in the high school debating society may make a speech that would be considered worthy of an A. Were that student to become president of the United States, his oratory would be judged by a different standard. Now his speech must motivate a Congress, move a nation, and lead the free world.

In short, every level of privilege involves a higher level of responsibility. Revolutions develop when those who are given wealth, privilege, and power fail to live up to their responsibilities. At no time in his life can a person say, "I have arrived at wealth and power. Therefore I can ignore my obligations to God and my fellow man." Unto whom much is given, much will be required.

---

12. What law guarantees the performance of impossible things?

The law of miracles guarantees the performance of impossible things. Miracles take place in Jesus' name, with power flowing from the invisible world where God is, through the spirit of man, where the center of our being is, through the mind of man, where doubts can arise, and out into the world around us through thoughts and the spoken word.

In Mark 11:22–24, there is the master key to miracles:

> Jesus answered and said to them, "Have faith in God. For assuredly, I say to you, whoever says to this mountain, 'Be removed and be cast into the sea,' and does not doubt in his heart, but believes that those things he says will come to pass, he will have whatever he says. Therefore I say to you, whatever things you ask when you pray, believe that you receive them, and you will have them."

First, have faith in God. With God nothing is impossible. He is the One who created all from nothing. The circumstances—the mountains that stand in your way—seem large in your eyes, but they are nothing to God.

Second, Jesus tells us to say to the mountain, "Be removed and be cast into the sea." He did not tell us to take a pick and shovel and move a mountain, but to *say* to the mountain "be removed." *Speak* to the disease. *Speak* to the financial load. *Speak* to whatever it is you want to have accomplished. Give that situation a direct order, springing from faith in God. Once a believer has received an order from God and knows His will, it helps to speak that order aloud. Do not ask the storm to stop. Tell it to stop!! Do not ask cancer to leave a sick body. Command it to leave.

But a condition must be noted. Jesus continues: "And shall not doubt in his heart." Those who are double-minded will not receive anything. There cannot be doubt in the inner man in the heart. In fact, there has to be such a strong persuasion in the heart that the believer knows the thing spoken of will happen. It is as if it already has been received.

You know without question the storm is going to be stopped. You know the finances are going to be provided. You know the little child is going to get well. I have experienced this. I actually begin to see the building I want to build. I begin to experience the opening of a nation to the gospel, or someone accepting Jesus Christ, or a financial matter being taken care of.

Begin to possess it. Taste it, touch it, feel it in your spirit. When it is already yours in the Spirit, it is also yours in the visible world.

However, Jesus goes on to say, "If you stand praying, and you have aught against any, forgive, that your heavenly Father might forgive you" (Mark 11:25). The great hindrance to miracles is a lack of forgiveness. Whether or not the attitude is justified by the circumstances, there must be freedom from bitterness and resentment or there will be no mountain-moving miracles. There can be no resentment, no bitterness, no jealousy, no envy—none of these things. To see miracles, there must be forgiveness and love.

13. How is it possible that a kingdom can be destroyed?

When some of Jesus' enemies charged that He was casting out devils, He said, "Every kingdom divided against itself is brought to desolation, and a house divided against a house falls."[26]

This is a universal truth. The best of all plans can be destroyed if we lack unity. When there is division, plans *cannot* succeed. This is the reason Satan does everything he can to cause division among Christians. Because we are so divided, suspicious, and focused on each other's weak points, we are breaking the most important key for corporate success: unity.

Jesus said that the world would know that God had sent Him if His disciples were one.[27] Unity is exhibit A to the world showing the supernatural origins of the Christian church. "How these Christians love one another" was the amazed observation of the people of the Roman Empire. With unity, the church can win the world. Without unity, it is powerless. Even evil men can find success through unity. God looked down on the tower of Babel and said, "Indeed the people are one and they all have one language . . . now nothing they propose to do will be withheld from them."[28] This is God's own appraisal of mankind in unity. Unity brings incredible strength! Nothing is impossible for people working in unity.

In Old Testament times, when God desired to destroy the enemies of Israel, He sent division among them and caused them to fight themselves. Israel often did not have to go into battle to fight because the enemy destroyed itself. Any time an organization begins to fight itself, it will go down. Any time it moves in unity, there is absolutely nothng it cannot do—for good or evil. If the Mafia, working together in harmony and unity, can accomplish incredible things until God or society stops it, think what God's people working in unity under His blessing can accomplish according to the laws of His kingdom!

---

14. Do the laws of the kingdom work, even if a person is not a Christian?

Yes. These are not just Christian and Jewish principles, any more than the law of gravity is Christian and Jewish. We are talking about universal laws. The laws of gravity, thermodynamics, and electromagnetism work for everybody. God lets His sun rise on the evil and the good; He sends rain on the just and the unjust.[29] The laws of God work for anybody who will follow them. The principles of the Kingdom of God apply to all of creation.

You must submit to a law before it does you any good, of course, and universal principles give us a system for organizing all society, not just the society of believers. If you follow these laws, you will benefit from them. If you rebel against them, even though you do not know them, you will be broken by them.

This would not be an instance of good working for evil. The laws of physics are impersonal. Ballistics laws, for example, work to drill an oil well or to shoot a bullet. They are truth, and truth works because it is true. However, few laws of the kingdom will benefit the unrighteous over a long period. Remember the warning of Jesus:

> Not everyone who says to Me, "Lord, Lord," shall enter the kingdom of heaven, but he who does the will of My Father in heaven. Many will say to Me in that day, "Lord, Lord, have we not prophesied in Your name, cast out demons in Your name, and done many wonders in Your name?" And then I will declare to them, "I never knew you; depart from Me, you who practice lawlessness!"[30]

Thus, Jesus was warning people against believing that success or even miracles in His name would guarantee a place in heaven.

Only those who are born again by receiving Jesus as Savior and Lord will gain eternal life and a place in God's kingdom. Although people who do not know Jesus can profit from the application of kingdom laws such as use, reciprocity, and unity, they will never see and enter the fullness of God's kingdom until they are born again.

---

15. How does one become great in the Kingdom of God?

The Lord Jesus chose men—ordinary fallible men—to be His disciples. Like men everywhere, they wrestled with pride and ambition. Who would be first? Who would sit at His left hand or His right in His kingdom?[31] Which of them was the greatest? Realizing their striving, Jesus set a little child down in their midst and said, "Whoever humbles himself as this little child is the greatest in the kingdom of heaven."[32] Later, when their concern for status surfaced again, he said:

> The kings of the Gentiles exercise lordship over them, and those who exercise authority over them are called "benefactors." But not so among you; on the contrary, he who is greatest among you, let him be as the younger, and he who governs as he who serves. For who is greater, he who sits at the table, or he who serves? Is it not he who sits at the table? Yet I am among you as the One who serves.[33]

In the kingdom, the great are humble like children. The greatest is the bond slave of all. A child has three significant characteristics that Jesus must have been referring to: a child is humble, trusting, and teachable. Instead of emperors and generals, the great in the kingdom are children and slaves—those who in Jesus' day had virtually no social status at all.

Is this standard something merely for heaven, or does it work today?

Some people want to be "great." They want to drive the biggest cars, employ the most servants, own the biggest houses, and have the most money. These people are not great, just self-centered. The great in our society are people like Albert Einstein or Mother Teresa or those who, like Florence Nightingale, serve the sick, the needy, and the wounded. These are the great people, because they have given themselves to serve others. Jesus Christ leads the list. He is the greatest of all because He gave Himself for the sins of the world.[34]

There is a very practical outworking of the law of greatness in the everyday world. Those who do serve the most people can often become the most famous and prosperous. Thomas Edison brought electric lights, phonographs, and other great inventions to people. In the process, he became enormously famous and rather wealthy. Henry Ford served people in our country by providing cheap transportation. He devised a means of assembling low-cost automobiles so that the average man could afford one. By serving many people, he became rich himself. J. C. Penney believed in serving. He tried to serve as many as he could with his stores. His early mottoes all spoke of honesty, integrity, and service. Because of this, he built up a huge chain of stores, and he became a multimillionaire.

---

16. How does power flow in the Kingdom of God?

The ultimate source of power is God Himself. He is the author of power. The sun, the moon, the stars, the galaxies, the light in our universe—all of this power flows from God. Since God is a Spirit, the ultimate source of life and energy is in the spiritual world.

From God's Spirit power flows to the human spirit, from the human spirit to man's mind. With God's enablement through the mind of man, there can be control over the natural world. Winds, storms, disease, sickness, death, finances, even demons must obey.

I believe that, in heaven, thought will become deed. We will have only to desire a thing to see it accomplished. We will travel at the speed of thought, which is faster than the speed of light. In heaven, we will be able to think of ourselves as being on a distant planet and instantaneously be there. Through thought, we can change ourselves and that which is around us. As the Bible says, "As he [man] thinks in his heart, so is he."[35]

Customarily, the flow of power comes from our minds through our mouths. We transfer power by the words we speak. The Bible says, "From the produce of his lips he shall be filled."[36] Few realize the power of the words we speak. We can kill with words, we can make alive with words, we can bring blessing with words, or we can bring a curse with words.[37] Our mouths are extremely important, because they can be the conduit for power from God—through the spirit, through the mind, and out to the world around us. If we realize the authority we have, it profoundly transforms the way we live.

Not understanding the power in the tongue, we say negative things like, "I feel terrible," which is almost a command for our bodies to hurt. We say: "I think I'm going to die." "I am exhausted." "I can't go another step." "I'm broke now and I'm going to stay broke." "The devil has me on the run." We make negative confessions constantly, thus assuring our failure.

By our months, we extend an invitation for Satan to dominate us. We submit to the forces around us, instead of exercising dominion and authority over them.

In our spirits, we must always see God. In God there is no sickness, no failure, no defeat, no problem. Our mouths must declare our victory in God. If we do that, we will see victory.

I do not mean that you should ignore material reality. Sickness and suffering are real, but God's reality is greater. For example, let's assume you had an accident in which your leg is broken. You can say, "I broke my leg. It hurts. But God's power is healing my leg right now. The pain is leaving. Jesus is doing a miracle, and I thank Him for it. I thank Him that regardless of what happened to my leg, a miracle is taking place. Therefore I command my leg to knit together and be healed. Praise God!" This type of confession will mobilize spiritual power toward healing and victory.

But suppose instead you say after the accident, "Oh, I can't stand the pain! It's the most horrible pain I've ever had! It will take a long time. My leg may never be healed." That negative confession admits defeat and directs the flow of spiritual power to ensure a long and painful convalescence.

The Bible neither denies the existence of evil and pain, nor teaches mere mind over matter. It does speak of a reality beyond the natural world that is so powerful that a mere mustard seed-sized portion of it would give virtually unlimited power over the visible material world.

---

17. What are the secrets of miracles?

The first secret is to have faith in God—to understand that in God all things are possible. In God, there is no suffering, no sorrow, no defeat, and no want.

The second secret is to recognize that God has total authority over everything in this world—over devils, angels, circumstances, and all of the physical world.[38] When you stand in His presence, you are standing in the presence of the One who can fix anything. All He has to do is speak the word.

The third secret is to learn God's will in any given moment.[39] "God, what are You doing in this situation? What do You want to do?" As you commune with Him and spend time with Him, you will discover what His intention is.[40] Then agree with it. The Bible says Abraham *amened* God, "And it was accounted to him for righteousness."[41] He assented to the word that was spoken by God. That is what we must do: amen God and agree with whatever He wants to bring about. Abraham agreed with God when God told him he was going to have a son, even though he and his wife were well past childbearing age. Instead of doubting or growing weak in faith, the Bible says he "was strengthened in faith, giving glory to God."[42]

The fourth secret is to disregard your own inability. Don't consider that there is no money in the bank. Don't consider that the whole world is against you. Don't consider that the task being assigned to you seems impossible. Don't think only about your own inabilities, or your previous failures; rather grow strong in faith, giving glory to God.[43]

The fifth secret is to be fully convinced. The Bible tells us that Abraham "[was] fully convinced that what He had promised He was also able to perform."[44] Abraham *was* fully convinced. In his spirit, he not only assented to God but also became fully convinced that what God had said was going to happen. Being fully convinced is what Jesus talked about when He said that if you believe, you will receive the thing that you say.[45] There is something inside you that says, "It's mine. It is mine. It is mine. Now I have it. There is no question about it. God has said it, and I believe it. I am fully persuaded. I am not considering the circumstances. I receive that now!"

Abraham began to live as if he were going to have a son. In time Isaac, "son of promise," was born.

Such belief cannot come from mere human effort. It comes only from depending on God, for "faith comes by hearing, and hearing by the word of God."[46] It has to come from the Lord. The attempt to force yourself to believe will come to nothing. You must use the faith God has given you. God's help comes to you when you consider Him, when you realize His power, when you praise Him, when you read His Word, when the Word is quickened to your heart, and when you have heard His spoken word in your heart saying, "This is what I am going to do. Believe it!"

---

18. What sin particularly blocks the flow of miracle power?

Lack of forgiveness blocks access to the kingdom and to miracle power.[47]

The first person you probably have not forgiven is

yourself. I think more people have a lack of forgiveness toward themselves than toward anybody else. They are unwilling to forgive themselves and to recognize that God says, "As far as the east is from the west, so far has He removed our transgressions from us."[48] If you are a believer, He has already cleansed your conscience from dead works so that you might serve the living God.[49] God cleanses us for service in order to not leave us with the guilt of past sin. That should be dead, buried, and forgotten.

People must forgive all who need forgiveness. If the first person to forgive is yourself, you need to say, "God, before You, I forgive myself. Whatever I have done, I accept Your forgiveness, and I forgive me." That's a very simple but profound statement, because as long as we feel that we are under condemnation, we will never have faith to see miracles.

"If our heart does not condemn us," the Bible says, "we have confidence toward God."[50] Obviously, we cannot have continuing sin in our lives and expect forgiveness. We have to be free from ongoing conscious sin and rebellion against God. But if we are walking in the light, and walking in forgiveness, then the blood of Jesus Christ is continuously cleansing us from all sin.[51]

The second person we have to "forgive," if we have bitterness, is God Himself. There are people who blame God because a child died, because a husband ran away, because they have been sick, because they have not had enough money. Consciously or unconsciously they think all of these things are God's fault. There is deep-seated resentment; yet you cannot be resentful toward God and experience miracles. You have to rid yourself of any bitterness toward God. That may take some soul-searching. You must ask yourself, *Am I blaming God for my situation?*

The third person you may have to forgive is a member of your family. I spoke to one woman in an Asian country, and I asked, "Do you have any resentment against anybody?" She said, "No." I said, "What about your husband?" She said, "Oh, well, I resent him, but I don't think he counts."

You have to get rid of resentment, especially toward

those closest to you. The husbands, the wives, the children, and the parents—all must be forgiven when slights and resentments have built up in family situations. Many people say, "Well, I didn't think that counted. I thought that was just a family matter." All lack of forgiveness has to be eliminated, especially toward every family member.

Finally, there has to be forgiveness for anybody else who has ever done anything against you. It may be that your resentment is justified. The person may have done a very evil, terrible thing to you. You may have every legal and intellectual right to hold a grudge and to hate that person. But if you want to see miracles in your life, it is absolutely imperative that you forgive.

Forgive them to the point where you actually feel yourself cleansed of resentment and bitterness and are actually praying for them. If you do not, the lack of forgiveness will make it impossible for God to forgive you. Every miracle depends 100 percent on your relationship to God the Father. That relationship is built strictly on the strength of His forgiveness of your sin.

Forgiveness is the key. Other sins can be present, and if your heart condemns you for something else, then of course you do not have confidence before God. But it is lack of forgiveness that most often comes between people and God.

---

19. What was God's intention for mankind?

The book of Genesis clearly shows God's plan for mankind. God created the world through a series of acts. And it follows that along with the creation came order and government. God made day and night, and the sun and the moon to govern the day and the night. He made the water; then He made the fish to occupy or rule the water. He made the sky, and then the birds to occupy it. He made the land and the creatures to occupy it. Finally, He made man to govern all of it.[52]

God's declared purpose for man was to be fruitful and

multiply, fill the earth, subdue it, and have dominion over it.[53] The key word is *dominion*. The Latin word *dominus*, from which it is derived, means "Lord." Man was created to have lordship over the earth and its creatures as a representative of God.

In the Hebrew, the word translated "dominion" speaks of something that is stretched out before man in submission, the way a rug lies on a floor. Man was to take charge of whatever would voluntarily submit to him. He was to walk over the ground and take charge of the trees, the plants, the herbs, the animals, the birds, the fish, and the reptiles.

The Lord God also told man to "subdue the earth." In Hebrew, the word translated "subdue" speaks of beating the dirt out of laundry. What does not voluntarily submit must be subdued. Satan is present on earth, and man's authority extends to taking dominion over Satan and subduing him and his forces. Man's sweeping grant of authority extends obviously to every manifestation of demonic power, especially disease, poverty, misery, and war.

In the beginning, man had the authority, in God, to restrict evil and to exercise benevolent leadership over all the earth—over rivers and seas, the air, the birds, anything that crawled upon the earth, and anything that walked upon it. It all belonged to man. It was his gift from God.

Instead of exercising his power, man surrendered his grant of dominion to Satan, who came to him in the form of a snake.[54] Subsequent to that tragic incident in the Garden of Eden, man has been a slave to the things over which he once had authority. We find today that man is not only a slave to Satan, but he is even a slave to fruits, and flowers, and vegetables. Tobacco, alcohol, and drugs are all vegetable and plant matter that man was supposed to cultivate and take authority over. Instead, he is a slave to these things. He is held hostage by disease and sickness, often a slave to natural disasters, and in most areas of this world, a slave to satanic power.

God is not happy with this situation. He desires that man's dominion be re-established. He is going to re-establish it when Jesus Christ comes back again. Meanwhile, His people have a mandate to understand His Word, to be filled with His Spirit, to enter His kingdom, and then to go forth in His Name to exercise dominion over the earth. The forces of evil will be subdued by the forces of good. Principalities and powers will learn God's order for the universe.[55]

God wants to demonstrate, through the church and through those who belong to Jesus, the great cosmic lesson of love. At the same time, He intends to re-establish His reign and His dominion. Proper order will be restored to the creation, and chaos and anarchy will be ended.

---

20. Has man blocked the advancement of God's kingdom?

The answer is yes and no. You cannot believe that God *intended* man to fall in the garden. But at the same time, God knew man was going to fall. He already had a plan of salvation, because the Bible calls Jesus "the Lamb slain from the foundation of the world."[56] Jesus Christ knew His role before the earth was created.

The Bible also tells us that God, in His foreknowledge, chose us to be His children.[57] God knew everything that was going to happen and had even planned how He was going to bring about a solution.

Nevertheless, the fall of man must have hurt God. It grieves God to see any perish. He is "not willing that any should perish but that all should come to repentance."[58] And God loves humankind very, very much. John's gospel tells us, "God so loved the world that He gave His only begotten Son, that whoever believes in Him should not perish but have everlasting life."[59]

God is grieved by sin, and He is grieved by rebellion. He grieves for those who will suffer for all eternity. So it is true that man's disobedience grieves God.

But man could never frustrate God's plan. God's plan is going to be accomplished, regardless of what man does.

Blessed are those who willingly accept a part in God's eternal purpose.

Scripture References

1 Luke 17:21
2 Matthew 6:10
3 John 3:3
4 John 3:5
5 1 Corinthians 2:14
6 2 Chronicles 7:14, James 4:10
7 See Proverb 22:4
8 James 4:6
9 Matthew 5:3
10 Psalm 59:12, Proberbs 8:13, 16:18, 29:23
11 James 4:6
12 See Matthew 18:3–4
13 Exodus 3:14
14 See Matthew 25:14–30
15 Matthew 25:29
16 See Leviticus 25:8–55, 27:17–25, Numbers 36:4
17 Matthew 7:12
18 See 1 Corinthians 2:10–16
19 Luke 6:38
20 See Matthew 13:23
21 Malachi 3:10
22 See Matthew 7:7–8, Amplified
23 2 Timothy 4:7
24 Galatians 6:9
25 Luke 12:48
26 See Luke 11:17–18
27 See John 17:20–23
28 Genesis 11:6

29 See Matthew 5:45
30 Matthew 7:21–23
31 See Matthew 20:20–23
32 Matthew 18:4
33 Luke 22:25–27
34 See Philippians 2:1–11
35 Proverb 23:7
36 Proverb 18:20
37 James 3:10
38 See John 14:12
39 See Romans 12:1–2, 1 John 5:14–15
40 See Psalm 85:8, Hebrews 12:25
41 James 2:23
42 Romans 4:20
43 See Psalm 84:11, Isaish 65:24, Jeremiah 32:27, Matthew 19:26
44 Romans 4:21
45 See Mark 11:24
46 Romans 10:17
47 See Matthew 5:23–24; 6:14–15, 18:21–25, Mark 11:25
48 Psalm 103:12
49 Hebrews 9:14
50 1 John 3:21
51 See 1 John 1:7
52 See Genesis 1:1–26
53 See Genesis 1:28
54 See Genesis 3:1–7
55 See Matthew 24:14, 28:18–19
56 Revelation 13:8
57 See 1 Peter 1:2
58 2 Peter 3:9
59 John 3:16

Index

(Cross references without numbers refer to the index)